19 New American Poets of the Golden Gate

19
New American Poets of the Golden Gate

EDITED BY PHILIP DOW

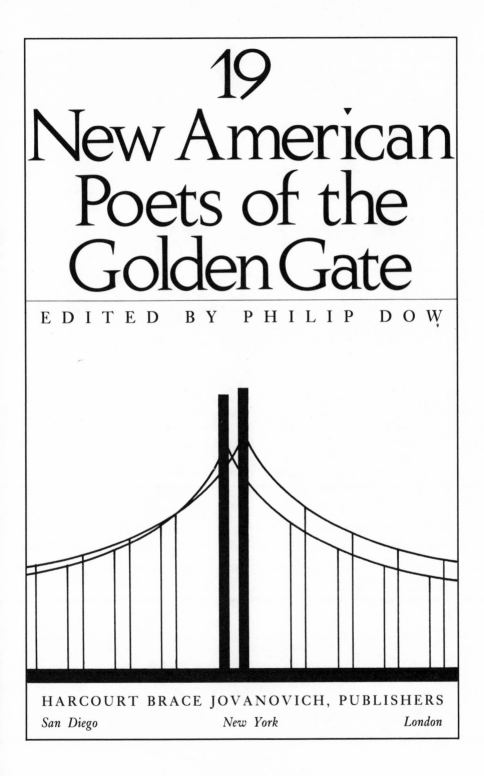

HARCOURT BRACE JOVANOVICH, PUBLISHERS

San Diego   *New York*   *London*

Requests for permission to make copies of any part of the work should be mailed to: Permissions, Harcourt Brace Jovanovich, Publishers, Orlando, Florida, 32887.

Library of Congress Cataloging in Publication Data
Main entry under title:
19 new American poets of the Golden Gate.
Includes index.
1. American poetry—20th century. 2. Poets, American
—20th century—Biography—Addresses, essays, lectures.
I. Dow, Philip. II. Title: Nineteen new American poets
of the Golden Gate.
PS615.A14   1983   811'.54'08   83-6124
ISBN 0-15-136418-4
ISBN 0-15-636101-9 (pbk.)

Designed by Jacqueline Schuman
Printed in the United States of America
First Edition

Acknowledgments

Jack Gilbert: "Real Nouns" printed by permission of author. "The Abnormal Is Not Courage," "Perspective He Would Mutter Going to Bed," "Don Giovanni on His Way to Hell," "Don Giovanni on His Way to Hell II," "On Growing Old in San Francisco," "New York, Summer," "Susanna and the Elders," and "Orpheus in Greenwich Village" reprinted by permission of Jack Gilbert from his book *Views of Jeopardy*, published by Yale University Press. Copyright © 1962 by Jack Gilbert. "A Bird Sings to Establish Frontiers," "All the Way from There to Here," "Pewter," "Sects," "Translation into the Original," "Burning and Fathering: Accounts of My Country," "The Fashionable Heart," "The Movies," "Byzantium Burning," "My Marriage with Mrs. Johnson," "The Revolution," from *Monolithos* by Jack Gilbert. Reprinted by permission of Alfred A. Knopf, Inc. Copyright © 1982 by Jack Gilbert. "Prospero without His Magic" reprinted by permission of Michael Cuddihy, editor of *Ironwood*. "The Lord Sits with Me Out in Front," "Playing House," and "Prospero on the Mountain Gathering Wood" reprinted with permission from *The American Poetry Review*, Vol. 11, Number 6. "Prospero Dreams of Arnaut Daniel Inventing Love in the Twelfth Century" used with permission of the author. Copyright © 1983 by Jack Gilbert. "The Lives of Famous Men" and "More Than Fifty" reprinted with permission from *The American Poetry Review*, Vol. 9, Number 4. Lines quoted in Mr. Gilbert's essay "Real Nouns" from "The Idea of Order at Key West" by Wallace Stevens are reprinted with the permission of Alfred A. Knopf, Inc., publisher of *The Collected Poems of Wallace Stevens*. The editor thanks Mr. Peter Jay, Anvil Press Poetry Ltd., London, for permission to reprint in Jack Gilbert's essay "Real Nouns," as follows: "for the extract from Odysseus Elytis's 'I lived the beloved name,' translation copyright © by Edmund Keeley and Philip Sherrard 1981, to Anvil Press Poetry Ltd, London and Viking-Penguin Inc., New York; from *Selected Poems* by Odysseus Elytis, edited by Edmund Keeley and Philip Sherrard, 1981."

Diana Ó Hehir: "Making Us Speak" printed by permission of author. "Summoned," "The Old Lady Under the Freeway," "Some of Us Are Exiles from No Land," "A Plan to Live My Life Again," and "They Grow Up Too Fast, She Said" reprinted from *Summoned* by Diana Ó Hehir by permission of the University of Missouri Press. Copyright © 1976 by Diana Ó Hehir. "The Power to Change Geography," "The Retarded Children Find a World Built Just for Them," "Alone by the Road's Edge," "House," "Learning to Type," "Anima," by Diana Ó Hehir, *The Power to Change Geography*. Copyright © 1979 by Princeton University Press. Reprinted by permission of Princeton University Press. "In the Water" and "Payments" first appeared in *Poetry Northwest*, copyright © Diana Ó Hehir; reprinted by permission of author. "Questions and Answers" and "Infant" are reprinted with permission from *Field*. "How to Murder Your Best Friend" first appeared in *Poetry*, copyright © July 1983 by The Modern Poetry Association, and is reprinted by permission of the Editor. "Tarantula" and "Private Rooms" are reprinted by permission of the author, copyright © 1983 by Diana Ó Hehir. "Shore" is reprinted with permission of the editor from *The Massachusetts Review*, © 1981, The Massachusetts Review, Inc. "Terminal Version" is reprinted with permission of the editor from *The Berkeley Monthly*.

George Keithley: "Dancing in the Doorway" printed with permission of author. The excerpt from *The Donner Party* is reprinted by permission from both the author and the publisher: from *The Donner Party*, published by George Braziller, Inc., copyright © 1972 by George Keithley. "Black Hawk in Hiding," "Morning Star Man," "Buster Keaton & the Cops," "A Song for New Orleans," "On Clark Street in Chicago" reprinted by permission from both the author and the publisher: from *Song in a Strange Land* published by George Braziller, Inc., copyright © 1974 by George Keithley. "The Thief's Niece" and "To Bring Spring" reprinted by permission from *Choice: A Magazine of Poetry and Graphics*. "The Child" is reprinted by permission from *The Iowa Review*. "Waiting for Winter" is reprinted by permission from *Antioch Review*. "The Woman" is reprinted by permission from *The Seattle Review*.

Kathleen Fraser: "Interview from a Treehouse" printed with permission of author. "Nuts and Bolts Poem for Mr. Mac Adams, Sr.," "The New," *Les Jours Gigantesques*/The Titanic Days," "La

Reproduction Interdite/Not To Be Reproduced," and "Locations" from *New Shoes* by Kathleen Fraser. Reprinted by permission of Harper & Row, Publishers, Inc. Copyright © 1978 by Kathleen Fraser. "Lily, Lois & Flaubert: the site of loss" reprinted from *Each Next: narratives* by permission of Geoffrey Young, Editor/Publisher, The Figures. Copyright © 1980 by Kathleen Fraser. "1930" reprinted by permission from *Ploughshares.* "These Labdanum Hours" reprinted by permission from *Exile.* "Joan Brown, about Her Painting" reprinted by permission from *Woman Poet.* "Interior with Mme. Vuillard and Son" reprinted by permission of author. Copyright © 1983 by Kathleen Fraser. "Medusa's hair was snakes. Was thought split inward" reprinted by permission of Michael Cuddihy, Editor/Publisher, *Ironwood.*

Philip Dow: "For the Nonce" printed with permission of author. "The Duck Pond at Mini's Pasture, A Dozen Years Later" (which first appeared in *The American Poetry Anthology*), "Drunk Last Night with Friends, I Go to Work Anyway," "It Comes During Sleep," and "Mother" reprinted by permission of Philip Dow from his book *Paying Back the Sea,* published by Carnegie-Mellon University Press. Copyright © 1979 by Philip Dow. "Doe" is reprinted by permission of William V. Spanos, editor, *Boundary 2, a Journal of Postmodern Literature,* Vol. IV, No. 1, 1975. "Elegy" is reprinted by permission of William V. Spanos, editor, *Boundary 2, a Journal of Postmodern Literature,* Vol. VI, No. 2, 1978. "Song" by Philip Dow (p.114) reprinted by permission; © 1976 *The New Yorker* Magazine, Inc. "Snow Geese in the Wind appeared in *Amphora Review,* Vol. I, No. 1, 1980 and is reprinted by permission of the author. Copyright © 1980 by Philip Dow. "Ghazal [So, we are ghosts of angels]" reprinted by permission of Michael Cuddihy, Editor/Publisher, *Ironwood.* "Goodbye 'Hello,' " "Bottom's Dream," "Letter," and excerpt from *Sussyissfriin* reprinted by permission of author. Copyright © 1983 by Philip Dow. Lines quoted in Mr. Dow's essay "For the Nonce" from "The Return of Artaud the Momo," translated by Clayton Eshleman & Norman Glass from *Artaud le Momo* by Antonin Artaud, published by Black Sparrow Press, 1976. Copyright © 1976 by Clayton Eshleman & Norman Glass. Reprinted with permission from Black Sparrow Press.

Dennis Schmitz: "First Person Singular" printed by permission of author. "Eclogues, I," "If I Could Meet God," "Virgil: Georgics, Book IV" reprinted by permission of Dennis Schmitz from his book *We Weep for Our Strangeness,* published by Big Table Publishing Company. Copyright © 1969 by Dennis Schmitz. "The Chalk Angel," "Star & Garter Theater," "The California Phrasebook" reprinted from *Goodwill, Inc.* by permission of The Ecco Press. Copyright © 1975 by Dennis Schmitz. "*Arbeit Macht Frei,*" "Planting Trout in the Chicago River," "Making Chicago" reprinted from *String* by permission of The Ecco Press. Copyright © 1980 by Dennis Schmitz. "A Picture of Okinawa" reprinted by permission from *Field.* "Dressing Game" and "Coma" reprinted by permission of David Hamilton, Editor, *The Iowa Review.* "Kindergarten" is reprinted by permission of Michael Cuddihy, Editor/Publisher, *Ironwood.* "Skinning-the-Cat" is published by permission of the author. "Gill Boy" and "News" reprinted by permission of Reginald Gibbons, Editor, *Tri-Quarterly,* where they were first published.

Al Young: "Breaking the Lightning Bug Code: Some Notes on Poetry and Childhood" printed by permission of the author. "Birthday Poem" from *Dancing* copyright © 1969 by Al Young. Reprinted by permission of Corinth Books. "The Song Turning Back Into Itself 3," "One West Coast," "Lonesome in the Country," "Ponce de León/A Morning Walk," "Moon Watching by Lake Chapala," "Dear Old Stockholm," and "Identities" reprinted by permission of Al Young from his book *The Song Turning Back Into Itself,* published by Holt, Rinehart and Winston. Copyright (1971) by Al Young. "Visiting Day," "Ho," "Boogie with O. O. Gabugah," and "The Old O. O. Blues" reprinted by permission of Al Young from his book *Geography of the Near Past,* published by Holt, Rinehart and Winston. Copyright © 1976 by Al Young. "Intimacy," "W. H. Auden & Mantan Moreland," "Lester Leaps In," and "The Blues Don't Change," from *The Blues Don't Change: New and Selected Poems* by Al Young, published by Louisiana State University Press. Copyright © 1982 by Al Young. Reprinted by permission of Louisiana State University Press.

Robert Pinsky: "Salt Water" printed by permission of the author. "Poem about People" and "Discretions of Alcibiades" from Robert Pinsky, *Sadness and Happiness: Poems by Robert Pinsky.* Copyright © 1975 by Princeton University Press. Reprinted by permission of Princeton University Press. "Serpent Knowledge" from Robert Pinsky, *An Explanation of America.* Copyright © 1979 by Princeton University Press. Reprinted by permission of Princeton University Press. "The Questions," "History of My Heart," "The Figured Wheel," and "The Changes" printed by permission of Robert Pinsky.

Robert Hass: "Some Notes on the San Francisco Bay Area as a Culture Region: A Memoir" printed by permission of the author. "Palo Alto: The Marshes" and "Maps" from Robert Hass, *Field Guide*, Yale University Press, copyright © 1973 by Robert Hass. Reprinted by permission of Yale University Press. "Meditation at Lagunitas," "Against Botticelli," "The Origin of Cities," and "Child Naming Flowers" reprinted from *Praise* by permission of The Ecco Press. Copyright © 1979 by Robert Hass. "Museum," "Churchyard," "Tall Windows," "A Story about the Body," "The Harbor at Seattle," "Paschal Lamb," "January," "The Apple Trees at Olema" printed by permission of the author. In his essay, "Some Notes on the San Francisco Bay Area as a Culture Region: A Memoir," Mr. Hass quotes copyrighted material with permission as follows: "The Domination of Black," by permission of Alfred A. Knopf, Inc., from *The Collected Poems of Wallace Stevens*, copyright © 1954 by Wallace Stevens; lines from "Howl" reprinted by permission of City Lights Books from *Howl and Other Poems*, copyright © 1956, 1959 by Allen Ginsberg; lines 61–75 of "Eye of God, Passages 29," by Robert Duncan from *Bending the Bow*, copyright © 1968 by Robert Duncan, reprinted by permission of New Directions Publishing Corporation; "Time Spirals" by Kenneth Rexroth, *The Collected Shorter Poems of Kenneth Rexroth*, copyright 1952 by Kenneth Rexroth, reprinted by permission of New Directions Publishing Corporation.

David Fisher: "O Come All Ye Faithful: a brechtian oratorio in five acts" printed by permission of the author. "Lost," "The Birds of Arles," "Rehearsal," "Why Do You Want to Suffer Less?," "The Emergency Room," "A Junkie with a Flute in the Rain," "Analyst," "The Mutilated Soldier," "The Retarded Class at F.A.O. Schwarz's Celebrates Christmas," "The Vietnamese Girl in the Madhouse," and "The Teacher," from *The Book of Madness*, Apple-wood Books, 1980. Copyright 1975 1980 by David Fisher. Reprinted by permission. "Death of Rimbaud," "Harvest Poem," "The Pastor Speaks Out," "The Keepsake Corporation" reprinted by permission of George Hitchcock, Editor/Publisher, *Kayak*. Copyright © by David Fisher. "The Old Man" reprinted by permission of Michael Cuddihy, Editor/Publisher, *Ironwood*. Copyright © 1982 by Ironwood Press. "A Child's Christmas without Jean Cocteau" appeared in *Pearl* (Denmark) and is reprinted by permission of David Fisher. "On the Esplanade des Invalides" is reprinted from *Alcatraz*, copyright © 1981 by David Fisher, by permission of author. "Mycenae" is reprinted by permission of David Ray, Editor, *New Letters*, Vol. 47, No. 1, copyright © Fall 1980 by the Curators of the University of Missouri.

Linda Gregg: "Not Understanding" printed by permission of the author. "We Manage Most When We Manage Small," "The Girl I Call Alma," "The Chorus Speaks Her Words as She Dances," "Gnostics on Trial," "There She Is," "Whole and Without Blessing," "Growing Up," "Eurydice," "The Gods Must Not Know Us," "As When the Blowfish Perishing," "Sun Moon Kelp Flower or Goat," and "Alma to Her Sister" are reprinted by permission of Scott Walker, Editor/Publisher, Graywolf Press, from *Too Bright To See*, Copyright © 1981 by Linda Gregg. "Trying to Believe" reprinted by permission of *Ploughshares*, copyright © 1981 by Ploughshares, Inc.; "Not Saying Much" reprinted by permission of *The Kenyon Review*, copyright © 1981 by *The Kenyon Review*; "Death Looks Down" reprinted by permission of *Columbia: A Magazine of Poetry and Prose*, copyright © 1981 by *Columbia: A Magazine of Poetry and Prose*; and "Marriage and Midsummer's Night" reprinted by permission of Michael Cuddihy, Editor/Publisher, *Ironwood Press*, copyright © 1980 by *Ironwood Press* are reprinted by permission of Scott Walker, Editor/Publisher, Graywolf Press, from *Eight Poems*, copyright © 1982 by Linda Gregg. "The Color of Many Deer Running" reprinted by permission of *Sonora Review*. "Not Wanting Myself" reprinted by permission of *13th Moon*. "Choosing the Devil" reprinted by permission of *Crazy Horse*. "Children Among the Hills" reprinted by permission of *Columbia: A Magazine of Poetry and Prose*, copyright © 1982 by *Columbia: A Magazine of Poetry and Prose*. "Being with Men" reprinted by permission of *Tendril*. "The River Again and Again," "Coming Back," "How the Joy of It Was Used Up Long Ago," "Things Not of This Union," and "Eurydice Saved" reprinted by permission of Michael Cuddihy, Editor/Publisher, *Ironwood*. Copyright © 1980 by Ironwood Press. Copyright © 1980 by Ironwood Press. Emily Dickinson's poem #512, in Ms. Gregg's essay "Not Understanding," reprinted by permission of the publishers and the Trustees of Amherst College from *The Poems of Emily Dickinson*, edited by Thomas H. Johnson, Cambridge, Mass.: The Belknap Press of Harvard University Press, Copyright © 1951, © 1955, 1979, 1983 by the President and Fellows of Harvard College.

Stan Rice: "Excess and Accuracy" printed by permission of author. "The Skyjacker," "America the Beautiful," "The Dogchain Gang," and "The Bicycle" are reprinted by permission of Stan Rice from his book *Whiteboy*, published by Mudra, copyright © 1976 by Stan Rice. "The 29th Month," "The Last Supper," "Incanto," and "Some Lamb" reprinted from *Some Lamb*, copyright (1975) by Stan Rice. Reprinted by permission of Geoffrey Young, publisher, The Figures. "History: Madness" first appeared in *The Grammercy Review* and is reprinted by permission of Stan Rice. "The Cry-Bird Journey" is reprinted by permission of Michael Cuddihy, Editor/Publisher, *Ironwood*. Copyright © 1979 by Ironwood Press. "Metaphysical Shock while Watching a TV Cartoon" was published as a broadside by Intersection (San Francisco) and is reprinted by permission of Stan Rice. "Poem Following Discussion of Brain" is reprinted by permission of *Berkeley Poetry Review*. "Flesh" and "Round Trip" reprinted by permission of Stan Rice. Copyright © 1983 by Stan Rice.

Susan Griffin: "Inside the Door" printed by permission of author. "Love Should Grow Up Like a Wild Iris in the Fields," "Chance Meeting," "Letter to the Revolution," "Chile," "Field," "Three Poems for Women," and "A Woman Defending Herself Examines Her Own Character Witness" reprinted by permission of Susan Griffin from her book, *Like the Iris of An Eye*, published by Harper & Row, Publishers, copyright © 1976 by Susan Griffin. "Prologue," "The Garden," "Silence," and "Acoustics" reprinted by permission of Harper & Row, Publishers, from *Woman and Nature: The Roaring inside Her*, copyright © 1978 by Susan Griffin. "Pot of Tea," "Tissue," "Teeth," "Sitting," "Distress," "Dogs," "The Awful Mother," "The Perfect Mother," "The Bad Mother," "My Child," and "Three Shades of Light on the Windowsill" printed by permission of author.

Joseph Stroud: "Geodes, Han-shan, The Tehachapis, Rexroth: Some Fragments" printed by permission of author. "Grandfather," "Poem to My Father," "Poem on the Suicide of My Teacher," "Monte Alban," "Poem to Hanshan," "Lament," "To Christopher Smart," "Exile," and "Memory" reprinted by permission of Noel Young, publisher, Capra Press, from *In the Sleep of Rivers*, copyright © 1974 by Joseph Stroud. "Dragon," "Below Mount T'ui K'oy, Home of the Gods, Todos Santos Cuchumatan, Guatemalan Highlands," "Signature (II)," "Documentary," "Signature (III)," "The Room Above the White Rose," "City," "Sibyl," "*As for Me, I Delight in the Everyday Way*," "Naming," "Proportions," "Above Machu Picchu, 129 Baker Street, San Francisco," and "The Gold Country: Hotel Leger, Mokelumne Hill, Revisited" from *Signatures* by Joseph Stroud. Copyright © 1982 by Joseph Stroud. Reprinted with the permission of the publisher, BOA Editions, Ltd. "*As for Me, I Delight in the Everyday Way*" appeared in *Ironwood*, 16; "City," "Dragon," and "The Room Above the White Rose" appeared in *Ironwood*, 19. "Machupuchare. What the Mountain Said. Shaking the Bones, Christmas Eve, 1974" printed by permission of Joseph Stroud.

Michael Palmer: "From the Notebooks" printed by permission of author. Copyright © 1983 by Michael Palmer. "Changes around the Bay" reprinted by permission of John Martin, Black Sparrow Press, from *The Circular Gates*, copyright © 1974 by Michael Palmer. "The Classical Style" and "On the Way to Language" reprinted by permission of John Martin, Black Sparrow Press, from *Without Music*, copyright © 1977 by Michael Palmer. "The Comet," "Song of the Round Man," "Documentation," and "Notes for Echo Lake 5" excerpted from *Notes for Echo Lake*. Copyright © 1981 by Michael Palmer. Published by North Point Press. ALL RIGHTS RESERVED. Reprinted by permission of North Point Press. "Symmetrical Poem," "Voice and Address," "The Village of Reason," "The Theory of the Flower," and Dearest Reader" are printed by permission of Michael Palmer.

Leslie Scalapino: Untitled essay printed by permission of author. Ten excerpts from *hmmmm* (8. "Haven't I said that part of having intercourse"; 9. "How can I help myself, as one woman said to me about wanting"; 10. "So I decided watching an *old* woman like her, who could rise so easily"; 13. "a woman who had been dressed by someone, in the same way that"; 14. "Seeing the Scenery"; 15. "As Rimbaud said, I thought today sitting in the library"; 19. "How was I to know that the woman seated next to me on the bus"; 21. "[EPILOGUE: *anemone*]"; 22. "'Having her under me,' the man said, 'in bed, and remembering'"; 24. "we put our heads into the windows of a car which was passing, and,") and *The Woman Who Could Read the Minds of Dogs* (first published by Sand Dollar, copyright © 1976 by Leslie Scalapino)—poems by Leslie Scalapino from *Considering how exaggerated music is*, North Point Press, 850 Talbot Avenue, Berkeley, CA 94706, copyright © 1982 by Leslie Scalapino. "A sequence" and "areas" printed by permission of Leslie Scalapino.

Laura Chester: "An Inclusive Poetry" printed by permission of author. "Simply," "Last Breath," and "Bees inside Me" reprinted by permission of Laura Chester from *Proud & Ashamed*, Christopher's Books, copyright © 1978 by Laura Chester. "On the Wallowy" and "Trellis" (formerly titled "Eden, Toward that Place of Pleasure") reprinted by permission of Geoffrey Young, publisher, The Figures, from *My Pleasure*, copyright © 1980 by Laura Chester. "Moved Towards a Future," "We Heart," "Go Round," "In a Motion," and "Returning to the World" printed by permission of Laura Chester. "Go Round" and "In a Motion" appeared in *Cream City*.

Jorie Graham: "Some Notes of Silence" printed by permission of author. "The Way Things Work," "Drawing Wildflowers," "Netting," "An Artichoke for Montesquieu," and "How Morning Glories Could Bloom at Dusk" from Jorie Graham, *Hybrids of Plants and of Ghosts*. Copyright © 1980 by Princeton University Press. Reprinted by permission of Princeton University Press. "The Age of Reason," "At the Long Island Jewish Geriatric Home," "In What Manner the Body Is United with the Soule," "History," and "Love" from Jorie Graham, *Erosion*. Copyright © 1983 by Princeton University Press. Reprinted by permission of Princeton University Press.

Gary Soto: "A Good Day" printed by permission of Gary Soto. "The Elements of San Joaquin" ("Field," "Wind," "Wind," "Stars," "Sun," "Rain," "Fog," "Daybreak") and "The First Born" reprinted from *The Elements of San Joaquin* by Gary Soto by permission of the University of Pittsburgh Press. © 1977 by Gary Soto. "The Street" from *The Tale of Sunlight* published by the University of Pittsburgh Press, copyright © 1978 by Gary Soto. Reprinted by permission of Gary Soto. "Mission Tire Factory, 1969" and "Brown Like Us" first appeared in *Revista Chicano-Requena* and are reprinted by permission of Gary Soto from *Where Sparrows Work Hard*, published by The University of Pittsburgh Press, copyright © 1981 by Gary Soto. "Heaven" is reprinted by permission from *Crazy Horse*. "Getting Serious" first appeared in *Poetry*, copyright 1983 by The Modern Poetry Association, and is reprinted by permission of the Editor of *Poetry*, John Frederick Nims. "Kearney Park" first appeared in *The American Poetry Review* and is reprinted by permission. "In the Madness of Love," "Cruel Boys," and "Black Hair" reprinted by permission of Gary Soto.

Epigraph in dedication from Kenneth Rexroth's "A Letter to William Carlos Williams," *The Signature of All Things* (1949), New Directions.

The editor thanks Esther Dow and Carol Haight for support and friendship during the time this book was in the making. Alan Goldfarb helped to get it started (and prepared all biographical notes not done by the poets themselves); Jean-Louis Brindamour, Publisher of Strawberry Hill Press, gave timely advice and encouragement; Howard E. Sandum, Trade Editor at HBJ, believed in the idea and made possible its realization as a book.

for Kenneth Rexroth

That is what a poet
Is . . . , one who creates
Sacramental relationships
That last always.

Preface

A good number of the best poets in America live in Northern California, a huge region with an expanding population. The cosmopolitan cities near the Golden Gate, around the shores of San Francisco Bay, comprise the nucleus of a vitality that flourishes also in the watershed expanse inland from Sacramento to Chico and along the coast from Santa Cruz to Eureka.

Poets thrive here, and in a variety befitting the vast range of natural features and remarkable cultural diversity. In some ways this region, a place of immigrants and not quite a melting pot, is to the rest of America what America has been to the Old World. The population's shift westward has accelerated since World War II and helped to generate profound changes in our nation's culture.

A new generation of poets came of age during the transformations of the last twenty years. Northern California has an exceptional number of very fine ones who have already earned strong national reputations and, perhaps not incidentally, an impressive array of honors.

19 New American Poets of the Golden Gate celebrates poets who began to publish no earlier than 1962, have completed at least a second full-length book of poetry, and have created a mature art both distinct and excellent.

The unique format of *19 New American Poets of the Golden Gate* provides the reader with the equivalent of nineteen books in one: approximately twenty pages of poems and an essay by each contributor. The devoted reader who knows all of the many books by these poets will find in this collection new and otherwise unobtainable material. The selections, spanning the poets' careers to date, draw outstanding poems from unpublished manuscripts as well as from earlier volumes and are complemented by essays written especially for this anthology. The equal and unusually large amount of space given to each poet allows the reader to get a fair sense of individual achievement, while the range of contrasting styles suggests the richness of poetry in America today.

No single compilation could encompass every noteworthy poet in Northern California and still maintain this generous format; early plans to include others therefore had to be changed. Poets of the previous generation, who made their mark in the 1940s and 1950s, have been anthologized often and for that reason fall outside the era represented here. Some collections of recent poets have done well at assembling one or two poems apiece by many scores of poets or by showcasing a particular group. But not since Donald M. Allen's *The New American Poetry, 1945–1960*, which restricted its California survey to members of the San Francisco Renaissance and the Beats, has a major anthology offered a significant exhibit of local talent. The achievement and promise of the diverse poets presented here is well known, yet *19 New American Poets of the Golden Gate* brings them together for the first time.

Although these poets reside within a well-defined area, they are not regional in the narrow sense. Born during the Great Depression and World War II (with few exceptions) and in distant places like Massachusetts, New York, Mississippi, Chicago, Oklahoma, Santa Fe, and Italy, these poets are typical nonnative Californians. Even those who were born in this state, who moved here as children, or who came here to be educated and put down roots have lived for extended periods elsewhere in America and abroad. As is natural, they sometimes employ elements drawn from their immediate environment; but just as their writing aims beyond local color, the presence of such motifs in these pages is incidental.

The best introduction to these fine poets is in their poetry—and in the prose they were asked to write to accompany it. The only stipulation they were given with regard to the prose concerned its length. Leaving the choice of its form and subject to each poet's discretion has elicited a delightful variety of responses: letter, poetics, journal notes, essay, memoir, collage, oratorio, and self-interview. In their aggregate, these informative pieces compose continuing chapters of an introduction to *19 New American Poets of the Golden Gate*.

Philip Dow
Napa, 1983

Contents

PREFACE *xiii*

Jack Gilbert

ESSAY: Real Nouns *3*

POEMS: § from *Views of Jeopardy*, 1962
The Abnormal Is Not Courage *9*
Perspective He Would Mutter Going to Bed *9*
Don Giovanni on His Way to Hell *10*
Don Giovanni on His Way to Hell II *11*
On Growing Old in San Francisco *11*
New York, Summer *12*
Susanna and the Elders *12*
Orpheus in Greenwich Village *13*

§ from *Monolithos*, 1982
A Bird Sings to Establish Frontiers *13*
All the Way from There to Here *14*
Pewter *15*
Sects *16*
Translation into the Original *16*
Burning and Fathering: Accounts of My Country *17*
The Fashionable Heart *17*
The Movies *18*
Byzantium Burning *18*
My Marriage with Mrs. Johnson *19*
The Revolution *19*

§ from manuscript, *Prospero Later On*
Prospero without His Magic *19*
The Lord Sits with Me Out in Front *20*
Playing House *20*
Prospero on the Mountain Gathering Wood *21*
Prospero Dreams of Arnaud Daniel Inventing Love in the Twelfth
    Century *21*
The Lives of Famous Men *22*
More Than Fifty *22*

Diana Ó Hehir

ESSAY: Making Us Speak 25

POEMS: § from *Summoned*, 1976
      Summoned 29
      The Old Lady Under the Freeway 30
      Some of Us Are Exiles from No Land 30
      A Plan to Live My Life Again 31
      They Grow Up Too Fast, She Said 32

      § from *The Power to Change Geography*, 1979
      The Power to Change Geography 32
      The Retarded Children Find a World Built Just for Them 33
      Alone by the Road's Edge 33
      House 34
      Learning to Type 35
      Anima 35

      § from manuscript, *Doubles and Twins*
      Courtship 36
      Questions and Answers 37
      How to Murder Your Best Friend 37
      Tarantula 38
      Payments 38
      Private Rooms 39
      Infant 40
      Shore 41
      Terminal Version 41

George Keithley

ESSAY: Dancing in the Doorway 45

POEMS: § from *The Donner Party*, 1972
      an excerpt 50

      § from *Song in a Strange Land*, 1974
      Black Hawk in Hiding 56
      Morning Star Man 57
      Buster Keaton & the Cops 58
      A Song for New Orleans 59
      On Clark Street in Chicago 59

      § from manuscript
      The Thief's Niece 60

The Child *61*
Waiting for Winter *62*
The Woman *63*
To Bring Spring *64*

Kathleen Fraser

ESSAY: Interview from a Treehouse *69*

POEMS: § from *New Shoes*, 1978
Nuts and Bolts Poem for Mr. Mac Adams, Sr. *75*
The Know *76*
Les Jours Gigantesques / The Titanic Days *77*
La Reproduction Interdite / Not to Be Reproduced *78*
Locations *79*

§ from *Each Next: narratives*, 1980
Lily, Lois & Flaubert: the site of loss *82*

§ from manuscript
1930 *84*
These Labdanum Hours *85*
Joan Brown, about Her Painting *86*
Interior with Mme. Vuillard and Son *87*
Medusa's hair was snakes. Was thought, split inward. *88*

Philip Dow

ESSAY: For the Nonce *93*

POEMS: § from *Paying Back the Sea*, 1979
The Duck Pond at Mini's Pasture, A Dozen Years Later *102*
Drunk Last Night with Friends, I Go to Work Anyway *103*
It Comes During Sleep *103*
Mother *104*

§ from manuscript, *Potlatch*
Doe *104*
Elegy *105*
Song *114*
Snow Geese in the Wind *114*

§ from manuscript, *Headwaters (The Ghazals)*
Ghazal ("So, we are ghosts of angels") *115*
Goodbye "Hello" *115*

Bottom's Dream   *115*
Letter   *116*

§ from manuscript, *Spindrift*
excerpt from *Sussyissfriin*   *116*

Dennis Schmitz

ESSAY: First Person Singular   *123*

POEMS: § from *We Weep for Our Strangeness*, 1969
Eclogues   *126*
If I Could Meet God   *128*
Virgil: Georgics, Book IV   *128*

§ from *Goodwill, Inc.*, 1975
The Chalk Angel   *129*
Star & Garter Theater   *129*
The California Phrasebook   *130*

§ from *String*, 1980
Arbeit Macht Frei   *132*
Planting Trout in the Chicago River   *133*
Making Chicago   *134*

§ from manuscript
A Picture of Okinawa   *136*
Dressing Game   *136*
Kindergarten   *137*
Skinning-The-Cat   *138*
Gill Boy   *139*
Coma   *140*
News   *141*

Al Young

ESSAY: Breaking the Lightning Bug Code: Some Notes on Poetry and Child-
hood   *145*

POEMS: § from *Dancing*, 1969
Birthday Poem   *149*

§ from *The Song Turning Back Into Itself*, 1971
The Song Turning Back Into Itself 3   *149*

One West Coast *150*
Lonesome in the Country *152*
Ponce de León / A Morning Walk *152*
Moon Watching by Lake Chapala *153*
Dear Old Stockholm *154*
Identities *155*

§ from *Geography of the Near Past*, 1976
Visiting Day *156*
Ho *158*
"Boogie with O. O. Gabugah" *159*
The Old O. O. Blues *159*

§ from *The Blues Don't Change*, 1982
Intimacy *161*
W. H. Auden & Mantan Moreland *161*
Lester Leaps In *162*
The Blues Don't Change *162*

Robert Pinsky

ESSAY: Salt Water *167*

POEMS: § from *Sadness and Happiness*, 1975
Poem about People *175*
Discretions of Alcibiades *176*

§ from *An Explanation of America*, 1979
Serpent Knowledge *178*

§ from manuscript, *History of My Heart*
The Questions *182*
History of My Heart *183*
The Figured Wheel *189*
The Changes *190*

Robert Hass

ESSAY: Some Notes on the San Francisco Bay Area as a Culture Region: A
    Memoir *195*

POEMS: § from *Field Guide*, 1973
Palo Alto: The Marshes *203*
Maps *206*

§ from *Praise*, 1979
Meditation at Lagunitas   *209*
Against Botticelli   *210*
The Origin of Cities   *211*
Child Naming Flowers   *212*

§ from manuscript
Museum   *213*
Churchyard   *213*
Tall Windows   *214*
A Story About the Body   *214*
The Harbor at Seattle   *215*
Paschal Lamb   *216*
January   *217*
The Apple Trees at Olema   *219*

David Fisher

ESSAY: O Come All Ye Faithful: a brechtian oratorio in five acts   *223*

POEMS: § from *The Revised Book of Madness*, 1980
Lost   *231*
The Birds of Arles   *231*
Rehearsal   *232*
Why Do You Want to Suffer Less   *233*
The Emergency Room   *233*
A Junkie with a Flute in the Rain   *234*
Analyst   *235*
The Mutilated Soldier   *236*
The Retarded Class at F.A.O. Schwarz's Celebrates Christmas   *236*
The Vietnamese Girl in the Madhouse   *236*
The Teacher   *237*

§ from manuscript
Death of Rimbaud   *239*
The Old Man   *239*
A Child's Christmas without Jean Cocteau   *240*
Harvest Poem   *241*
The Pastor Speaks Out   *242*
On the Esplanade des Invalides   *243*
The Keepsake Corporation   *243*
Mycenae   *244*

Linda Gregg

ESSAY: Not Understanding *249*

POEMS: § from *Too Bright To See*, 1981
We Manage Most When We Manage Small *253*
The Girl I Call Alma *253*
The Chorus Speaks Her Words as She Dances *254*
Gnostics on Trial *254*
There She Is *255*
Whole and Without Blessing *256*
Growing Up *256*
Eurydice *256*
The Gods Must Not Know Us *257*
As When the Blowfish Perishing *258*
Sun Moon Kelp Flower or Goat *258*
Alma to Her Sister *259*

§ from manuscript
Trying to Believe *259*
The Color of Many Deer Running *260*
Not Wanting Myself *260*
Choosing the Devil *261*
Children Among the Hills *261*
Not Saying Much *262*
Death Looks Down *263*
Being with Men *263*
The River Again and Again *264*
Marriage and Midsummer's Night *264*
Coming Back *264*
How the Joy of It Was Used Up Long Ago *265*
Things Not of This Union *265*
Euridice Saved *266*

Stan Rice

ESSAY: Excess and Accuracy *269*

POEMS: § from *Whiteboy*, 1976
The Skyjacker *272*
America the Beautiful *273*
The Dogchain Gang *274*
The Bicycle *275*

§ from *Some Lamb,* 1975
The 29th Month *276*
The Last Supper *276*
Incanto *277*
Some Lamb *280*

§ from manuscript, *Body of Work*
History: Madness *280*
The Cry-Bird Journey *281*
Metaphysical Shock While Watching a TV Cartoon *282*

§ from manuscript
Poem Following Discussion of Brain *283*
Flesh *284*
Round Trip *284*

Susan Griffin

ESSAY: Inside the Door *291*

POEMS: § from *Like the Iris of an Eye,* 1976
Love Should Grow Up Like a Wild Iris in the Fields *297*
Chance Meeting *298*
Letter to the Revolution *299*
Chile *300*
Field *301*
Three Poems for Women *302*
A Woman Defending Herself Examines Her Own Character
    Witness *303*

§ from *Woman and Nature,* 1978
Prologue *305*
The Garden *305*
Silence *306*
Acoustics *306*

§ from manuscript *Our Mother*
Pot of Tea *308*
Tissue *309*
Teeth *309*
Sitting *309*
Distress *310*
Dogs *310*
The Awful Mother *310*
The Perfect Mother *311*
The Bad Mother *312*

My Child *313*
Three Shades of Light on the Windowsill *313*

Joseph Stroud

ESSAY: Geodes, Han-shan, The Tehachapis, Rexroth: Some Fragments *317*

POEMS: § from *In the Sleep of Rivers*, 1974
Grandfather *322*
Poem to My Father *322*
Poem on the Suicide of My Teacher *323*
Monte Albán *325*
Poem to Han-shan *325*
Lament *326*
To Christopher Smart *326*
Exile *327*
Memory *327*

§ from the manuscript, *Signature*
Dragon *328*
Below Mount T'ui K'oy, Home of the Gods, Todos Santos
   Cuchumatán, Guatemalan Highlands *328*
Signature (II) *329*
Documentary *330*
Signature (III) *330*
The Room Above the White Rose *331*
City *332*
Sibyl *332*
As for Me, I Delight in the Everyday Way 333
Naming *334*
Proportions *334*
Above Machu Picchu, 129 Baker Street, San Francisco *336*
The Gold Country: Hotel Leger, Mokelumne Hill, Revisited *336*

§ from manuscript
Machupuchare. What the Mountain Said. Shaking the Dead Bones,
   Christmas Eve, 1974 *337*

Michael Palmer

ESSAY: *From the Notebooks* 341

POEMS: § from *The Circular Gates*, 1974
Changes Around the Bay *350*

§ from *Without Music,* 1977
The Classical Style *351*
On the Way to Language *354*

§ from *Notes for Echo Lake,* 1981
The Comet *355*
Song of the Round Man *356*
Documentation *357*
Notes for Echo Lake 5 *358*

§ from manuscript
Symmetrical Poem *359*
Voice and Address *360*
The Village of Reason *361*
The Theory of the Flower *362*
Dearest Reader *364*

Leslie Scalapino

ESSAY: Untitled *367*

POEMS: § from *Considering how exaggerated music is,* 1982
hmmmm [ten excerpts from the twenty-eight-part sequence]: *370*
8. Haven't I said that part of having intercourse *370*
9. How can I help myself, as one woman said to me about wanting
   370
10. So I decided watching an *old* woman like her, who could rise so
    easily *370*
13. a woman who had been dressed by someone, in the same way
    that *371*
14. Seeing the Scenery *371*
15. As Rimbaud said, I thought today sitting in the library *371*
19. How was I to know that the woman, seated next to me on the
    bus, *372*
21. [EPILOGUE:*anemone*] *372*
22. "Having her under me," the man said, "in bed, and
    remembering *372*
24. we put our heads into the windows of a car which was passing,
    and, *373*
The Woman Who Could Read the Minds of Dogs, 1976 *373*

§ from manuscripts
A sequence *379*
areas *381*

Laura Chester

ESSAY: An Inclusive Poetry *387*

POEMS: § from *Proud & Ashamed,* 1978
Simply *390*
Last Breath *390*
Bees Inside Me *391*

§ from *My Pleasure,* 1980
On the wallowy *392*
Trellis *397*

§ from the manuscript, *We Heart*
Moved Towards a Future *400*
We Heart *401*
Go Round *403*
In a Motion *404*
Returning to the World *404*

Jorie Graham

ESSAY: Some Notes on Silence *409*

POEMS: § from *Hybrids of Plants and of Ghosts,* 1980
The Way Things Work *416*
Drawing Wildflowers *416*
Netting *417*
An Artichoke for Montesquieu *418*
How Morning Glories Could Bloom at Dusk *419*

§ from manuscript
The Age of Reason *420*
At the Long Island Jewish Geriatric Home *423*
In What Manner the Body Is United with the Soule *426*
History *429*
Love *430*

Gary Soto

ESSAY: A Good Day *435*

POEMS: § from *The Elements of San Joaquin,* 1977
The Elements of San Joaquin *440*
Field *440*

Wind *440*
Wind *440*
Stars *441*
Sun *441*
Rain *441*
Fog *442*
Daybreak *442*
The Firstborn *443*

§ from *The Tale of Sunlight*, 1978
The Street *444*

§ from *Where Sparrows Work Hard*, 1981
Mission Tire Factory, 1969 *449*
Brown Like Us *449*

§ from manuscript
In the Madness of Love *451*
Heaven *452*
Cruel Boys *453*
Getting Serious *453*
Black Hair *454*
Kearney Park *455*

INDEX *457*

19 New American Poets of the Golden Gate

Jack Gilbert

Jack Gilbert grew up in Pittsburgh, where he was born in 1925. He was educated at the University of Pittsburgh and San Francisco State University. When he is not living abroad, he makes his home in San Francisco. He has lived for many years in Europe, Japan, and on the island of Paros in Greece. From time to time he returns to teach here so that he can earn enough to travel and write. His first book of poems, *Views of Jeopardy*, was the 1962 winner of the Yale Series of Younger Poets Award. His long awaited book of poetry, *Monolithos*, was published in 1982. His poems have been featured in *The American Poetry Review, Poetry, Ironwood, The Kenyon Review, The New Yorker*, and other magazines.

Real Nouns

Dear Father Alberto Huerta,

Forgive my taking so long to reply. It is hard to answer your questions. Especially your asking why I "don't like to adorn, ornamentate (my) poetry." It is difficult because the obvious reason is a lesser one.

Obviously, ornament has been out of fashion with most good poets in the United States for half a century—since Pound and Eliot and Williams promulgated the use of natural speech, informal tone, economy, rhythm of the ear instead of metrical regularity, and Williams' maxim about "no ideas but in things." This was even more true after the great spread of poetry workshops across the nation and the realization that the Williams style is something beginners can get moderately good at quickly. (It has become so familiar that it is now going out of favor.)

All of which you know, so you are probably asking about another thing. You are probably asking why I choose against the richness common to the Latin-American poets you are translating, as well as to contemporary Spanish, Greek and Italian poets. In our conversations, we drifted into calling this rhetorical poetry. Or I did, and you allowed it for convenience: a poetry of rhetoric strongly influenced by French surrealism.

The plain style that was so common until recently in this country is a reflection of the North American sensibility as well as a legacy from Whitman. Which in turn have roots farther back in the Protestant, North-European, Anglo-Saxon soul. A kind of ancestral mistrust of easy eloquence, bright colors and slack beauty.

Besides which, you must remember I grew up in Pittsburgh, Pennsylvania: a city of rusted iron, brutal winters, old trains at night, robber barons and steel mills. A Pittsburgh of the Dark Ages. Not a place for charm or decoration. (But a major place. Three impressive rivers, grand romantic summer storms, dinosaurs and unmistakable reality.)

I don't mean it was grim or that I came out damaged. I came out of Pittsburgh as the only serious romantic I've ever met, a person who woke up happy nearly every day for 35 years after leaving—even though always conscious of mortality.

But whether these are the cause or not, poetry has always been a serious matter for me. I don't get off on it. A couple of years ago I wrote:

> The Greek sailors don't play
> on the beach, and I don't
> write funny poems.

I'm not saying others shouldn't. If people want to write funny or fancy, that's their business. I'm not prescribing. I'm trying to explain why my poetry seems "stripped" to you. Poetry for me does not come from an instinct to play, as Auden insisted it did and as all the psychologists I know of who have studied creativity assume it does. Poetry, for me, is about something important; and I am in love with trying to implement that importance.

So my disinclination for ornament may be partly out of temperament, but it is even more because I think it is a poor way to get the poem to do what I want it to. Rhetorical poetry and poems of highly visible formal elegance seem to me usually for recreation. It is sometimes recreation of an admirably refined sort, and other times it is recreational in the sense of "fun" architecture. In either case, it seldom makes anything happen that is truly significant for me.

I know, of course, that many intelligent people would insist that much of the Latin-American poetry is of major importance, and they are probably right. But it is hard for me to believe in. Just as it is hard for me to believe in Verdi's *Requiem.* I feel that same lack of trust when I read the poetry of Odysseus Elytis. I see the immense gesturing and theatrical assertions and all that "fine" writing, but am left feeling like I do when somebody in a sestina tells me passionately that his heart has just been broken. It reminds me of how I felt after reading the famous poem by Elytis, *Axion Esti*—in which he emotionally tells of his reverence and love for the lovely island of Lesbos where his parents and ancestors lived—and then discovered he had never bothered to take the ferry over to see it. So much for rhetoric passion.

It is so easy to induce emotion in oneself or in the reader with rich language. Like those people in bars who have a gift for words. I sometimes wonder, listening, whether that is what Plato had in mind when he said he didn't want poets in his Republic because they told lies.

There is no way to test the reliability in rhetorical poetry. If the poet lowers his voice a little and uses real nouns, I feel I have a much better chance to tell. By *real* I mean concrete particulars which are not rhetorical flourishes. Not similes and symbols, but honest to god nouns. Let me take an Elytis poem as an example—taken at random:

I Lived the Beloved Name

I lived the beloved name
In the shade of the aged olive tree
In the roaring of the lifelong sea

Those who stoned me live no longer
With their stones I built a fountain
To its brink green girls come

Their lips descend from the dawn
Their hair unwinds far into the future

Swallows come, infants of the wind
They drink, they fly, so that life goes on
The threat of the dream becomes a dream
Pain rounds the good cape
No voice is lost in the breast of the sky

O deathless sea, tell me what you are whispering
I reach your morning mouth early . . .

and so on. Not a real noun anywhere.

I've lived five years of the last fifteen on those Greek islands. With those fork-tailed swallows morning and evenings. Big olive trees by the outhouse window month after month. The dawns, capes, skies, Aegean . . . and I don't believe a word of this. The most noticeable thing about Greece is exactly the opposite: the sea is water and the stones rock. The sky is the sky, without a breast; the capes are points of land extending out into blue water—with pain never, never rounding into view. Not even O deathless sea has a mouth. And I very much doubt he ever built that fountain. Aphrodite and Apollo and Poseidon may be there, but not those green lips. I don't care how many Nobel prizes Elytis has. (Oddly, Elytis himself has said that Greek "is a lean language which elicits a lean content.")

Here's the beginning of a poem full of real nouns, again taken almost at random:

The Unmoving Cloud

The clouds have gathered and gathered,
        and the rain falls and falls,
The eight ply of the heavens
        are folded into one darkness,
And the wide, flat road stretches out.
I stop in my room toward the East, quiet, quiet,
I pat my new cask of wine.
My friends are estranged, or far distant.
I bow my head and stand still . . .

—To-Em-Mei, translated by Pound

Not only do I believe that, I know that man and I know he pats the full cask of wine sadly. Those are *nouns*. I can bite them like people used to bite coins to see if they were genuine. How can you test a pretend-noun, a noun that turns out to be a trope? Rhetorical language is like lawyers, it can be put to the use of any master.

I'm not talking about literalism. I'm not against all figurative use of language. I rejoice when Christopher Smart writes,

> For in my nature I quested for beauty, but God, God
> hath sent me to sea for pearls.

And I believe him. As much as when he writes about his cat, Jeoffrey—though differently.

And the same with Wallace Stevens:

> It was her voice that made
> The sky acutest at its vanishing.
> She measured to the hour its solitude.
> She was the single artificer of the world
> In which she sang. And when she sang, the sea,
> Whatever self it had, became the self
> That was her song, for she was the maker.

And Linda Gregg:

> Ghosts and the old are gathered here.
> Bored of being gathered without waltzes,
> one asks for music and the bird says soon.

I believe these people. I believe they believe, and I believe the evidence can be felt in their language. With Elytis, and with most rhetorical poetry, I feel the poet constantly curtsying and whispering, "Look how marvelously I did that. And look how astonishing I'm being now!" A lot of Elytis and the others feels like lazy language-mongering. A pretend-surrealism with no need behind it. The Mediterranean delight in the dance of the mind over a subject without trying to get anywhere. The subject being merely an occasion for the performance. Like poets giving birth without getting pregnant.

I suppose there is something in my Scottish blood which distrusts the Baroque, feeling there is something vaguely dishonest in using structural devices for decorative purposes. But it is more importantly true that my reservations are because it is an approach that dotes on the surface—whereas my chief interest is focused on the interior of things. I *enjoy* surfaces, I delight in Italy, I find great pleasure in Veronese; but the Rembrandt self-portraits are far, far more important to me. As the Giotto Madonnas are more valuable than those of Raphael. I relish the physical surface of a woman, but I am importantly haunted by the ghost inside.

My poetry is largely about ideas and perceptions, about knowing or understanding. Seldom careful detailing of foreign landscapes or requests that the reader sympathize with how much someone has hurt me. Even my love poems are likely to be a perception about love or marriage, or trying to distinguish between two aspects of the heart which seem the same, or working to register a particular tonality of the spirit. Gorgeousness of language is likely to distract from that kind of attention. The music or richness may dance the reader into a mood or beguile him into enlisting, but it is a conversion without substance. Like becoming Catholic because you like the vestments.

On the other hand, I'm not interested in abstract language. That would be fine if I were interested in *telling* the audience what to believe. Kurosawa, the film maker, said that if he wanted to deliver messages he would paint signs. I want the reader to experience the knowledge or understanding I have. I am not interested in his assent. And because it is that felt knowing I am trying to transfer rather than an abstraction to be decoded, real nouns are central to my strategy. When you try to communicate something, quite apart from poetry, the other person is likely to ask for examples. We seem to assemble reality inside from concrete details. If you say a brown dachshund was suffocated, the message is felt. If you say an animal was eliminated, the mind says yes. That's why major nations in the West are finding it hard to wage war. Not many people will mind when the radio says terrorists were executed. But when people see on their television ordinary Palestinians or Vietnamese being slaughtered, there is a drastic drop in support. It becomes real.

In somewhat the same way, I want the reader to encounter the human matter I am writing about. Pleasuring the reader is not likely to accomplish that. A dazzle of language can increase the pulse rate, but soon after it will be like television shows that grow dim in the viewer by the time the commercials are over. If I pour even the finest honey over the reader, it will not augment him. Used right, the concrete image can become a real thing inside.

Finally, I find the employment of rhetoric unsatisfying to my instincts as a craftsman. It is the art of expansion, multiplication, indulgence. I am by nature drawn to exigence, compression, selection. One of the special pleasures in poetry for me is accomplishing a lot with the least means possible. Maybe because I was influenced right at the beginning by the Arthur Waley translations of ancient Chinese poetry, and by The Greek Anthology of classical times. Both of these stress almost more than anything else the human, the concrete particulars, and a pleasure in the scantness of means. Both the Chinese and the Greeks were in love with what mathematicians mean by elegance: not the heaping up of language, but the use of a few words with utmost effect. The Chinese in their greatest paintings limited themselves to little more than blacks, white and grays. And the ancient Greeks used so little ornamentation that when the Victorians translated them they felt it necessary to pretty up the work to make it seem like real poetry.

I hope it is understood that I am not choosing against the splendor of Shakespeare. But even there, I prefer *King Lear* and *The Tempest* to the rich decorativeness of *Richard II.* Partly because the first two are larger and deeper and more seminal, but also because the language feels more truly felt. Part of the reason that Aeschylus, Samuel Beckett, Ingmar Bergman and Graham Greene are important to me is because they are so powerfully *made.*

On the other hand, I feel much the same about ornament in things as unserious as well-designed gowns, fine cooking, furniture, cars and chess. There is usually a minimum of decoration in the best.

As James Thomson wrote:

> loveliness
> Needs not the foreign aid of ornament,
> But is when unadorned adorned the most.

But in a deeper sense, it has to do with something of my spirit probably. I am reminded of many years ago when Gerald Stern and I lived in Paris, very shortly after the Second World War. It got to be near Christmas and I took him to a yuletide service at the American Church. Something he had never seen. Candle-light and carols and bringing in the yule log and all. When it was over and we were walking back along the Seine, I asked how he liked it. He said it was beautiful and that he was glad I'd taken him. "But you have to understand," he said, "that when we go to the temple, we don't go to have a good time."

Cordially,
Jack

P.S. I hope the weather in Rio is good now. Is it true that the colonial Brazilian artists didn't paint the jungle for a hundred years?

THE ABNORMAL IS NOT COURAGE

The Poles rode out from Warsaw against the German
tanks on horses. Rode knowing, in sunlight, with sabers.
A magnitude of beauty that allows me no peace.
And yet this poem would lessen that day. Question
the bravery. Say it's not courage. Call it a passion.
Would say courage isn't that. Not at its best.
It was impossible, and with form. They rode in sunlight.
Were mangled. But I say courage is not the abnormal.
Not the marvelous act. Not Macbeth with fine speeches.
The worthless can manage in public, or for the moment.
It is too near the whore's heart: the bounty of impulse,
and the failure to sustain even small kindness.
Not the marvelous act, but the evident conclusion of being.
Not strangeness, but a leap forward of the same quality.
Accomplishment. The even loyalty. But fresh.
Not the Prodigal Son, nor Faustus. But Penelope.
The thing steady and clear. Then the crescendo.
The real form. The culmination. And the exceeding.
Not the surprise. The amazed understanding. The marriage,
not the month's rapture. Not the exception. The beauty
that is of many days. Steady and clear.
It is the normal excellence, of long accomplishment.

PERSPECTIVE HE WOULD MUTTER GOING TO BED

"Perspective," he would mutter, going to bed.
"Oh che dolce cosa è questa
prospettiva." Uccello. Bird.

And I am as greedy of her, that the black
horse of the literal world might come
directly on me. Perspective. A place

to stand. To receive. A place to go
into from. The earth by language.

Who can imagine antelope silent
under the night rain, the Gulf
at Biloxi at night else? I remember

in Mexico a man and a boy painting
an adobe house magenta and crimson
who thought they were painting it red. Or pretty.

So neither saw the brown mountains
move to manage that great house.

The horse wades in the city of grammar.

DON GIOVANNI ON HIS WAY TO HELL

The oxen have voices
the flowers are wounds
you never recover from Tuscany noons

 they cripple with beauty
 and butcher with love
 sing folly, sing flee, sing going down

the moon is corroding
the deer have gone lame
(but you never escape the incurably sane

 uncrippled by beauty
 unbutchered by love)
 sing folly, flee, sing going down

now it rains in your bowels
it rains though you weep
with terrible tameness it rains in your sleep

 and cripples with beauty
 and butchers with love

you never recover
you never escape
and you mustn't endeavor to find the mistake

 that cripples with beauty
 that butchers as love
 sing folly, sing flee, sing going down

sing maidens and towns, Oh maidens and towns
folly, flee, sing going down

DON GIOVANNI ON HIS WAY TO HELL II

How could they think women a recreation?
Or the repetition of bodies of steady interest?
Only the ignorant or the busy could. That elm
of flesh must prove a luxury of primes;
be perilous and dear with rain of an alternate earth.
Which is not to damn the forested China of touching.
I am neither priestly nor tired, and the great knowledge
of breasts with their loud nipples congregates in me.
The sudden nakedness, the small ribs, the mouth.
Splendid. Splendid. Splendid. Like Rome. Like loins.
A glamour sufficient to our long marvelous dying.
I say sufficient and speak with earned privilege,
for my life has been eaten in that foliate city.
To ambergris. But not for recreation.
I would not have lost so much for recreation.

Nor for love as the sweet pretend: the children's game
of deliberate ignorance of each to allow the dreaming.
Not for the impersonal belly nor the heart's drunkenness
have I come this far, stubborn, disastrous way.
But for relish of those archipelagoes of person.
To hold her in hand, closed as any sparrow,
and call and call forever till she turn from bird
to blowing woods. From woods to jungle. Persimmon.
To light. From light to princess. From princess to woman
in all her fresh particularity of difference.
Then oh, through the underwater time of night,
indecent and still, to speak to her without habit.
This I have done with my life, and am content.
I wish I could tell you how it is in that dark,
standing in the huge singing and the alien world.

ON GROWING OLD IN SAN FRANCISCO

Two girls barefoot walking in the rain
both girls lovely, one of them is sane
hurting me softly
hurting me though
two girls barefoot walking in the snow
walking in the white snow
walking in the black
two girls barefoot never coming back

NEW YORK, SUMMER

I'd walk her home after work,
buying roses and talking of Bechsteins.
She was full of soul.
Her small room was gorged with heat,
and there were no windows.
She'd take off everything
but her pants,
and take the pins from her hair,
throwing them on the floor
with a great noise.
Like Crete.
We wouldn't make love.
She'd get on the bed
with those nipples,
and we'd lie
sweating
and talking of my best friend.
They were in love.
When I got quiet,
she'd put on usually Debussy,
and,
leaning down to the small ribs,
bite me.
Hard.

SUSANNA AND THE ELDERS

It is foolish for Rubens to show her
simpering. They were clearly guilty
and did her much sorrow. But this poem
is not concerned with justice.
It concerns itself with fear.
If it could, it would force you to see
them at the hedge with their feeble eyes,
the bodies, and the stinking mouths.
To see the one with the trembling hands.
The one with the sun visor.
It would show through the leaves
all the loveliness of the world
compacted. The lavish gleaming.

Her texture. The sheen of water on her
brightness. The moon in sunlight.
Not only the choir of flesh.
Nor the intimacy of her inner mouth.
A meadow of warmth inhabited.
Personal. And the elders excluded
forever. Forever in exile.
It would show you their inexact hands
till you acknowledged how it comes on you.

I think of them pushing to the middle
of Hell where the pain is strongest.
To see at the top of the chimney,
far off, the small coin of color.
And, sometimes, leaves.

ORPHEUS IN GREENWICH VILLAGE

What if Orpheus,
confident in the hard-
found mastery,
should go down into Hell?
Out of the clean light down?
And then, surrounded
by the closing beasts
and readying his lyre,
should notice, suddenly,
they had no ears?

A BIRD SINGS TO ESTABLISH FRONTIERS

Perhaps if we could begin some definite way.
At a country inn of the old Russian novels,
maybe. A contrived place to establish manner.
With roles of traditional limit for distance.
I might be going back, and there would be a pause.
Late at night, while they changed the horses on your sled.
Or prepared my room. An occasion to begin.
Though not on false terms. I am not looking for love.
I have what I can manage, and too many claims.
Just a formal conversation, with no future.
But I must explain that I will probably cry.

It is important you ignore it. I am fine.
I am not interested in discussing it.
It is complicated and not amiable.
The sort of thing our arrangements provide against.
There should be a fireplace. Brandy, and some cigars.
Or cheese with warm crackers. Anything that permits
the exercise of incidental decorum:
deferring to the other's preceding, asking
for a light. Vintages. It does not matter what.
The fireplace is to allow a different grace.
And there will be darkness above new snow outside.
Even if we agree on a late afternoon,
there would still be snow. Inside, the dining room must
have a desolate quality. So we can talk
without raising our voices. Finally, I hope
it is understood we are not to meet again.
And that both of us are men, so all that other
is avoided. We can speak and preserve borders.
The tears are nothing. The real sorrow is for that
old dream of nobility. All those gentlemen.

ALL THE WAY FROM THERE TO HERE

From my hill I look down on the freeway and over
to a gull lifting black against the grey ridge.
It lifts slowly higher and enters the bright sky.
Surely our long, steady dying brings us to a state
of grace. What else can I call this bafflement?

From here I deal with my irrelevance to love.
With the bewildering tenderness of which I am
composed. The sun goes down and comes up again.
The moon comes up and goes down. I live
with the morning air and the different airs of night.
I begin to grow old.

The ships put out and are lost.
Put out and are lost.
Leaving me with their haunting awkwardness
and the imperfection of birds. While all the time
I work to understand this happiness I have come into.

What I remember of my nine-story fall
down through the great fir is the rush of green.
And the softness of my regret in the ambulance going
to my nearby death, looking out at the trees leaving me.

What I remember of my crushed spine
is seeing Linda faint again and again,
sliding down the white X-ray room wall
as my sweet body flailed on the steel table
unable to manage the bulk of pain. That
and waiting in the years after for the burning
in my fingertips, which would announce,
the doctors said, the beginning of paralysis.

What I remember best of the four years of watching
in Greece and Denmark and London and Greece is Linda
making lunch. Her blondeness and ivory coming up
out of the blue Aegean. Linda walking with me daily
across the island from Monolithos to Thira and back.
That's what I remember most of death:
the gentleness of us in that bare Greek Eden,
the beauty as the marriage steadily failed.

PEWTER

Thrushes flying under the lake. Nightingales singing underground.
Yes, my King. Paris hungry and leisurely just after the war. Yes.
America falling into history. Yes. Those silent winter afternoons
along the Seine when I was always alone. Yes, my King. Rain
everywhere in the forests of Pennsylvania as the king's coach
lumbered and was caught and all stood gathered close
while the black trees went on and on. Ah, my King,
it was the sweet time of our lives: the rain shining on their faces,
the loud sound of rain around. Like the nights we waited,
knowing she was probably warm and moaning under someone else.
That cold mansard looked out over the huge hospital of the poor
and far down on Paris, grey and beautiful under the February rain.
Between that and this. That yes and this yes. Between, my King,
that forgotten girl, forgotten pain, and the consequence.
Those lovely, long-ago night bells that I did not notice grow
more and more apparent in me. Like pewter expanding as it cools.
Yes, like a king halted in the great forest of Pennsylvania.
Like me singing these prison songs to praise the grey,
to praise her, to tell of me, yes, and of you, my King.

SECTS

We were talking about tent revivals
and softshell Baptists and the one-suspender Amish
and being told whistling on Sunday made the Madonna cry.
One fellow said he was raised in a church that taught
wearing yellow and black together was an important sin.
It got me thinking of the failed denomination
I was part of: that old false dream of woman.
I believed it was a triumph to have access to their mystery.
To see the hidden hair, to feel my spirit topple over,
to lie together in the afternoon while it rained
all the way to Indonesia. I had crazy ideas of what it was.
Like being in a dark woods at night
when an invisible figure crosses the stiff snow,
making a sound like some other planet's machinery.

TRANSLATION INTO THE ORIGINAL

Apollo walks the deep roads back in the hills
through sleet to the warm place she is.
Eats her fine cunt and afterward they pretend
to watch the late movie to cover their happiness.
He swims with his body in the empty Tyrrhenian Sea.
Comes out of that summer purple with his mind.
Cherishes and makes all year in the city.
But Apollo is not reasonable about desire.
This wolf god, rust god, lord of the countryside.
God of dance and lover of mortal women. Homer said he
is fierce. His coming like the swift coming of night.
That the gods feel fear and awe in the presence
of this law-giver, explainer of the rules of death.
Averter of evil and praiser of the best.
The violent indifference of Dionysus makes nothing
live. Awful Apollo stands in the brilliant fields,
watching the wind change the olive trees.
He comes back through the dark singing
so quietly that you can hear nothing.

BURNING AND FATHERING: ACCOUNTS OF MY COUNTRY

The classical engine of death moves my day. Hurrying me.
Harrowing. Tempering everything piece by piece
in a mighty love of perfection, and leaving each part
broken in turn. I walk through the energy of this slum,
walking there by the Loire among the châteaux of my country.
"Banquets where beautiful and virtuous ladies walked
half-naked, with their hair loose like brides." Or François
Premier blossoming in that first spring of France.
                                        Flickering.
As Diane de Poitiers flickers. As the ladies of Watteau flicker.
As these fine houses blur to tenements. Beyond, in the park,
the great eucalyptus are clearly provisional, waning in time.
And there are gods in the palace of leaves, their faint glaze
showing briefly as they promenade in the high air, going away.
François Premier dimming. The trees shuddering. The gods,
the Loire, flickering at night. My country, which does not exist,
failing. I walk here singing there by the river with all times
and places flickering and singing about me in their dialects
as I go back into the slum dreaming of Helen washing her breasts
in the Turkish morning.
                    But she wavers and cracks. Suddenly
the towers go down everywhere. Everything is breaking.
Everything is lost in the fire and lost in the gauging. Fire
burning inside of fire, where love celebrates but cannot preserve.
The marble heart of the world fractures. The unrelenting engine
tests everything with a steel exigence, and returns it maimed.

And yet all we have is somehow born in that murdering.
Born in the fire and born in the breaking. Something is perfected.
François Premier changes as he watches the dying Leonardo drag
through the splendid corridors. Pressure of that terrible intolerance
gets brandy in the welter. Such honey of that heavy rider.

THE FASHIONABLE HEART

The Chinese, to whom the eighteenth-century English
sent for their elaborate sets of dishes,
followed the accompanying designs faithfully:
writing red in the spaces where it said red,
yellow where it said yellow.

THE MOVIES

He realized that night how much he was in their power.
Ludwig was insolent from the time he arrived
and insisted the projection should be on a plum.
The purple made a poor screen, and at that distance
it was impossible to get any sort of real focus.
He could see the phosphorescence of her body
in the stamp of light, but not her expression
as she turned from kissing the Japanese. The man and bed
drifted smaller and smaller as she came forward.
He could feel his heart as he strained to see.
She showed herself, as usual, naked except for
the black stockings he sent last time. She continued
toward the camera until the screen was an even white.
He sat there in the kitchen thinking it had gone on
so long now these people were the only family he had.

BYZANTIUM BURNING

When I looked at the stubborn dark Buddha
high in the forest, I noticed crimson
just along where his lips closed.
And understood Byzantium was burning.
So there would be no more injustice.
Unless everyone can sit on a throne
that rises and has enameled birds that sing,
no one should sit on such a throne.
Such a city measures the merit of villagers.
So it was all perishing in there at last.
The definitions of space by basilicas.
The shape of law in the mind of Justinian.
But how could he dare, this opulent Buddha
with his temples and everyone adoring,
preach to me of the ordinary? Who was he
to subtract Byzantium from the size of my people?
So I begin to sing. Build and sing.
Sing and build inside my thin lips.

MY MARRIAGE WITH MRS. JOHNSON

When the storm hit, I was fording the river
and thinking of Doctor Johnson. Garrick, as a boy,
spied on that bulbous man doting on his blowsy wife.
For years did the famous imitation for London society
of those walruses pretending to be lovers. I was
thinking of Johnson's permanent sadness after she died.
I looked up at the palms floundering in the warm rain
and out at the waves piling up in the cove.
I thought of the foolish earth and how we dally
in my bed. The absurd exaggeration of her.
She lies with me after singing, singing, singing,
singing—Oh, it is such a marriage, however it looks
through any keyhole. I went on, carrying the fish,
feeling for the bottom, and dreaming of us entering
the great hall at Versailles: everyone gaping
and elaborate Louis Quatorze wondering at his envy.

THE REVOLUTION

Robinson Crusoe breaks a plate on his way out,
and hesitates over the pieces. The ship begins
to sink as he sweeps them up. Sets the table
and stands looking at history for the last time.
Knowing precision will leak from him
however well he learns the weather or vegetation,
and despite the cunning of his hands.
His mind can survive only among the furniture.
Amid the primary colors of the island, he will
become a fine thing, perhaps, but a different one.

PROSPERO WITHOUT HIS MAGIC

He keeps the valley like this with his heart.
By paying attention, being capable, remembering.
Otherwise, there would be flies as big as dogs
in the vineyard. Cows made entirely of maggots.
Cruelty with machinery and canvas. Sniggering
behind the canebreak, and the sea grossly vast.
He struggles to hold it right. The eight feet
of Paradise by the well with geraniums and the tree

and basil. If the shepherdess will not pass
anymore through the twilight with her few sheep
and her head never again change color just before
she goes behind the bamboo because she looked back,
he will nevertheless rejoice in having seen her.
Whether or not she ate the two lambs with her family
at Easter. He does not keep it fine by innocence
or leaving out. How paltry is the Devil's power
to destroy compared to what can momentarily be.

THE LORD SITS WITH ME OUT IN FRONT

The Lord sits with me out in front watching
a sweet darkness begin in the fields.
We try to decide whether I am lonely.
I tell Him about waking at four a.m. and thinking
of what the man did to the daughter of Louise.
And there being no moon when I went outside
He says maybe I am getting old.
That being poor is taking too much out of me.
I say I'm fine and He asks for the Brahms.
We watch the sea fade. The tape finishes again
and we sit on. Unable to find things to say.

PLAYING HOUSE

I found another baby scorpion today. Tiny,
exquisite, and this time without his mother.
Alone in the bag of onions. I wonder
what is between them, this mother and babe.
Does she grieve now someplace up there hanging
by her claws as she makes her way awkwardly
back and forth across my bamboo ceiling?
Is there a bewildered sound like the goat
calling her eaten kid for three long days?
Is there a thin, whispery voice I can't hear
going back and forth? Which the Chinese elm
hears. Which the grapes and ants, the spiders
and the-rat-I-won't-let-in hear. Or is it insectal?
The sound of apparatus? Did she feed him incidentally
beside her? Did they sleep unafraid? Merely alert?
Not needing to touch the other's arm first?

PROSPERO ON THE MOUNTAIN GATHERING WOOD

I

He gets mostly dead sage and thornbush,
warned that oleander can kill in the fire.
The small farms in the long valley below
are miniature. The green is where the grapes are.
Two separate cows and then the sea.
Up here terraces of bracken and vetch.
If there was water once, there isn't now.
Only rock and hammering sun. He tastes all
of it again and again, his petite Madeleine.
The augury he followed so far maybe worn out.

II

The wild up here is not creatures, wooded,
tangled wild. It is absence wild.
Barren, empty, stone wild. Worn away wild.
Only the smell of weeds and hot air.
But a place where differences are clear.
Between the mind's severity and its harshness.
Between honesty and failure of belief.
A man said no person is educated who knows
only one language, for he can't distinguish
between his thought and the English version.
Prospero is translated to a place where it is
possible to distinguish between age and sorrow.

PROSPERO DREAMS OF ARNAUD DANIEL
INVENTING LOVE IN THE TWELFTH CENTURY

"Let's get hold of one of those deer
who live way up there in the mountains.
Lure it down with flutes, or lasso it
from helicopters, or just take it out
with a 30-30. Anyhow, we get one.
Then we reach up inside its ass and maybe
find us a little gland or something
that might make a hell of a perfume.
It's worth a try. You never know."

THE LIVES OF FAMOUS MEN

Trying to scrape the burned soup from my only pot
with a spoon after midnight by oil lamp
because if I don't cook the mackeral
this hot night it will kill me tomorrow
in the daily vegetable stew. Which on a budget
of three dollars a day for everything is twice
wasteful. Though it would be another way of
cutting down I'm thinking as I go out to get
more water from the well and happen to look up
through the big stars. Yes, yes, I say,
and go on pulling at the long rope.

MORE THAN FIFTY

Out of money, so I'm sitting in the shade
of my farmhouse cleaning the lentils
I found in the back of the cupboard.
Listening to the cicada in the fig tree
mix with the cooing doves on the roof.
Look up when I hear a goat hurt far down
the valley and discover the sea
exactly the blue I used to paint it
with my water colors as a child.
So what, I think happily. So what!

Diana Ó Hehir

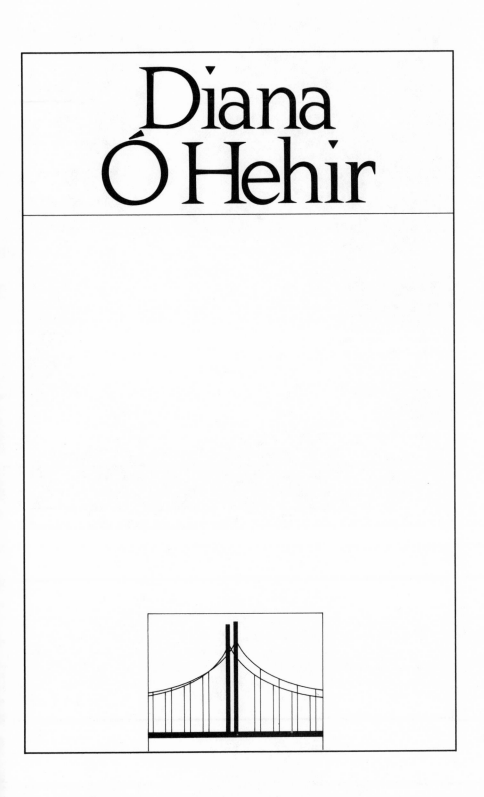

Diana Ó Hehir grew up in Berkeley near the University of California, where her father was head of the English Department. She dropped out of Johns Hopkins University for ten years to work in the labor movement, then returned there to earn her M.A. (in writing) and Ph.D. (in humanities). She has taught at Mills College for twenty years, where she is Professor of English and Creative Writing. She began writing poetry in 1974. Two years later she received the Devins Award for a first book of poetry. *The Power to Change Geography* was published in 1979 in the Princeton Series of Contemporary Poets. In 1980 she won The Poetry Society of America's Di Castagnola Award for a work in progress, *Doubles and Twins*, which is not yet published. Her novel, *I Wish This War Were Over*, is scheduled for 1984 publication. She is married and has two children.

Making Us Speak

In 1974 I taught a class in the Romantic poets for the first time.

I went into this teaching project with a set of very childish and dated "free-poetry-from-its-shackles" high-school prejudices: Shelley was that laughable figure who had cried out, no doubt in a high falsetto: "I fall upon the thorns of life; I bleed"; Byron was a rhymester, admirable for the ironic disengagement of *Don Juan*. The high point of the Romantic movement was Keats' banquet, a sensuality necessarily (because of the prudery of the age) expressed as soothest syrups. I liked *The Ancient Mariner* for the Doré illustrations, but not for the ones involving angels. Blake I approved of; approval rising inversely to the ease with which he could be understood. (No on *Songs of Innocence and Experience*. Yes on *Urizen*.)

Fortunately for my students, I experienced during that Romantic semester the equivalent of an esthetic religious conversion. The class was one of those groups of brilliant, perceptive, innovative inquirers that a really fortunate teacher collides with occasionally, at needy moments in her history. They and I adored, explored, were astonished. Lamia, Melancholy, Kubla Khan, Shelley! How all of us loved Shelley. That was the year in California when, as I say in one of my poems, "it never rained at all." My marriage was breaking up; I went home from classes through an eternal heavy hot autumn haze. I was drunk on personal emotional impact and on Shelley; his brilliant Italian landscape and my brilliant California landscape—I saw it all for the first time as if it were happening for the first time—the poetry and the real world were inextricably merged in my perception and in that stock of things we carry around with us to say about life:

> Lo! the sun upsprings behind,
> Broad, red, radiant, half-reclined
> On the level quivering line
> Of the waters crystalline;
> And before the chasm of light
> As within a furnace bright,
> Column, tower, dome and spire
> Shine like obelisks of fire
> Pointing with inconstant motion
> From the altar of the ocean
> To the sapphire-tinted skies . . .

> —Shelley, "Lines Written
> among the Euganean Hills"

There's no question that one sees, feels, remembers in an accelerated way in a time of stress and growth. Shelley and that fall and winter:

We dip into books as if they were
Wells of pity, cups of
Futures, lending of light from the genuine owners of light,
Shining for miles into the awful garden
Where, deep enclosed, is the Rajah's frightening jewel . . .

—my own poem, "January Class: It Hasn't Rained for Seven Months"

Shelley remains an influence, one of the strongest on my poetry.

Keats, with his enormously subtle subterranean conjunctions of images, was slower to surface in my work; I'm just beginning to feel him now. And I continue to love Blake, *especially* for the *Songs*.

As to modern poets who have influenced me, I think again of a somewhat dramatic event. I'm in the library of a Northern California town named Dutch Flat. Dutch Flat is a former mining town in Placer County; its streets are asphalt laid over bright red dust; there are many pine trees; the air is electric blue and smells good. The population of the town is 154. The library is in the back of the notions store, which sells fishing tackle, thread, greeting cards. There are about three hundred volumes in the library; the stock is replenished monthly by a book bus from Auburn, the county seat. (We know everyone in the area; the driver of the book bus is a good friend.) There are usually about four volumes of poetry in this library; I always look at them; I'm not myself a poet at this time (about fifteen years ago), not even a very assiduous reader of poetry. I pick up a volume: Plath's *Ariel*. Electricity. Astonishment. How do you feel when you meet between book covers a voice which speaks for you, economically, concisely? I stand as astonished as Helen Keller with the water rushing over her hand. Someone has said this for me. I, too, want to learn to talk.

No, I don't admire the suicide cult which has grown up around Plath; I think it degrades her poetry's precision, exactitude, lyric form, vision, power. I admire her work enormously.

And, yes, I did begin to write poetry late in life as a result of Plath, Shelley, Keats, Blake, and a year of life crisis. But it is somewhat misleading to say this; I had been a childhood and high-school poet; probably the poetic possibility had been simmering at less than a boil for the twenty years that I didn't write, the poetic receptors accepting and stashing away material. There were two short occasions of poetic explosion during this twenty-year period; both of them produced outbursts of tight, rhymed, epigrammatic verse resembling early Eliot, heavy on metaphysical metaphor, the theme usually that of reality vs. illusion. Reality and illusion are safe subjects when you're afraid to explore your real concerns.

Almost every poet I have ever talked to has been a childhood versifier. I don't think any particular childhood encouragement was necessary to me; I probably would have written regardless of any discouragement except constant hungry poverty. But in my case there were two causes, one positive, one negative, both incitements to write: on the one hand, a perceptive and loving father, on the other, loneliness and estrangement from most of the rest of my world. My father read my poems and told me what was good; as for the estrangement, the poems were my escape from that; I would retire to the attic, sit in the unfinished room with my back against the boxes balanced on planks over a raw ceiling, write with a pad on my knee; everything was forgotten; I could do at least one thing right. The attic was hot and smelled of lumber; I loved wrapping its silence and warmth around me.

My childhood poems were like other people's childhood ones: fairly bad. There were sonnets (not necessarily bad in themselves, but not the right vehicle for a self-conscious ten-year-old); there was one poem which won the Hallowe'en contest from Aunt Flo of the *Berkeley Daily Gazette* with a first line: "The aged priest knelt at the altar . . ."

Poetry isn't the only kind of writing that I've tried. For years and years I wrote prose—short stories, akin to poems in their attempt to grasp image and meaning from experience; novels, which are very little like short stories. My prose is not as good as my poetry. I was writing prose at a time when I was afraid to talk about my real concerns; some of these concerns of course appear, but muffled, disguised. And the style of narration is curiously quick, flip, and knowing—a prose style somewhat resembling my social self.

I don't expect now ever to write a great or good novel, but neither do I regret the energy I've spent on this enthusiasm. The feelings of actually writing were the same enclosing and comforting ones I had known with my early poetry; the exercise of working hard and lovingly day after day on a project which never met my ideal model was a curiously salutary one. Most of us are admirers of some art we ourselves aren't good at; we love and receive examples of this art as viewers rather than as creators; we read, listen, and look at every novel, symphony, picture that comes by, recognizing and enjoying in other people's talent what we could have done if we had had the gift. I'm an excellent critic of fiction and a good teacher of its craft; I look back with pleasure on my apprenticeship to it.

What do I think are the strengths of my poetry? First of all, there is intensity, feeling. My poems never work unless they are about subjects I really care about. This personal engagement, inward vision, self-centeredness of course give the poem power. The danger is that the poet may fall into the trap of thinking that *any* deeply felt experience can make a poem. I have recently been learning things about throwing poems away, or, if not literally that, about working and reworking, striving for the distilled expression that lies behind the readily accessible.

A second strength of my work is imagery. When I move away from imagery into words (seductive rhythms and sounds), the poems immediately get weaker.

An absolute weakness is an inability to transmit philosophical insight. I would like to do this; I can't. The poems in which I try for it are message conveyers, dreary, pious, sentimental.

And, finally, for a strength which may not show in my work, but is a strength for me: I love poetry, its process, world, people. I admire the poetry of others; enjoy my own poetry (even when unredeemable), delight in the safe-house where it is created, the warm attic smelling of cedar with the flies buzzing on the windowpane. I like other poets and have been enormously and generously helped by them. A friend recently pointed out to me the strange siblinghood enforced on us: creative artists, conjoined by mutual enthusiasms, separated by inevitable rivalries. I like that brother/sisterhood, even its rivalries and defeats.

> The sun comes through the window in knife patterns,
> And none of us can say how it happens,
> That loving turns to shapes so fierce,
> Aiming for the lids, the corners of the lips,
> Wedging the voice. The edges of heat are square. They
> stop the voice.
>
> But the jewel in the garden pulls like rain. Can it open
> Our hard blue sky, can it
> Make us speak.

—again, from "January Class: It Hasn't Rained for Seven Months"

(Since composing this essay I have rewritten one of my novels. It is to be published next year, and, of course, I am delighted.)

Summoned

Summoned by the frantic powers
Of total recall, sleeping pills, love;
Come down, come down, come down;
Wear red if you can, wear red
For suffering, jade for rebirth,
Diamonds in your front incisors,
A rope of orange stars—you were martyred, weren't you?
So wear a circle of gold thorns, prongs capped
In scarlet shell.

And bring with you, down, down, down,
A recollection of how you fell
Like Lucifer, morn to morn and night to night
For at least a year, your hair alight
Your rigid corpse a spoked wheel
Meteor trails ejecting from each thumb,
Sun eyes, a black light in your chest
Where the bare heart burned.

Oh, love, my love, my failure,
I can hardly bear, barely recall
The nights I ate ghosts, the nights
My shuttered, shivered window held
Three million savage stars and you;
Your spread arms splitting my sky, the light
Reflected in my own eye: your light, your might, your burn.

Come down. My sky-chart shows
Your cold corpse turning slowly, a black sun
Giving no light at all, reflecting none,
Aimlessly gentle, a twig on a pond
Circling. Gone, they say, gone, truly gone.
The eyes as blank as buttons, the mouth
Only an O. Never mind. Come down.
I can revive you. My passion is Judah, all artifice, all God.
I care with my breasts. I care with my belly's blood.
Come down.

The Old Lady Under the Freeway

I've come down here to live on a bed of weeds.

Up there are white spaces with curving ceilings,
Harsh wide silver-fitted cars,
Marching squads of freckled-armed men.

My world is depths of green, a water of fern.
No one would guess that a safety hides here below,
Secretly jeweled, dropped in this special pocket.

I'm the mad old lady under the ledge. The good
Who fall headlong off the freeway bridge,
I salvage their nail files, pen knives;
I carve my way in with them;
I make a tunnel with green sides.

At night I lie on my back;
The ferns meet over my face like lover's hair.
They nestle my ear. Their words are unsafe.
The words they say are harsh and green.

I'm roasting shreds of leaf, roasting soup in a can.
My air is as solid as the inside of a honeydew melon.

Some of Us Are Exiles from No Land

We march into the suburbs led by a six-year-old kid
Whose only memory is the inside of a cardboard box
Where an electric light shone twenty hours a day.
He is as innocent as a white rock;
His banner carries a fringed open eye.

We don't have memories of white spaces,
Or skies with the right kind of clouds;
Our blood remembers the beat of no better sea.

Living a day at a time is easy, you others say.

You say, I do it the way my Aunty Minna did,
That old lady, crosser than most;
She wears Keds with the sides cut out;
Her nonsense gives life an arrow.

But we must invent it all: relatives out of ads,
Grandfathers shaped into American senators, a lost country
Painted by Dali.

Our army moves in on the hills like picnickers.
Watch out. We will fodder it all.
We can turn rocks into paper;
A bit of sidewalk grass becomes a green, marbled sea,
Opened for us, its chosen jewel.

Our new country will be as artful as Tashkent;
If we get there we will all be real.

A Plan to Live My Life Again

I would adore doing it over.

I wouldn't marry the prince and live in his Mediterranean palace;
No marble vistas of stairs, no
Peacock's tails unfurled; clematis falling from porticos;
The electric sea silent for some other feet; the lover,
Curls brushed, teeth flashing like road signs,
Holds out his arm for another fainting mate.
That glass-slipper cramps,
A slipper of notions; a little cold vise.

My other country has white roads and static skies.
Once, flashing a car across Utah, I saw
A crown of mountains upside down in the vague air;
Peaks, echoes scraping the earth,
But only in the mind's camera,
A machine as ominous
As dynamo, creasing water into electric light.

There can be no prince in such finality.
He'd blow away like a cry across white sand
End over end, his little arms flailing.
A puff in the uncanny air. Those mountains crush
Upside down, founder to all logic
A terrible problem:

Particles scraping against an interior lining.

They Grow Up Too Fast, She Said

Out under the sprinkler, naked as toads,
Popping each other face down on the grass,

I imagined her children, lemon-naked,
Jeweled in her dream like dragonflies.

My thoughts also go homeward at noon.
They climb the stairs sneaky footed
To covet a solemn face
With eyelashes like fans; they snoop into the garden
Drawing blue Xs on the children: MINE.

That woman and I would like our babies back.

We want to sag out a warm wide huddle of love
Over our children, our little warm rocks,
Solid-backed in their world fenced by light,
Under sunshine twice-powered, under bird's arms of sprinkler,
Revolving a charm to keep off the crows.

Inside those wings of safe water,
The children turn their golden backs,
They shed our pale voices, crying for time.

The Power to Change Geography

For all the ungainly ones, the awkward, silent ones, for
The pinched faces,
The hand trying to hold no shape, for that smile
That means: Wait for me, for corridors
Without doorways, walkways,
For all my other treasons, for the times I didn't return in time

Someone forgive me, absolve me, let me
Try to regain my light

That hovers still at the edge of my fingertips, walks up my arm, is of no use
To me only.

You sat in your chair with your head lowered,
You said my name without belief,
There was a tan plastic bandage over both your eyes,
I wanted to burn for you.

But the force lay behind me elusive as electricity, silent as sunshine,
Colorless, transparent,
Hovering outside of me,
Waiting to be summoned,
Promising
To take a shape.

The Retarded Children Find a World Built Just for Them

The doors of that city are ninety feet high,
On their panels are frescoes of ships, of mountains.

Inside is the children's kingdom
Where the mad ones, the foot-draggers, garglers,

Askew as a tower of beads,
Are sustained by the air. Buildings, like great gold chains

Emboss themselves around
The crazy children, their jewels.

The children turn and turn like dancers,
Their sweaters whirl out at their waists, their long chopped hair

Scrapes the sides of the archways,
They're happy, they're famous.

They walk on the streets in crystal shoes, lapis flows in the gutters;
Around the edge of each building there's a scarlet halo.

And those children with eyes like scars, with tongues sewed to the
                              roofs of their palates, with hands that jerk

Like broken-backed squirrels,
Feed the writing of light from the buildings;

They forgive us ninety times over;
They sing and sing like all the birds of the desert.

Alone by the Road's Edge

> "You don't know what loneliness is until you've been left by the edge of the
> road, in the middle of nowhere, with nothing for company but a dancing
> chicken."
> —Owner of a traveling animal show

The myth-maker drags his myth
Legs tethered together, squawking in chicken,

Down the cold nightroad unrolled
Into a world of rabbits.

Behind him the table-square mountain
Creases in jet-frost flakes; his own
World used to be bright and forward, his
Green suit smelled of candy

And his mother was a waitress named Helen.

Past every quartz rock he goes, flat lake soaked in stars,
To a restaurant named EAT. He'll wrench melodies out of the percolator,
Old crag of counter, streaked like jade,
House where all hopes come down. The performing egg
Glitters its wildest gold. Reflects

Memory's cozy auditorium hung with cellophane
In Hamtramck, Michigan.
Hordes of flash-toothed people there
Clap the roof down, wipe out the white odd desert;
Fill up our ears with clamor, wild acclaim

Applause for the magic-maker's heaven bird,
Its harsh dance, its grave eccentric song.

House

Erased off the face of my earth, all that remains is a white space,
On it the possible ghost
Of roofline, window. I travel
Looking for myself in all the empty rooms
That say, why did you leave us.

Country of no-one. An open door, a dropped book, a photo of me at the age
                                                                    of four.

I wait for myself on the stairs,
Touching a hand along the walls,
Move up behind myself, saying: Stop that.

In the upstairs room is the memory of another solitude; it once
Made a bright oxygen that raised my ribcage,
Touched against the insides of the windows, glowed out,
Filled up the whole house

To roofline, timbers, where now my own ghost climbs,
And the sparrow swings in under the roof ridge
Her wings beating
Searching for something she's hidden there.

Learning to Type

> A laboratory chimpanzee has been taught to communicate
> by means of a symbol-keyed typewriter

The sign for anger could be a felled pine tree.
Arbitrarily, love is a glass of orange juice.

On this machine you can type only declarative sentences:
My eyes hurt;
I have two tears sliding down the ridges of my nose;
My father lies on his hospital bed. His eyes are open.

A chimpanzee has no voice-box
And a machine must teach it the difference between make and give.
Make me a heart for giving; give me time.

I am sitting now at a machine like a middle aged woman.
Its panel is intricate and garbled; there are symbols for leave-takings:

Pictures of the crowd praying outside the cathedral,
Of the red train moving slowly off down the station.

If I study long enough I can find out how:
Machine, make me fingers to manage the dangerous keys.

Anima

But why are you sleeping, your wispy black hair
Touching your face in fern shreds, your eyes fringed shut, your own
Reflection painted below you, a reminder
Of something gone entirely away, my shadow's edge?

Because the dark-haired child that sleeps on the shelf over the pond
Must be my vanished mirror's face,
Jewels bloom around her, blue, green, hidden,
The water's as even
As a washed glass window. In it are pearls, ropy moss,
Feathered and dense, to climb higher than the ankle, glove the foot in green
fur.

I have always known her, a hidden listener, resting,
Living in this closed way. In her glass are jewels more variant
Than a maharanee's treasure, than all my hoardings;

Than the strange train of artifacts
Hiding, water-polished, under our sleep's blue shelf.

Courtship

How I loved him.
With his damp white skin, his damp blue eyes, his
Tan hair stuck to his forehead in wet leaves,
His crepey fingers that found easily the fevers and suns of my body.
How I opened for him like an anemone, how I
Turned under him like sand, how the water came down,
Loud and black outside the window, how his cold phallus grew in
                              my hand to
The ice shard in the gut,
The lizard mouth at the breast,
The black water blocking the door,
The rock coming loose at the fall's base,
Our hut melting, its reed spikes stuck together.

He's killing you, they called out. *Fight free.*
Who didn't understand even the simplest thing about us:
His teeth marks like flowers, ridged fish chest, spiky brain
                              with its webbed thoughts,
His world of drowning.

Over the fall we went,
Down into the water. Love soaked my lungs.
Across dark rocks, black sand,
We turned like logs,
I clutching him tightly
Even after they had pulled us up,
I shaking, entranced, head to foot in a scheme of bubbles,
And he with his bleached hands drifting;
He with his head swung backward.

Questions and Answers

Who'll marry me? Cold Saturday. *Will he leave me?* With the
                     blinds half-pulled. *How will I*
Love him? Hastily. Now,
Can you finish your trip before dark?

You must go by the top of the hill, the bus, the bridge, the hedge,
                     the bench;
There you'll be a child,
Your scrawny arms together,
Your hands clutching a pocketbook. You have a dime and a nickel.
                     You're going
Down the road, across the town,
To the school, the store; you'll dance once across the supermarket
                     parking lot,
Flare like a lighted pine cone,
Fade dull gray.

And there your coffin will be waiting, old lady.
Row it home
With your own two hands.

Now who'll marry me?
The green man, with eyelashes like cornsilk, the tall boy with
                     the dripping wet hair, the lover
With a valley full of wheat.

How to Murder Your Best Friend

With poisoned apple, comb, ring, garment,
Word in the ear.

How heavy she'll be when I carry her stretched on my arms,
Elongate eyes, sunflower hair, questions clutching
My sleeve, kiss like a spoiled child's, feathery
Cries.

I got to you first, you beautiful desperate
Bitch, I'll say. Here's
Passion, love, acclaim. Here's your view
Of the kingdoms of earth, your open window to review the troops
                     from.
I push her through it.

This film can be stopped at any point;
We can run it backward.
Tonight outside my house I meet my friend, hauling my
Sharp white crime. Hello, I say,
What's that beautiful hard object? I ask.

And before I can count to ten she raises it high,
Slices it into my chest.

Tarantula

Don't look, the woman says.
The child's small, salivating head is held against her skirt, he
                                        listens to
Fear thudding through the vein in her wrist,

Squeezes his eyes gray at the corners, imagines
Whatever is gray with too many
Quivering parts,
Climbs the wall in a cluster of legs,
Clump of hair, patch of the body yanked loose and set in motion.

Came in on the bananas, the woman says. How shall I kill it?

(Something is always moving here)
Floater behind the eyeball, ring at the edge of the windowpane,
                                        snatched-back breath
Just before sleep, cavity in
The encyclopedia photo of the Milky Way—
All those heaven miles of palest gray, pocked with needle-hole stars;
In the middle of them
A creature with its terrified
Arms reaching out.

Payments

That memory like a derelict plane
Appears on the horizon and steers straight at me,
Aged propellers clunking,
Motor spitting pieces;
I can't dodge it, forget it, run; I lie down flat,
Bury my nose in the grass,
It zooms over me, dropping rivets.

It doesn't have to hunt for me, it knows where I am,
I promised it something that I never came through on.

An aged hospital:
Dirty rain outside, walls paved in fingerprints; on the bed
My child is dying; in the opposite wall
Is a window I'd like to jump out of.
I don't believe in God, but I try anyway: God in your creaking
                                        plane,
I'll do anything,
Reform, get poor, worship you,
Anything.

God hears.
The child is better.
He acts in a play,
Gives me a tin butterfly,
Falls in love, into debt, writes a poem
About salvation, grows up.

God in your fierce old plane,
This country understands perfectly,
We're waiting for the day raid, the night raid,
We know all about broken agreements;
Every scrap of disaster's your
Privilege.
Anything.

Private Rooms

I *Autistic Child*

There is a gray enameled sky,
A smooth black floor.
The boy lies on his back with his hands under his head,
He watches the shapes on the sky:
A pump handle, a winch, a suitcase, a razor blade.

Outside, the father and mother
Hammer on the roof of his world.
Their voices are cubes, their hammering is ice water, their hammering is
Panels, their voices chairs.
They tell him they go hungry and thirsty to reach him.
Their voices are wheels.

The parents find a cranny in his roof.
Their fingers sprinkle blood on the floor.

When they are gone the boy gets up and walks around his world.
He is needles, he is triangles, he is
Iron filings.

II *The Blonde Child*

Come here, blonde child, the grown-up visitor says,
With your neat flat hair and your smile
Attached to my motions.
Who'd believe that her world,
After the print dress, the patent leather shoe,
Is dark and heavy, and rustles in the underbrush?

Green rayed eyes look out from under the jacaranda bush,
And the blonde child runs like a ghost in her white nylon nightgown
Down and down her slanting country, her hair straight out behind her
Like a sail.

Infant

The head tilts back, like a heavy leaf, the eyes sew shut
With a row of grains, the hand wavers under the chin, fingers
Splayed; this is
Exactly the way I remember it;
No syllable different; navy-blue
Boiled eyes, and cuckoo-mouth, cuckoo
Child; all of us always have known,
Recognition printed on the cells
Of the primitive body chart.

Every night that month I dreamed the baby was born,
It was fragile, creased like an overseas envelope; it was mislaid;
I had forgotten to feed it.
I woke up, moved my awkward belly into the bathroom,
Stood gasping at the edge of the washbasin. I would never
Be used to this.

And when I picked up the real baby it settled its heavy weight
                              between my arm and my body
Like a sullen beanbag,
Turned its face against me,
Pulled me into it.

Shore

For my father

I remember, you tell me, a daughter, a love, as high as my kneecap.
That was me, I say.
You're 87 years old. We walk by the sea at Carmel.
You say: she slept in the upper berth of the train.

And now you forget me and I have to reach after you;
You're captious, like a plunging Japanese kite.

The ocean's harsh today, the wind's rising,
Our path lies along the edge of the cliff.
Hold my hand.

She had yellow hair, you say.
I know, Father. I love you
Because you're old, because you need me, because you look like someone
                    I am forgetting.

Is his height like yours, does his head turn like yours, is he
Going to be dead, like you? Should I order us both a boat
For that long journey over daylight, up to the cold zone

Where you go whenever I ask you a question,
Where the kite dips, pulling
Its long bright anxious chain.

Terminal Version

It will happen in the summer,
The air dry and still,
Hills yellow, silence warm; we'll look up into the air,
And there, halfway down the sky,
Their machines like bubbles or old planes or
Emptiness, or the sky.

They don't have human faces,
Their bodies are electric edged patches of cold,
They make blanks in the perspective, places where birds collide,
                    insects die.

Those dreams we've been having, surely
They spoke of this; the circles that pulled us onto the narrow rim,

The vast gray
Sweeps of sky.

Everything we've ever known is futile now. We understand this
In the first twenty minutes while the grass shrinks,
Our fear is too great to be absorbed,
The clear blue California sun surrounds us.

George Keithley

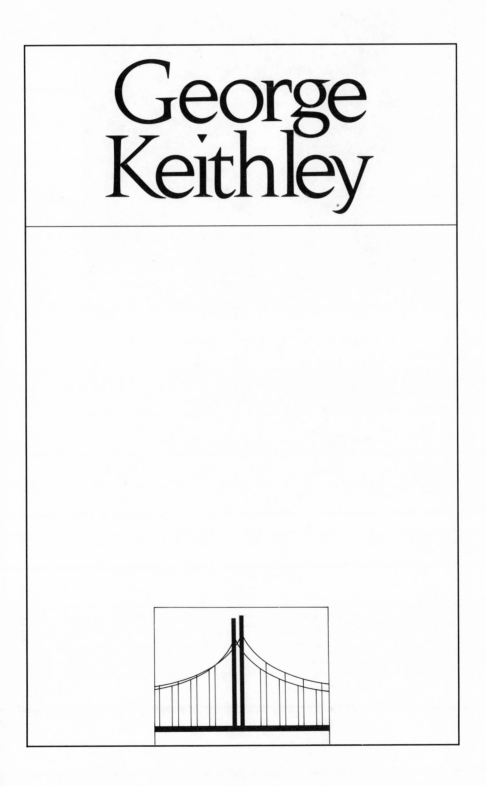

"I grew up in Illinois and worked as a racetrack groundskeeper, road repairman, warehouse stockman, hotel desk clerk, magazine writer; eventually a teacher. Educated at Duke, Stanford, and Iowa, I then spent six years writing the long poem, *The Donner Party*. After it became a Book-of-the-Month Club selection, I was asked to write the stage adaptation, and the play has had 23 performances. Recently, the opera of *The Donner Party* has been performed several times, and a radio play based on the poem is in production.

My second book, *Song in a Strange Land*, won the Di Castagnola Award of The Poetry Society of America. It's part of a poetic series which includes *The Donner Party* and a verse play, *The Best Blood of the Country*. A finalist in the National Poetry Series competition, this drama has won three awards for playwriting. It was first presented in a staged reading by The Playwrights' Center, in San Francisco.

The father of three children, I now live in Chico, California. My poems and stories have appeared in *Harper's*, *TriQuarterly*, *The Yale Review*, *The New York Times*, *Antioch Review*, *New Letters*, *American Poetry Review*, *The North American Review*, and other publications."

Dancing in the Doorway

I think we ought to abandon the severe distinction between conscious and unconscious life. All mind is one. I don't mean to say that our ideas lead us to unity; anyone can see that they don't. At least not for very long. Mentality is many-faceted in its images and its conclusions, but it is united in the primary functions of imagination and reason. However, to speak of the unconscious is to suggest that part of our mentality is ordinarily stunned or dulled. And yet, what we regard as the work of that aspect of mind—dreaming, visioning, impulsive image-making, impulsive desire—very quickly makes its interest known to us by welcome suggestion or unwelcome conflict. In other words, the imagery brought to mind may be lively, intriguing, appealing, threatening.

If we must use a negative term to describe that aspect of our being, it will be more accurate to speak of it as the *unmet,* the *unencountered.* It will be even more helpful to think of what this *is,* than what it is not. For it is the dwelling place of the new. The strange, original, different, unique, mysterious, enigmatic. All of that. And when we meet its imagery in a dream or vision or poem, often the encounter makes us more alert and aware than we usually are. What we feel is not that we've escaped from the stupor of an unconscious state, but that we have entered the magic of a theater which involves us in a heightened awareness.

It's an unfortunate fact that our understanding of mentality is influenced by the economic order of our society. Only those aspects of thought which are *productive,* which lead to the making of careers or objects or money, are considered *conscious* and *real.* And so our dreams, intuitions, impulses, fantasies, poetry, all are confined to what we call an inner world, while the *real* world rolls on, with or without the diversity of the imagination. In this whirling world we hear the words *myth* and *poetry* used in a pejorative sense, to indict ideas that lack empirical validity; notions that cannot survive the test of experience. But we know that these newly met, newly encountered images work within us with a vitality and force and purpose at least as strong as anything in that pragmatic world. Why then do we say that the material world is the *real* world?

I suspect the distinction between inner and outer worlds, and between conscious and unconscious thought, is a false dichotomy. A metaphor meant to suggest the psychic distance between one state of being and another; but not meant to insist on any actual difference between the two. For the sake of argument, let's extend the spatial metaphor and say that our image-making activity has its origin in some realm we cannot reach by physical means. If we dread the messages of those images, then we're likely to think they come from a dark region that is somehow beneath us. If we believed in Satan we could say they were sent to us from his Hell. Delusions and temptations sent from a demonic underworld. When that kind of hell lost its credibility, it became a lost landscape, an entire continent closed like the ancient Orient to our eyes. A realm which our repressions forbid us to see, so the theory goes, although according to its metaphor it is still beneath us. It has become, we say, the subconscious.

But there's an even older metaphor for the image-making mind, a metaphor that does not confine it to a realm of dread or irrelevance or blindness. In fact, it assumes for this essentially poetic activity of envisioning, an appropriate sense of wonder. And an appropriate mixture of humor and ridicule. Puts it not on a pedestal, where it would turn to stone, but on a far mountain whose unbounded slopes glimmer within us. In this metaphor the imagination is Mount Olympus. (And occasionally heaven.) The dwelling place of the gods, those prototypes of all imagined acts. What takes place in that metaphorical world is every act of creation and destruction. Image-making, transforming, always changing, manifesting in powerful visions, articulating in poetry, shaping in stories and dramas, urging to action. Urging us into hiding too, as with the young Achilles, and Moses, and Jesus, and as in solitude, forgetting, and repression.

So it's not surprising that an old alchemist and surgeon, Paracelsus, who has been called the founder of modern medicine, should say there is in every person a complete heaven. He says further that all of us are one heaven, and heaven is only one person. Again, all mind is one.

Very well, but poems are not written by angels. Anyone who has been acquainted with a poet will vouch for that. The point is that the activity of envisioning, of bringing visual or rhythmic images into being, is the work of the imagination. It is a basic activity which seems to originate within us, not always at our command. At times it even seems to rise up and overthrow our sense of command, as if it obeys some other master, or none at all.

And what are angels, anyway?

It's tempting to dismiss the question. To say it doesn't matter because, whatever they are, we don't believe in them. Never mind that Jacob wrestled for his life with one; that was a very long time ago. Still a poet might let the question linger longer than other people would, remembering that the first modern poet, William Blake, spoke with angels and thought it only proper that he should. And in our own century, Rainer Maria Rilke saw the angel as a fully achieved life of the spirit. The angel appears in Rilke's *Duino Elegies* as evidence that the human spirit can become wholly realized, wholly fulfilled. Yet that solitary creature stands among those poems as a quiet condemnation of the fact that it hardly ever happens.

Clearly this messenger is not some aberration of a mind which is trying to avoid itself. Always it asks us to see things differently, but also to see distinctly. As far as possible, to see truly. In the final poem of *The Auroras of Autumn*, Wallace Stevens writes:

I am the angel of reality,
Seen for a moment standing in the door.

. . . I am the necessary angel of earth,
Since, in my sight, you see the earth again.

To see again. Re-vision. Revising the earth, the material world, the world that wants us to call it the real world. But then the terrible dichotomy would begin again. No. Let's look for a moment longer at the figure of the angel, that intermediary figure standing, perhaps even dancing now, in the doorway between imagination and event.

Why didn't we see it before? Wasn't it there? Apparently not. It's not always apparent. The possibility is there, but it's not always fleshed out for us to recognize. Like the figure in that enigmatic rhyme:

Yesterday upon the stair
I saw a man who wasn't there.
He wasn't there again today.
I wish to hell he'd go away!

A figure that seems to come and go, independent of our will. Perhaps opening and closing the door. But we do not see the door into the world of the imagination; we see the image at the entrance. That is what is always possible, and that is what is essential. Because that figure *is* the entrance, the angel is the image. David Miller has noted that in Syriac the same word is used for "icon," "image," and "angel," and in the Greek version of Genesis, Jacob named the place where he encountered God's angel, "Image of God."

In the mind's eye we see suddenly the image we had not seen before, or had not seen clearly. The unmet, the unencountered. New, strange, original, mysterious . . . It comes now to command our attention, to clarify our vision. And this is why Stevens says it is the necessary angel that will enable us to see the earth again.

If we have any humanity we'll recognize that the figure has not come to mind for its own sake, to be admired or feared. If we have any humility we'll admit that it's not there for our sake, to show how clever we are. It is there because something is happening.

You try to understand what is happening. What is it that is being shown to you? You look closely at it, and you listen to it. For some people the initial image which begins a poem will be visual. For some a phrase or line. For me it is always a line that has an interplay of sounds, and a particular spring or tension to it. As a writer or a reader, my primary impression of a poem is of a movement of rhythm and sound.

Rhythm is the central nervous system of the poem, the particular energy that influences tone, form, content. It's the rhythm of that unexpected line that catches my attention, and at once I become more alert to the line and listen for more of that energy, the rhythm flowing through the line. At the same time, since you've noticed the line outside of any context, you're struck by the strangeness of it; you don't know what it means. But you listen for the pleasure of the current moving, as if you had stopped beside a stream to watch the water flowing. You listen ahead, to hear the rhythm continue. Because it is words that carry the rhythm, you're listening for language to continue the flow of energy. Inviting the poem to appear. If the flow stops, you listen back the other way. What must have been said before this point, you wonder, to bring this line along?

William Stafford wrote a poem called "Listening In," and I think that title suggests this activity at the beginning of a poem. Whether it's visual or auditory, the initial image induces a momentary trancelike state in which you are very alert but may not appear to be doing anything. All your attention is concentrated on the movement of language. This encounter is experienced in the mind and body and spirit, and I'm convinced these three are not nearly so separate as we pretend they are.

I'll write the first draft of the poem as rapidly as possible. I do alter a few phrases but not many; I want to be uncritical and keep the current of energy coming. I know that later I will revise, rewrite, countless times. Sometimes a poem will require months or even years before it is complete. And yet I sense that it *is* complete, in my mind and in the world, if only I could see it and hear it more clearly. This is the search for the exact language and the necessary form. Revising the manuscript is a form of learning. Attempting to articulate the poem, by bringing its language to light I hope to discover it.

Always, too, there's the sense that the poem is something which I need to learn. An experience which I need to feel, or a story I have to hear. There's an urgency to pursue it, to enter into its situation; a sense of discovery but also of necessity. A very strong hint that once you have become aware of *this* material, you cannot live fully unless you discover what it has to say to you.

In that regard, Stafford wrote another poem called "Reporting Back," and that title suggests the other side of the process. Having entered the state of mind in which you are exploring the rhythm and language of the poem, you then bring back, across that psychic distance, what you have found.

I don't mean to say that poems are sacred documents or psychological treatises. Let's hope not! Everyone knows that good poems can be funny, grubby, bawdy, sad, and beautiful. But in the writing and reading of the poem, something transpires in the writer and the reader, and I think we need to acknowledge the value of that activity. In a world that shouts its political and economic *realities*, we must insist that this too is basic to what we are. Much of the work of art is mysterious. But men and women have participated in this mystery, it seems, forever. We might have to admit to something essentially mysterious about our humanity. Something we glimpse when the light alters along the slopes of that mountain far within us.

No wonder such moments once were called a gift of the gods. Or that someone might think of the inspiring image as an angel, an enigmatic figure that comes to command our attention to the imagination, and then its work is done. But at that moment *our* work has just begun. Heaven help us!

FROM *The Donner Party*

Old Graves fell asleep
with his head in Mary's lap,
that evening he was dead.

In the morning
Mary went snowblind
seeing a steep green gully

and a stream of smoke
rising from a cabin closeby,
where there was only a canyon covered with snow.

"They're anxious for me!"
She ran off more than once,
slipped in the drifts up to her hips.

The last time she was told,
"You don't see a damned thing.
All you do is dream."

During the fourth day
all the beef had been consumed
and so people sucked on the sugar

as they paused
protected from the wind, waiting
in a sunny cleft

for Stanton to find his way.
He came in on his knees at night.
"I can't climb," he said, "my legs are gone."

By dawn it was plain he was dying.
He kept back against the rock
when the others started out.

The day after he was left for dead
nobody had any food—
beef or flour or whatever—

Foster went first
and the rest followed him
in a ragged line

under the sun.
Eddy said he felt
the snow was on fire.

He shut his eyes
and heard the soft noise
of his shoes caving into the crust.

Night found them on a ridge,
they heard the wind
above and below.

Eddy sat down
on the snow and Dolan drew
his pistol from his coat.

"We can't help it.
We need to kill someone for food."
Eddy set one condition . . .

"It must be someone with flesh
enough to feed these people.
Either you or me."

When Foster walked over and announced,
"Antoine has froze both feet,"
they decided to wait.

This man who had herded
cattle for the company was found
to be out of his head.

He passed the night in pain.
It departed and he drowsed all day
in a queer calm on the snow until he died.

Working with knives in the evening
they carved enough to cook
by a whistling fire.

It began to appear
that the loss of more men
might sustain them:

the Fosdicks fell sick
and the Murphy boy lame from frostbite
and the guides

could not tell
where they were
nor where they were going.

On the ninth day
everyone watched the clouds
passing over the peaks.

Sitting in a circle
they held their blankets behind their backs
to serve as a wall

but the wind
ripped the ring apart;
people let go, the fire flared up.

Eddy said nothing
they tried was any help.
They put on one piece of pine at a time.

The branches burst into light as though they were straw.
The flames flapped like flags.
They spit sparks onto the snow.

A pool formed underfoot from the sudden thaw.
Amanda McCutchen found her legs lying
in the water and crawled away crying.

When the party pulled together
and lifted their quilts like a tent
the snow wove a mound around the wool

and they were sealed inside
where they sat in the dark air.
The Murphy boy died there.

Later Dolan dragged the roof away.
It was morning, on the next day.
The sunlight leaped over the snow

as he stumbled downhill.
The mountainside was ribbed with pine
where he seated himself

to pull his boots off.
He stood barefoot in the snow
and pulled his pants off.

He looked up when he heard his name
but he wouldn't come.
He began to bury his body in the snow.

He was carried up the spine
of the mountain by two men.
Mary Graves gave him her quilt

but he died before night fell.
As dusk came down it was snowing.
No one moved. In the morning

the storm stopped,
and people crept out from beneath
their blankets and the dead

were uncovered for food—
Dolan and Murphy and the herder.
The flesh was fixed onto long sticks.

People were careful to set aside
what meat could be put into their packs.
Foster liked the liver and prepared it for himself.

If anyone was unwilling
he let his eyes fall from the fire
and ate in silence like a shadow.

By now none of the party said, "No—"
Each person consumed his course
and crawled off to sleep in his quilt.

Soon the men had gained
enough strength to go on.
Among the women

Amanda had to be carried;
Sarah Foster sickened and hung on her husband's shoulder;
only Mary Graves was much revived.

One guide sat stripped to the waist.
The two of them shared his shirt
to bandage their feet.

The party limped out
on the lip of a canyon and came down
ledge by ledge and finished the last of the flesh

on the floor and followed a stream
wherever they heard it hissing underfoot.
Then in the third week

they reached a pleasant plateau.
Patches of brown grass glowed in the snow.
They burned a bush

and took the thongs from their shoes
and singed them in the flame
and chewed them for the juice.

Foster asked Eddy for his gun.
"What good are the guides to us
if we die here?"

Sarah supported
her husband:
"Let him kill them.

Let him shoot
one at least,
so we can eat."

Mary Graves agreed.
"If you will
kill one,

we can feed
everyone else
with that meat."

Eddy kept his gun.
When they were alone
he talked to the quiet guides

and they fled
into the woods after dark.
By dawn a red trail was visible

where their feet bled
leaving the clearing and slipping across the snow.
Besides these smears

they discovered the sharp
prints of a deer
cut into the crust—

he walked off with Mary
and they made their way
among the oak trees that grow

at that low height
and the bushes struck with frost,
the thin stems thrust up from the snow.

"Soon we were tired,"
he said. "I sat on a stone
and rested the gun on my knees.

'Have you lost him?'
she wondered.
I answered, 'No.'

Then we saw the oval place
where the deer slept
and we tracked him

into the sun.
We saw how he stopped
to hold

his head erect,
his ears alert
listening for us.

I shot wild once.
My second shot missed.
The third one hit.

'Merciful Jesus!'
Mary cried.
'O yes, yes!'

He slumped in the snow.
We hooted and ran
and jumped on him.

Raising his jaw
we attacked his neck
with my knife.

Letting out
the last life we cut
a huge hole there.

'God bless us, blood!'
Mary screamed and I sank
my arms in the gore.

We drank
by bowing our heads
and licking our hands.

We giggled with glee.
I kissed Mary once
and we embraced.

We kissed again.
Her face red.
Both her hands red.

We pulled out the innards
and sat chewing on the strands
and I hugged her

my hands sticking
to her hair—
when we laid down to rest

I propped my rifle toward heaven
and fired a shot in the air
for the others to hear."

Black Hawk in Hiding

Everyone can see me standing in the center
of the stockade, which I hear was built to contain
white soldiers who got drunk or disobeyed
their officers—now it houses their prisoners of war.
The soldiers grow sober looking at us
in the sunlight over the fence.

*

A chain runs around my wrists and under my balls.
It circles both my legs like an iron vine.
A black bar is fastened to both feet
to make certain I won't run far
and I don't try, I just stand still.

*

I hope I will die soon
so I can go into the woods around Rock River
and stop knee-deep among the mesh
of creepers growing under the trees,

and breathe the brown bittersweet stink
of stale fish and grass, keeping back
in the wet shade where no one can see me.

Morning Star Man

juggles old bones
and odd stones. He lofts these long bones
end over end, and they land in one hand.

The stones he flips fast and high,
higher still, so they will drop
one by one on his other palm.

> Along his spine a red fox fur
> has spread like fire. His thin arms and legs
> sprout small paws on which he prances

> among the maples with a merry smile
> below his snout. When he walks upright
> again it's the grin of a grown man.

In green daylight a kettle is set
upon a rock—level full
of maple syrup steaming hot—

He leans over its brim to thrust
his hand, his wrist, his whole human arm
into the thick liquid while we scream.

The shaman scrubs his skin and shows
how his flesh glows from the heat:
no burns or blisters, no sign of harm.

He calls a young couple to come forth.
The girl refuses to let their eyes meet.
She won't lift her gaze from her feet.

In her hands he lays two figures
carved from wood. Male and female tied
together with one leather thong.

She pries these two apart. Their faces
are their own—hers and the man
looking on, whose heart she will not have.

The belly of the female is a box
hollowed below her bosom to hold
inside her a crouching animal—

the meticulous image of a fox.
She shudders. Then a cold shriek
as she feels the creature within her

and flings herself into the arms
of her neglected lover. Death
alone can loosen their embrace.

Their eyes find only one another.
Their host has burst into flames of hair
that hide his flanks; his ribs bristle.

Into the trembling shade he trots
quickly to cover on all fours;
his tail flails between his thighs.

*

Asked how he came to make his home
among us, he gives this reply:

"At night did you never see a small
ball of flame hurled out of heaven?

How it scorched poor earth!
The pain my mother bore at my birth—

This fire that flies from the night sky
is no star. Look up—It is I! It is I!"

Buster Keaton & the Cops

Stone Face is the likeness of all lovers.
Under a flower cart he keeps his seat,
hiding his hopes from the crowd
until some clown discovers
his hat in the cop-cluttered street.

The officers fall on their knees
in the flowers and find his hiding-place.
He remains undismayed.
He rubs his cuffs and dusts his collar.
The cops crawl up and greet him face to face.

He throws his roses in their eyes.
In retreat he duels for his life,
with daffodils he clouts their clubs.
He creeps from his cart, he tries
to lose them in the lilies which he spills.

When he impeccably plucks his hat
and races through the swirling street,
his shirt-tail hangs unfurled
and waves goodbye to his heart
and goodbye to the fragrant world.

A Song for New Orleans

Oh the wine's fine
but listen you drink too
damn much. I drink too damn

much fine wine eating
salty fish, we have to
get out of this place

I can't whistle
you can't kiss
eating salty fish.

On Clark Street in Chicago

On Clark Street in Chicago
the faces that you see

are rising on the river
of immortality—

Washed by the warm water
that floods the floor of hell

they circle in the current
their voices climb and fall.

O listen when they pass us
on the sunny shore

they're calling out to Jesus
no more no more no more.

Don't you ever worry
Sugar we
found us a place to lay—

Don't ever worry
Sugar we have
found us a place to lay—

O you give me
some sweetness, pay
you soon as I can

I'll get me my
sweetness now
here comes the honey-man.

On Clark Street in Chicago
your face was wet with fear

hearing the summer morning
awaking as before.

O listen to the sparrow
singing so long and clear

in the daylight slowly drying
the street outside your door—

Someone will come tomorrow
someone who wants to hear

your sweetness and your sorrow
no more no more no more.

The Thief's Niece

While the women sliced bread and cold meat
the thief's niece rolled and unrolled the white sheet
and their old men leaned at the wall to count
how many night guards the oniongrowers
ordered for the ride. She walked out so hers
was the first face he might see from his mount
now it came groping into the black street.

Between two guards the council-treasurer
shrugged the priest toward his niece to comfort her.
As the horses stepped uphill in the dark
the girl said there were no growers she'd seen.
"They have their money back." On high ground clean
of brush one guard reined in his horse to mark
widths of limb. The old men haunched where they were.

The guard riding in front held the pistol
the treasurer fired in the hotel
lobby, wounding a clerk. He roped the limb
and the girl asked the priest, "Pray he may live!"
And he explained, "Mercy is relative;
yes, we'll pray now." He called the men to him
who read the Grange receipts in the council.

The wives and girl sat by the tree. Nearby
the guards and jailor on horse watched the sky.
At dawn the first guard cut the councilman's
horse with a belt. It bolted and he hung
while they rode downhill. Then his friends among
the growers' younger sons and the farmhands
drew down upon his heels to help him die.

The Child

In my dream the brooding child
I was ten years ago leans back
far, tilting his kitchen chair,
to hear the Chicago Symphony
of the Air. No one else is home
until the strings and horns grow still.
How soon my family fills the room—
Grey-eyed uncles and aunts, and father
and mother. My sister, Julia, too.
It might be every holiday reunion.
If I were younger I would guess
my First Communion. It's not,
though someone has invited Father Tein,
who thought he was a friend of mine.

Each face is flame. The gleam or glow
of flesh without its weight of guilt.
All their voices know my name—

"Gerhardt!" they cry. Or simply
"Gary!" if it's my sister. Always
I look as if I'm listening.
Now they command my attention
their mouths form an important shape—

    "You can be anyone you want.
    Anyone at all!"

                              I smile.
They blaze into ordinary air.
Why should they stay? I recall
their message vividly. They dare
not fester in restless sleep
like some hallucination out of hell.
Mostly they're my family, you see.

And because I was taught every dream
is a delusion, telling you this
just now I smiled. Still
in the dream I understand they mean
what they say: "Be anyone at all"

but not that child.

Waiting for Winter

1

I think of my name, Julia Grahm,
and hold my hands so in a circle,
making my mind obey my mind.
Alone in a harsh room in some home,
no sound but my breathing for hours.
Light cleanses the floor of its color.
On the walls no mirrors, no chairs
in the corners or tables or flowers.

My flesh has forsaken its shadow.
My eyes wander to one window
which offers a view of the orchard,
apples and pears long since picked
and packed. Leaves purple the grass.
Rubbed to its sheen like a pewter plate,
behind bare branches sleeps the lake.

In all that ache of autumn
the only woman— Why must I wait
for the weather to turn? And turn again?
Caught up in a crowd of acquaintances
I want to feel the wishes of my flesh,
though I know that I'm dreaming—
No one is here, no one is coming.

2

It's impossible to move one muscle
even to music, unless you love.
Look at me, I want to see
the swift sex of birds!
Spring sun melting the mud!
To be born in a warm season like the bulbs—
The first sound of sin that you hear in your skin.

But it's almost the end
of November and over blue fields
flakes are sown or scattered without care.
A pocket of snow collects in the crotch
of every available tree,
and I'm frozen in my fortieth year
of this dream, waiting for winter.

I keep my wits. I say I'm a wise woman.
Then an ice storm strikes so deep
it chokes the springs in the lake for weeks
and won't warm. Well water sleeps.
The orchard claws at the wind.
My bones are blind but they believe
what they are told of cold despair.
Now it is coming, now it is here.

The Woman

1

Where is the woman who unmoored this morning,
rowing upriver to visit her sister?
Toward noon her skiff rides so high
its keel climbs free of the current.

No one to work the oars,
they drag silver ribbons like whispers
her children trail through the sedge grass.

2

Into blue shadow her boat
drifts under the arch of the stone bridge.

3

It brightens now floating in crimson light,
more earth than air in it.

Light at the last hour
downstream where the yolk of the sun breaks,
bleeding in the water.

To Bring Spring

        all it takes is girls
        arriving at the end
        of a gun blue day
        dancing on
the screen porch and passing over
the lawn. A breeze tails
off Rock Lake cold
with the steel smell
        of rainwater making
lanterns in the paper evening air
blow half-way dark
and half-way back.

        Most of the morning
        a dead season lies
        on the hill
or leans at the porch in the sun.
The white colt his winter
        legs slack strolls
up from his hay, like anyone
he's heard about the rain and
tramples the littered hill, down
and up the hill the apple branches
blossom . . . A slow girl
her black hair braided

---

and two tall sisters come stripping
the lanterns off. The sisters
                with a certain arch,
                like divers, loft
                the lamp shells down
to their friend. They walk out
the drive, the three girls now,
where sunlight blows under
the eaves. The last girl
cradling several globes
in her bare arms
yellow and blue and rose.

Kathleen
Fraser

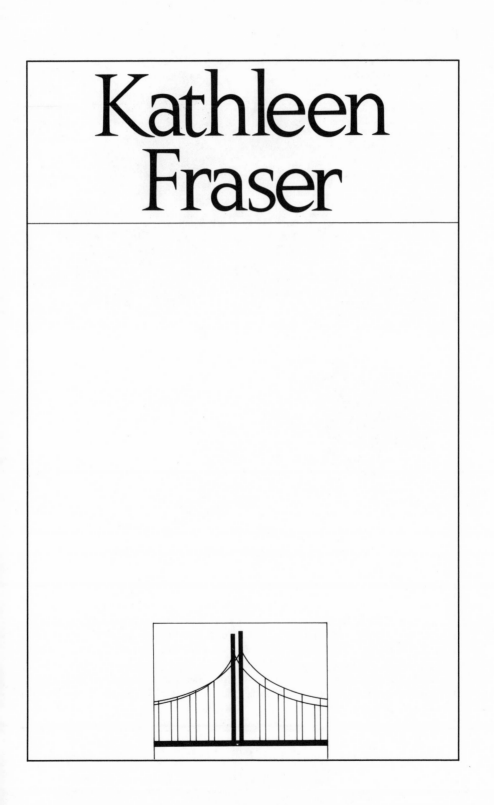

Kathleen Fraser lives in San Francisco, teaching in the graduate writing program at San Francisco State University during the week and studying Italian conversation and jazz singing on weekends. Much of her Guggenheim Fellowship (1980–1981) was spent in Rome and the Tuscany region of Italy working on a new book, *Something (even human voices) in the foreground, a lake.* Other awards include a grant and a fellowship from the National Endowment for the Arts. She has published eight books, including *Change of Address, What I Want,* and *New Shoes. Each Next, narratives,* is a poetic narrative reflecting her own experience of discontinuous time, published in 1980 by The Figures. She has one son, David, age 16, and lives with the playwright and philosopher, A. K. Bierman.

Interview from a Treehouse

What the new writer does is to throw light on things never noticed before
. . . Revolutionary art is tied to the new persons who make themselves heard
in this world . . . Suddenly, they *see:* things that were always there, but which
the light didn't reach.

—Grace Paley

(*Note:* This interview took place in the somewhat plain but lofty treehouse
chosen by the Poet at the time of her formal retirement from the world of letters
and was done on a day when unexpected gusts of wind punctuated the conversa-
tion and prevented a certain drawing-room stuffiness from making its demands.
Often, as an illustration to the Interviewer's question, the Poet would reach to
one tree limb or another, opening, with a tiny key, one of many small doors
revealing a chamber in which single objects were poised, and she would take each
object into her hands while recalling, as if through touch, the answers to particu-
lar questions she'd struggled with for much of her writing life.)

Interviewer: What shall we talk about?

Poet: I'm glad you didn't say what *should* we or what *ought* we to talk about.
There are so many things to see between these branches and how can you
possibly know ahead of time, until you look closely, what is *there* to be interested
in? I remember one afternoon, about 5 o'clock, I was driving from the top to the
bottom of the same hill I traveled every day, and the sky seemed to slowly bloom
into a luscious flesh of persimmon, uncommon for that time of year. There were
theories of weather floating about. I knew that. I heard people putting things in
their place every day. But their convictions didn't account for the unsettling in
me. I wanted to hold this persimmon light in my throat. I was *un*placed and the
feeling resonated in me.

I: But why not ask a weather expert who'd studied these phenomena? There
are explanations. Why not let yourself rest easy?

P: You mean take it easy. (The Poet broke off at this point to unlock one of
the doors and take out a thermometer and put it under her arm.)

I: Excuse me, but what's that for . . . are you feeling feverish?

P: Not exactly. But I've always taken my own temperature. One *does* change,
you know. And reading the path of the mercury is difficult . . . you think you
see something shining, you think you've finally learned how to measure heat,
you look closely . . . and it turns out to be as difficult to track as it ever was.

I: Have you always been elliptical?

P: I've been accused of many things. Those are marvelous buttons on your
jacket.

I: Well, thank you, they're antique bone. I found them in a little button shop in Soho . . . but what about Poetry?

P: Oh, it's something significant you're after, is it . . . well, listen to this, then. (The Poet opened another door and took out a journal covered with Italian paper. Its white pages appeared to be only partly filled.) This is Gerard Manley Hopkins writing to his friend Baillie, in 1864, about the language of inspiration: "I mean by it a mood of great, abnormal in fact, mental acuteness, either energetic or receptive, according as the thoughts which arise in it seemed generated by a stress and action of the brain, or to strike into it unasked. This mood arises from various causes, physical generally, as good health or state of the air . . ."

I: Ah, Hopkins . . . instress, inscape. . . . I remember: "The world is charged with the grandeur of God."

P: "It will flame out like shining from shook foil.

It gathers to a greatness, like the ooze of oil

Crushed . . ."

(The Poet glanced at the Interviewer triumphantly.)

I: Those poems really move me, but his theory sounds as if another, entirely different person were writing it . . . it just confuses me. I like a writer to be clear, so that you know what to expect and how to prepare yourself to read the work.

P: But not many people thought of Hopkins's poems as "clear" when he was writing them. What we think of as his ecstatic re-invention of the poetic line, his piling up of sound upon sound, was often considered to be eccentric, obscure and ambiguous, even by his poet-friend Bridges, who wrote the preface to his First Edition. Hopkins was a remarkably conscious craftsman, constructing his own stress patterns from such disparate sources as nursery rhymes and the complicated rhythms of the Welsh poetry called *cynghanedd,* in which stresses were grouped together in a way that suggested excitement and intensity to Hopkins. He was a high-roller in Jesuit robes, whose ear heard and measured a different music than the English poets had been hearing. He noticed everything and it clamored in him.

I: Hopkins, that sensualist, a Jesuit?

P: That's how he happened onto Duns Scotus . . . he was reading medieval philosophy, in preparation for the priesthood, when he found in Scotus what reinforced his own thought, that: "Each poet is like a species in nature and can never recur."

I: You mean Hopkins thought each one of you poets is an original?

P: Precisely . . . at least potentially we are. Scotus coined a word, *haecceity,* to mean "thisness." He composed it from the Latin feminine form of the demonstrative pronoun, *haec* (this), combined with the feminine suffix, *-eity* (-ness). Thus: *haecceity:* thisness. He must have been referring back to the Greek word for "being," *ousia*, which is a feminine word meaning: that which is one's own essence, one's true nature. Scotus found a soulmate in Hopkins. "Thisness" lit up his mind.

I: *Thisness* lit him up?

P: Hopkins was responding to something ultimately important to any poet trying to write about the world and human experience in fresh terms. Scotus declared that the individual is immediately knowable by the intellect in union with the senses. He gave Hopkins's disturbing intensity a sanction, fuel for discovering new ways to put words together. To Scotus, *haecceity* was the property of things that marks their identity and differentiates each thing from each other thing. Hopkins's task was to transform the individuality of observed things into language. (The Poet reached for the Interviewer's hand and turned it over, examining its palm.) Like your hand. Its individuality isn't only its common anatomical designation—hand—nor simply the unusual patterning of lines on the palm, or the texture of skin determining this particular hand, but also its being *this*, not that. You can see why Hopkins was so excited.

I: I wish I *could* see.

P: Well, *haecceity* is very close to what Hopkins meant by his term *inscape*, which he defined as "that individually distinctive form which constitutes the rich and revealing oneness of the natural object." Not a landscape, but an *interior*-scape.

I: This seems very removed from *you* . . . what about *your* poetry?

P: Inscape, instress—that's what makes my work process, as a poet, so exacting. Instress describes that *stress*ing energy which is coming *from* the inscape of each thing and which acts upon *my* senses and through them, to actualize the inscape in *my* mind.

For Hopkins, instress was the *sensation* of the inscape of a particular bird or wave or . . . a kind of quasi-mystical shedding of light on the deeper structures of things, one's sudden understanding of how phenomena reveal themselves. But, of course, the poet can't *know* this deeper structure until she approaches it through the act of writing.

I: Are you saying that this idea is actually exciting to you? I don't understand how a woman like you could love an idea like that . . . (The Poet leaned deep into the tree and picked an apple for her interrogator.)

P: Can you feel the inscape of this particular apple pulling on you? (The Interviewer took a bite.)

I: Want a bite? Or aren't apples your subject?

P: It depends. If that particular apple happened to suddenly flag me down . . . but it occurs to me that I *did* write about an apple, once . . . "How the apple says/tart!/Perfidious green/and roundness,/endless. Its stem/snaps; the ceiling/cracks/with pressure./I am saved from perfection . . ."

I: That must be from one of your earlier poems. It sure doesn't sound like your recent work . . . and it certainly doesn't sound like Hopkins.

P: Good lord, I had to give up long ago on ever *sounding* like Hopkins . . . or Stein, or Woolf, Stevens, cummings, Zukofsky, O'Hara, Oppen, Barbara Guest. I was in love with every one of them, of course. I've always wanted to be other people, as well as myself—not just other poets, but to feel what it's like to live in another sort of body, to taste a different kind of speech on my tongue . . . I suppose that's why I love speaking Italian.

I: Excuse me, but . . .

P: But it has usually been the peculiar movement of the language *against* tradition that has finally thrilled me in the work of the poets I've been most drawn to. The way they've broken away from the beautiful smooth lull of the prevailing poetry breezes. (At this point, a wind banged against the branches of the treehouse and the Poet cautioned the Interviewer to hang on.) The poets I've loved most were innovators . . . they took pleasure in making their own.

I: But don't you think the quest for originality can become a fetish? I mean quirkiness, oddness for its own sake, can get a bit precious at times, wouldn't you agree?

P: Anything can get overbred, if that's what you mean. Poetry *can* get too dependent on its own hothouse temperature controls so that its ability to sustain life in less than perfect circumstances makes it overly fragile, groomed to predictability and finally useless. I mean, I don't go to look at paintings to be lulled into drowsiness. And I don't read poetry to tell me what I already know. TV and most newspapers can do that for me. I want to be put *on alert*. To be reminded I'm mortal.

I: Is that partly how you use your writing, to remind you of your mortality?

P: That sounds pretty literary . . . but I *do* know that when I am in the state-of-alert instress has described, it is then I feel most alive and unpredictable. I am a witness, rather than an ego with its daily complaints. I am being led by the thing that is suddenly calling me to attention, *and* I am trying to record it as faithfully and originally as my language sense will allow. This means I'm not interested in saying it in the way it has already been said. Otherwise *my* instress is fogged in by someone else's language preferences. To work in this way means to re-construct, to question the habits I've been taught . . . to try to give *it* the new form-of-being it has revealed to me.

I: It? You mean Hopkins's "Windhover" or his "rose-moles all in stipple"?

P: No. I mean my apple.

I: But you don't strike me as a nature poet.

P: Good. I never cared to be classified in *any* way, because classification interferes with one's appreciation of the uniqueness—the inscape—waiting to be discovered in each poem. Changing forms is my pleasure. I was someone else, after all, when I first read Hopkins, *not* the woman you are talking to right now. But don't you see, that's his point. That who *you* are, at this very moment of continuous change, is called forth by the peculiar qualities of *what* you are witnessing. It is in this collaborative act, this process of engaging, that the poet experiences a rebirth of imagination and is given the authentic chance to pass this on in her poems. The poet is participating in bringing into existence the thisness of the thing perceived, *and* the thisness of the perceiver herself.

I: But what about me? I really liked those poems in your first book. I could understand them. You were really a singer . . . in love with life. Now, I have to try harder to get at what you're talking about. It just seems less poetic . . . less recognizable. Where's the old music, I keep asking myself . . . where's the old thrill?

P: But, I'm not writing for your good *old* thrill. That would be entertainment. My eye is on the new. Who I am, what I witness—these are infinitely more complicated than when I was twenty-two and someone else's. Why do you think I moved up *here?* That other place was very nice, you know. But I couldn't hear myself think. I talk to myself about things when I'm alone. (The Poet unlocked another of the doors and pulled out a crazy quilt, patched together from odd pieces of silk and satin fabrics from the Twenties. She tossed it over the Interviewer's shoulder like a shawl.)

I: Oh, thanks. Now let me get this straight. If you are hoping for Hopkins's perfect bliss of instress to hit you, so that you can write, I would think you'd want to *quiet* your mind, not listen to its ramblings.

P: Are you sure you aren't getting uncomfortable up here? The wind's so unpredictable. Maybe I should make some tea?

I: Tea *would* be soothing.

P: Look . . . part of who I am is *how* I think, *how* I talk to myself. In my mind, I'm never a smooth talker. I worry, I repeat myself, I dream and stutter along, trying to sort out things. This is a kind of movement that has its own changing patterns. Sometimes there is this frantic, chaotic character lurching around in there. Other times, a hermetic, contained observer. In fact, I am a female person living through specific moments in history, who was impressed at an early age, like a lovely pat of butter in a fancy restaurant, with certain designs other people found attractive. I was taught attitudes of femininity, of poetry, of survival . . . *through* language. But it was someone else's idea of how to be. It didn't include my changes. It didn't make room for me to respond to the inscape in everything out there. That witness I told you about, who is watching through these branches, is also watching a mind struggling to free itself of the old designs. There are times when the inscape of my mind—its subject of thought, or the way that thought is moving around—is alerting me to pay attention. As a poet, I'm continually learning how to track that calling from the world, listening for whatever most moves *me* . . . subjects which haven't necessarily been included, thus far, as appropriate content in the canons of literature. It's a question of learning to trust one's own. So that what *you* may call "ramblings" or babble *might* be, for me, as interesting a flight pattern as the movement of a bird in the wind.

I: I'm glad you said might . . .

P: Well, obviously . . . any mind, without some wind blowing through it, is going to be as dank as a hothouse or a smog-clogged city. One doesn't want to repeat oneself. That's what art is about. That's what Hopkins reminds us of. The inevitability and the potential excitement of being our own unique poet.

Nuts and Bolts Poem for Mr. Mac Adams, Sr.

May I put my head on your shoulder, Mr. Mac Adams, Sr.?
My future takes on bubbles and substance
like a new sourdough formula and I know I can sell it
and convince them on the continent to take a bite,
with you as my lap, my Platonic cigar,
but more whiff to it, more longevity in the face
of disbelief, unlike the ideal, and thus
the kind of thing I can trust.

Where *do* you get your information
about Oswald's letter of tender regard? How is it, living
in Dallas, you have found the key to this century's thickness
in the *L.A. Times?*

       Drinking French wine in L'Etoile, the shadow of
the Orient whisking by in his white cotton jacket, I notice
your wife is radiant and exquisitely intact. Her face
reveals a preference for the emotional.

        You wave to her like two flags
a swimmer carries in his teeth, making signals, trying
to remember what the codebook said before the boat collapsed;
               he wants to say "Help!"
but he gets the syntax of red and blue confused
and it comes out "nuts and bolts."
        Now it's coming out from *your* mouth,
          you are the carrier of the code,
           it presents itself
in a white balloon above the table at L'Etoile,
above your son's devotion,
above your wife's gold belt shining,
next to me, discovering the thread
of the nut and bolt with its solid visual bite,
how much I need this silvery connection,
how much I want to sit on your lap and be small again,

to tell you about my father who held me,
whose study had a wooden desk with drawers full of
colored chalks, T-squares, compasses
and little metal pencils with pieces of lead held intact
by tiny nuts and bolts, which he'd show me how to use,
sitting on his lap, my head against his shoulder,
               connecting the points

at the edge of the circle with arc after arc of fuchsia
and gold and fishy green pastels that crumbled and came off
                                        in my fingers.

This is sentimental material, Mr. Mac Adams, Sr.,
and when my father got hit, head-on, he was just gone.
All his perfect body.
And when he never came back, we had to lock up.
                                        But here you are, ready
for a second round, with your Texas-size cigar
                        and your sourdough formula
about to launch a revolution in the dining rooms of Europe,
                                        and your belief
in the day after next.

The Know

     For Laura Wessner

Not overwhelming, this morning's little dream
            hot white squares
                    of sun soaking through
                        opaque tattered shades, then
    window   wind   oh window light falls in
                on a vision of future neat stacks:
                    papers letters announcements falling,
        now filed under   "mouth" or "flower"

    Just pressing them together   pushing them flat
with glass paperweight
            depicting beige cliffs and
                half a curved bridge   diagonal trestles
                    vertical in white puffy clouds
                        and the intimate blur of somebody's house
        under trees   at the edge of a thought
                called "paradise"

            All that
                    calls for absolute attention
        at each moment   separate
            Being in the now is not
    what they called "the know"   or is it   I am
            solidifying into a constant flow
                    roots going down sideways for water

In sleep fragments,
        I jogged with D. in pasture   passed long slabs
of old wood   brownish grey from smoothing of water
     our thought   between us running

as this attempt to reach you, Laura,
        through air
Still shots, of purple under your eyes   spread of blood vessels
      rooted   like some new Japanese eye-shadow
where they   broke your nose   on the inside   to let you
        breathe
          The bruises made me think "pain"
      when you walked in   that someone had hit you
but it was just you   coming through time
         and trying to evolve into the air
    borne species you sense
      in those wingtips at your heels
          you imagine for someone else . . .

     . . . your "cowboy," I think
You give him your best shots, always
      and in between   tender
      towards his "testicles like petals"
        the pink soft wrinkled edge of both
   your warm shores
        There is more, I wish I knew where
the corner is   to turn   Still poised
   in this light, feeling all digital glow
        this message is a conviction
from someone sprung into the joy of not knowing

Les Jours Gigantesques / *The Titanic Days*

Have you noticed the little shadow?
   How when you are in the middle of brushing your teeth
   there is something gathering around the corner?
She is dreaming this thought to a self
awake in the world
when she feels a tug, something like a hand pressing
down upon her thigh
   and she remembers she is naked and alone in the room
   and wishes for her silk blouse
   and the zipper with its three silver hooks at the top.

In her body's emptiness
a growing sense of intimacy,
the pressure of a shadow in its black suit,
its right hand moving
around her waist, as if looking
for a pocket,
        or the push of a head against
        her shoulder, as though
        this movie from some little light booth
        on the opposite wall was focusing,
        on her, and the image was him,
        his half head
moving towards her nipple,
with the thirst in him, black
against her white body. She looks down,
        she looks down at, oh, the hand, or is it
        the shadow of a hand
        pressing in on the thigh that is hers.
Her muscles bulge with effort
and become tremendous
in their flex. The color drains
from every part of her, but
        the red mouth,
        holding its shape steadily,
        the scream, at first uncertain,
        enters the air
        and becomes the third,
        the knowing, between them.

La Reproduction Interdite / *Not to Be Reproduced*

For Dick

I am interested in the logic of secrets, how it has always moved me, in
particular, to be invited by a face into the aura of its withholding, as though
we were designed to bring forward two opposing sets of facts and bathe
ourselves in the resulting struggle, as in watching a tightrope walker move
from one point in space to another, each foot brought precisely from behind
and placed in front of the other, but without the delicious possibility of
falling, were it not for the rope stretched tautly beneath him, cutting the air
with its odor of hemp.

The secrets between men and women are of peculiar fascination. My father, for example, invited me into a dream last summer where I discovered that he was making preparations to die. He was busy doing small errands, rushing about in his impeccably tailored suit and polished shoes, with a face so sad, so preoccupied with its secret, so designed to escape observation that I immediately began to pay attention, invited as I was by that closed-off expression to become the rope upon which he demonstrated his journey.

As I watched him moving to get everything in order before leaving, my sense of dismay began to take on its own life, expanding into anger and then curiosity. "How does he know?" I asked my mother. The fibers in me were twisting and vibrating. A conviction was growing. I became filled with the possibility of his life continuing and decided to speak to him directly, hoping to convince him that his death need not be imminent.

I go to my father and I say "Why do you think you are going to die?" His feeling is more one of resignation or tiredness than any specific illness. I ask him matter-of-factly to take off his clothes so that I may look at his body. He does so and his body appears to be fine, a bit shorter and stockier than I remember, but ruddy and glowing. I see immediately that he is perfectly well and able to live for a very long time. I tell him with conviction and energy that there is no reason for him to continue on this course of dying, that he is wholly alive and has many things to do. As I tell him this, we are walking outside through a woods, now up a slight incline to a clearing. My father seems very joyous and happy to hear the news. He accepts it, but with a kind of privacy that he's always had, savoring it for himself, indicating that he hopes I won't make a public issue of it. There is a kind of charged excitement between us, a flirtation with the possibilities that now lie ahead.

In 1965, my father was hit by a car and pronounced dead. I asked for his first set of architect's drawing tools, wrapped in a chamois case he'd sewn himself, each metal pencil and compass enclosed in its own soft pocket, each a potential source of precision and invention, given a hand to hold it.

Locations

For Bill Evans, jazz pianist

Light forgetting itself   light falling loosely
deep into May

Trying to listen to all that presses up
from under each side
of the seam

Holes where something gives in
to a pulse   careful stitches unraveling

cross-hatch of insulated wires
black slow curves among the poles
street slopes   here
in shadow where houses
lean on each other

but light still
catching white oil tank   distinct against
blue haze above bay water

Pollution soothes us in early evening
we breathe in and forget
coffee no longer hot   wind coming up
flapping the shades

Red metal pot the color of poppies

His love
the spot on the white tablecloth
after dinner

·

To give up
finally   to stop holding
the infant idea   how deep
you've been told to hurt,

to dissemble the structure
of wounds which choose
to resemble one another

Someday, because he was an exquisite set
of gestures, you thought
still   you would escape
the yearning to be surprised infinitely

A home inside yourself.

Your body held unto itself.

There were ways of talking.

·

He plays his piano in big cities
and now you are alone with him

in the full amplification
of ambiguous chords which he trusts
silence to justify

What is waiting for you
to fall into

big saxophone body
pulling from another side
of the seam
of music no longer
automatically
dropping

An effort to leave the window
justifies the question of
which is more important:

to witness
last light of mauve sponge sky

or, an inclination towards sound
drifting through the cities
where you listen
to what he isn't telling you,
clearly ambiguous
and totally intimate

·

How she notices, is a formal fact
clearly evident as a chip of paint
knocked off perfect white flow

where someone's brush tried to see a wall

Amplification attempts to make it all
all right

and in times of sorrow
a voice turned up loud
can be a true resonance

Still, some sound was too pretty

an easy beat
where you could get stuck,
not finding out

Two trout bought for supper, to please his mouth,
now softening under their scales
She'd know if their eyes were dead
Lights just went out

Their scales were silver and excited her
in a room she didn't talk about

·

Summer, such a little place

full of fish in rivers leaping   The apples out,
red with yellow streaking their sides,
not so glamorous as stores promised
but pulling low on branches next to the road

All in heaviness
to be crushed into softness   Her sweet throat
Cider drinks   gravel you hear first
from the driveway
before the shadow appears   and then
the visual body of the guest

·

These acts of attention   to fill in
all the gaps
where his body keeps going away

Lily, Lois & Flaubert: the site of loss

For Robert Glück

"How is she?" I asked.

"She is well. She is just fine," he said. "My Lily is back. I have my family back. I can take the sitter home now. Would you like me to do that? The tires are bad, so I go up hills slowly. But Lily doesn't mind."

Who is Lily? I think. I try to remember which one Lily is. I feel she is probably one third of his nuclear family. The other third is his Aunt Cora, sitting in an airplane above Los Angeles. Her ambiance hovers—a thin trail of white smoke drifting always above and behind him. One can almost hear the gossamer command of her voice in his childhood, filtered like light falling perpetually upon him. Her shadow is a light jacket, his little coat from the third grade.

Listening to him speak of Lily, I decided that he must be speaking of his lover. I thought I understood him. That is, I immediately provided a set of images from which to identify this object of his affection. To my ear, his all-embracing acceptance of Lily sounded romantic and excessive. I felt a bit jealous. I compared his feeling for her to a cloud of dust escaping from a vacuum cleaner. Yet as the dust cleared, things took on their true shapes. I understood that Lily was his dog. "White Lily of my family," he called her. "I wanted a family," I once heard him say to himself.

His voice was a kind of scenery behind the scrim one sees at the front of the stage, at the apron of the stage where Lily was forever wagging her tail. Lily, who had been lost, was now back in his arms. There existed among us a scenario, stitching together our lives at intervals: this tin can of dogfood he opened and spooned into a dish for her, linked Lily's love of dogfood to his love of Lily to my romantic projection of his "other life."

.   .

Phillipe S. has a dog called Lois. From the beginning of our friendship, this fact was clearly established. Phillipe feeds Lois *blanquette de veau* to gain her trust. He likes to think of Lois as something sacred, a sacrament as only the French can know it. He likes to lick his chops when he thinks of the pure prosody of life with Lois, the sheer grammar of Lois when she gushes her dog speech—often a series of sharp barks, as though a ribbon of sound were emitted spontaneously, yet inviting certain ritual progressions to soothe the air.

Phillipe often imagines Lois ordering a five course meal with all the correct wines. Her commanding use of the vernacular provides him with clear directives, a perpetual reassurance of order in his otherwise muddled life.

Lois gives him vigorous argument as well as propriety. And her wag assures him, even in those hours alone, when he feels the subject falling away from the predicate and that odd chill rise up to drench his solar plexus, when the sentence, as he's known it, begins to dismantle itself.

.   .

We have a dog at our house. His name is Rover. He's hardly ever around. Sometimes we call him Flaubert, to introduce a second possibility—as, for instance, on a greyish day when you pull up the shade on waking, with the hope of orange emerging somewhere among the cloud layers—just a small gash, even, as when my friend's old work pants developed a rip and you could see his muscular thigh showing through, a bit of tawny skin, though the trousers were loose and not normally the kind of garment you'd attribute to sexual arousal.

Flaubert, as a nickname, provides an immediate source of imagery. A guest walking in and hearing you call out "Flaubert . . . Flaubert???" might enter a different context than he thought his steps were leading to—a configuration of narrow lanes and dark doorways opening onto courtyards, or an acknowledgement of certain social issues he had hoped to dismiss as buried.

The wine you serve at dinner takes on an entirely different bouquet, a brickier color, haunted by an aftertaste of vineyards in the Dordogne. It hardly matters that Flaubert does not come in, wagging his tail and performing the set of tricks his former master taught him. His name is enough.

"Flaubert . . . Flaubert?" Now the guest begins to ease toward that seam where the stretch of his former life is stitched to this room, where Flaubert's remembered barks form a discourse that still perforates the common silence.

1930

Because the shadows are sepia

all the little precisions seem soft, a quaking
of leaves that extend their tenuous web
We imagine it gold because it is August

there is Marjorie   there is Ian

eyes averted, modestly, so great is their pleasure

And you see his bare arm, exactly as graceful as
the other young trees   long and willow yes limb yes
compare it

Everywhere, aspens shiver

The weight of her breasts how the light floats
there

Flowers open
because it is summer, their great dark heads lean

into this sexual composure he pretends
against the sapling   seeking balance
in its appearance

while all around them the possibility of doubt hums

wingspans slap and break loose in the hot dust
a tremor behind the leaves

You are the one, my shining, oh kisses I never knew
mother   father

These Labdanum Hours

You couldn't find it in the bird's weight
pulling an arc through the twig. You must

catch yourself somewhere or fall anywhere.
Four cherries, red showing through

green webs. This surprise may not catch you
and that is the trouble. A whole new life

may be just another tree. Now the floor
is as clean as vinegar. It shines

from rubbing. Sleeping inside your little
and constant coughs, you could hear

someone helping you, finally waking.
The helper has her rags and tools.

With tenacity she hangs on to the dimming
vision. You are trying too hard

to enter this world. The door is open.
What can you find in this

that is yours wholly? A belief,
not to be divided into silken strands

in air. This childish hope. I give you up,
each day, to another. Abstract acts

of generosity, as we dream in two positions
on the bed, with the softer, lighter pillows

just under our heads, some slight elevation.
Whole sentences are subtracted from

conversation. Darkness moves continuously
towards that line where the sun gives in.

To let go of shapes held in peaches,
the bruise of a thumb and forced sweetness.

You are the lightest of all the silver-white metals.
Jade was never what I wanted.

Joan Brown, about Her Painting

There is a black dog in my painting.
He says Woof.

You recognize this message, don't you?

It is a gesture
as typical
as the mechanical pleat of laughter.

I have decided to give up my palette knives
and my "typically vivid" colors. He approved
of me so much

I couldn't hear, so for months I stood
before the canvas   and made tiny strokes
on a "highly irregular" still-life,
still
breaking the pattern of woof and bow-wow.

I loved so much my red and black.

I needed confidence   and the tiny brushes whispered
to me.

I mean I could hear each stroke like a pointing finger

so that I could walk into the paint
or one side of me be there
like a nude faced frontally to show her bulges
flatly.

I pay attention to my fingernails
and   when the moons disappear and under the long part
yellow gets stuck
then I know it's time to be lonely.

You will think I am intentionally careless
and spontaneous.
You will love me,
describing the familiar bow-wow
as I make my plans.

Interior with Mme. Vuillard and Son

Yellow's unstitching itself from the sun,
Madame Vuillard. Take off your black dress.

Your thimble will rust inside
the moist scullery of another's vividness.

That cobalt blue chiffon, Madame,
left over from the mayor's youngest daughter—

take it! Cover yourself in ruffles.
A rare Sunday has dropped its perfume

upon us, we are its prisoners, it is time
to marvel at tulips! The air annoints

itself. My body is running away. I am
Edouard, your son, and I say that

under your lamp it's always nighttime,
stitching and piecing for the banquet gowns

of those who are constantly feeding.
Their sleeves puff with your lightness.

Our father's marching now, away in his big dream,
down from Senegal to the Red Sea. He's a toy

soldier, tin and commanding thousands to mass
like ants across the full cloth of a continent.

He's stuck in the old two-step, Madame. Let him
be. Your sitting-room's buzzing with women

before mirrors, behind screens, considering
their long torsos or short waists pinned

and tucked into place by your needle.
Let us study the facts, Madame. Your neck

carries the light, the imagined movements
of a lovely arm trussed in taffeta

reaching for a glass of Dom Perignon.
Have a drink, Madame! A day such as this

is worth a thousand flounces.
The earth is still kind to us on Sunday,

coaxing away all thoughts but those which compel
our bodies to give everything away

to the green leaves and the blue shadows.

Medusa's hair was snakes. Was thought, split inward.

For Frances Jaffer

I do not wish to report on Medusa directly, this variation of her
writhing. After she gave that voice a shape, it was the trajectory itself
in which she found her words floundering and pulling apart.

Sometimes we want to talk to someone who can't hear us.
Sometimes we're too far away. So is a shadow
a real shadow.

When he said "red cloud," she imagined *red*
but he thought *cloud* (this dissonance in which she was feeling
trapped, out-of-step, getting from here to there).

Historical continuity
accounts for knowing what dead words point to,

a face staring down through green leaves as the man looks up
from tearing and tearing again at his backyard weeds. His red dog sniffs
at what he's turned over. You know what I mean.
We newer people have children who learn to listen as *we* listen.

M. wanted her own.
Kept saying *red dog. Cloud.*
Someone pointing to it while saying it. Someone discovering stone.

Medusa trying to point with her hair.
That thought turned to venom.
That muscle turning to thought turning
to writhing out.

We try to locate blame, going backwards.
I point with my dog's stiff neck
and will not sit down,
the way that girl points her saxophone at the guitar player
to shed light
upon his next invention. He attends her silences, between keys,
and underscores them with slow referents.

Can she substitute *dog* for *cloud*, if *red* comes first?
Red tomato.

Red strawberry.
As if all this happens on the ocean one afternoon in July,
red sunset soaking into white canvas. The natural world.
And the darkness does eventually come down.
He closes her eye in the palm of his hand.
The sword comes down.

Now her face rides above his sails, her hair her splitting tongues.

Flashes of light or semaphore waves, the sound
of rules, a regularity from which the clouds drift
into their wet embankments.

Philip Dow

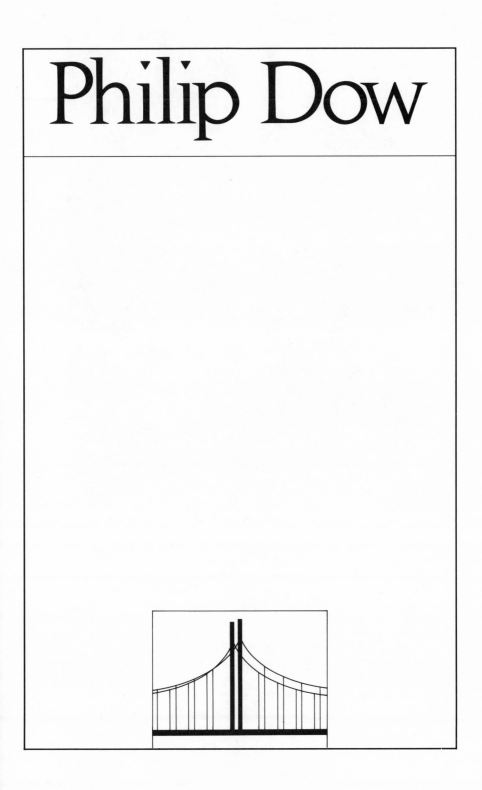

Philip Dow was born in Santa Fe, New Mexico, in 1937. He grew up and went to public schools in Vallejo and Napa, California. He lives in Napa now, and has two sons. He was educated at San Francisco State University and the State University of New York at Buffalo. He has taught at SUNY, Buffalo, and SUNY, Binghamton, San Francisco State, and has also been teacher and poet-in-residence at Carnegie-Mellon University, Reed College, the University of Texas, El Paso, and Louisiana State University. His awards include a grant from the National Endowment for the Arts, the Joseph Henry Jackson Award, and a Creative Artists Public Service Fellowship in Poetry from New York State. He has been Consultant in Literature to the Texas Commission on the Arts, and has participated in numerous poetry residencies in California, New York, and Pennsylvania, where he has organized prison workshops. His first book, *Paying Back the Sea*, was published in 1979. His work has appeared widely in magazines and in such anthologies as *Quickly Aging Here*, *Best Poems of 1976*, and *The American Poetry Anthology*.

For the Nonce

I believe in contradiction and synthesis, because observation and thinking reveal that unstable alliance to be the way of things.

I believe in most of the Gods, except when they preach against one another, but pray to none singly because the rigid doctrine that elevates one to banish the others inures itself to doubt. When I am thankful, I need no protection against doubt, it simply vanishes; when I am in doubt to allay it would be delusional.

I have written one prayer, to a fly.

This piece will be a prayer to mouse-brain.

*

For me, the poem that celebrates tends to be pure, arising from unalloyed emotion. Dread as well as joy.

The poem that begins in doubt tends to be impure, embodying the process of a struggle towards clarity, insight, or tentative resolution.

The dumb world is an unmediated, inchoate fiction.

Language is a symbiotic organism.

The mind is and isn't the one and the other.

Art is connection, whether it imitates or scorns to plagiarize God and invents. It is, inescapably, an image of mind in one of its phases. Everything is itself-alone in eternity and monad, and metaphor: the purest energy of connectedness.

A poem may concentrate on any aspect or phase, to isolate and purify in an heroic effort of integrity to escape the terror or despair of the open, or to celebrate the irreducible, elemental. My poem "Snow Geese in the Wind," aims to do the latter, as does "Song" in another fashion.

Or a poem may open itself to the dynamic process of energies interacting in the poet's faculties during the actual time of the poem's composition in a particular locale, improvising a form consistent with the temporal patterns of consciousness, the alternating stimuli of the senses and internal feeling, the collisions of concept and perception and memory. This is to render lyric dramatically, the way action painting contains and exhibits its own genesis. "Elegy" is a poem that attempts to do this.

*

In the dumb world of my youth, in Northern California, I hunted and fished a lot and in a great variety of terrains and weathers.

Patterns of repetition and variation revealed connectedness, giving a sense that everything operated on the basis of natural laws you could detect and study and understand.

In creatures was something subtler: alertness, instinct, intelligence, cunning, defiance, a will to survive. When I killed one I took my life in hand, holding palpable mystery. Elusive life gone made me prayerful in one way, and the beautiful body in another: elegant form adapted to elements, intricate detail of plumage, say, or scales, or fur, simultaneously texture and tincture.

I cleaned my own game, as I was taught; I took nothing I would not eat.

*

The Imagination, says Coleridge, is esemplastic and molds disparate elements into a unity. Character is a unity molded by experience. Raw, material experience of the dumb world gives the mind a shape, as well as a jumble of content; that order or disorder (what Wittginstein calls "the order you didn't expect"), where intellect, emotions, experience, sensation, memory, bodily energy, temperament and tone intersect, composes character and is the source of style.

*

In the city garden was a tame order, lovely and succulent. In the wilderness, two modes of discipline, ways of knowing, forms of devotion: to sit, alert and patient, for as long as it took; to pursue, reading sign, using stealth and strength and endurance, for as long as it took.

Failure was part of the process. And luck, though only a fool counted on it.

It occurred to me recently that two diverse modes of poems I feel comfortable with and tend to alternate the writing of, may well be related to that formative experience of hunting.

The ghazal: a kind of sitting, meditative, concentrated, formed of autonomous elements, the mind putting things together.

The dithyrambs (I don't know what else to call "Elegy" and the other long poems like it): tracking something elusive over shifting terrain, the body in motion.

*

What is wanted in impure poems of the kind I have described is the virtues not the defects of spontaneous consciousness. The fluent muscularity of thought and feeling rising from the cells out of need to celebrate or rediscover wholeness.

There's nothing sacrosanct, in terms of poetry, about a transcript of crude thought bombarded by sensations and skittering over surfaces of random matter. That just leaves in its wake a sense of fatigue for the hurry, of fragmentation for the loss of possibilities hinted at but scattered and undeveloped. Certain poems of performance can make this work to some extent, but only during the act and with a loss of energy at each subsequent performance.

The drama of the psyche at work is, for the sake of the poem, only a possibility, like a resolved state of mind: in need of art; otherwise they are like any other immaculate conceptions.

Assertion is not proof.

Belief is not success.

There is an inexhaustible image, multiplied by thought and feeling, from which a poem arises. It may seem only the tremor of a current in a word or two, but electro-chemical events in the brain's synapses are connected to their source in matter and spirit as you perceive them or not. Sun, gravity, static electricity, magnetism, humidity; peristalsis and the cat on your lap.

Exclusion is a fine line between, a rift or chink, or a fine blade that may probe them. It begins in the center of the universe, as does inclusion with its compost heap sprouting seeds. The universe has many centers.

A poem is made of words and is not made of words.

It is an image of that place in the psyche where soul intersects with matter. It is also a transformation of that image into the recalcitrant body of language which it fragments and re-orders, to form a new word of all the words in the poem. For the nonce.

*

These are provisional notions, intuitions and associations as well as reasoned conclusions, and that is fine with me. Definitions are no more interesting to me than the process that brings them to mind. I prefer, therefore, to have them after the fact, as a hunch about something I have done. I prefer the wilderness to marked trails and have never hunted with a hired guide nor hunted for *sport*.

*

Like any other outsider, when I look at poems I've written I can use my literary-critical skills and describe what's going on. It's not that I forget such stuff when I'm writing, but that I'm involved with the dance and my partner and music, using the basic stuff without being restrained by it when it would hold back discovery and delight.

*

The dithyrambs, as I look back at them, seem to favor a three-beat line that ignores unaccented syllables and sometimes subsumes a phrase into one measure, adapting from hovering accent and sprung rhythm. This is subliminal work done by the body as voice guides hand in the scribble: the process of mind when not subordinated to will, an improvisatory syntax. The poem responsive to the impulse it grows from, reciprocal and heuristic, acting upon the mind as it evolves, trying to synthesize simultaneous chain-reactions, multiple themes. Like jazz improvisation.

The ghazals (over a hundred and fifty, now, in three manuscripts), leave silent that singing energy between the points of resolution, wanting quick flashes to leap between those points. Like the spark between points in the car engine, it's a problem of adjustment: too little space they burn up, too great a gap and nothing happens. Problems of analogy, association, and metaphor, complicated by mixed tone and diction, unmediated by comforting Authorial guidance. Like collage, or mobile.

*

That a psyche is unified doesn't mean that its distinctive components must be puréed, or welded into a seamless sphere. Poems that don't examine themselves may project an image superior to life. There are fine ones that do and I won't speak against them, but confess my suspicion of flattery. Which is not the same thing as doubting grace.

*

Poetry is not an escape from emotion, or anything else. It is confrontation. Not bribery, confession or objet d'art, but a mixture of provocation and sacrifice. You say grace between the slaughter and the eating: poetry is all of that, and the singing afterwards with loved ones and guests.

*

What I call the *lyric impulse* is a sudden access of pure feeling. Few poems manage, or even attempt, to express it directly. It is difficult and infrequently desirable to be so artless as:

pain drips

—the surviving fragment of a Sappho poem dismembered by time and translated by Guy Davenport who admirably resists any temptation to reconstruct with expert conjecture what, presumably, is missing.

From the perspective of our literary traditions, this piece seems almost pre-linguistic; a DNA molecule of feeling, perhaps, yet isolated both from the rhythmic and melodic body of sound that composes the physical poem we enjoy singing or reciting, and from the structured argument by which we make sense of such an isolated point. It may strike us as an insight but still seem a truism shorn of a context, like the complete poem it has survived, which could make it matter.

To my mind, however, it is a poem as given, nothing missing and nothing left over, an ideal marriage of form and feeling. I don't know the Greek but the choice of verb in English is exquisitely suited to its subject, an exacting registration of scale and process.

Haiku is a perfected form for this; here's Bashō:

> Along this road
> Goes no one,
>   this autumn evening.

*

In a little book called *Symbolism*, Whitehead claims the poet differs from other men. He says other men are reminded by the word *tree* of something which they have seen, whereas the poet walks among trees being reminded of words.

Baby-puke!—that's what the odor of the unfamiliar fruit reminded me of and what I blurted, spontaneously, to the empty street, with a gasp of delight. A twenty-year-old body-memory swarmed over my left chest and shoulder: the heft of my infant son as I burped him and sweet milk returned from his gut wetting my skin with its warmth. I took a sample of leaves from the tree and looked it up in a book—*Ginko.*

Is Whitehead speaking for me if I find myself divided and stretched between his "poet" and other "men" by the power of words and sentence? The points of rest strung together by the elastic time of the sentence (which speed-reading, spatialized logic, and genteel declaratives ignore) can pull one feeling right out of the insides of a different one and leave you throbbing. Language at its simplest has this power to enact tragic delight, especially as it begins to sing in lines. "Old Mother Hubbard" did it to me when I was learning to read, pulling my child's mind-and-feelings against resistances, dividing them in different directions but carrying them through the same channels to the same end, united in conflict. It stirred confidence and hope and affection, as she went to the cupboard (which anachronistic reason knew should contain no bone, and which experience had proved did not), and hurt my feelings by failing the trust it had created, leaving me unexpressably sad that her dog always got "none."

Does the poor "poet" never have trees, other men never "words"?

A theorem governed by definition in a limited case may feel like a vicious dream masquerading as reverence for the poet, and send one for relief to Stein's *Four Saints in Three Acts,* McClure's *Ghost Tantras* or Creeley's *Words.* Relief doesn't necessarily mean getting off the hook.

What "Mother Hubbard" did naively, Creeley does with genius. The tension of his abrupt enjambments, the stuttered definitions, shifting vectors in syntax which, cut by line-breaks, knotted by anacoluthon (to effect metaphor of locutions rather than images), yet ends up, like a magician's rope, in one piece

—these haunt me with *felt* time: agons of alert animality pacing in thought. Yet, even the conceptual purity of "A Piece,"

> One and
> one, two
> three.

—begins to multiply in the mind, like its biological implication. Words in the flesh echo: Count Basie launching his orchestra, Euclid articulating space. A *piece* implies a whole.

*

Hume said we cannot see consciousness, only that we are conscious of something. Heisenberg tells us our instruments distort our observations. The brave luminosities of Philosophers pretend or devise *Principia Mathematica*. Gödel reminds us of mortality.

Language evolves a rebellious spirit, turning upon its maker or proving an alien origin. How servilely it clarifies the dilemma it makes for thought, Creeley shows in "The Pattern" (from *Words*, Scribners, 1967),

> As soon as
> I speak, I
> speaks. It
>
> wants to
> be free but
> impassive lies
>
> in the direction
> of its
> words . . .

Frost's "The Road Not Taken" looks and sounds like a conventional poem. That gives some readers reassurance, others dread. It gives a country feel to treasured norms, fit for the avuncular tone. Platitude has such familiar designs on the reader, he knows A Moral lurks at the road end. Admirers follow, detractors stray, but both swallow it whole, taking the poet at his word. Its positive statements have a self-swallowing order, however, assertions disproving themselves. The Epimenides paradox hides in the hedge of metaphor. Behind the Currier & Ives calendar scene, a hole in the wall of the skull.

That's where Artaud comes in? (*Artaud le Mômo*, as translated by Clayton Eshleman and Norman Glass, *Sparrow*, 47:1976.)

"The anchored mind / screwed in me / by the psycho- / lubricious thrust / of the sky / is the one who thinks / every temptation, / every desire, / every inhibition.

O dedi
O dada orzoura
O dou zoura
Adada skizi
. . .

Artaud strains against the anchored mind to liberate himself from terror first by naming it and next by pulling another feeling out of its insides by chanting nonsense. Crammed from without, he empties the psyche from within by producing nonce words that mean only themselves yet carry the charge of his feeling. This is a kind of ecstasy. The effect of these syllables "reminds" me of a constellation of things, which cannot be said all-at-once in the temporal-sequential nature of language, although I experience them internally like a chord, a collage. To list them is not to explicate Artaud's nonce words but to hint at the kind of complex response which feeling evokes and from which a poem may gather its being into language, forming a nonce word that is the aggregate and otherwise unsayable:

* Embryology shows the brain develops from the ectoderm. Some of its surface develops a shield against external stimuli, a tinier portion becomes the organs of sense. Internal excitation can be defended against only by acting as if it were external and could be shielded out. This is the origin of "projection." (Freud, *Beyond the Pleasure Principle*; condensed and paraphrased from the Strachey translation, Liveright, 1950.)

* Novalis: "any absolute sensation is religious."

* *Please, Mommy, Please, Please, Please* & The bleating of a lamb &
"*E-li, E-li, la-ma sa-bach-tha-ni?*"

* Issa's sweet, melancholy pity fierce in its contempt of remote power:

Once it happened
a child was spared a whipping
through earnest solicitation

My neglecting to mention mordant humor doesn't dispose of it. It only helps to underscore the idiocy of explication.
The live nerve is in the poem.

* The cannibal eating kin whose soul was snared by demons, inoculates himself (incarnating a science of hygiene unknown to its

practitioner), by propitiation destroying disease. So, the demons live on.

*   Primitive masks. Cell-memories of mute evolutionary stages: angel and fish and sheep. Dumb infancy. Child-magic to enter other bodies and to become the beasts we adored and feared. We grew like the red-spotted newt that sheds and eats its gossamer outer skin.

*

Where I duck-hunt on the prairie between Suisun Marsh and Sacramento Valley farmlands, it's common to find the carcass of a ewe that died lambing-out, or of a cow. The early stage of decay is foul and repulsive, but short-lived. That must sound odd, I know, but the transformation from carrion to skeleton is furiously alive. Days of vultures or crows or yellow-billed magpies; nights of coyotes, skunks, and mice. Assiduous scavenging complemented by weather and insects.

From one hunt I carried back the horned skull of one creature and weathered it atop a clothes-line post for a year of additional curing.

I use the word *creature* not out of sentiments of kindredness but as a compromise for an accuracy denied me, oddly, by our language. If I simply called it a *cow-skull* the story could go on without a hitch. However, I don't know the skull's gender.

Cow is female, though frequently used as if it were the equivalent of *horse*, neuter. *Bovine* seems pretentious. "Is there any secret in skulls, / The cattle skulls in the woods . . . ?" Wallace Stevens asks in "The Pleasures of Merely Circulating." Gender is one that occurs to me, and our language's lack of a neuter singular. Maybe the long history of animal husbandry's domestication and control of cattle explains it, bulls penned separately for breeding, cows pastured and herded for milking, bullocks castrated and fattened as beef—precise particulars.

As I gave that skull, *cow-skull*, I guess, a final cleaning before mounting it on a wall, I found the foramen magnum, the hole into the floor of the brain cavity, through which the spinal cord passes into the vertebrae, obstructed by a mass of coarse, gray tufts. I had to use a butter knife to dig them out, the entire brain cave was packed densely with it: raw wool. The discovery gladdened me, and sent me leafing through work sheets for some quick notes jotted down ten years back, between Steamboat Springs, Colorado, and Heber City, Utah.

While my sons and I fished in a sage flats reservoir, their mother hiked around. Later, she led us to a sheep-herders' abandoned winter camp where we poked about in decades of trash for old bottles and the like. We lifted a rusted blue enamel washtub against the sky, admiring the lace of holes rusted in its bottom.

Setting it back, we saw something it had hidden. That's what my notes were about:

> *a cloud of fleece under the rusted can / mouse-turds in it / bright-wet ones / the tiny mother's eyes. // I lifted a tuft / a row of blind babies sucked onto her belly. / Nothing moved. / I let the lid down, carefully / afraid of the light / loving the close dark / of her world, its scale / vaster, more intimate / than mine— / chilled by the sudden bright / emptiness crossed by the shadow of thought: / hawk dropping, coyote's thrust paw.*

That's not a draft of a poem, just an extension of memory cells on a scrap of paper, so I couldn't have the excuse of forgetting. Only underneath my mind was it connected to the following, until this writing remembered it. Between them is something I need to find out more about. Provisionally, I'll think about that unknown as the unknowable: "mouse-brain."

> . . . *"Ace took me out to his shed to show off the rattler he'd captured and put in a new 50 gallon drum half-filled with sand. Said he'd put two mice in a week back and the one it swallowed is still a lump about ten inches down the snake. 'The other one has gotten so it scrambles all over that torpid rattler, frantic to find a way out. He's got a couple of weeks yet before the snake's hungered again.' When he lifted the lid we saw the mouse jump away from the snake and then freeze. The rattler was dead, the spinal cord just back of its head bit through by the mouse. Ace snorted like disgust and laughter at a bad joke and dropped the lid. As we walked back, I asked what he'd do with the mouse. 'We'll see.' I was passing though, so I never did."*
> . . .

The Duck Pond at Mini's Pasture, A Dozen Years Later

Walking out, I flushed some meadowlarks—
Now they're down, and redwings gone into cattails.
A loose strand of barbwire begins softly thrumming.
Out over San Pablo Bay, clouds
Blow up from sunset, fading yellow
Off the Indian Tobacco.

Remembering all those nightfalls
Spent anywhere rain gathered
In corn or barley fields and ducks flew,
I hunch in pickleweed, shooting distance
From the pond, make a raspberry
With my lips and roll a whistle for Greenwing Teal
The old way learned from my brother.

Mosquitos rise out of sedge. White faces
Of Herefords bob dreamily as they graze.
In quirky teal-like flight, bats
Startle. Oil slickens my thumb on the safety
And I rub it into the marred walnut stock
Of the Winchester double, sniffing
Hoppe's lubricant, souring weeds in the flooded pond.
Behind me, darkness comes on.
A shitepoke crosses the Evening Star.

Far off, beyond the eucalyptus groves,
A pair of mallards
Cross the powerlines—
And I call, rough-voiced. They weave, dip,
Then flare. Afraid they'll pass,
I call again and my throat burns. They circle,
But I dont turn. I know to watch over water.

Out of darkness overhead, drake first,
Slowly they drop, rocking gently
On set wings, down
Slowly, into the last light—

Drunk Last Night with Friends, I Go to Work Anyway

The boss knows what shape I'm in. He tells me
about the twenties, when he was my age,
how he drank all night and woke up in strange rooms
with strange dolls. He tells me *Get lost.*

Out back, a weedbank I'd never noticed—
I head for it in cold air, remembering
dogs and cats eating grass when sick.

I sit shoulder deep in weeds.
Beneath the leaves
in green air, black beetles shoulder
enormous stems, dew quivering
between stalk and leaf.
In the pale moss I see ants
the size of salt grains
and budding red flowers
smaller than these ants.
A snail
dreaming in the throat of an old wine bottle.

It Comes During Sleep

The cry in my mouth wakes me (thirty years later)
to hear the cry is now my son's.
He sleeps with a stick
in case something tries to get
into his bed. I go to his room, listening
to the rain
raining on the roof, and pull the covers over him.

I used to get up about this time and walk
miles in the rain, duckhunting
with my father—he's an old man now, far away,
dying year by year
of lung disease. He smokes
most of the night, alone,
telling the same old hunting stories.

Is this the dream that wakes us?

Mother

I awoke hot, startled in daylight, calling
you: ashamed: black waters were streaming over
faces, shell-blue fungi on fallen maples,
trestles in crumbling

fires collapsed: kingfishers above, my children
yelling *Mom, wake Daddy, I caught a big one*:
oh, so that's who you are, my Mother: *Mother*:
Father's-old-widow.

Doe

I held on her neck
& dropped her where she stood
beneath the apple tree,
she keeps on dropping in my mind.
My wife shrieked from her window
the only shriek I've heard.
She cried out as a doe.

Love! I was afraid:
I felt my anus pucker
when I pulled her by the legs
and the loose thighs
tightened: the kick
went through my nerves:
with that rhythmic shudder
fucking brings:
and through my anger.

Love! I hated death:
I hated my midwife hands.
That night in bed
far from my wifely sleep
I felt my throat
blown open
by exploding light
& bloodied wind.
I've waited for these words.

the pattern of the house
jerked through the brambles

on a noise
the pattern of the house
& I collapsed
it dimming in my mind.

I open the ribs again.
I hack them into meat.
In this dream they are my wife's
and mine, all meat and bone,
all loss and hope
in my mind.

I put her in my belly.
I pour Irish whiskey in.
The world's so rich and good
it sickens in my gut.
I've waited for these words.
I like that sickness here.
It brings to life the deer.
My mind moves like a doe

the blackberry vine slides along my flank
I slip beneath the broken apple branch
drawn breathing musk of apples softening
into mush where they fall in the wet grass
& fan my ears toward a sudden music
swelling from the house below the meadow
and toward everything I fear in my dark
mind lost to my suddenly brilliant throat

Elegy

And if our lives spill
the way dark honey flows
flowering up out of the nocturnal earth,
the dark inward sleep of the soil,
into roots and burns
beneath the skin
yielding its heat
to those green intuitions
voiced in the wind,

No window shows this,
nor the combustion
in the leaves

straggling like minnows
in a shrinking pond.

It's hard to approach
the exposed inward-scapes
where ritual falters
and we move along paths
shaped by breath, jellyfish
shaken, every current
a bell in the medulla
radiant through fragile oceans of air,—

This is something in my veins,
these spidery plucked elderberry stems
skim my window, ride
a mid-day breeze, silent
and edgy as my wife
right now in another room

While my body feels
heavy summer crumble
under the dolor of dull rays
into the same bold forms again.

Spring comes again
I know, but this cruel prelude
I wouldn't willingly choose
sings of all there is
anymore to be,

but not Chaplain Vermillion's theme
rehearsing the empty heart,
lacerated for raptures,
that lame trawler in the choppy bay
succumbs to its haven of myth

And I don't believe Death
if you listen to the heart's
exclusive pain
is there all the while:
gravel in the grosbeak's craw

& that's where summer goes:
into the gristle—the panicles
of seed that rub and seethe,
pine nuts and sumac, fox grapes
souring on the high thick vines.

The creek winds downhill
spilling over whale-colored slabs
of slate its loose, swollen body
that overnight thickened
and froze a white shell—

Yes there's still a brittle trickle
there at its heart,
a wounded harpsichord
that backtracked upstream
to elude the hunter and collapsed in a pool
wide-eyed as the ice closed over,
its breathing leaks stiffly,
flutters its frail antlers
against a numbed lip of shale.

Is this what we shall have,
the flowing torso's plunge
into a calm plane, as memory
spills its music into the present,
frozen by Vermillion's ritual?

A delicate gray-white bird, alone,
in dying elm twigs,
flits,
as the few pale leaves lift,
between my window and the creek—
and ruby-crowned kinglets
sift through failing elderberries
skimming aphids from the leaves' undersides,
the scarlet pulse,
when the male looks away, gleams—

That's how I feel.
My body hasn't failed
to titillations by galaxies
of extinct cynic mumble
nor the pulse in my skull
been numbed by a vascular hegemony
of heart treacle and rot,
becrazed, wrangling,
a sweaty, riddling, finical cunt
whispering in nostalgia's ear
To Die today.

I listen for impulse
the way my eyes have taught me
to listen for the shallow scarlet harp
yoking the Flicker's skull,
male and female, to its nape.

Roots of the great willow
begin to speak in the womb
and pollen sleeps in the plums and
the thawing creek flows out of itself
surfing in the cells—

My body feels swollen,
slumps towards new balance,
off-center, precarious, a little numb,
scribbly, dull-sighted,
my head drawn by my chest,
arms folding in,

As if a woman felt
the unformed voice
in her budding womb begin,
beginning to croon,
and leaned in, listening—

Roots of the great willow stretch
through mulch and stones
squeezing further down and out
through grains of soil, the pulsing
cells, its tremulous fretwork of thirst

To lift upwards
the hovering green angel
of earth it is, my wife,
and you cross the floor overhead
into my pulse, wedding the moment,

I feel the heft of your feelings
sink like footsteps
beginning to form
gestures around the core of silence,
like elderberries
retaining their tartness in the pie
you bake with globs of honey

Or retaining their blueblack stain
in the spurt the Flicker shits
onto the porchstone.

So last night's snow
erased the eye's appetite for detail?
So all that falling
brought clouds beneath us,
brought us beyond the ripe
putrescence of feed lots
and the body's greeny sweet
ditchwater—
brought us into a world of forms
where purity only
isn't hollow, musical, lost,
like a dying tree

And that's why the hemlock split
in the gale and the maple
flushed scarlet down one side
like an old farmer
with a stroke
and yesterday's false thaw
woke the bees to die?

For purity? The world a dream
to blunder into and forget?
And nothing left but to mull over love,
prolonging into winter's shrinkage
summer and its passion to destroy
floating like cream upon milk?

After distant thunder
in a grove of bare trees
near the pond half-lidded by ice
I heard a soft terrible voice,
as if a clam being opened
were what it is: a mouth,

a heart wrenched
from its snug socket
and shucked of blue-tinged muscle—
not a blue mussel-shell
purged of gristle,

gristle burnt to a coal,
for purity against loss

But, as the snow
blown from high boughs
sifted brilliance around me,
I heard a tree letting go,
a wail begin to rise
from delicate tentacles
clenched unsuckled and brittle
in somnolent stratas of slate
and shale where its suck slackened,
and the honey that pulsed
in fluent eddies beneath
its skin as it swayed
in layering wind
I heard shiver into splinters,

I heard the voice of a tree
about to die,
but not for purity.

We are shamed by the body's wisdom,
its indifference to the mind,

That's why Emilio's hired hand
sawing a limb from the dead elm
thought the green sawdust
curdling in the raw cut
and blowing back, smelled like baby shit,
and why the half-cut limb
dropped twisting shreds
of heartwood out of the trunk
and bounced back splintering
the ladder, and the hired hand
went over pinned in the bramble
cradling the chainsaw carefully
against his breast like a baby,
the ribs its crib & drifting stars
staves upright and musical.

In the stereo's weak right speaker
Mahler's percussion fuzzes
behind the sad violins,
the heavy breathing of a cow in labor,
the calf they'll castrate

and fatten without remorse
as the violins swell and we move together
in the crystalline hive
where Chaplain Vermillion
comforts the bereaved—
but the city passes through us,
yielding to our present,

rolling slopes of dried cornstalks,
leaves flames flickering
in wind, pennants
of the battalions of dead
rushing from the cloudy earth
into sun.

Insomnia, the angel sleepless
ripens me along the pale ranges,
and I turn from the dark room
toward sunlit fields
& my sons.
I have been holding my breath,
secrets in darkness released
stain this windowpane I look through,
separating me from their ease
wholly to live there
in sunlit fields,
to live, holy, there.

They bring a turtle up from the pond,
snug in its intaglio
of green horn, and
while their friend Milton holds it,
this Kessler who has taught himself
to wear the fontanel again,
the scalp as skullcap,

with a candle flame they
gently shuck a leech
tucked in the snug folds under its left leg,

then return both the turtle
and the leech unharmed
to the pond.

They know the heart is a well,
a tight disc of light, flame-rippled
in its bone-dark socket,

their innocence mirrors
the spirit's memory:
that ritual God's undismembered face
whatever it may be
must look back at
for its unrepeatable purity
not of renunciation
but communion,
those moments so despised for their pain
or the pain of their loss
we would die
rather than lose them,
the fuel of the present.

When I go down to join my sons
distance skins me,
they see how tentatively I belong
among them
with my soul sometimes confused
because the world fails to resemble
my pain of it
gained through those faults it seeps out
into me
like electrons
homing into the hive
with dust of the present
storing the world's twin,
the honey burning inaudible,
breath swelling the window pane
with destination.

I sought a woman
whose beauty distracted,
soothed me, submissive to the body,
released into happy laughter,
its aftermath of lucidity
at death's inconsequential brink
where I rise
not into sticky fragments
of silence chipped from
posthumous scaffoldings of joy
lost to sorrow, but careless
into a poem—

And if, my love,
I have sometimes hammered
your weakness into rage,
at last to grief and sleep,
and drank while the fire died,
I feel you lift me now
the way time lifts the acorn
(the tree furled in that egg
like a stunned god
in rapt contemplation),

On this acorn dew shines
as daybreaks surface first
on waters, and the sheen reflects me,
a dark core in a pool of light,
eye I am the pupil of,

shadowseed locked in light's core,
word, spore,
dissolves the cell's walls,
the germed womb swells
into springs twilit—
a child there, sings
and swings in its great oak,
dark then bright
lithe motion wakes the air,
shakes its acorn free—

This kernel of wet sight
I hold in my hand
& return to that child
a man's song, seed, child-joy,
to say *I* truly
is to see,
seed,
sing, my distant
grandchild,

the *sweet*
sweet sweet of the phoebe
skittish
nears its nest
over the porch door.

Song

What binds the atom together
must be like these hives,
this cluster of white bee boxes near the creek,
this exhaling and breathing of wings
like sparks, bits of a mirror,
tracing over the meadow
the petals of a transparent blossom,

                         opening—

these veins flow into a dark armature,
heart or brain, a globular,
interior mirror
of ignited cells about which
the mind whirls: this sibilant,
            luminous pulp,
                  one cell
or one cell's shadow
         in the great body of growing
                  we grow in.

Snow Geese in the Wind

        That tremor rising
in the heart of mind, surprising
      with a swift knot
        from disparate
strands combining into one thought
          may be the *Spirit*—

      since *spirit* is air:
its secret form one sees appear
      like streaming light
        as scattered geese
suddenly weave a line of flight
          from the wind's release.

Ghazal

So, we are ghosts of angels
in a landscape abandoned by deicides, & the world is shit?

That stammering head, awash,
is a cask or sodden husk rocked by surf.

The reef of solipsism, iced over like the moon
it favors, breaks the sea. Uselessly.

At the edge of love we find another country: these are the mountains
of the mind, older than the mind & rivers grieving.

The dung-beetle is sister to Sisyphus & father
to Ptolemy—in whose mind we lived so long.

Goodbye "Hello"

Each time we lose grief, Friend, we are free from joy & cross into eternity.
Rice wine for Li-Po; for you—that's your secret. And that's why you know

about this petal torn from a yellow rose: that I am a dew-drop on it,
lazing in the current, a hog on the raft floating to town.

Drum and flute in the lady cardinal, Kabuki dancer, sweet-rotting-peach,
scum on the pond letting light float, iron fry-pan giving its secret to drying
water.

These tinctures of saffron and rose, on the gauze bandage. This is it, no?
Each time, Friend, it's good not even this saves us, not even a pocket full of
spoons.

Right now, forever, only a breath more, it's a fine boat, hilarious-rough-sea,
no? Eternity is where we forget we are as we call out: *Hello! Hello!*

Bottom's Dream

Come to the window & see sweet dawn shine on this wonder: a man
with a *man's*-head. Thoth was not so wise a God as this, not for all

his ibis-head moon-God gifts to Egypt—hieroglyphics magic math & poetry.
We humans so excel, you see, at his spate of hobbies, we've probed

the dark side of the moon. As the *God's-scribe-incarnate,* Thoth changed
into a baboon. We cage that primate in a class beside its cousin's royal ass.

Done with Gods, we toy with mystery—or feed our song ourselves. Though
                                                                    each human
birth is the rebirth of all Gods once adored, they died to be reborn
                                                                    abhorred?

Titania saw as a mortal for a brief spell and so (as few *will*) loved well.
We claim the ordinary *Good* and in the name of *Love* love to be cruel.

Letter

One word in your letter &, again, that quail trots from the vineyard, spurts
up onto a grape-stake & holds as the covey scuds into the creek-bottom.

Intervals of those fluting whistles in Tomales echo through this El Paso
                                                                    noon,
sweet to our native ear as any melancholy glissando of human yearning.

Each of us, these ten years, has had a marriage & two passions fail
& here we are, still joined across distance by a few words, birds we know.

Picking blackberries of varying ripenesses from the tangle and thorns,
how much your hand resembles the bird the silly will say love is free as.

I give thanks & wonder how we manage—is it lack of ecstasy & rage, like
                                                                    quail?
Last time together we bathed each other, chaste. I remember as I masturbate.

FROM *Sussyissfriin*

My son & I, between *Fu-Sang* and
Cathay—Chinatown USA.
Does this dim, empty bakery serve dinner?
we inquire in *American* (that dialect of phrases,
grins & gestures) and are seated at a round table
by a family of gesticulations, smiles & sweet lyric.

At once, a silhouette in a gust of light
comes from a swinging door to swirling cloud—
pilgrim from a T'ang scroll, translating
sweet *Chinese* tray by tray
into 19 delicacies:

Egg flower soup with pork sausage
Steamed bok choy with pork sausage
Pork sausage balls and black mushrooms

Almond sub gum gai ding pork sausage
Fried won ton filled with pork sausage
Pork sausage balls sweet & sour
Blue willow pork sausage
Pork sausage and quartered ice-berg head lettuce
Cartesian pork sausage with poppyseed
Pork sausage Rockefeller with spats and dum-dums
Barbecued pork sausage à la Karloff
Infallible pork sausage wafers in watered wine
Pork sausage prosthesis
Pork sausage tea and fortune cookie with kosher dill kumquats
Praxitelean pork sausage
Special theoretical pork sausage
Erogenous pork sausage
Orphic pork sausage dyscrasia
Pork sausage hotchpotch in a soggy carton forgotten in the taxi

Familial feasting, for a song.
Prodigious pig & variation
that sticks to your ribs.
Like Bach's two-part inventions
or the prodigal changes, orthodox
permutations, of
Father
& son & son &
Father:

minced & stuffed into intestine:
sensorium of universal pig, lights
& liver, sweetbreads, heart,
swine-snout, -eyeball, -ear, -tongue,
hog-jowl, -sphincter, -eyelid,
-epididymis, -ballocks,
ubiquitous pig-god's corkscrew pizzle. . . .

Execrate
the pig
& gorge to your heart's content

or, bless
this gorgeous pig
& abstain, pure to the core.

The sacred *profane*, the profane *sacred?*
Sweet-heart, Koré,
pig-heart unjeered:

valve
of my sister's life.

In the window of The Celestial Palace
a row of golden-brown ducks
hang by their heels,
plucked & roasted whole:
webbed feet furled,
shorn tucked-up flippers,
the snake-like neck straight & rigid,
the spatulate lips clamped shut—

obscene & edible.
Like a bag-limit of dead poets
spurned by the Deer Park custodian,
the Swan-keeper:

That's wild Hart Crane of the incandescent plumage & sordid ritual,
              caught at the apex of his plunge;
That's gregarious Lindsay who quacked up storms among flocks;
Sandburg—a varnished gourd-guitar, mute as the vanished mill-town
              hiring hall;
Jeffers, once the cormorant of Big Sur's sea cliffs, looking like
              a pterodactyl preserved in amber.

A thousand years, the Imperial Court will serve them up
              —golden roasted whole duck, like Marlowe "lucky
              to have been murdered before he was burned."
Serve & carve them with pomp, to cultivate the young & to sate
              the dilettante rich & to busy the dabblers

as do we:
Li Po, migratory, ubiquitous, scattering poems like molted feathers,
              pickled in rice wine;
Po Chü-i, stripped of warmth by heavy taxes;
Wang Wei, imprisoned in a monastery to show the Emperor
              "what kind of animal a poet is";
beneath the splendid golden skin, tender Tu Fu's true colors:
              "war's blue smoke, men's white bones."

In what window of the Celestial Palace
does History deposit the remains
of the poets' mothers? Look again:

here they hang
like a row of Chinese roast duck,
but not so whole. Reduced to essence, hollowed

like fact, dried-seasoned-shellacked—an octet
of uteri

shafted-fretted-strung with an octave
of wires, they are strung-up

like chamois-skin douche-bags
in a trophy-case, to jangle and spur
the warrior-heart; or

like mandolins in a pawn-shop window (made to lure
and lull and snare—between interludes
of war—a gentle virgin)

Persephoneous lutes
to be redeemed,
to swell the spring.

Dennis
Schmitz

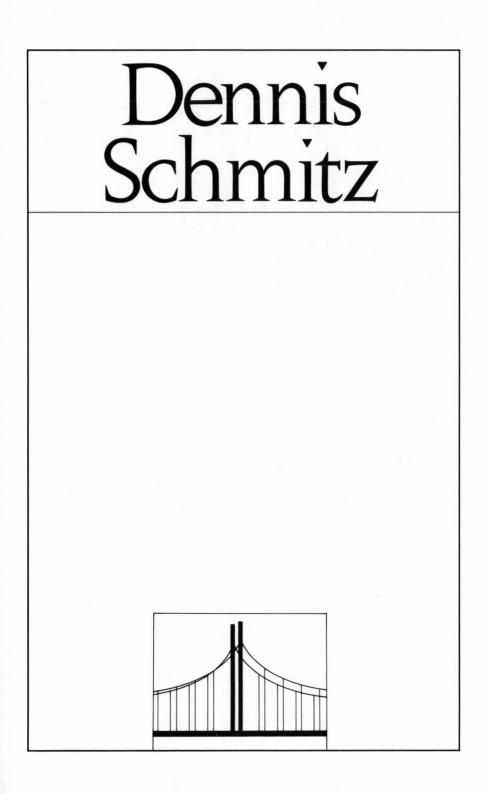

Dennis Schmitz was born in Dubuque, Iowa, in 1937. He was educated at Loras College and the University of Chicago. He lives in Sacramento, and has five children. He has taught at Illinois Institute of Technology; University of Wisconsin, Milwaukee; and is now professor of English at California State University, Sacramento. He is the recipient of the YM-YWHA Poetry Center (New York) Discovery Award, a grant from the National Endowment for the Arts, and a Guggenheim Fellowship. His books of poetry include: *We Weep for Our Strangeness; Double Exposures; Goodwill, Inc.;* and *String.* His poems have appeared in numerous anthologies, including: *The Young American Poets; New Voices in American Poetry;* and *The American Poetry Anthology.*

First Person Singular

I

A few years ago, William Bennett, a physics professor at Yale, programmed a computer according to the rules of probability to simulate the hypothetical monkeys-writing-Shakespeare. He found, in his simplest formulation, that if a trillion monkeys were to type ten randomly chosen characters a second, it would take more than a trillion times as long as the universe has been in existence just to produce "To be or not to be." However, with a more sophisticated formulation, Bennett found that he could project that a single monkey, typing ten characters per second nonstop, could write all of Shakespeare in 10^{36} years. One could ask a further question of the experiment: how long would it take Shakespeare to write Shakespeare using the method available to the monkeys?

Bennett's initial statement of the problem is at once a phrasing of its limitations and insolubility—Achilles and the Tortoise. Bennett's second formulation demonstrates intention—randomness is less a factor. In what ways was Shakespeare Hamlet?

Poet Gary Thompson says that the first question one asks of a poem when one knocks is "Is there anyone at home?" Who should be there? Merely oneself? And I'm asking this last question for the reader as well as for the writer (who asks first). Both reader and writer expect a real presence, not an echo, not the nameless "Occupant" of the junk mail delivery.

A poem must have a speaker and one who answers, an Other, thing or person. In the poems that say "I," the speaker must find in himself the Other. Shakespeare, the man, the speaker whose consciousness unifies the speech of his poetry, writes the poetry, makes the transfer of personae—his poetry is not a series of arbitrary utterances, not solipsisms, not random.

In some poets, no number of "I" assertions will make you believe that anyone is there. How seldom George Oppen says "I" in his poems, but attendance, the attention to the Other, vibrates each abrupt sound forced from him. There seems to be an infinite waiting behind the speech of his poems—the poem seems a resolution of silence.

In Czeslaw Milosz there is a powerful race memory. His attention achieves focus in distancing; the individual becomes historical by taking on connection after connection in "From the Rising of the Sun." The responsibility of the poet is responsibility—I'm not advocating a Bull Moose Party poetry, but noting that the poet does suffer with the suffering. And assesses. Milosz's distancing gives perspective if not hope.

"Genuine responsibility," Martin Buber says, "exists only where there is real responding." In his essay "Dialogue," Buber defines what he terms *reflexion*, which he says is the movement of monologue, of the inhibited self. He tells of visiting his favorite horse on his grandfather's estate when he was eleven. In that animal he experienced the Other, not merely another, which he says "placed itself elementally in the relation of *Thou* and *Thou* with me" as he stroked the horse.

And the horse approved him. Only when Buber became conscious of his hand stroking and the pleasure that stroking gave him did he betray the Other and lose the relation. The horse then ignored him. Buber says that it "is not that a man is concerned with himself, considers himself, fingers himself . . ." it is *reflexion* "when a man withdraws from accepting with his essential being another person in his particularity."

When Robert Lowell in one of his later poems says, "Is getting well ever an art/ or art a way to get well?", he is ironic perhaps in a way he didn't intend. The so-called confessional poem which fails is self-criticism which tries to excuse itself. It is doggedly circular in its movement. *Reflexion.*

The poetic generation which includes Kinnell, Levertov, Levine, Logan, Rich and James Wright has variously extended the concerns of the personal poem. In an earlier generation, when he didn't project the idealized self which sometimes flaws his work, Kenneth Rexroth wrote wonderful poems of transcendence. In the remarkable poem "The Signature of All Things," he shows the intent of things is mutual definition. That the numinous informs but is not limited by the visible. That identity in world memory is not reactive but accepting. That re-cognition is not confrontation but association.

But the chief tone, the middle voice, of contemporary magazine verse only seems conversational—the level delivery, the soft sell, is not real speech anticipating exchange—at best it is the speech of men, not angels. It thinks small; it is correct and well-mannered because it has an agreement with the reader that they share the test-key. "Every religion," says Pascal, "that does not affirm that God is hidden is not true."

II

Context was created in the five days before Adam. Adam, in a sense, had memory without having experience—or responsibility. He had nothing to rescue. He was chosen before he had to be self-chosen.

Commentators ritually complain that the self seems less available to one these days. In a time of mass media and archival storage, personal memory becomes an extension of public memory. How do we know who we are? Memory, however, is both a faculty and a context. The choice of self is a borrowing. Even distortions of the self can be the self.

"Memory is the medium of the must-have-been," Julian Jaynes says in *The Origin of Consciousness in the Breakdown of the Bicameral Mind*. Ancient man received messages from inside, right-brain broadcasts, which directed his behavior. Poets in some way, sometimes, are vatic receivers of inner messages delivered in a similar way. At such times, the remembered or narrated event the poet uses is a way to bring on the poem. Episode is occasion.

In his *Autobiography*, Benvenuto Cellini, the great Renaissance sculptor, tells of watching a salamander in the fireplace. Salamanders were thought to be impervious to flame, to be essential cold, to be magically generated perhaps or rejected by flame. Cellini's father, who was watching with him, cuffed the boy so that he would remember the manifestation. The blow was a teaching device. As poets, what blow calls us to vision, to memory of transcendence? At what point are we changed?

The monkeys-writing-Shakespeare story with which I began this essay has a hidden message about spontaneity. If there is randomness in the choice of means, it is only the first searching, the clumsy but exhilarating abandonment to process. Adam's names for the beasts may have been misapplied, unrelated to function or any proto-rational standard Adam could've used. Poetic speech is parenthetical.

Obviously, one doesn't say "I" in a poem merely for verisimilitude (i.e., to engage the reader), nor merely to say what one is, but to find what one could be. The urge in the poem is to find the *present*. The reader must share that present for the poem to succeed. In seeking the present, the poem follows the natural process of self-orienting, using the analogue, in the sense that Jaynes defines the term: the mind presents a version of the past action happening *now* as a rehearsal of the future act. In finding what one could be, memory and the decision process are congruent—the notion of time we communally agree to is like a vernier scale on the arrangements of the single consciousness.

Eclogues

where I lived the river
     lay like a blue wrist
between the bluffs & the islands
were tiny unctions of green. where
     every morning the horses outside
my house woke the sun & their breath
was like wet foliage
     in the cool air. but in my house
my bedroom poised
     between shadow & light & the light
was flawed by angles of glass
till night disappeared in a moment
     of wonder. the farm fed
on the full hillsides & sheets
of grain seemed to fall
     almost to the river's shore.
but from my window the farm
     was less real: the river & at noon
the fish I could almost hear fading
in its cool depths distracted
     the boy of twelve. my brother
beside me
     slept. he was oldest & duty
has deliberate solitude: even my sisters
kept their dolls
     quietly.

the second son: his father
is silent. whose hands are fouled
     with the birth of a new foal & the brother
fixes the blanket
over the mare's belly. the blood! & the younger
     boy thinks the flesh
a burden & at fault
     for its own pain. the others
lift the foal & pull
the small genital till it flexes
with full life.
     I stood in the barn
born second of God's beasts
     & alone in the days of my making.

my grandfather's God
guided him to the river & the Holy
        Ghost, he said, hung
like a white hand over this hill. our farm
        was his & when he died
my father (his son) worked a stone
in the shape of a bird, wings
        upraised as if startled
by my grandfather's death.

my name came from the river
the Fox called "Father" &
        "Source" as if a man's semen
were the only cause & my mother's fluid
        a mere aspiration. my mother
told of monsters who may
have died in the river-bed & she read
        that ice a mile high once
moved over their bones. at night
        the river with cold friction
pushes my slumbering flesh
        & my manhood moves
new
& in its own seed.

my father
        died, feeder of many horses & so fine
an ear he had
he heard the birds with feathered weight
        drop between the green rows
of corn. a gothic
man knowing
no wisdom & in that field we
        no longer plant. the birds
forever float
        above his grave & the ground
gives
more each year.

that winter the farm
        dozed, its tillage deep
in snow. the river
backs a cruel spine against
        the bluffs & boyhood's
dim fish ride

up under the ice, Mother:
        your children. inside
the fire rubs
itself for warmth & the windows
go white with frost.

If I Could Meet God

if I could meet God
as an animal
my mouth filled with grass
I would not talk
for he knows the smell
of grass
& the great choking
one must have
who seeks to swallow
his world
when an animal dies
his choking is not laughter
he does not shuffle
like a man who forgets
his key
he knows there is no door
he walks inside himself
his belly full
his ears erect with certainty

Virgil: Georgics, Book IV

the wonder
of the bees who
do not mate
for love nor bear
children
in birth-throes
they take their kind
from flowers
in their mouths
they take
their young
the king is kept

in ritual
for ritual they fashion
halls of wax
often
in wandering their wings
are crushed
against a rock
& the heavy body
dies
such is their love
of flowers
& their pride
in honey-making

The Chalk Angel

even though he falls
across it, not the drunk's

outline, nor the dog's
who drifts in
& out of the shape

scenting meat.
this is not what the child
was assigned who copied

the figure with stolen
schoolroom chalk.
tomorrow his teacher

too might have
used it for a math
problem: a measurement

of astral bodies.

Star & Garter Theater

      For Roger Aplon

it is always night here
faces close but never heal
only the eyes develop

scabs when we sleep & head
by head the dream is drained
into the white pool

of the screen. we go on rehearsing
THE REVENGE OF FRANKENSTEIN:
my arm is sewn to your shoulder.
your father's awful hand
& an actual criminal brain

take root under the projector's
cold moon. I wanted to do
only good. I planted my mouth
& kisses grew all over skid row.
now the fat ladies of the night

are lowered into the lace
stockings & strapped into their black
apparatus. this body is grafted
to theirs. alone we are helpless,

but put together winos, whores
& ambivalent dead, we walk the daytime
world charged with our beauty.

The California Phrasebook

west of the Sierras where
the central valley
drifts on its crusts of almond
orchards the fields
die in a holiday accident
the freeways snapping
back in the dust like severed
arteries while the accomplished
doctor of silence stitches the evening
closed with stoplights which
never hold. gardens go
on their knees to the sun
all summer turning
over the brief counterfeit the rain
leaves, looking for a real
coin. in the arbors the Italian
uncles sit stirring anise-flavored
coffees, red bandanas

over their knees pulsing
with the sweating
body's rhythm like an open
chest in which the transplanted
organ of the homeland has not yet
begun to function.

in East Bay beyond the valley
towns pore to pore
the children black & brown
press out a test pattern
of veins, their faces rigid with long
division. they stand
in front of the blackboards looking
for their features, refusing
to draw the white mark
of a dollarsign while the mayor
waits & all the examining
board of cops waits, the correction
texts trembling in their hands.
why must we repeat our lessons,
let us go. in the alleys we rehearse
the lonely patrol of hands
over each other's bodies.
if we unfold a woman's creases
we are afraid to read
the platitudes. the black
penis is the last piece
of the puzzle we put in place
before the streetlamps have slipped
away in the wet fingers of the April
night, before the pathways
through the asphalt gardens
disgorge the feathers of the black
angel.

you who arrive late
from some forgotten Kansas
laminated of wheat & the sweet
alfalfa wasted with incurable winter
take root in the familiar
flat valley where the only
winter is overweight with rain
again & again welling up in fallen
wet fruit an early unearned

bitterness like the bum who drowses
under the indelible azaleas scrawled
against the capitol's white
walls. his life too
is a fragrant perennial.
he is less foreign than you,
but you must learn his difficult
language full of inflections for another
self palpable as the stone in spoiled
fruit. another self! the cheap
foundations of love shift—
before you always built in the quake-
proof plains where small rivers
pillow their heads in poplar
roots & turn all night
in the drought's persistent
insomnia. the cellar was dirt
still alive with roots
from which your father cut
your life in rigid board walls
incredibly steady
on the rippling floor of yellow
grain. in California the cellarless
houses sway at the slightest
tremor.

Arbeit Macht Frei*

his first day they asked
him to remove the swallows
so he hosed the mud
nests high up under

the sign while we watched, hats
off. once such ladders ran
out above a man's house
to touch frayed clouds.
now, a man is hired to wash the sky

or urge grass.
if you are uncomfortable in our world,
stop for a minute & put your eye

*"Work sets you free"—inscription on the gate at Auschwitz.

---

to the entrance hole, the swallow's
exit, hose pointed to another

nest. you look
inside: a woman is sprawled, legs
wide. you peer into her

hole too & see
a third hole or original
of your mouth hatching

the word "human,"
pretty feathers the spit
fades. press your face to the nest
& reach out with your liberated
tongue remembering
other words it kneaded into love
as many climb the ladder
behind you.
underneath, mud darkens

the tidy yard.
is that a guard kneeling
by a hole accidently washed
from a nest? as he reaches down
the hole closes
over his ring finger.
this is how birds are made.

Planting Trout in the Chicago River

> fishers of men
> —Mark I, 17

because it is lunchtime
we lean from offices high over the river.
at a holding tank below the mayor
is on his knees as he mouths
the first fish coming down the hose.
his wife pulls back crepe
so aldermen & ethnic reps can help themselves

to rods as he bends
over the awful garbage, as his lips let go
this fish rehearsed four nights
in which his tongue grew

scales, the Gospel epigram hooking
his mouth both ways
until he talked fish-talk
but still hungered for human excrement.
even in sleep he can will the river:
the midnight bridges folded

back for a newsprint freighter,
the Wrigley Building
wrinkling off the spotlit
water—he submerges a whole city

grid by grid to make one fish.
four nights he dreamt the different
organs for being fish,
but out of the suckhole soft
as armpit flesh a face always bobbed,
on the eyes a froth of stars.
in turn each of us

will have to learn to cough
up fish, queue from Lake St. Transfer
at the river to disgorge
& after, wade at eye level

under Dearborn bridge, intuitive,
wanting flesh, wanting
the warm squeeze & lapse
over our skeletons because the fin repeats
fingerholds, the gills
have an almost human grin.

Making Chicago

> We cannot take a single step toward heaven. It is not in our power to travel
> in a vertical direction. If however we look heavenward for a long time, God
> comes and takes us up. He raises us easily. —Simone Weil

let it end here where the blueprint
shows a doorway,
where it shows all of Chicago
reduced to a hundred prestressed floors,
fifty miles of conduit & ductwork

the nerve-impulse climbs to know God.
every floor we go up is one more down
for the flashy suicide, *for blessed man who*
by thought might lift himself

to angel. how slowly we become only men!
I lift the torch away, push up the opaque
welder's lens to listen for the thud
& grind as they pour aggregate,

extrapolating the scarred forms resisting
all that weight & think
the years I gave away to reflexive anger,
to bad jobs, do not count
for the steps the suicide
divides & subdivides in order not to reach

the roof's edge. I count the family years
I didn't grow older with the stunted
locust trees in Columbus Park,
the ragweed an indifferent ground crew
couldn't kill, no matter the poison.
now I want to take up death more often

& taste it a little—
by this change I know I am not what I was:
the voice is the voice of Jacob
but the hands are the hands of Esau—
god & antigod mold what I say,

make me sweat inside the welding gloves,
make what I thought true turn heavy.
but there must be names
in its many names the concrete can't take.
what future race in the ruins
will trace out our shape from the bent

template of the soul,
find its orbit in the clouded atmosphere
of the alloy walls we used as a likeness
for the sky? the workmen stagger
under the weight of the window's nuptial
sheet—in its white reflected clouds
the sun leaves a virgin spot

of joy.

A Picture of Okinawa

Out of adult hearing
the birds stammer this place
the animals intact
the remembered trees mismade
because a child painted them

from radio news & the interdicted
marsh back of Catfish Slough—
no GI drab but the Rousseau greens
snakes shed in their turnings

from heaven-held aquas & cerulean.
When the last Japanese soldier
gave up thirty years late
crashed down in some islander's

backyard, the sniper webbings cradling
his navel to the bandoliers
& commando knife with the four
metal knuckle-rings, I still looked
for my soldier uncle in this picture

my aunt never sent
to show how I imagined the enemy
condemned to eat close to heaven
the lonely madness for another's flesh,
his greenish waste wrapped in leaves

& stabbed on treeforks,
the mottled arm reaching for birds,
leaf by leaf making himself
innocent of his weapons—
only thirty years to come down human.

Dressing Game

After the men hunt,
the woman cleans the game.
She follows the puckered skin with a match
to burn off pin feathers,
pushes & kneads squirrels from their hides,
printing against a haunch,

against the suddenly revealed
scraped breastbone, her live flesh.
Over the oiled underskin
her fingermarks, her scars,
the thick crown of a wart,

maybe a hair between her flesh & theirs.
The knife-nick will be cooked in,
the touches-for-nothing.
Even the trash organs

pick up her image as she sorts,
breaking the membranes, turning the joints
180 degrees to break their lock
on remembered fields,
burrows & slide-holes in burdock.

Afterwards she soaks in the stream—
the red curling off,
the current clotting around rocks.
She lets her soiled shirt fill,

removes it & wrings it. & her pants
as she swings them,
emptied of herself, fill too with a clear
though invisible body
which passes, shivering the denim, back
into the stream.

Kindergarten

Bee-logic: each small life
for the hive,
but not one of them lived out

at the same speed—
your heart thuds *fortissimo* but slow,
my heart trots to its death.

Proto-druggist pickpocket or priest
begin as mysteries to themselves.
Big-head Vincent who chews his pastels

& wipes spit with the blue
over his squat trees,
& Levonn too who wets himself

is one of us.
Our keeper Sister Agnes,
wrinkled as a peach-nut & left-handed,

sings Latin, whose inside
is God's, she says, but we can go in
too with our tongues & the head

will follow, simplifying
heaven. Vincent went to heaven
in wet April. We sang a few words

of "Nunc Dimittis" among the gladiolas
& floribunda wreaths,
gripping each other's fingers

as we knelt all points in a compass,
expecting somehow to sing
Vincent up. But we belonged

to the headless Vincent
someone crayoned on the cloakroom
wall under his coathook,

the feet broken
right-angles, the heavy
arms straining against gravity—

a child's unfinished body,
waxy & insistent.

Skinning-The-Cat

& this is the organ which was made last
I said, nine years old & proud
to go back & forth with the pan brimming

from my aunt's kitchen into the dark.
Because sight is burned out
the hand-linked adults around the dining
room table overload the other senses

sharing distaste, afraid of the future.
My grandmother passes from her wet hands
into my mother's something slippery

with unknown fluid.
I am too young to play the WW II games
they did when electricity was uncertain

or during lights-out practice drills,
so I am chosen to carry
these common objects felt in common

turned by dark & suggestion
into an animal's insides: cantaloupe waste
slimy with seeds, a few grapes heated . . .

to this day I don't recall
what stood for which organ, the quivering
unborn, the one like a prickly
tree-gall. The not-dead groaning

of the party-goers keeps on
as they feel individually & pass on
the perfect animal, the group animal.

Gill Boy

For John, my son

The toys I bought for you
splash down in your brothers' tub,
are rubbed paintless,
protean, in the 15 yrs coming down:

the space vehicle Apollo,
the rubbery aliens,
& the tooth-scarred astronaut
who trails air-hose,
prepared to go breathless

into the child's world.
You lived only five days,
unable to surface, cyanotic

in the isolette, then cold—
the way I've learned to accept you
when I wash your two brothers real,
when I shape each

of their small parts over
& over again with soap.

I tried to forget, to sublimate,
but under seven inches of bathwater,
out of reach,

you learned to breathe.
The suds your brothers leave,
the soapy waste

webs galls & scaley eyelets
all over your skin
so cruel no one could love you

& want to survive.

Coma

Done with myself, I asked
to lie down with the stroke victims,
to be one with those who keep themselves
in being by concentration—
the war-deaths who wake in a civilian eternity,

the army re-ups, the cancer-sufferers
who adore their own dying
for whom the fear of living again

blurs the fear of death:
a fatigue not with pain, but with habit.
Already I've practice-slept

the Vietnam War through—
if My-Lai happens it happens in this unrelieved
dreaming that blooms white-haired

out of the brainlight traced on the monitor
by my bed—an aging the technician
waits for before he calls the White House

& Mr. Truman answers that
he remembers me as a boy spread
sleeping across a pew tired of the Lord

who let the Chinese cross the Yalu.
My wife has grown older
by the same relentless science that keeps her

awake. Why can't I die
of this blindness rusted into my head?
What I once saw I saw unable to be moved,

a scapegoat, a second-born—
in group therapy the last one to answer,
to make a memory. Only the prosthetic

heroes can will to pick up
this world—sweating, they flail, they tap,
they pinch for it as it rolls

out of the therapist's hands, very small.

News

The CHRONICLE "Green Sheet" dries out
BIC pens mustaches & goggles,
underwear women
the boys decorated with paisley lesions,

interpreting the news.
Extinction seems a protracted, ironic task:
though Hitler's
manager Albert Speer dies

only a few pages ago,
I remember Hitler's death
on the radio was the work of an age,

a whole industry;
Eva Braun was anyone's sister gone wrong.
Finally I go on my belly
with the children to highlight

what is real. Newsprint bruises
ripple all over me;
faces come off on my sleeves

as I sweat & fill
page after page, call for new stacks.
Captions pull off like scabs,

but reversed:
this news understood only in mirrors,
accepted by the body,

will teach me shame.
My wife kneels too
on what we once thought important:

boldface sex crimes,
ferocious nations & burneddown discos.
Unaware of all they carry,

both boys stagger
in with old TRIB issues,
the GUARDIAN, THE BERKELEY BARBs

so yellow from garage weather
that they flake & snow
down on us lost, unrecoverable lives.

Al Young

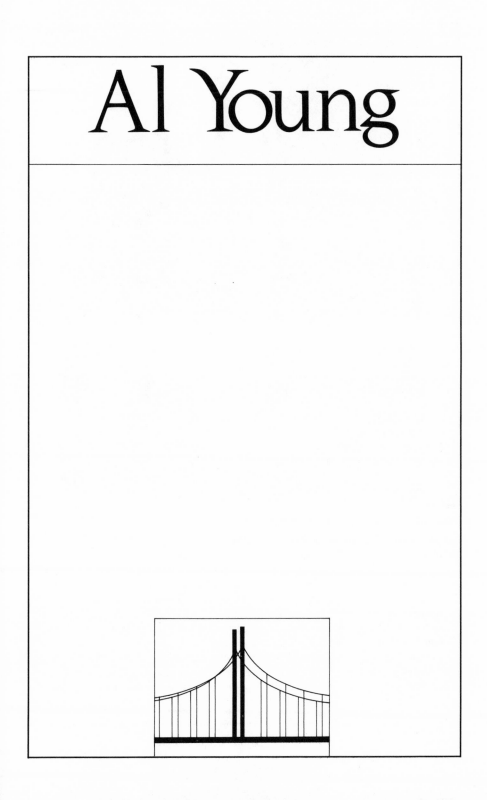

Al Young was born in 1939 in Ocean Springs, Mississippi. He was educated at the University of Michigan, Stanford University (where he was a Wallace E. Stegner Creative Writing Fellow), and the University of California, Berkeley. His home is in Palo Alto. He has one son. He has worked as a free-lance musician, a disc jockey, and has taught at the University of California, Berkeley, the University of Washington, and Stanford University; in the fall of 1982 he was Distinguished Andrew Mellon Professor of Humanities at Rice University in Houston. Since 1972 he has edited with Ishmael Reed *Yardbird Reader*, and *Quilt Magazine*. His verse includes: *Dancing; The Song Turning Back into Itself; Geography of the Near Past;* and *The Blues Don't Change*, which contains new and selected poems. His work also includes four novels and two plays. He is the recipient of grants from the National Endowment for the Arts, the San Francisco Foundation Joseph Henry Jackson Award, and a Guggenheim Fellowship.

Breaking the Lightning Bug Code:
Some Notes on Poetry and Childhood

I grew up in homes where the verbal jam session was a floating and usually festive fixture. Clusters of people were forever talking with one another, telling stories, sharing experiences, observations, jokes, riddles, conundrums, and swapping lies. Our talk was musical. The old folks often quoted scripture and we all mimicked the voices and gestures of others, marbling the fat of our utterance with lean strips of proverbial wisdom: "A dog that'll *carry* a bone will *bring* you one." Much later I would become aware of the Kenyan proverb that goes: "Talking with one another is loving one another." For then it was enough to take delight in the pictures and emotions that flooded my imagination as I went about learning, by ear and by heart, the nature of the world that lay beyond my childhood walls and fields.

I used to curl up on floor pallets in a corner or in warmly quilted beds with the door ajar and, while pretending to be asleep, listen to the grown folks carry on into the night by kerosene lamplight—with crickets or rain or wind in the background—way back up in rural Pachuta, Mississippi, and other distant settings.

Language and its stitched-together patterns of sound and beat and melody and pitch was real for me. Those crazy-quilt patches of bright and somber and giddy sound formed the literal fabric of my tender world. They were to be taken every bit as seriously as the very tree stump by the side of the dust road winding into town; that stately chinaberry stump where Uncle John, my maternal grandfather's brother, boasted that he'd once seen a hair-raising haint trot past one autumn long ago, hundreds of midnights before I was born. "He was ridin on a moon-white steed," said Uncle John, "and he was as close to me as you sittin from me now. Old Jack seen it too, like to sked him half to death. Rared back, commence to buckin and jeckin so bad I got gooseflesh!"

But I knew Old Jack. He was still alive and he was Uncle John's favorite riding mule. And I knew what Papa, my grandfather, meant when he'd haul off and say in the dead of winter, "I'm tireda hurryin down there to see bout John's mules. Only thing John's mules sufferin from is the miss-meal colic."

It was all as clear and mysteriously evident as lightning bugs pinpointing the summer-starved nights, winking out their starry morsels of code. My Cousin Jesse and the other kids even held long discussions about this. That was probably the way fireflies talked with one another. We figured there had to be some luminous cipher involved that was none of people's business. All the same, we spent hours trying to break the lightning bug code; that is, when we weren't dashing around trapping them in mason jars to make our own special flashlights.

The rise and fall of locust choirs on sizzling afternoons was equally magnetizing. Locusts, in fact, provided the background music for a signal incident that buzzes through my memory circuits to this day.

I'd just finished feeding the chickens and was resting on the edge of the back porch, lazily scrawling letters in the yard dirt with a prized stick, when an old, raggedy, smiling hobo appeared out of nowhere. He wore a faded, floppy straw hat and was carrying a burlap croaker sack. I stood, startled, and looked at once to see what Claude was going to do. Claude was our sleek, black farm dog whose jet keen nose usually picked up everything. But Claude didn't stir; he didn't let out so much as a low growl. That tattered stranger, armed with nothing but a grin, crouched at the porch steps where Claude had been dozing and, nodding a friendly "Hi do?" in my direction, patted the dog on his tick-tortured head just as gently as anyone in the family might have done.

Mama, my grandmother, was coming from her garden with an apronful of fresh-cut okra, snapbeans, and green tomatoes. I could see she was as puzzled as I was. Nevertheless, she put on a smile, walked around to where we were and she and the hobo exchanged pleasantries. He wasn't asking for a handout or odd jobs to do; he was only passing through and had somehow lost his way. Mama, her gold tooth fittings flashing in the late sunlight, patiently rerouted him, invited him to pluck a few figs and gather some pecans, then sent him on his way. He seemed harmless enough. But when he was gone, she studied Claude and looked at me, then stepped into the shadows of the porch. Narrowing her lucent brown eyes, she said, "I do believe that old rascal musta hoodoo'd that dog." She said this low under her breath, just loud enough for me to hear.

"Hoodoo!" I said. I must've been seven, maybe eight, and I'd heard the term but never from her lips until now. Its meaning had long been hidden from me. "What's hoodoo, Mama?"

"Hoodoo?" she repeated with a slow smirk that wasn't easy to read. "Aw, that's a kinda magic, whatchacall conjure. You burn candles, you mix these powders, get a holt to a locka somebody's hair or a piece of they clothes, say these words over and over. It's magic, but it's the Devil's magic. See, God got his magic and the Devil got his. Myself, I don't like to be foolin with them hoodoo people, never did."

"Well, how come you say that man done hoodoo'd Claude?"

"Cause that dog ain't got no business layin up and lettin that Negro pet him like that. Didn't bark, didn't even budge hardly."

"But how could the man put a hoodoo on him if he hadn't even seen Claude before?"

"That's what we don't know. He coulda slipped round here one night while we was sleep and sprinkled around some goofer dust. Mighta even had some in his hand or up his sleeve just now for all we know."

"But, Mama, wouldn't we'da heard him sneakin round the house here at night?"

"Don't know that either. Them kinda folks know all this lowdown stuff; that's all they study. The man coulda run up on Claude back there in the woods someplace and hoodoo'd him then."

"But why would he wanna hoodoo Claude in the first place?"

Mama trained her gaze on the chickens and the chicken coop and said, "Can't answer that neither, but I can tell you one thing. If I hear any kinda devilment goin on in the night, yall'll hear me shootin my pistol."

This was the same woman who moaned and hummed and sang spirituals all day long while she worked, and who taught me table blessings and the beautiful Twenty-Third Psalm.

It was in such settings that poetry began for me. Perhaps it is children who understand poetry best. I know for certain that, unlike most people, I never outgrew the need for magic or the curative powers of language. The quiescent greenness of those pastures in which I pictured myself lying down is more vivid than ever, and I can see the shapes of cloud and sky reflected in those still waters. I do not take John lightly when he declares, "In the beginning was the Word, and the Word was with God, and the Word was God." Even now in the Nuclear Era when we're constantly only a micro-chip blip away from graceless extinction; even at a time when the functions of poetry have been denigrated and trivialized, when postliterate societies largely regard poetic expression as a mere amusement at best, I've come to view Creation itself as the actualized speech of the Divine; the unnameable, dreamlike essence of some marvelous cosmic presence. Sustained and intensive personal experience and involvement with language have opened both my ears and eyes to the magnitude of the Word and its power to transmute perception and consciousness: reality, if you will.

Such lofty realizations have never been uncommon among traditional preliterate peoples, nor among the so-called civilized. Hindu, Taoist, Christian, Buddhist, and Islamic cosmologies abound with them. Leslie Silko opens *Ceremony*, her fecund novel about Indian life on a New Mexico reservation, with a poem that begins: "Ts'its'tsi'nako, Thought-Woman/is sitting in her room/and whatever she thinks about/appears." And in his moving book, *Eskimo Realities*, the humanist anthropologist and filmmaker Edmund Carpenter notes: "In Eskimo the word 'to make poetry' is the word 'to breathe'; both are derivatives of *anerca* —the soul, that which is eternal, the breath of life. A poem is words infused with breath or spirit. 'Let me breathe of it,' says the poet-maker and then begins: 'I have put my poem in order on the threshold of my tongue.' "

It took me quite some time to learn how poetry has always functioned and flourished among all peoples in all times and places, customarily as a natural component of song, dance, work, play, prophecy, healing, exorcism, ceremony, ritual, or communal worship. It was the printing press, among other innovations —to say nothing of altered notions about the place of the individual in the scheme of things—that helped change the way we think about poetry and the Word.

Long before the printed word and stuffy ideas about literature turned up in my life, and certainly long before I became the willing ward of schoolteachers, I was sleeping with words. I fondled and sniffed and placed my ear to their secret meanings. I soaked up the silences between syllables, tested them, tasted the saltiness or sweetness of them, and stared off into their bottomless eyes and down their dark, rosy throats. In a world innocent of ABC's, I dreamed in word-pictures and word-objects and word-feelings. And, like most children who live poetry all day long, I disappeared in between the spaces words made. It is this early enchantment with electrifying speech that abides with me still, in spite of the literature industry, in spite of poet-careerists and their ambitions, and quite in spite of the poetry scene itself.

"I always knew you were gonna be strange," Mama reminded me recently. She's closing in on a hundred now; a tough and beautiful little country woman whose light-drenched eyes can still see clean through me. My father's long gone from this world, and my mother just slipped away too. I've wandered and rambled from Mississippi to Michigan to California; all over this country, all over the world. And Mama's still here, telling me things I need to hear. "Always knew you were gonna be strange. From the time you could babble, you had your own way of talkin and understandin. We would put you on the floor with a funnybook or a magazine while you was still a baby, and you'd start turnin pages and feelin on em, and drift right off into some other world. Never would cry hardly. Long as you had them books to look at, you was happy. I never seen anything like it."

All my life I've been trying to hold onto and expand the joyous purity of those early moments and the magical talk that nourished it. Word by word, line by line, season upon season, poetry keeps teaching me that the only time there is is now.

Houston, Texas
October 1982

Birthday Poem

First light of day in Mississippi
son of laborer & of house wife
it says so on the official photostat
not son of fisherman & child fugitive
from cottonfields & potato patches
from sugarcane chickens & well-water
from kerosene lamps & watermelons
mules named jack or jenny & wagonwheels,

years of meaningless farm work
work Work WORK WORK WORK—
"Papa pull you outta school bout March
to stay on the place & work the crop"
—her own earliest knowledge
of human hopelessness & waste

She carried me around nine months
inside her fifteen year old self
before here I sit numbering it all

How I got from then to now
is the mystery that could fill a whole library
much less an arbitrary stanza

But of course you already know about that
from your own random suffering
& sudden inexplicable bliss

The Song Turning Back Into Itself 3

Ocean Springs Missippy
you don't know about that
unless youve died in magnolia
tripped across the Gulf
& come alive again
or fallen in the ocean
lapping up light
like the sun digging
into the scruffy palm leaves
fanning the almighty trains
huffing it choo-choo
straight up our street

morning noon & nighttrain
squalling that moan
like a big ass blues man
smoking up the sunset

Consider the little house
of sunken wood
in the dusty street
where my father would
cut his fingers
up to his ankles
in fragrant coils
of lumber shavings
the backyard of nowhere

Consider Nazis & crackers
on the same stage
splitting the bill

Affix it all to
my memory of Ma
& her love of bananas
the light flashing
in & out of our lives
lived 25¢ at a time
when pecans were in season
or the crab & shrimp
was plentiful enough
for the fishermen
to give away for gumbo
for a soft hullo
if you as a woman
had the sun in your voice
the wind over your shoulder
blowing the right way
at just that moment in history

One West Coast

For Gordon Lapides

Green is the color of everything
that isnt brown, the tones ranging
like mountains, the colors changing.

You look up toward the hills & fog—
the familiarity of it after so many years
    a resident tourist.

                A young man walks
toward you in vague streetcrossing denims
& pronounced boots. From the pallor of
    his gait, the orange splotch twin gobs of sunset
in his shades, from the way he vibrates
    his surrounding air, you can tell, you can tell
        he's friendly, circulating,

            he's a Californian: comes to visit,
                stays for years, marries, moves a wife in,
            kids, wears out TV sets, gets stranded on
                        loneliness,
                    afternoon pharmaceutica,
                so that the sky's got moon in it by
                3 o'clock, is blooo, is blown—

                The girls: theyre all
            winners reared by grandmothers & CBS.
            Luckier ones get in a few dances with
            mom, a few hours, before dad goes back
        in the slam, before "G'bye I'm off
            to be a singer!" & another runaway
                Miss American future drifts
                    over the mountain &
                    into the clouds.

            Still
        there's a beautifulness about California.
It's based on the way each eyeblink toward
the palms & into the orange grove leads backstage
        into the onionfields.

Unreachable, winter happens inside you.

Your unshaded eyes dilate at the spectacle.

You take trips to contain the mystery.

Lonesome in the Country

How much of me is sandwiches radio beer?
How much pizza traffic & neon messages?
I take thoughtful journeys to supermarkets,
philosophize about the newest good movie,
camp out at magazine racks & on floors,
catch humanity leering back in laundromats,
invent shortcuts by the quarter hour

There's meaning to all this itemization
& I'd do well to look for it in woodpiles
& in hills & springs & trees in the woods
instead of staying in my shack all the time
thinking too much,
                falling asleep in old chairs

All those childhood years spent in farmhouses
& I still cant tell one bush from another—
Straight wilderness would wipe me out
faster than cancer from smoking cigarettes

My country friends are out all day long
stomping thru the woods all big-eyed &
that's me walking the road afternoons,
head in some book,
           all that hilly sweetness wasting

Late January
Sonoma Mountain Road
in the Year of the Dragon

Ponce de León / A Morning Walk

You too if you work hard enough
can end up being the name of a street
in a drowsy little Indian town
a day's drive from Mexico City
where orphans like bold Joselito
hustle in the taxi burro streets,
where cosmetic fragrances mingle
with scents of ripe & overripe fruits
& vegetables, where the smell of breakfast
& dinner are almost the same.

The natural odor of dung & bodysweat
rises from the zócalo into a sky, semi-
industrialized, housing the spirits of
blue señoritas with sun soaking into
their rain-washed skirts dried dustier
& wrinklier than red or green pepper.

While a crazy rooster's crowing late
a brown baby delights in orange & yellow
balloons floating up like laughter
to tenement windows where a whole family
of older kids wave happy soap wands
that yield fat bubbles part air part
water part light that pop in the faces
of prickly straw behatted gents
rambling by below, ragged & alive—

One morning's moment in this ageless
stone thoroughfare named after just one
dead Spaniard who wanted to live forever

Moon Watching by Lake Chapala

> I love to cross a river in very
> bright moonlight and see the
> trampled water fly up in chips
> of crystal under the oxen's feet.
> —The Pillow Book of Sei Shōnagan,
> 10th Century

IT CAN BE beautiful this sitting by oneself all alone except for the world,
the very world a literal extension of living leaf, surface & wave of light: the
moon for example. American poet Hazel Hall felt,
       "I am less myself
        & more of the sun"
                         which I think upon these cool common nights
being at some remove, in spirit at least, from where they are busy building
bombs & preparing concentration camps to put my people into; I am still
free to be in love with dust & limbs (vegetable & human) & with lights in
the skies of high spring.

IN THE AFTERNOON you watch fishermen & fisherboys in mended
boats dragging their dark nets thru the waters. You can even buy a little
packet of dried sardines like I do, a soda, & lean against the rock & iron
railings but you wont be able to imagine the wanderings of my own

mustachio'd dad who was a fisherman in Mississippi in the warm streams of the Gulf of Mexico. How time loops & loops! Already I'm drunk with the thought of distances. I do that look skyward & re-chart the constellations. No one to drop in on. No one to drop in on me. It's been a long time since I've had nothing better to do than establish myself in one spot & stare directly into the faces of the moon, the golden orange white brown blue moon, & listen to the tock of my heart slowing down in the silence. I can almost hear in the breeze & picture in the sniffable award-winning moonlight the doings & dyings of my hard-working father, of all my heartbroken mamas & dads.

WHO WILL LIVE to write The Role of Moonlight in the Evolution of Consciousness?

IN NEW YORK, San Francisco & points in between the sad young men & women are packaging their wounds & hawking them; braggadocios cleansing old blood from syringes & sly needles in preparation for fresh offerings of cold hard chemical bliss: ofays wasted on suburban plenitude; not-together Bloods strung out on dreams.

I'M OUT HERE alone, off to one side, in the soft dark inspecting a stripe of tree shadow on my moonlit hand, dissolving into mineral light, quivering donkey light, the waters churning with fish & flora, happiness circulating thru my nervous system like island galaxies thru space.

MEXICO CAN BE Moon can be Madness can be Maya. But the rising notion that we are in the process of evolving from ape to angel under the influence of star-gazing is the Dream.

Dear Old Stockholm

Of course it is snowing
but two city girls,
one blonde the other black-
haired, are preparing for bed
in a warm apartment they share.
One is washing her hair in the bathroom sink
while the other does hatha yoga exercises.
They have been dancing with some young men
who spoke nothing but north american english,
one of them from Pittsburgh
(from Crawford's Grill up on the Hill)
& the other
a fingerpopper from Leamington, Ontario.

Suddenly, recalling the evening,
the rushing from taxis up inside music clubs,
all of them pleased that it should be so,
the bathroom blonde
who,
like a great many scandinavians,
played some instrument in secondary school
whistles John Coltrane's whole solo
from the Miles Davis *Dear Old Stockholm*
which had been an old swedish folk song.
In fluorescent abandon.
& in time
she massages her foamy scalp
with delight.

The young black-haired woman,
hearing all this
—tensed in a shoulderstand,
head full of new blood,
filling with new breath—
is overcome with unexpected happiness.

Each girl smiles in private
at the joyfullness of the evening
& at the music & the men, wishing
it would never end

Identities

So youre playing
Macbeth in Singapore
1937 before you were
even born perhaps

The lady is warm,
your lines are waiting
in your stomach
to be heard.

An old seacoast drunk
in pullover blue cap
stomps up one-legged
onto the stage to
tell you youve got no
business playing this

bloody Macbeth,
not a lonely black boy
like you, lost like
himself in a new world
where it's no longer
a matter of whom
thou knowest so much
as it is who you know.

(Say the lady warming
is a career bohemian
with OK looks & a
Vassar education)

Say the future seems
fractured in view of
the worsening wars
in Europe & Asia &
the old man's just
shattered your last
chance illusion.

Well, do you go on
& Shakespeare anyway
or reach for the sky
for the 500th time?

Visiting Day

For Conyus

This being a minimum security facility, it feels more like being on a reservation
than in a touchable cage

Books are allowed, smiles, eats (you could slip a .38 inside a baked chicken or
a file inside a loaf of sourdough french easily enough, but there's really not
much to shoot or saw thru)

You sign up, take a seat at one of the open-air picnic tables, & yawn from hours
of driving into the beautiful chilled morning

All the black inmates trudging by or hanging out of barracks windows give you
the power salute as you consider yourself again strapped down in their
skins

You walk, you talk, you toy around with words, you steal guarded looks down
into one another

A little food, fruit juice, a lot of gossip, & the sun on the trees under blue sky surrounding us is magnified into one big silly-looking halo

"I'm not into meat all that much anymore, man, & there's a whole lotsa books I wanna talk about &—here, these're some things I wrote last month—thinking about that last letter I wrote you where I said my head was getting peaceful—what's the bloods on the block woofing about these days?"

He looks healthier than he did in the old macrobiotic city yogi wild bustling days when you'd both get zonked on sounds in the middle of the afternoon & reminisce for midnights about stuff that probably never happened

This is what's known as a conservation camp where you cut & prune trees, dig up the earth, seed the ground, weather watch, sweat a lot, do a little basketball, sun on the run, sneak peeks at crotch shots in magazines smuggled in from outside

You think of his woman, you think of his son, you think of them holed up alone in the city, waiting & waiting for him to come home

You think of all the professionals involved: pipe smokers with advanced degrees from state colleges—penologists, criminologists, sociologists who minored in deviate psychology; in clean, classy ghettos where they never take walks, their children snort coke on an allowance

Three tables away from where you sit consoling one another, a slim young man up on a burglary rap is splitting his attention between a 2-year-old daughter & a 22-year-old wife who's shown up thoughtfully in tight-fitted jeans ripped generously enough to allow him to see what she hasn't bothered wearing

Well, it isn't San Quentin, it isnt Attica, & it's no one's official prisoner of war camp, yet you cant help thinking there's a battle going on somewhere out there in the bloodstreams of men

You say good-bye, you shake hands good-bye, you stare good-bye; you wave what you havent said, you grin what you cannot say, you walk away & turn again to wave what neither of you has to say

You gun your engine good-bye & roar off down the California road back out into your own special prison

Weeks later you hear about the steel file some white inmate's driven into the heart of another white inmate found by your friend by some bushes in the rain—dead—because he was your friend's good friend, because he was a nigger lover, a nigger lover

The news chills the tips of your fingers & you sweat

Could it have been the father of the sweet little girl, husband of the gal whose
   ass was showing?

Could it have been the marijuana dealer who read the *Bhagavad Gita* & medi-
   tated nightly?

Could it have been the small-boned cat thief who spoke Spanish with an Italian
   lilt like an Argentinian?

Could it have been the crinkly eyed loser who made you laugh & laugh when
   he talked about his life inside & outside the joint like a stand-up comic?

You think about the first person you ever screamed at

You think about the first thing you ever stole, or lied about, or killed

Ho

She coulda been somethin
like the Supremes or somebody
Her folks give her everything she need
I use to know her family pretty good
They dont have that much but they
         aint on relief
She call herself in love

Her money it go for that stuff, I guess,
         & for strong mouthwash, I know
I see her buyin Baby Ruths & Twinkies too
         down at the liquor store

Every night she start her day
right under my window when the lights
         come on
She aint bad-lookin neither, just little

She just a skinny little sister
bout big as my fist
but even she done slipped & found out
heaven aint the only H in the dictionary

"Boogie with O. O. Gabugah"

Note—

O. O. Gabugah writes that he "was born in a taxicab right smack on 125th and Lenox in Harlem on Lincoln's Birthday, 1945. Franklin Delano Watson was the name my poor brainwashed parents gave me but I had that racist tag legally altered once I got old enough to see what was going down. The O.O., by the way, stands for Our Own, i.e., we need to do *our own* thing, can you dig it?"

In addition to being one of our strongest young Black revolutionary voices, Brother Gabugah is the author of half a dozen volumes, all of which have appeared since last year. *Slaughter the Pig & Git Yo'self Some Chit'lins* is the title of his most popular work which is presently in its sixth big printing. Other volumes include: *Niggers with Knives, Black on Back, Love Is a White Man's Snot-Rag* and *Takin Names and Kickin Asses.* His plays—*Transistor Willie & Latrine Lil* and *Go All the Way Down & Come Up Shakin* (a revolutionary Black musical)—received last month's Drama Authority Award.

The brother is presently the recipient of both a Federal Arts Agency grant as well as a Vanderbilt Fellowship to conduct research on Richard Wright. Currently vacationing in Australia, he is preparing a collection of critical essays tentatively titled *Woodpile Findings: Cultural Investigations into What's Goin On.*

His last critical work, *Nothin Niggers Do Will Ever Please Me,* is also a favorite.

"O. O. Gabugah draws strong folk poetry from the voice of a strident but vital revolutionary who attacks the Uncle Tom," states *The Nation* in its March 19, 1973 issue.

A militant advocate of the oral tradition, he chooses to dictate his poems through me rather than write them down himself.

The Old O. O. Blues

Like right now it's the summertime
    and I'm so all alone
I gots to blow some fonky rhyme
    on my mental saxophone

Brother Trane done did his thang
    and so have Wes Montgomery,

both heavyweights in the music rang,
    now I'mo play my summary

It's lotsa yall that thank yall white
    (ought I say European?)
who thank Mozart and Bach's all right,
    denyin your Black bein

Well, honkyphiles, yall's day done come,
    I mean we gon clean house
and rid the earth of Oreo scum
    that put down Fats for Faust

This here's one for-real revolution
    where aint nobody playin
We intends to stop this cultural pollution
    Can yall git to what I'm sayin?

Sittin up here in your Dior gown
    and Pierre Cardin suit
downtown where all them devil clowns
    hang out and they aint poot!

We take the white man's bread and grants
    but do our own thang with it
while yall bees itchin to git in they pants
    and taint the true Black spirit

I'm blowin for Bird and Dinah and Billie,
    for Satch, Sam Cooke, and Otis,
for Clifford, Eric, and Trane outta Philly
    who split on moment's notice

Chump, you aint gon never change,
    your narrow ass is sankin
Like Watergate, your shit is strange
    You drownin while we thankin

My simple song might not have class
    but you cant listen with impunity
We out to smash your bourgeois ass
    and by *we* I mean The Community!

Intimacy

Right up under our noses, roses
arrive at middleage, cancer blooms
and the sea is awash with answers.

Right here where light is brightest,
we sleep deepest; ignorant dreamers
with the appetites of napping apes.

Right this way to the mystery of life!
Follow your nose, follow the sun or
follow the dreaming sea, but follow!

W. H. Auden & Mantan Moreland

In memory of the Anglo-American poet & the Afro-American comic actor
(famed for his role as Birmingham Brown, chauffeur in those ancient Charlie
Chan movies) who died on the same day in 1973

Consider them both in paradise,
discussing one another—
the one a poet, the other an actor;
interchangeable performers
who finally slipped backstage
of a play whose cast favored lovers.

"You executed some brilliant lines,
Mr. Auden, & doubtless engaged our
innermost emotions & informed imagination,
for I pondered your *Age of Anxiety*
diligently over a juicy order of ribs."

"No shit!" groans Auden, mopping his brow.
"I checked out all your Charlie Chan
flicks & flipped when you turned up again
in *Watermelon Man* & that gas commercial
over TV. Like, where was you all that
time in between? I thought you'd done
died & gone back to England or somethin."

"Wystan, pray tell, why did you ever eliminate
that final line from 'September 1, 1939'?—
We must all love one another or die."

"That was easy. We gon die anyway no matter
how much we love, but the best thing I like
that you done was the way you buck them eyes
& make out like you runnin sked all the time.
Now, that's the bottom line of the black
experience where you be in charge of the scene.
For the same reason you probly stopped shufflin."

Lester Leaps In

Nobody but Lester let Lester leap
into a spotlight that got too hot
for him to handle, much less keep
under control like thirst in a drought.

He had his sensitive side, he had
his hat, that glamorous porkpie whose
sweatband soaked up all that bad
leftover energy.

       How did he choose
those winning titles he'd lay on favorites
—Sweets Edison, Sir Charles, Lady Day?
Oooo and his sound! Once you savor its
flaming smooth aftertaste, what do you say?

Here lived a man so hard and softspoken
he had to be cool enough to hold his horn
at angles as sharp as he was heartbroken
in order to blow what it's like being born.

The Blues Don't Change

> "Now I'll tell you about the Blues. All Negroes like Blues. Why? Because
> they was born with the Blues. And now everybody have the Blues. Sometimes
> they don't know what it is."   —Leadbelly

And I was born with you, wasn't I, Blues?
Wombed with you, wounded, reared and forwarded
from address to address, stamped, stomped
and returned to sender by nobody else but you,
Blue Rider, writing me off every chance you
got, you mean old grudgeful-hearted, table-
turning demon, you, you sexy soul-sucking gem.

Blue diamond in the rough, you *are* forever.
You can't be outfoxed don't care how they cut
and smuggle and shine you on, you're like a
shadow, too dumb and stubborn and necessary
to let them turn you into what you ain't
with color or theory or powder or paint.

That's how you can stay in style without sticking
and not getting stuck. You know how to sting
where I can't scratch, and you move from frying
pan to skillet the same way you move people
to go to wiggling their bodies, juggling their
limbs, loosening that goose, upping their voices,
opening their pores, rolling their hips and lips.

They can shake their bodies but they can't shake *you.*

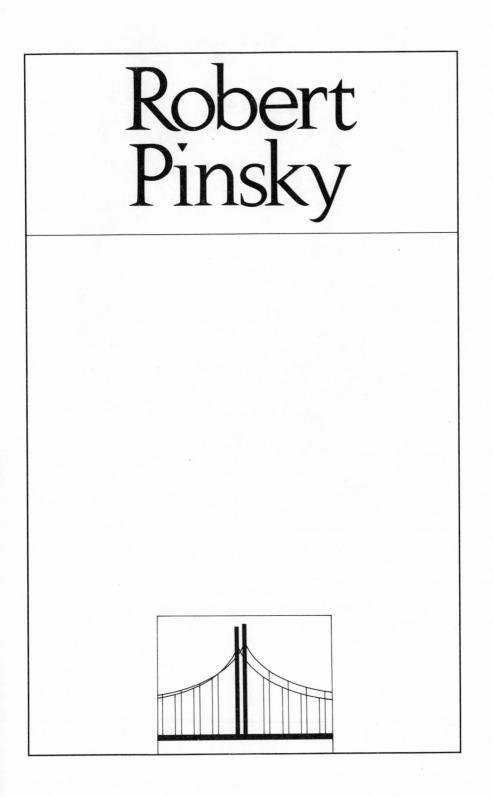

Robert
Pinsky

PETER SOUTHWICK

Robert Pinsky's first two books of poetry are *Sadness And Happiness* (Princeton, 1975) and *An Explanation of America* (1979); a new volume, *History of My Heart*, will be published in 1984. He has also written a book of criticism, *The Situation of Poetry* (1976).

A native of the seashore resort of Long Branch, New Jersey, he went to school there. He graduated from Rutgers, and first came to California as a graduate student at Stanford, where he held a Stegner Fellowship and studied with Yvor Winters. After three years, he left California in 1965 and lived for a long time in Wellesley, Massachusetts. In 1980, he returned to the Bay Area and now teaches at the University of California, Berkeley.

His poems have won many awards, including fellowships and prizes from the Guggenheim Foundation, the American Academy and Institute of Arts and Letters, and *Poetry* magazine. Since 1978, he has been poetry editor of *New Republic*.

Salt Water

All four of my grandparents came to live in Long Branch, New Jersey, when they were young people. Long Branch is an ocean resort, once a famous watering spot painted by Winslow Homer, visited by Abraham Lincoln and Diamond Jim Brady: "the Newport of its day," people said. But in the days when my grandparents raised their families in Long Branch, and later when I grew up there, the town was decayed: the beach eroded, the boardwalk on the famous bluffs given over to honky-tonk, many of the immense Victorian "cottages" on Ocean Avenue converted to hotels or to "cook-alones" or gutted by Jewish Lightning, as arson for insurance purposes was known.

I have an early memory of going down to the ocean in a car to watch a hurricane. From across the boardwalk, through sheets of rain, feeling the car rock on its springs in the mighty gusts, we saw the water spill in exhilarating sheets over the sea-wall, submerge the jetties, and break off chunks of pavement and boardwalk. As a climax, the hurricane that year tore a hot dog stand right off its wooden stilts and into the ocean.

Except for one unhappy year I spent in Chicago, I have always lived near salt water; so have my brother and sister and cousins. My grandfather Dave Pinsky was among other things a bootlegger during Prohibition; since one or two of the family stories from those days involve boats, the ocean may have had a practical, commercial importance to him. But it is not easy to picture him with the spray in his face, or even with his clothes wet. He is a figure from *Roaring Twenties*, not *Man of Aran*. He was a professional fighter for a time, and there is a picture of him in a black turtleneck, scowling and putting up his fists in the traditional pose.

His raffish, rowdy confidence has always appealed to me. Grandpa Dave, with his bar (the Broadway Tavern), his big hands and ape face, his gentile wife (number three), and his enormous Christmas tree, exerted a thuggish swank, an attractive counterforce away from another conception of being Jewish, a cerebral timidity epitomized by debate about Christmas carols. Should Jewish kids in public school sing them as "just songs"? A boy called Barney Hirsch took the opposite view that one must stand mute and immobile. Some compromisers lip-synched without vocalizing, while others omitted the religious parts only:

La-la the Savior is born!

The point about Grandpa Dave was not assimilation, but something like assurance.

It was partly a small-town assurance. The bar and his past made him firmly a local character. My father, an optician rather than a barkeeper, had a certain small-town outlook as well. I can hear him asking me, about an encounter with a teacher, storekeeper, cop, doctor: "Did he know who you were?" This wasn't said with arrogance, but with respect for the idea that we fit into the fabric of the place. The other side of the question was something like: "I know who he is; his uncle is an asphalt contractor. He used to do a specialty dance at dance marathons."

This small-town element, and a kind of criminal element, and what I'll call the salt-water element, have seemed left out, to me, in the many American novels about Jewish life in New York or Chicago. I am tempted to distinguish between New York Jews and salt-water Jews. This may explain why I love Isaac Babel's Odessa stories, with their romanticized Jewish gangsters:

> Reb Arye-Leib was silent, sitting on the cemetery wall. Finally he said: "Why he? Why not they, you wish to know? then see here, forget for a while that you have spectacles on your nose and autumn in your heart. Cease playing the rowdy at your desk and stammering while others are about. Imagine for a moment that you play the rowdy in public places and stammer on paper. You are a tiger, you are a lion, you are a cat. You can spend the night with a Russian woman, and satisfy her. You are twenty-five. If rings were fastened to heaven and earth, you would grasp them and draw heaven and earth together. . . . that's why he's the King, while you thumb your nose in the privy.

And then the old man tells the youth the comical epic tale of Benya's rise to become king of the dockside gangsters. One of the many things that interest me in the quotation is the process of mythologizing and glamorizing. I recognize that process, independently of content. (And Odessa is, of course, a seaport.) I recognize the scene of the old man telling the youth a story that he probably knows already.

One of the main junkyards in Long Branch used to belong to a man called, oddly enough, Ash. I went to Izzy Ash's junkyard in the summer of 1962 to get a part for a 1953 Dodge convertible which I proposed to drive out to California. I was going to be a poet, and I was going to Stanford. Mr. Ash took this in as he grunted and tugged at a long-handled wrench, removing the part I needed from a wrecked Coronet.

I told Mr. Ash that I was going to graduate school, not that I was going to be a writer. As it happens, he knew more than might be expected about going to graduate school. And I had already, that summer, been embarrassed by the idea that I was a writer.

A Long Branch boy called Danny Pingitore was having some minor success under another name as a television actor at this time. The absurdity of the ambitions I was carrying West with me had been driven home when Danny phoned me earlier that summer. I didn't really know him, he was at least five years older than me, but our mothers had run into one another in a store, and he was in Long Branch for part of July.

"Robert, this is Danny Pingitore. Your mother says you are going out to California to be a writer."

"Well, yes."

"There's something I really want to tell you."

"What's that?"

"Don't go."

"What?"

"Don't go, Robert, I mean it. I know a lot of writers in L.A. and they all say this is the worst year for it. It was okay for a while, but they aren't producing any more hour shows at all. Everything is half-hour shows. That's all they're making, and most of the writers out there already can't get work."

So I simply told Mr. Ash that I was going to Stanford, to graduate school. In Izzy Ash's class at Long Branch High School there were two outstanding students, both from Jewish families. Both went to Harvard: Mike Abrams and Barry Green, two brilliant and ambitious Long Branch boys whose stories still meant something to Mr. Ash as he braced his feet against the sandy, shadeless, oil-stained dirt of his junkyard and pulled a part free along its channeled bracket. He had his generation's respect for what doing well in school could do for somebody whose family had no money or power. So he told me about Mike and Barry.

Mike Abrams went from Harvard College to graduate school and became a distinguished professor, the author of a famous book (*The Mirror and the Lamp*, a study of the two Romantic images for poetry; though I had not exactly read it, I knew that it was—as it did prove to be—very good). Barry Green became a rich, clever lawyer, but sadly—as Mr. Ash told me the myth he knew I knew —in the course of his climb to success he got in deep with the Mob, including a deal that involved selling orange peels to the government for the production of synthetic sugar. The deal was saturated in fraud, bribery, chicanery—even, when you think about it, despoiling the Treasury in wartime; and the dukes and generals of the Mob (in Long Branch, where Vito Genovese had his once-famous yellow eyeglasses made by my father, "Mafia" always sounded almost highbrow or literary), protecting the myth of their patriotism, declared that Barry Green would have to go to prison, and so he did. The alternative was testifying, and sudden disappearance. His wife and daughters—both beautiful, they took elocution lessons, and the younger one was the first girl in town to play Little League —were taken care of by the dukes.

Meanwhile, the story concluded, Mike Abrams continued the idyllic life of an honored professor at Cornell University, an Ivy League college in a class with Harvard itself.

Mr. Ash sighed emphatically. He knew from his children, my classmates, that I had not been a very good student in high school, and his telling me this story was a way of indicating respect for my new seriousness. Wiping his head with his forearm, he finished with a moral:

"Yes, Robert, there's two different paths in life: it's just like North Broadway and South Broadway."

Having said this, Izzy Ash held out to me the extracted, rebuildable fuel pump of the Coronet. Broadway's two forks, North and South, form a Y just a couple of blocks from the beach. One of the things that seemed funny to me about Mr. Ash's allegorizing of the town, even as I nodded solemnly, is that North Broadway and South Broadway extend only to arrive at exactly the same place—the Atlantic Ocean.

On Broadway not far from where it divides there was a string of Jewish-owned businesses; those shops produced a number of distinguished names. One —was it a paint and hardware store?—belonged to the parents of M. H. Abrams. Norman Mailer's aunt had a dress shop called, I think, Estelle's. Another store of some kind paid for the first lessons of the noted pianist Julius Katchen. And I think that the parents of Jeff Chandler, the movie star who played Cochise in *Broken Arrow*, owned the delicatessen. Their name was Grossel.

The feeling about a place that makes people pass on such lore—I probably have the details all wrong, but those people really were born in Long Branch —is a feeling of importance. To mythologize or inflate a community, or even to make anecdote (or allegory) of it, is both to submerge one's identity partway into the communal identity and to assert one's importance. To make one's native place illustrious is an acceptable, ancient form of claiming personal significance. As a kind of impersonal boasting, it raises the great conflict and accommodation between self and community, figure and background.

The sense of importance, or heroic weight, is a big part of what thrills me in Edwin Arlington Robinson's *Eros Turannos*, the power of the plural *we* and the way that uncomprehending, smugly provincial *we* vibrates and gives a greater power to the singular *her,* in the closing stanzas:

> The falling leaf inaugurates
>   The reign of her confusion:
> The pounding wave reverberates
>   The dirge of her illusion;
> And home, where passion lived and died,
> Becomes a place where she can hide,
> While all the town and harbor side
>   Vibrate with her seclusion.

We tell you, tapping on our brows,
    The story as it should be,—
As if the story of a house
    Were told, or ever could be;
We'll have no kindly veil between
Her visions and those we have seen,—
As if we guessed what hers have been,
    Or what they are or would be.

Meanwhile we do no harm; for they
    That with a god have striven,
Not hearing much of what we say,
    Take what the god has given;
Though like waves breaking it may be,
Or like a changed familiar tree,
Or like a stairway to the sea
    Where down the blind are driven.

The excitement of this gloomy grandeur and glory—"they/That with a god have striven"—depends upon the peculiar relationship between the rather mean-minded, brow-tapping townfolk and the woman. Though she does not hear much of what they say, they help give her isolation heroic scale, as surely as she gives them something worth talking about.

This relationship of the tragic individual to the provincial community comes through so powerfully that it almost obliterates the equally brilliant first half of the poem, where the woman's choice of a terrible love affair over no love at all is etched with enormous conviction. The poem is charged with all the pride and frustration Robinson must have felt as a penniless, ailing provincial, successful neither in the terms of small-town life nor in the terms of the standard literary culture of the 1890s and after, whose magazines wanted no part of his work.

I think I love the poem partly for the detail that Long Branch shares with the Maine town Robinson was thinking of—the "stairway to the sea." And just as large, spooky vibrations course between "her" and "we," other tremendous, old forces pass between the Homeric opposites "sea" and "home":

And home, where passion lived and died,
Becomes a place where she can hide,
While all the town and harbor side
    Vibrate with her seclusion.

Her house is near the ocean, and her hometown, where we think we know so much, is right on the ocean. Stairs go right down to where the waves crash. Her fate and glory, her *doom* in the original sense, all seem located out there, in the same dangerous, productive waters where the swarthy, piratical sea-trading businessmen who made a first ideal audience for the *Odyssey* located glory, death, wonder, and profit. Telemachus is sent out onto it in order to make a name for himself. "Home" and "sea," being of a place and leaving it: Robinson's poem makes Izzy Ash seem less ludicrous, more an intuitively bardlike figure. Only Harvard, Hollywood, New York seem inadequate to their half of the Homeric equation. Broadway, with its two forks and its ambitious, cunning sons, seems Ithaca enough, when one reads Robinson's poem.

In Babel's story "Awakening," the Jewish fathers of Odessa run a "lottery, building it on the bones of little children." That is, since Mischa Elman and Jascha Heifetz were Odessa babies, all of the kids in that circle were taught music, by Mr. Zagursky, who ran "a factory of Jewish dwarfs in lace collars and patent-leather pumps," girls "aflame with hysteria" pressing violins to their "feeble knees," "big-headed, freckled children with necks as thin as flower stalks and an epileptic flush on their cheeks."

The narrator, at fourteen, is beyond "the age limit set for infant prodigies," but he is short and weak, as small as an eight-year-old: "Herein lay my father's hope." The father, significantly, is hopelessly and insanely obsessed not with money but with glory: "though my father could have reconciled himself to poverty, fame he must have."

But the boy props a book by Turgenev or Dumas on the music stand, while "the sounds dripped from my fiddle like iron filings, causing even me excruciating agony." And one day, on the way to Zagursky's for a lesson, the boy sets out on his own course for glory. He begins secretly cutting the lessons and heads in another direction, the direction in which Athene tells Telemachus to seek glory in Book One of the *Odyssey*. He heads for the ocean.

Down by the docks, he accompanies his friend Nemanov onto an English ship to get a consignment of smuggled handmade pipes. (The boy Nemanov will grow up to find glory as "A New York millionaire, director of General Motors, a company no less powerful than Ford.") Torn in "a struggle of Rabbis versus Neptune," the would-be writer, on one of these days by the docks, meets an old man who teaches him how to swim, encourages him as a writer, and commands him to look for the first time at the natural world. ("In my childhood, chained to the Gemara, I had led the life of a sage. When I grew up I started climbing trees.") As Babel puts it, "the local water-god took pity on me."

This water-god, proofreader of the *Odessa News,* reads a work of the boy's, "a tragedy I had written the day before." The old man reads, runs a hand through his hair, paces up and down; then—

> "One must suppose," he said slowly, pausing after each word, "one must suppose that there's a spark of the divine fire in you."

The water-god then immediately takes the boy outside:

> He pointed with his stick at a tree with a reddish trunk and a low
> crown.
> "What's that tree?"
> I didn't know.
> "What's growing on that bush?"
> I didn't know this either.

And so forth, with the names of birds, where they fly away to, even—astound-ingly, yet credibly—on which side the sun rises.

What seems important is not the old man's perception that "a feeling for nature" is essential to a writer, but the truth that the boy has been led somehow to neglect not merely the natural world, but the very physical world itself, in which his own body must live. It is fitting and deeply traditional that in order to encounter this truth the boy must head down toward the docks, the Mol-davanka district where the Jewish gangsters like Benya Krik rule: that is, toward the earth-shaking, massive, threatening and challenging domain of Poseidon, Odysseus's opponent.

Something I like in the story is that there is enough glory to go around for everyone: Nemanov at General Motors, Gabrilowitsch playing a recital before the Czar, the young writer deciding to climb trees. The scale of the ocean, and its message of possibility—any pitfall or wonder imaginable is in it somewhere —seems to encourage the idea of measuring human life, with its names and desires, against the preposterously enormous backdrop. That is why the woman in *Eros Turannos* appears against that heroic backdrop. Such characters prove worthy of salt water.

It is ridiculous, but Izzy Ash's venture into allegory or Danny Pingitore's venture into Hollywood, toward fame, the whole Long Branch pantheon of Jeff Chandler, Barry Green, Vito Genovese, Norman Mailer, seems in my imagina-tion also related to the overwhelming size and perpetual movement of the ocean. It is so big and changing and unchanging, its various noises are so evocative and musical, it suggests so much of heroic risk or gaudy pleasure, that the imagina-tion is nudged by its presence in extravagant directions.

Everybody carries their own rulers and scales with them. When I arrived in California, I had never seen land elevated beyond the hundred feet or so of Atlantic Highlands, or the rolling hills near the Delaware. The Sierras perma-nently astonished me. The clarity and immensity of the air and rock, the extent and nakedness of the light, were things I had not imagined. Kodak dyes fail to indicate the penetration and subtlety of the colors. In a sense, I was like the archetypal provincial gaping at the towers of Manhattan. But, for the scope and grandeur of size—though here the first big impression is of how much can be seen, while at home it is how much may remain hidden, out and below—I did have a standard to bring. And there is an ocean here, to help me feel at home and to remind me that I come from someplace.

Berkeley
1982

Poem about People

The jaunty crop-haired graying
Women in grocery stores,
Their clothes boyish and neat,
New mittens or clean sneakers,

Clean hands, hips not bad still,
Buying ice cream, steaks, soda,
Fresh melons and soap—or the big
Balding young men in work shoes

And green work pants, beer belly
And white T-shirt, the porky walk
Back to the truck, polite; possible
To feel briefly like Jesus,

A gust of diffuse tenderness
Crossing the dark spaces
To where the dry self burrows
Or nests, something that stirs,

Watching the kinds of people
On the street for a while—
But how love falters and flags
When anyone's difficult eyes come

Into focus, terrible gaze of a unique
Soul, its need unlovable: my friend
In his divorced schoolteacher
Apartment, his own unsuspected

Paintings hung everywhere,
Which his wife kept in a closet—
Not, he says, that she wasn't
Perfectly right; or me, mis-hearing

My rock radio sing my self-pity:
"The Angels Wished Him Dead"—all
The hideous, sudden stare of self,
Soul showing through like the lizard

Ancestry showing in the frontal gaze
Of a robin busy on the lawn.
In the movies, when the sensitive
Young Jewish soldier nearly drowns

Trying to rescue the thrashing
Anti-semitic bully, swimming across
The river raked by nazi fire,
The awful part is the part truth:

Hate my whole kind, but me,
Love me for myself. The weather
Changes in the black of night,
And the dream-wind, bowling across

The sopping open spaces
Of roads, golf-courses, parking lots,
Flails a commotion
In the dripping treetops,

Tries a half-rotten shingle
Or a down-hung branch, and we
All dream it, the dark wind crossing
The wide spaces between us.

Discretions of Alcibiades

First frost is weeks off, but the prudent man
With house-plants on his front porch marks the season
And moves the potted *ficus* back indoors

While windows can be open for a while.
(The plant prefers a gradual transition.)
—The kid who did his homework, washed his face

And never wore tight pants, kept cherry bombs
And nasty photos in his briefcase (think:
A seventh-grader with a briefcase)—Hantman,

In Student Council with his red-hot bag:
His picture of a lady on all fours,
A Great Dane on her back, was not for sale.

And though he may have sold a bomb or two,
And must have set some off, I like to think
He preferred, like Presidents, their deep reserve.

Speaking of gradual transitions, "plant
Prefers" of course is only an expression.
You might say that the plant prefers to die,

Or wishes it were home, in Borneo,
Preferring never to have seen a window.
The stars are similar: "The wheeling Bear,

One white eye on the Pleiads, rolls another
At glowering Orion." Autumn stars.
On this first chilly dusk, a furry bat,

Warm-blooded, dips and flutters in the sky.
(Some constellations might be called, "The Bat.")
The roles are arbitrary too. The man

Who sleeps with Socrates and Leontes' wife,
Who knocks the cocks from his own effigies,
Or not, simply prefers—to use another

Expression—to hide his briefcase in a bomb.
Consider gods and heroes, how they merge:
(I speak as one believing in the gods,

Especially in quick, reflective Hermes,
So sensitive and practical—like a thief,
Or like long-suffering, shrewd Odysseus).

Apollo, sullen and glamorous obverse
Of Hermes, shrouds himself in dark, or shines,
Like bold Achilles in his tent—or out,

As he prefers. All one. Tithonus, too,
And Alcibiades, balling Lady Luck
Until she dried him up. When people say

"How was your summer?" who is there alive
Who wouldn't like to change sides, go to Sparta
Like Alcibiades, cut your hair, live clean . . .

And then knock up the king's wife on the sly.
That's where the inner briefcase is revealed:
He hoped his heir would be the King of Sparta—

More screwing with Fortuna, man with goddess . . .
From a god's point of view, it is perhaps
Disgusting, if exciting in a way,

Like a dog doing a lady from behind.
The sundry dogs from along the road prefer
To conduct ferocious gang-fucks in a field:

Dogs Only, in the end-of summer fest.
But people, on Cape Cod, the Costa Brava,
Borneo, emulate gods and goddesses:

Rubbing their skin with oil, they sun it brown
Until they all are Spaniard, Jew or Greek—
Wear sandals; ply their boat; keep simple house

Cooking red meat or fish on open fires;
Market for salt; and dance to tinkly music.

Serpent Knowledge

FROM *An Explanation of America*

In something you have written in school, you say
That snakes are born (or hatched) already knowing
Everything they will ever need to know—
Weazened and prematurely shrewd, like Merlin;
Something you read somewhere, I think, some textbook
Coy on the subject of the reptile brain.
(Perhaps the author half-remembered reading
About the Serpent of Experience
That changes manna to gall.) I don't believe it;
Even a snake's horizon must expand,
Inwardly, when an instinct is confirmed
By some new stage of life: to mate, kill, die.

Like angels, who have no genitals or place
Of national origin, however, snakes
Are not historical creatures; unlike chickens,
Who teach their chicks to scratch the dust for food—
Or people, who teach ours how to spell their names:
Not born already knowing all we need,
One generation differing from the next
In what it needs, and knows.
                                        So what I know,
What you know, what your sister knows (approaching
The age you were when I began this poem)
All differ, like different overlapping stretches
Of the same highway: with different lacks, and visions.
The words—*"Vietnam"*—that I can't use in poems
Without the one word threatening to gape
And swallow and enclose the poem, for you
May grow more finite; able to be touched.

The actual highway—snake's-back where it seems
That any strange thing may be happening, now,
Somewhere along its endless length—once twisted
And straightened, and took us past a vivid place:
Brave in the isolation of its profile,
"Ten miles from nowhere" on the rolling range,
A family graveyard on an Indian mound
Or little elevation above the grassland. . . .
Fenced in against the sky's huge vault at dusk
By a waist-high iron fence with spear-head tips,
The grass around and over the mound like surf.

A mile more down the flat fast road, the homestead:
Regretted, vertical, and unadorned
As its white gravestones on their lonely mound—
Abandoned now, the paneless windows breathing
Easily in the wind, and no more need
For courage to survive the open range
With just the graveyard for a nearest neighbor;
The stones of Limit—comforting and depriving.

Elsewhere along the highway, other limits—
Hanging in shades of neon from dusk to dusk,
The signs of people who know how to take
Pleasure in places where it seems unlikely:
New kinds of places, the "overdeveloped" strips
With their arousing, vacant-minded jumble;
Or garbagey lake-towns, and the tourist-pits
Where crimes unspeakably bizarre come true
To astonish countries older, or more savage . . .
As though the rapes and murders of the French
Or Indonesians were less inventive than ours,
Less goofy than those happenings that grow
Like air-plants—out of nothing, and alone.

They make us parents want to keep our children
Locked up, safe even from the daily papers
That keep the grisly record of that frontier
Where things unspeakable happen along the highways.

In today's paper, you see the teen-aged girl
From down the street; camping in Oregon
At the far point of a trip across the country,
Together with another girl her age,
They suffered and survived a random evil.
An unidentified, youngish man in jeans

Aimed his car off the highway, into the park
And at their tent (apparently at random)
And drove it over them once, and then again;
And then got out, and struck at them with a hatchet
Over and over, while they struggled; until
From fear, or for some other reason, or none,
He stopped; and got back into his car again
And drove off down the night-time highway. No rape,
No robbery, no "motive." Not even words,
Or any sound from him that they remember.
The girl still conscious, by crawling, reached the road
And even some way down it; where some people
Drove by and saw her, and brought them both to help,
So doctors could save them—barely marked.

                                        You see
Our neighbor's picture in the paper: smiling,
A pretty child with a kerchief on her head
Covering where the surgeons had to shave it.
You read the story, and in a peculiar tone—
Factual, not unfeeling, like two policemen—
Discuss it with your sister. You seem to feel
Comforted that it happened far away,
As in a crazy place, in *Oregon*:
For me, a place of wholesome reputation;
For you, a highway where strangers go amok,
As in the universal provincial myth
That sees, in every stranger, a mad attacker . . .
(And in one's victims, it may be, a stranger).

Strangers: the Foreign who, coupling with their cousins
Or with their livestock, or even with wild beasts,
Spawn children with tails, or claws and spotted fur,
Ugly—and though their daughters are beautiful
Seen dancing from the front, behind their backs
Or underneath their garments are the tails
Of reptiles, or teeth of bears.

                              So one might feel—
Thinking about the people who cross the mountains
And oceans of the earth with separate legends,
To die inside the squalor of sod huts,
Shanties, or tenements; and leave behind
Their legends, or the legend of themselves,
Broken and mended by the generations:
Their alien, orphaned, and disconsolate spooks,

Earth-trolls or Kallikaks or Snopes or golems,
Descended of Hessians, runaway slaves and Indians,
Legends confused and loose on the roads at night . . .
The Alien or Creature of the movies.

As people die, their monsters grow more tame;
So that the people who survived Saguntum,
Or in the towns that saw the Thirty Years' War,
Must have felt that the wash of blood and horror
Changed something, inside. Perhaps they came to see
The state or empire as a kind of Whale
Or Serpent, in whose body they must live—
Not that mere suffering could make us wiser,
Or nobler, but only older, and more ourselves. . . .

On television, I used to see, each week,
Americans descending in machines
With wasted bravery and blood; to spread
Pain and vast fires amid a foreign place,
Among the strangers to whom we were new—
Americans: a spook or golem, there.
I think it made our country older, forever.
I don't mean better or not better, but merely
As though a person should come to a certain place
And have his hair turn gray, that very night.

Someday, the War in Southeast Asia, somewhere—
Perhaps for you and people younger than you—
Will be the kind of history and pain
Saguntum is for me; but never tamed
Or "history" for me, I think. I think
That I may always feel as if I lived
In a time when the country aged itself:
More lonely together in our common strangeness . . .
As if we were a family, and some members
Had done an awful thing on a road at night,
And all of us had grown white hair, or tails:
And though the tails or white hair would afflict
Only that generation then alive
And of a certain age, regardless whether
They were the ones that did or planned the thing—
Or even heard about it—nevertheless
The members of that family ever after
Would bear some consequence or demarcation,
Forgotten maybe, taken for granted, a trait,
A new syllable buried in their name.

The Questions

What about the people who came to my father's office
For hearing aids and glasses—chatting with him sometimes

A few extra minutes while I swept up in the back,
Addressed packages, cleaned the machines; if he was busy

I might sell them batteries, or tend to their questions:
The tall overloud old man with a tilted, ironic smirk

To cover the gaps in his hearing; a woman who hummed one
Prolonged note constantly, we called her "the hummer"—how

Could her white fat husband (he looked like Rev. Peale)
Bear hearing it day and night? And others: a coquettish old lady

In a bandeau, a European. She worked for refugees who ran
Gift shops or booths on the boardwalk in the summer;

She must have lived in winter on Social Security. One man
Always greeted my father in Masonic gestures and codes.

Why do I want them to be treated tenderly by the world, now
Long after they must have slipped from it one way or another,

While I was dawdling through school at that moment—or driving,
Reading, talking to Ellen. Why this new superfluous caring?

I want for them not to have died in awful pain, friendless.
Though many of the living are starving, I still pray for these,

Dead, mostly anonymous (but Mr. Mank, Mrs. Rose Vogel)
And barely remembered: that they had a little extra, something

For pleasure, a good meal, a book or a decent television set.
Of whom do I pray this rubbery, low-class charity? I saw

An expert today, a nun—wearing a regular skirt and blouse,
But the hood or headdress navy and white around her plain

Probably Irish face, older than me by five or ten years.
The Post Office clerk told her he couldn't break a twenty

So she got change next door and came back to send her package.
As I came out she was driving off—with an air, it seemed to me,

Of annoying, demure good cheer, as if the reasonableness
Of change, mail, cars, clothes was a pleasure in itself: veiled

---

And dumb like the girls I thought enjoyed the rules too much
In grade school. She might have been a grade school teacher;

But she reminded me of being there, aside from that—as a name
And person there, a Mary or John who learns that the janitor

Is Mr. Woodhouse; the principal is Mr. Ringleven; the secretary
In the office is Mrs. Apostolacos; the bus driver is Ray.

History of My Heart

I

One Christmastime Fats Waller in a fur coat
Rolled beaming from a taxicab with two pretty girls
Each at an arm as he led them in a thick downy snowfall

Across Thirty-Fourth Street into the busy crowd
Shopping at Macy's: perfume, holly, snowflake displays.
Chimes rang for change. In Toys, where my mother worked

Over her school vacation, the crowd swelled and stood
Filling the aisles, whispered at the fringes, listening
To the sounds of the large, gorgeously-dressed man,

His smile bemused and exalted, lips boom-booming a bold
Bass line as he improvised on an expensive, tinkly
Piano the size of a lady's jewel box or a wedding cake.

She put into my heart this scene from the romance of Joy,
Co-authored by her and the movies, like her others—
My father making the winning basket at the buzzer

And punching the enraged gambler who came onto the court—
The brilliant black and white of the movies, texture
Of wet snowy fur, the taxi's windshield, piano keys,

Reflections that slid over the thick brass baton
That worked the elevator. Happiness needs a setting:
Shepherds and shepherdesses in the grass, kids in a store,

The back room of Carly's parents' shop, record-player
And paper streamers twisted in two colors: what I felt
Dancing close one afternoon with a thin blonde girl

Was my amazing good luck, the pleased erection
Stretching and stretching at the idea *She likes me*,
She likes it, the thought of legs under a woolen skirt,

To see eyes "melting" so I could think *This is it,*
They're melting! Mutual arousal of suddenly feeling
Desired: *This is it: "desire"!* When we came out

Into the street we saw it had begun, the firm flakes
Sticking, coating the tops of cars, melting on the wet
Black street that reflected storelights, soft

Separate crystals clinging intact on the nap of collar
And cuff, swarms of them stalling in the wind to plunge
Sideways and cluster in spangles on our hair and lashes,

Melting to a fresh glaze on the bloodwarm porcelain
Of our faces, Hey nonny-nonny boom-boom, the cold graceful
Manna, heartfelt, falling and gathering copious

As the air itself in the small-town main street
As it fell over my mother's imaginary and remembered
Macy's in New York years before I was even born,

II

And the little white piano, tinkling away like crazy—
My unconceived heart in a way waiting somewhere like
Wherever it goes in sleep. Later, my eyes opened

And I woke up glad to feel the sunlight warm
High up in the window, a brighter blue striping
Blue folds of curtain, and glad to hear the house

Was still sleeping. I didn't call, but climbed up
To balance my chest on the top rail, cheek
Pressed close where I had grooved the rail's varnish

With sets of double tooth-lines. Clinging
With both arms, I grunted, pulled one leg over
And stretched it as my weight started to slip down

With some panic till my toes found the bottom rail,
Then let my weight slide more till I was over—
Thrilled, half-scared, still hanging high up

With both hands from the spindles. Then lower
Slipping down until I could fall to the floor
With a thud but not hurt, and out, free in the house.

Then softly down the hall to the other bedroom
To push against the door; and when it came open
More light came in, opening out like a fan

So they woke up and laughed, as she lifted me
Up in between them under the dark red blanket,
We all three laughing there because I climbed out myself.

Earlier still, she held me curled in close
With everyone around saying my name, and hovering,
After my grandpa's cigarette burned me on the neck

As he held me up for the camera, and the pain buzzed
Scaring me because it twisted right inside me;
So when she took me and held me and I curled up, sucking,

It was as if she had put me back together again
So sweetly I was glad the hurt had torn me.
She wanted to have made the whole world up,

So that it could be hers to give. So she opened
A letter I wrote my sister, who was having trouble
Getting on with her, and read some things about herself

That made her go to the telephone and call me up:
"You shouldn't open other people's letters," I said
And she said "Yes—*who taught you that?*"

—As if she owned the copyright on good and bad,
Or having followed pain inside she owned her children
From the inside out, or made us when she named us,

III

Made me Robert. She took me with her to a print-shop
Where the man struck a slug: a five-inch strip of lead
With the twelve letters of my name, reversed,

Raised along one edge, that for her sake he made
For me, so I could take it home with me to keep
And hold the letters up close to a mirror

Or press their shapes into clay, or inked from a pad
Onto all kinds of paper surfaces, onto walls and shirts,
Lengthwise on a Band-Aid, or even on my own skin—

The little characters fading from my arm, the gift
Always ready to be used again. Gifts from the heart:
Her giving me her breast milk or my name, Waller

Showing off in a store, for free, giving them
A thrill as someone might give someone an erection,
For the thrill of it—or you come back salty from a swim:

Eighteen shucked fresh oysters and the cold bottle
Sweating in its ribbon, surprise, happy birthday!
So what if the giver also takes, is after something?

So what if with guile she strove to color
Everything she gave with herself, the lady's favor
A scarf or bit of sleeve of her favorite color

Fluttering on the horseman's bloodflecked armor
Just over the heart—how presume to forgive the breast
Or sudden jazz for becoming what we want? I want

Presents I can't picture until they come,
The generator flashlight Italo gave me one Christmas:
One squeeze and the gears visibly churning in the amber

Pistol-shaped handle hummed for half a minute
In my palm, the spare bulb in its chamber under my thumb,
Secret; or, the knife and basswood Ellen gave me to whittle.

And until the gift of desire, the heart is a titular,
Insane king who stares emptily at his counselors
For weeks, drools or babbles a little, as word spreads

In the taverns that he is dead, or an impostor. One day
A light concentrates in his eyes, he scowls, alert, and points
Without a word to a pass in the cold, grape-colored peaks—

Generals and courtiers groan, falling to work
With a frantic movement of farriers, cooks, builders,
The city thrown willing or unwilling like seed

(While the brain at the same time may be settling
Into the morning *Chronicle*, humming to itself,
Like a fat person eating M&Ms in the bathtub)

IV

Toward war, new forms of worship or migration.
I went out from my mother's kitchen, across the yard
Of the little two-family house, and into the Woods:

Guns, chevrons, swordplay, a scarf of sooty smoke
Rolled upwards from a little cratewood fire
Under the low tent of a Winesap fallen

With fingers rooting in the dirt, the old orchard
Smothered among the brush of wild cherry, sumac,
Sassafras and the stifling shade of oak

In the strip of overgrown terrain running
East from the train tracks to the ocean, woods
Of demarcation, where boys went like newly-converted

Christian kings with angels on helmet and breastplate,
Bent on blood or poaching. *There are a mountain and a woods*
Between us—a male covenant, longbows, headlocks. A pack

Of four stayed half-aware it was past dark
In a crude hut roasting meat stolen from the A&P
Until someone's annoyed father hailed us from the tracks

And scared us home to catch hell: We were worried,
Where have you been? In the Woods. With snakes and tramps.
An actual hobo knocked at our back door

One morning, declining food, to get hot water.
He shaved on our steps from an enamel basin with brush
And cut-throat razor, the gray hair on his chest

Armorial in the sunlight—then back to the woods,
And the otherlife of snakes, poison oak, boxcars.
Were the trees cleared first for the trains or the orchard?

Walking home by the street because it was dark,
That night, the smoke-smell in my clothes was like a bearskin.
Where the lone hunter and late bird have seen us

Pass and repass, the mountain and the woods seem
To stand darker than before—words of sexual nostalgia
In a song or poem seemed cloaked laments

For the woods when Indians made lodges from the skin
Of birch or deer. When the mysterious lighted room
Of a bus glided past in the mist, the faces

Passing me in the yellow light inside
Were a half-heard story or a song. And my heart
Moved, restless and empty as a scrap of something

Blowing in wide spirals on the wind carrying
The sound of breakers clearly to me through the pass
Between the blocks of houses. The horn of Roland

V

But what was it I was too young for? On moonless
Nights, water and sand are one shade of black,
And the creamy foam rising with moaning noises

Charges like a spectral army in a poem toward the bluffs
Before it subsides dreamily to gather again.
I thought of going down there to watch it awhile,

Feeling as though it could turn me into fog,
Or that the wind would start to speak a language
And change me—as if I knocked where I saw a light

Burning in some certain misted window I passed,
A house or store or tap-room where the strangers inside
Would recognize me, locus of a new life like a woods

Or orchard that waxed and vanished into cloud
Like the moon, under a spell. Shrill flutes,
Oboes and cymbals of doom. My poor mother fell,

And after the accident loud noises and bright lights
Hurt her. And heights. She went down stairs backwards,
Sometimes with one arm on my small brother's shoulder.

Over the years, she got better. But I was lost in music;
The cold brazen bow of the saxophone, its weight
At thumb, neck and lip, came to a bloodwarm life

Like Italo's flashlight in the hand. In a white
Jacket and pants with a satin stripe I aspired
To the roughneck elegance of my Grandfather Dave.

Sometimes, playing in a bar or at a high school dance, I felt
My heart following after a capacious form,
Sexual and abstract, in the thunk, thrum,

Thrum, come-wallow and then a little screen
Of quicker notes goosing to a fifth higher, winging
To clang-whomp of a major seventh: listen to *me*

Listen to *me*, the heart says in reprise until sometimes
In the course of giving itself it flows out of itself
All the way across the air, in a music piercing

As the kids at the beach calling from the water *Look*,
Look at me, to their mothers, but out of itself, into
The listener the way feeling pretty or full of erotic revery

Makes the one who feels seem beautiful to the beholder
Witnessing the idea of the giving of desire—nothing more wanted
Than the little singing notes of wanting—the heart

Yearning further into giving itself into the air, breath
Strained into song emptying the golden bell it comes from,
The pure source poured altogether out and away.

The Figured Wheel

The figured wheel rolls through shopping malls and prisons,
Over farms, small and immense, and the rotten little downtowns.
Covered with symbols, it mills everything alive and grinds
The remains of the dead in the cemeteries, in unmarked graves and oceans.

Sluiced by salt water and fresh, by pure and contaminated rivers,
By snow and sand, it separates and recombines all droplets and grains,
Even the infinite sub-atomic particles crushed under the illustrated,
Varying treads of its wide circumferential track.

Spraying flecks of tar and molten rock it rumbles
Through the Antarctic station of American sailors and technicians,
And shakes the floors and windows of whorehouses for diggers and smelters
From Bethany, Pennsylvania to a practically nameless, semi-penal New Town

In the mineral-rich tundra of the Soviet northernmost settlements.
Artists illuminate it with pictures and incised mottoes
Taken from the Ten-Thousand Stories and the Register of True Dramas.
They hang it with colored ribbons and with bells of many pitches.

With paints and chisels and moving lights they record
On its rotating surface the elegant and terrifying doings
Of the inhabitants of the Hundred Pantheons of major Gods
Disposed in iconographic stations at hub, spoke and concentric bands,

And also the grotesque demi-Gods, Hopi gargoyles and Ibo dryads.
They cover it with wind-chimes and electronic instruments
That vibrate as it rolls to make an all-but-unthinkable music,
So that the wheel hums and rings as it turns through the births of stars

And through the dead-world of bomb, fireblast and fallout
Where only a few doomed races of insects fumble in the smoking grasses.
It is Jesus oblivious to hurt turning to give words to the unrighteous,
And is also Gogol's feeding pig that without knowing it eats a baby chick

And goes on feeding. It is the empty armor of My Cid, clattering
Into the arrows of the credulous unbelievers, a metal suit
Like the lost astronaut revolving with his useless umbilicus
Through the cold streams, neither energy nor matter, that agitate

The cold, cyclical dark, turning and returning.
Even in the scorched and frozen world of the dead after the holocaust
The wheel as it turns goes on accreting ornaments.
Scientists and artists festoon it from the grave with brilliant

Toys and messages, jokes and zodiacs, tragedies conceived
From among the dreams of the unemployed and the pampered,
The listless and the tortured. It is hung with devices
By dead masters who have survived by reducing themselves magically

To tiny organisms, to wisps of matter, crumbs of soil,
Bits of dry skin, microscopic flakes, which is why they are called "great,"
In their humility that goes on celebrating the turning
Of the wheel as it rolls unrelentingly over

A cow plodding through car-traffic on a street in Iasi,
And over the haunts of Robert Pinsky's mother and father
And wife and children and his sweet self
Which he hereby unwillingly and inexpertly gives up, because it is

There, figured and pre-figured in the nothing-transfiguring wheel.

The Changes

Even at sea the bodies of the unborn and the dead
Interpenetrate at peculiar angles. In a displaced channel

The crew of a tanker float by high over the heads
Of a village of makers of flint knives, and a woman

In one round hut on a terrace dreams of her grandsons
Floating through the blue sky on a bubble of black oil

Calling her in the unknown rhythms of diesel engines to come
Lie down and couple. On the ship, three different sailors

Have a brief revery of dark, furry shanks, and one resolves
To build when he gets home a kind of round shrine or gazebo

In the small terraced garden of his house in a suburb.
In the garden, bees fumble at hydrangeas blue as crockery

While four children giggle playing School in the round gazebo.
(To one side, the invisible shaved heads of six priests

Bob above the garden's earth as they smear ash on their chests,
Trying to dance away a great epidemic; afterwards one priest,

The youngest, founds a new discipline based on the ideals
Of childlike humility and light-heartedness and learning.)

One of the sailor's children on his lunch hour years later
Writes on a napkin a poem about blue hydrangeas, bees

And a crockery pitcher. And though he is killed in a war
And the poem is burned up unread on a mass pyre with his body,

The separate molecules of the poem spread evenly over the globe
In a starlike precise pattern, as if a geometer had mapped it.

Overhead, passengers in planes cross and recross in the invisible
Ordained lanes of air traffic—some of us in the traverse

Passing through our own slightly changed former and future bodies,
Seated gliding along the black lines printed on colored maps

In the little pouches at every seat, the webs of routes bunched
To the shapes of beaks or arrowheads at the black dots of the cities.

Robert Hass

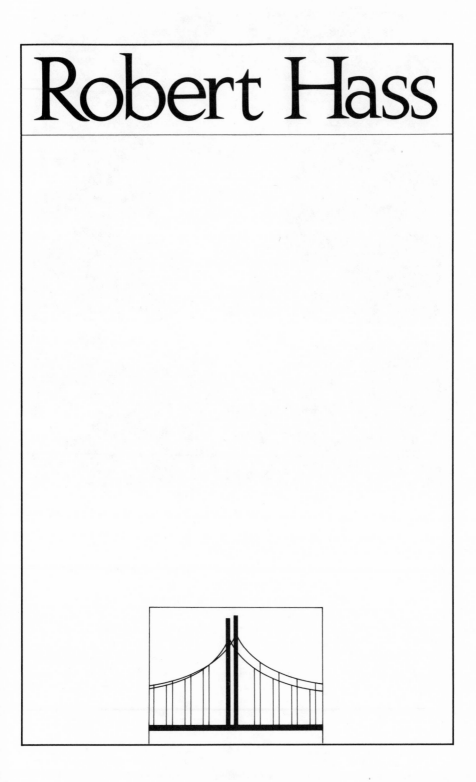

Robert Hass is the author of *Field Guide*, 1973, and *Praise*, 1979. He was born in San Francisco in 1941 and grew up in San Rafael. Educated at St. Mary's College Moraga, California, and Stanford University, he has taught literature for a living at various institutions, including SUNY Buffalo, the University of Virginia, Goddard College, and Columbia University. In 1976–77, he was a fellow of the U.S.–U.K. Bicentennial Exchange Program in the Arts and lived in a village near Cambridge, England. In 1978 he was Poet-in-Residence at The Frost Place in Franconia, New Hampshire. He received a Guggenheim Fellowship in 1980. His most recent publication is a translation, together with the author and Robert Pinsky, of Czeslaw Milosz's *The Separate Notebooks*, 1983. His essays and reviews have appeared widely in American magazines and he has lectured on American poetry in the Netherlands, Yugoslavia, and Hungary. Currently, he works at St. Mary's College and lives in Berkeley with his wife and three children.

Some Notes on the San Francisco Bay Area as a Culture Region: A Memoir

One of the women who babysat for me when I was a child was Portuguese. She had lived most of her life in Marin County, but her English was halting. I don't know why she lived in town, whether she was widowed or unmarried. Her name was Marianna Sequieros and her brothers were dairy farmers. They lived a few miles away on their ranch in an old white clapboard house, choked with lilacs when I knew it, with a dilapidated palm tree in the front yard and a half dozen peacocks trailing their tails in the dust. The brothers were selling off their land parcel by parcel to real estate developers, and by the time I was in the eighth grade the newest tract abutted the house itself.

I had just entered an essay contest sponsored by the National Legion for Decency in Motion Pictures. We were supposed to read a book and say why it would make a good movie. My teacher, Sister Reginald, a tall woman who used to play Robert Burns songs for us in music appreciation on rainy days and then sit at her desk dreamily listening and weeping, was very keen on the project. She assigned us each a book to read and made us write an essay. I didn't like the book I read, and with the encouragement of my older brother—for I understood that it was an act of rebellion—I wrote an essay on why it was a bad book and wouldn't make a good movie. I thought it was a vigorous composition and Marianna—though she could not read English, she checked our work when she arrived in the morning to see that it had a look of orderly diligence—examined and approved its appearance. But Sister Reginald did not like it much. She had long beautiful hands which she waved in the air like doves when she conducted us at Mass in the singing of the *Tantum Ergo* and *Pange Lingua* (in the recently rebuilt chapel of the Mission San Rafael, very nearly the last to be founded and built as a hospital because by that time the native Californians were dying of European diseases in great numbers) and, in the silent period, she beckoned me to her desk with a brief movement of her exquisite, tapering fingers. Her face was not beautiful. She was nicknamed The Beak. Face and hands were all we saw of the bodies of the nuns, who were covered otherwise by a whirling mass of white cloth which the Dominican order had worn since it was founded in the twelfth century in Spain and Northern Italy as a kind of papal CIA to root out the gnostic heresy of the Cathars.

I became interested in the Cathars, years later, from reading Robert Duncan. He must have acquired the interest from reading Ezra Pound and he also studied medieval history at Berkeley under the great historian Kantorowicz. At that moment, I think, he was in New York hanging around the edge of a literary group which had Anaïs Nin at its center and working on the poems in *Caesar's*

Gate. A poisonous portrait of the young man can be found in the first volume of Nin's spider web of a diary. Duncan's foster parents were theosophists, which also explains his interest in occult lore—it belonged to his world as naturally as singing *Eat, tongue, the body of the mystery* in Latin belonged to mine—and he used that knowledge in *Bending the Bow* to draw an analogy between the American war in Vietnam and the final massacre of the Cathars at Montsegur. One poem lists the names of men and women killed by the crusaders:

> At Montsegur
> that the heart be tried,
>
> Corba de Perella,
> Ermengarde d'Ussat,
> Guilleline, Bruna, Arssendis,
>
> Guillame de l'Isle,
> Raymond de Marciliano,
> Raymond-Guillame de Tornabois,
> Arnald Domerc,
> Arnald Dominique . . .
>
> these among the seventeen
> receiving the *consolamentum* to join the two hundred
>   and ten *perfecti*
> at the field of the fiery martyrs, *Champs de Cramatch*,
> until the name of the Roman Church with its heaped honors
> stinks with the smell of their meat burning

Also at about this time, a young writer, Allen Ginsberg, looked out of the window of his Nob Hill apartment at the glowering face of an office building and was given his own *gnosis*, a vision of the very god of money and power:

> What sphinx of cement and aluminum bashed open their
>   skulls and ate up their brains and imagination?
> Moloch! Solitude! Filth! Ugliness! Ashcans and unob-
>   tainable dollars! Children screaming under the
>   stairways! Boys sobbing in armies! Old men weeping
>   in the parks!
> Moloch! Moloch! Nightmare of Moloch! Moloch the loveless!
>   Mental Moloch! Moloch the heavy judger of men!
> Moloch the incomprehensible prison! Moloch the cross-
>   bone soulless jailhouse and Congress of sorrows!
>   Moloch whose buildings are judgement! Moloch the
>   vast stone of war! Moloch the stunned governments!
> Moloch whose mind is pure machinery! Moloch whose blood
>   is running money . . .

Reading these passages later would give me one idea of what it was that writing could be faithful to, but just then, Sister Reginald—dressed, I suddenly see, in exactly the style, solidly middle class, sexually modest, of the Cathar women who had been burned alive seven hundred years before—was explaining to me why *Stranded on an Atoll* would make a very educational Walt Disney film —snapping turtles, whole colonies of exotic sea birds, an octopus. She had freckles, Sister Reginald. And, though she was not beautiful, up close I thought her skin was pretty. She must have been younger than I am now, Italian probably, gone straight from a San Francisco high school to the convent—and what a romantic name she had chosen for herself! I found her account of the Walt Disney film completely convincing. I could see it, in technicolor, the boys running down the reef to get their fish that the turtle was dragging off for himself. She told me I could ignore the regular class work and rewrite my essay through the afternoon, which I did, and I think I was as much pleased by my rhapsody about the book as I was by my attack on it. I remember that I was able at one point to use the word "sylphin" got from an historical novel by F. Van Wyck Mason, but I also had the feeling that my brother would think I had knuckled under, so at the end of the day I told her that I wanted to take it home and recopy it; in fact I covered it with scrawls and erasures so that I had to recopy it. I wanted to explain to my brother that I had realized what a great movie *Stranded on an Atoll* would make.

We had a long conference that night in our upstairs room before pretending to go to sleep and turning on the radio. It was a ritual in our house—which was too disorganized to have very many rituals—that we had to go to bed at 9:45, which was fifteen minutes before our favorite radio show came on. Every night we went downstairs, kissed our parents—or our father, if my mother who was ill a lot wasn't there—goodnight, went upstairs, turned off the light, waited ten minutes, turned on the radio to warm it up, and listened to *I Love a Mystery*. My father knew perfectly well what we were doing and I think he approved. Two of his favorite books were *Penrod* and *Penrod and Sam*, by Booth Tarkington. They are about freckled, charming, disobedient boys from Indiana. I think it amused him that we were upstairs secretly listening to the radio—a Norman Rockwell cover from *The Saturday Evening Post*, which arrived at our house every Tuesday and to whose humor page my brother and I had already submitted poems, neatly written out in pencil. My father could have let us stay up until 10:15—he was at his desk, lodged in the corner of the dining room, writing on long yellow legal pads a book on strategy in contract bridge which was never published—but he didn't, and it taught me an attitude toward the truth I am still trying to unlearn, so that, years later again, when I read the opening lines of Robert Duncan's "In Place of Passage 22" from *Bending the Bow*,

> That Freedom and the Law are identical
> and are the nature of man—

I knew instantly that I couldn't understand what he meant and felt sick to my stomach.

That morning, though, I felt sick to my stomach because I had to walk to school, up D Street to Fifth—San Rafael, a little valley under a hill, was laid out by developers, after the Mission had failed and the Indians scattered, in the grid pattern of American urban development dreamed onto the blank land by Thomas Jefferson's love of land surveying and by economic convenience; the expressions "square deal" and "square meal" emerged, I read somewhere, from those rare speculators who didn't squeeze a few feet off each lot to jam in an extra one at the end; and the arrangement suggested the possibility of infinite expansion, though here it had only got as far as E Street and Fifth Street. Anyway, up those I walked to tell Sister Reginald that I was sticking to my first essay.

The nuns arrived from the convent in a taxicab. That started the day, if one were not serving early Mass for Father O'Meara, who liked plenty of Dry Sémillon in the chalice at six-thirty in the morning. All of the kids I couldn't stand lined up at the curb to greet the sisters and carry their briefcases to the classroom. This day I hovered at their edges, followed Sister Reginald into the classroom, and told her that I wanted to submit my first essay because it was what I really thought, not the second essay which was what she thought. The speech was prepared by my brother and I am ashamed to say that I think it was exactly as real or unreal to me as each of the essays. She heard me out, with chalk in her hand, standing at the desk, and then asked me gently, rather impressively, or at least there was something impressive about her tone, if I understood that I had very little chance of winning a contest having to do with why a book would make a good movie by writing an essay on why a book would make a bad movie. I said that I did, trying to match her tone, but in fact I didn't; she asked me if I would consider adding a sentence to the end of my essay saying that there were many interesting animals in the book and that it might make a good Walt Disney movie. She said it would improve my chances of winning, and I said I would, and I did. It turned out to be two sentences and she made me rewrite them several times.

I won second place in the essay contest. A kid from E Street School won first place with an essay on *Catcher in the Rye,* and it made me resent the public school kids for being allowed to read daring books. My prize was a ten dollar money order from the Cottage Bookshop. It was presented at a luncheon ceremony in the dining room of the Rancho Rafael Motel. I went to the bookstore—for the first time, I think; it was where, four years later, I would buy Ginsberg's *Howl* because I read in the newspaper that it was a sexual book. But this first time I was at a loss. Out of all the books, which one to buy? I browsed, dizzy. It seemed impossible to choose, to have a basis for choice. In the end, I grabbed a small red book, a Modern Library Classic, entitled *A Comprehensive Anthology of American Poetry*. I chose it, I think, because its title was so clear that I thought I knew exactly what I was getting.

To my disappointment almost everything in the book was incomprehensible to me. But there was one poem I liked. I liked it so much, if "like" is the word, that it made me swoon, and made me understand what the word "swoon" meant. The poem went like this:

> At night, by the fire,
> The colors of the bushes
> And of the fallen leaves,
> Repeating themselves,
> Turned in the room,
> Like the leaves themselves
> Turning in the wind.
> Yes: but the color of the heavy hemlocks
> Came striding
> And I remembered the cry of the peacocks.
>
> The color of their tails
> Were like the leaves themselves
> Turning in the wind,
> In the twilight wind.
> They swept over the room,
> Just as they flew from the boughs of the hemlocks
> Down to the ground.
> I heard them cry—the peacocks.
> Was it a cry against the twilight
> Or against the leaves themselves
> Turning in the wind,
> Turning as the flames
> Turned in the fire,
> Turning as the tails of the peacocks
> Turned in the loud fire,
> Loud as the hemlocks
> Full of the cry of the peacocks?
> Or was it a cry against the hemlocks?
>
> Out of the window,
> I saw how the planets gathered
> Like the leaves themselves
> Turning in the wind.
> I saw how the night came,

Came striding like the color of the heavy hemlocks.
I felt afraid.
And I remembered the cry of the peacocks.

I read it over and over. I read it exactly the way I lined up for a roller coaster ride with a dime tight in my fist at Playland across the bay in San Francisco. I see certain things about it now. I was full of not very conscious fear for my mother and it filled my days with gusts of childish terror and, obscurely, with a small boy's desire to do good. I suppose it was the acknowledgement of terror, of terror and beauty, in the poem that seemed to so wake me up, or hypnotize me, that I wanted to hold it close. Then, of course, I didn't see anything, or need to. The poem was as unambiguously thrilling, as definite as any physical experience. A year later, in high school, I went on my first date. To Playland, and rode the roller coaster with a girl from my ninth grade class whom I thought the most beautiful being I had ever come close to in my life, which may also account for something of the previous year's swooning. And, as it happened, when we grew up, I married that girl.

But in the year of the essay contest, I was more interested in baseball than girls. Little League had arrived in Marin County, a small puddle of that organizing energy which seems to characterize nations in their empire phase. I played for a team sponsored by a businessmen's club. My best friend played for a team sponsored by an insurance company. His colors were green and white, mine were purple and gold. We wore our uniforms constantly, OPTIMISTS emblazoned across my chest, CALIFORNIA CASUALTY across his. His father was a Basque who had run away to sea, worked in the galleys of ships, married an Australian woman, and become a chef at a restaurant on Fisherman's Wharf. He, my friend, studied Slavic Languages at Berkeley and is now a translator of Milosz and Gombrowicz, living in Toronto. Sometimes we played games against other towns. When we played against Fairfax, we played at White's Hill School. My position was center field and just in back of it—so that if you hit a home run, it went in their yard—was the ranch house of the Sequieros brothers, completely surrounded by the new school and the tract of suburban houses from which issued every morning the men who took buses to work in the banks and insurance companies of San Francisco.

Playing center field in the late innings that summer, I heard the irritated, prenocturnal cries of the peacocks in the Sequieros brothers' yard. The cry of a peacock sounds like some hardwood being scraped against slate. It is not a pleasant sound, but on those summer evenings in the twilight, the game would be coming to an end, we would be winning or losing, I liked to listen—with a hollow in my stomach and the body of the mystery still to be lived—to the cries of those birds.

I never once associated them with the Wallace Stevens poem. Art hardly ever does seem to come to us at first as something connected to our own world; it always seems, in fact, to announce the existence of another, different one, which is what it shares with gnostic insight. That is why, I suppose, the next thing that artists have to learn is that this world is the other world. A creek ran by the baseball diamond at White's Hill School, just by the third baseline. It was called Papermill Creek and it winds through western Marin and empties into the Pacific at Tomales Bay. I read many poems that pleased and startled me after "Domination of Black" but the first one to teach me that there could be an active connection between poetry and my own world was in a book by Kenneth Rexroth. Flipping through it, I came across this:

> Under the second moon the
> Salmon come, up Tomales
> Bay, up Papermill Creek, up
> The narrow gorges to their spawning
> Beds in Devil's Gulch. Although
> I expect them, I walk by the
> Stream and hear them splashing and
> Discover them each year with
> A start. When they are frightened
> They charge the shallows, their immense
> Red and blue bodies thrashing
> Out of the water over
> The cobbles; undisturbed, they
> Lie in pools. The struggling
> Males poise and dart and recoil.
> The females lie quiet, pulsing
> With birth. Soon all of them will
> Be dead, their handsome bodies
> Ragged and putrid, half the flesh
> Battered away by their great
> Lust . . .

Rexroth died this past spring. He was, like Penrod, a bad boy from Indiana. He came to San Francisco in the late 1920s, and in 1941 he published the first readable book of poems ever produced by a resident of the city. There were less than four hundred English-speakers in all of California in 1841, so it took about a hundred years for colonization to produce the city that produced the book of poems. There had been earlier writers born here. But all that remains of California in the poems of Robert Frost, though he spent his summers in the Nicasio Valley through which Papermill Creek flowed, was the fear of his father's violence, and that has been transformed into the dark interiors of New England farms. Gertrude Stein took only the genteel provincial culture, imported here like horses, chairs, the machine age, and the English language, which she reacted against. Jack London and Robinson Jeffers, of roughly the same generation as Frost, were the first California writers, with the important exception of John Muir. Rexroth and Steinbeck belong to the second generation.

But *In What Hour,* Rexroth's first book, seems—with its open line, its almost Chinese plainness of syntax, its eye to the wilderness, anarchist politics, its cosmopolitanism, experimentalism, interest in Buddhism as a way of life and Christianity as a system of thought and calendar of the seasons, with its interest in pleasure, its urban and back country meditations—to have invented the culture of the West Coast. It is a phenomenally fresh and enlivening book to read still; not perfect and flawed when it is flawed in ways that I find unattractive, but very much alive. None of which mattered to me then. I was stunned by the presence of the creek in a poem. It made it seem possible that the peacocks in Wallace Stevens and the scraggly birds under the palm tree could inhabit the same place and made me think of Kenneth Rexroth with gratitude when I heard that he died. His poem ends like this:

> . . . I sit for a long time
> In the chilly sunlight by
> The pool below my cabin
> And think of my own life—so much
> Wasted, so much lost, all the
> Pain, all the deaths and dead ends,
> So very little gained after
> It all. Late in the night I
> Come down for a drink. I hear
> Them rushing at one another
> In the dark. The surface of
> The pool rocks. The half moon throbs
> On the broken water. It is black,
> Frosty. Frail blades of ice form
> On the edges. In the cold
> Night the stream flows away, out
> Of the mountains, towards the bay,
> Bound on its long recurrent
> Cycle from the sky to the sea.

Palo Alto: The Marshes

For Mariana Richardson (1830–1891)

1

She dreamed along the beaches of this coast.
Here where the tide rides in to desolate
the sluggish margins of the bay,
sea grass sheens copper into distances.
Walking, I recite the hard
explosive names of birds:
egret, killdeer, bittern, tern.
Dull in the wind and early morning light,
the striped shadows of the cattails
twitch like nerves.

2

Mud, roots, old cartridges, and blood.
High overhead, the long silence of the geese.

3

"We take no prisoners," John Fremont said
and took California for President Polk.
That was the Bear Flag War.
She watched it from the Mission San Rafael,
named for the archangel (the terrible one)
who gently laid a fish across the eyes
of saintly, miserable Tobias
that he might see.
The eyes of fish. The land
shimmers fearfully.
No archangels here, no ghosts,
and terns rise like seafoam
from the breaking surf.

4

Kit Carson's antique .45, blue,
new as grease. The roar
flings up echoes,
row on row of shrieking avocets.
The blood of Francisco de Haro,

Ramon de Haro, José de los Reyes Berryessa
runs darkly to the old ooze.

5

The star thistles: erect, surprised,

6

and blooming
violet caterpillar hairs. One
of the de Haros was her lover,
the books don't say which.
They were twins.

7

In California in the early spring
there are pale yellow mornings
when the mist burns slowly into day.
The air stings
like autumn, clarifies
like pain.

8

Well I have dreamed this coast myself.
Dreamed Mariana, since her father owned the land
where I grew up. I saw her picture once:
a wraith encased in a high-necked black silk
dress so taut about the bones there were hardly ripples
for the light to play in. I knew her eyes
had watched the hills seep blue with lupine after rain,
seen the young peppers, heavy and intent,
first rosy drupes and then the acrid fruit,
the ache of spring. Black as her hair
the unreflecting venom of those eyes
is an aftermath I know, like these brackish,
russet pools a strange life feeds in
or the old fury of land grants, maps,
and deeds of trust. A furious dun-
colored mallard knows my kind
and skims across the edges of the marsh
where the dead bass surface
and their flaccid bellies bob.

9

A chill tightens the skin
around my bones. The other California
and its bitter absent ghosts
dance to a stillness in the air:
the Klamath tribe was routed and they disappeared.
Even the dust seemed stunned,
tools on the ground, fishnets.
Fires crackled, smouldering.
No movement but the slow turning
of the smoke, no sound but jays
shrill in the distance and flying further off.
The flicker of lizards, dragonflies.
And beyond the dry flag-woven lodges
a faint persistent slapping.
Carson found ten wagonloads
of fresh-caught salmon, silver
in the sun. The flat eyes stared.
Gills sucked the thin annulling air.
They flopped and shivered,
ten wagonloads. Kit Carson
burned the village to the ground.
They rode some twenty miles that day
and still they saw the black smoke
smear the sky above the pines.

10

Here everything seems clear,
firmly etched against the pale
smoky sky: sedge, flag, owl's clover,
rotting wharves. A tanker lugs silver
bomb-shaped napalm tins toward
port at Redwood City. Again,
my eye performs
the lobotomy of description.
Again, almost with yearning,
I see the malice of her ancient eyes.
The mud flats hiss as the tide turns.
They say she died in Redwood City,
cursing "the goddamned Anglo-Yankee yoke."

II

The otters are gone from the bay
and I have seen five horses
easy in the grassy marsh
beside three snowy egrets.

Bird cries and the unembittered sun,
wings and the white bodies of the birds,
it is morning. Citizens are rising
to murder in their moral dreams.

Maps

Sourdough french bread and pinot chardonnay

*

Apricots—
the downy buttock shape
hard black sculpture of the limbs
on Saratoga hillsides in the rain.

*

These were the staples of the China trade:
sea otter, sandalwood, and bêche-de-mer

*

The pointillist look of laurels
their dappled pale green body stirs
down valley in the morning wind
Daphne was supple
my wife is tan, blue-rippled
pale in the dark hollows

*

Kit Carson in California:
it was the eyes of fish
that shivered in him the tenderness of eyes
he watched the ships come in
at Yerba Buena once, found obscene
the intelligence of crabs
their sidelong crawl, gulls
screeching for white meat
flounders in tubs, startled

---

*

Musky fall—
slime of a saffron milkcap
the mottled amanita
delicate phallic toxic

*

How odd
the fruity warmth of zinfandel
geometries of "rational viticulture"

*

   Plucked from algae sea spray
cold sun and a low rank tide
   sea cucumbers
lolling in the crevices of rock
they traded men enough
to carve old Crocker's railway out of rock
to eat these slugs
bêche-de-mer

*

The night they bombed Hanoi
we had been drinking red pinot
that was winter the walnut tree was bare
and the desert ironwood where waxwings
perched in spring drunk on pyracantha

squalls headwinds days gone
north on the infelicitous Pacific

*

The bleak intricate erosion of these cliffs

   seas grown bitter
with the salt of continents

*

Jerusalem artichokes
raised on sandy bluffs at San Gregorio
near reedy beaches where the steelhead ran

Coast range runoff turned salt creek
in the heat and indolence of August

*

That purple in the hills
   owl's clover stiffening the lupine
while the white flowers of the pollinated plant
   seep red

the eye owns what is familiar
   felt along the flesh
"an amethystine tinge"

*

Chants, recitations:
Olema
Tamalpais Mariposa
Mendocino Sausalito San Rafael
Emigrant Gap
Donner Pass

Of all the laws
that bind us to the past
the names of things are
stubbornest

*

Late summer—
red berries darken the hawthorns
curls of yellow in the laurels

your body and the undulant
sharp edges of the hills

*

Clams, abalones, cockles, chitons, crabs

*

Ishi
in San Francisco, 1911:
it was not the sea he wondered at
that inland man who saw the salmon
die to spawn and fed his dwindling people
from their rage to breed
it was the thousands of white bodies
on the beach
"Hansi saltu . . ." so many
ghosts

The long ripple in the swamp grass
is a skunk
he shuns the day

Meditation at Lagunitas

All the new thinking is about loss.
In this it resembles all the old thinking.
The idea, for example, that each particular erases
the luminous clarity of a general idea. That the clown-
faced woodpecker probing the dead sculpted trunk
of that black birch is, by his presence,
some tragic falling off from a first world
of undivided light. Or the other notion that,
because there is in this world no one thing
to which the bramble of *blackberry* corresponds,
a word is elegy to what it signifies.
We talked about it late last night and in the voice
of my friend, there was a thin wire of grief, a tone
almost querulous. After a while I understood that,
talking this way, everything dissolves: *justice,
pine, hair, woman, you* and *I.* There was a woman
I made love to and I remembered how, holding
her small shoulders in my hands sometimes,
I felt a violent wonder at her presence
like a thirst for salt, for my childhood river
with its island willows, silly music from the pleasure boat,
muddy places where we caught the little orange-silver fish
called *pumpkinseed.* It hardly had to do with her.
Longing, we say, because desire is full
of endless distances. I must have been the same to her.
But I remember so much, the way her hands dismantled bread,
the thing her father said that hurt her, what
she dreamed. There are moments when the body is as numinous
as words, days that are the good flesh continuing.
Such tenderness, those afternoons and evenings,
saying *blackberry, blackberry, blackberry.*

Against Botticelli

In the life we lead together every paradise is lost.
Nothing could be easier: summer gathers new leaves
to casual darkness. So few things we need to know.
And the old wisdoms shudder in us and grow slack.
Like renunciation. Like the melancholy beauty
of giving it all up. Like walking steadfast
in the rhythms, winter light and summer dark.
And the time for cutting furrows and the dance.
Mad seed. Death waits it out. It waits us out,
the sleek incandescent saints, earthly and prayerful.
In our modesty. In our shamefast and steady attention
to the ceremony, its preparation, the formal hovering
of pleasure which falls like the rain we pray not to get
and are glad for and drown in. Or spray of that sea,
irised: otters in the tide lash, in the kelp-drench,
mammal warmth and the inhuman element. Ah, that is the secret.
That she is an otter, that Botticelli saw her so.
That we are not otters and are not in the painting
by Botticelli. We are not even in the painting by Bosch
where the people are standing around looking at the frame
of the Botticelli painting and when Love arrives, they throw up.
Or the Goya painting of the sad ones, angular and shriven,
who watch the Bosch and feel very compassionate
but hurt each other often and inefficiently. We are not in any painting.
If we do it at all, we will be like the old Russians.
We'll walk down through scrub oak to the sea
and where the seals lie preening on the beach
we will look at each other steadily
and butcher them and skin them.

2

The myth they chose was the constant lovers.
The theme was richness over time.
It is a difficult story and the wise never choose it
because it requires a long performance
and because there is nothing, by definition, between the acts.
It is different in kind from a man and the pale woman
he fucks in the ass underneath the stars
because it is summer and they are full of longing

---

and sick of birth. They burn coolly
like phosphorus, and the thing need be done
only once. Like the sacking of Troy
it survives in imagination,
in the longing brought perfectly to closing,
the woman's white hands opening, opening,
and the man churning inside her, thrashing there.
And light travels as if all the stars they were under
exploded centuries ago and they are resting now, glowing.
The woman thinks what she is feeling is like the dark
and utterly complete. The man is past sadness,
though his eyes are wet. He is learning about gratitude,
how final it is, as if the grace in Botticelli's *Primavera*,
the one with sad eyes who represents pleasure,
had a canvas to herself, entirely to herself.

The Origin of Cities

She is first seen dancing which is a figure
not for art or prayer or the arousal of desire
but for action simply; her breastband is copper,
her crown imitates the city walls. Though she draws us
to her, like a harbor or a rivermouth she sends us away.
A figure of the outward. So the old men grown lazy
in patrician ways lay out cash for adventures.
Imagining a rich return, they buy futures
and their slaves haunt the waterfront for news of ships.
The young come from the villages dreaming.
Pleasure and power draw them. They are employed
to make inventories and grow very clever,
multiplying in their heads, deft at the use of letters.
When they are bored, they write down old songs from the villages,
and the cleverest make new songs in the old forms
describing the pleasures of the city, their mistresses,
old shepherds and simpler times. And the temple
where the farmer grandfathers of the great merchants worshipped,
the dim temple across from the marketplace
which was once a stone altar in a clearing in the forest,
where the nightwatch pisses now against a column in the moonlight,
is holy to them; the wheat mother their goddess of sweaty sheets,
of what is left in the air when that glimpsed beauty
turns the corner, of love's punishment and the wracking
of desire. They make songs about that. They tell

stories of heroes and brilliant lust among the gods.
These are amusements. She dances, the ships go forth,
slaves and peasants labor in the fields, maimed soldiers
ape monkeys for coins outside the wineshops,
the craftsmen work in bronze and gold, accounts
are kept carefully, what goes out, what returns.

Child Naming Flowers

When old crones wandered in the woods,
I was the hero on the hill
in clear sunlight.

Death's hounds feared me.

Smell of wild fennel,
high loft of sweet fruit high in the branches
of the flowering plum.

Then I am cast down
into the terror of childhood,
into the mirror and the greasy knives,
the dark
woodpile under the fig trees
in the dark.
        It is only
the malice of voices, the old horror
that is nothing, parents
quarreling, somebody
drunk.

I don't know how we survive it.
On this sunny morning
in my life as an adult, I am looking
at one clear pure peach
in a painting by Georgia O'Keeffe.
It is all the fullness that there is
in light. A towhee scratches in the leaves
outside my open door.
He always does.

A moment ago I felt so sick
and so cold
I could hardly move.

Museum

On the morning of the Käthe Kollwitz exhibit, a young man and woman come into the museum restaurant. She is carrying a baby; he carries the air-freight edition of the *Sunday New York Times*. She sits in a high-backed wicker chair, cradling the infant in her arms. He fills a tray with fresh fruit, rolls, and coffee in white cups and brings it to the table. His hair is tousled, her eyes are puffy. They look like they were thrown down into sleep and then yanked out of it like divers coming up for air. He holds the baby. She drinks coffee, scans the front page, butters a roll and eats it in their little corner in the sun. After a while, she holds the baby. He reads the book review and eats some fruit. Then he holds the child while she finds the section of the paper she wants and eats fruit and smokes. They've hardly exchanged a look. Meanwhile, I have fallen in love with this equitable arrangement, and with the baby who cooperates by sleeping. All around them are faces Käthe Kollwitz carved in wood of people with no talent or capacity for suffering who are suffering the numbest kinds of pain: hunger, helpless terror. But this young couple is reading the Sunday paper in the sun, the baby is sleeping, the green has begun to emerge from the rind of the cantaloupe, and everything seems possible.

Churchyard

Somerset Maugham said a professional was someone who could do his best work when he didn't particularly feel like it. There was a picture of him in the paper, a face lined deeply and morally like Auden's, an old embittered tortoise, the corners of the mouth turned down resolutely to express the idea that everything in life is small change. And what he said when he died: I'm all through, the clever young men don't write essays about me. In the fleshly world, the red tulip in garden sunlight is almost touched by shadow and begins to close up. Someone asked me yesterday: are deer monogamous? I thought of something I had read. When deer in the British Isles were forced to live in the open because of heavy foresting, it stunted them. The red deer who lived in the Scotch highlands a thousand years ago was a third larger than the present animal. This morning walking into the village to pick up the car, I thought of a roof where I have slept in the summer in New York, pigeons in the early morning sailing up Fifth Avenue and silence in which you imagine the empty canyons the light hasn't reached yet. I was standing on the high street in Shelford Village, outside the fussy little tea-shop, and I thought a poem with the quick, lice-ridden pigeons in it might end: this is a dawn song in Manhattan. I hurried home to write it and, as I passed the churchyard, school was letting out. Luke was walking toward me, smiling.

He thought I had come to meet him. That was when I remembered the car, when he was walking toward me through the spring flowers and the eighteenth century gravestones, his arms full of school drawings he hoped not to drop in the mud.

Tall Windows

All day you didn't cry or cry out and you felt like sleeping. The desire to sleep was lightbulbs dimming when a powerful appliance kicks on. You recognized that. As in school it was explained to you that pus was a brave army of white corpuscles hurling themselves at the virulent invader and dying. Riding through the Netherlands on a train, you noticed that even the junk was neatly stacked in the junkyards. There were magpies in the fields beside the watery canals, neat little houses, tall windows. In Leiden, on the street outside the university, the house where Descartes lived was mirrored in the canal. There was a pair of swans and a sense that, without haste or anxiety, all the people on the street were going to arrive at their appointments punctually. Swans and mirrors. And Descartes. It was easy to see how this European tranquility would produce a poet like Mallarmé, a middle class art like symbolism. And you did not despise the collective orderliness, the way the clerks in the stores were careful to put bills in the cash register with the Queen's face facing upward. In the house next to the house where Descartes lived, a Jewish professor died in 1937. His wife was a Dutch woman of strict Calvinist principles and she was left with two sons. When the Nazis came, she went to court and perjured herself by testifying that her children were conceived during an illicit affair with a Gentile, and when she developed tuberculosis in 1943, she traded passports with a Jewish friend, since she was going to die anyway, and took her place on the train to the camps. Her sons kissed her goodbye on the platform. Eyes open. What kept you awake was a feeling that everything in the world has it own size, that if you found its size among the swellings and diminishings it would be calm and shine.

A Story About the Body

The young composer, working that summer at an artist's colony, had watched her for a week. She was Japanese, a painter, almost sixty, and he thought he was in love with her. He loved her work, and her work was like the way she moved her body, used her hands, looked at him directly when she made amused and considered answers to his questions. One night, walking back from a concert, they came to her door and she turned to him and said, "I think you would like to have me. I would like that too, but I must tell you that I have had a double mastectomy," and when he didn't understand, "I've lost both my breasts." The radiance that he had carried around in his belly and chest cavity—like music—withered, very quickly, and he made himself look at her when he said, "I'm sorry. I don't think I could." He walked back to his own cabin through the pines, and in the morning he found a small blue bowl on the porch outside his door. It looked to be full of rose petals, but he found when he picked it up that the rose petals were on top; the rest of the bowl—she must have swept them from the corners of her studio—was full of dead bees.

The Harbor at Seattle

They used to meet one night a week at a place on top of Telegraph Hill to explicate Pound's *Cantos*—Peter who was a scholar; and Linda who could recite many of the parts of the poem that envisioned paradise; and Bob who wanted to understand the energy and surprise of its music; and Bill who knew Greek and could tell them that "Dioce, whose terraces were the color of stars," was a city in Asia Minor mentioned by Herodotus.

And that winter when Bill locked his front door and shot himself in the heart with a Webley service pistol, the others remembered the summer nights, after a long session of work, when they would climb down the steep stairs which negotiated the cliff where the hill faced the waterfront to go somewhere to get a drink and talk. The city was all lights at that hour and the air smelled of coffee and the bay.

In San Francisco coffee is a family business, and a profitable one, so the members of the families are often on the society page of the newspaper, which is why Linda remembered the wife of one of the great coffee merchants who had also killed herself; it was a memory from childhood, from those first glimpses a newspaper gives of the shape of the adult world, and it mixed now with the memory of the odor of coffee and the salt air.

And Peter recalled that the museum had a photograph of that woman by Minor White. They had all seen it. She had bobbed hair and a smart suit on with sharp lapels and padded shoulders, and her skin was perfectly clear. Looking directly into the camera, she does not seem happy but she seems confident; and it is as if Minor White understood that her elegance, because it was a matter of style, was historical, because behind her is an old barn which is the real subject of the picture—the grain of its wood planking so sharply focused that it seems alive, greys and blacks in a rivery and complex pattern of venation.

The back of Telegraph Hill was not always so steep. At the time of the earthquake, building materials were scarce, so coastal ships made a good thing of hauling lumber down from the northwest. But the economy was paralyzed, there were no goods to take back north, so they dynamited the side of the hill and used the blasted rock for ballast, and then, in port again, they dumped the rock in the water to take on more lumber, and that was how they built the harbor in Seattle.

Paschal Lamb

Well, David said—it was snowing outside and his voice contained many registers of anger, disgust, and wounded justice—I think it's fucking crazy. I'm not going to be a sacrificial lamb.

In Greece sometimes, when she walked on the road above the sea back to her house from the little village in the dark, a friend told me, and the sky seemed immense, the moon terribly bright, she wondered if her life would be a fit gift.

And there is that poor heifer in the poem by Keats, all decked out in ribbons and flowers, no terror in the eyes, no uncontrollable slobber of mucus at the muzzle, since she doesn't understand the festivities.

And David, after he had quit academic life, actually bought a ranch in Kentucky near a town named Pleasureville and began to raise sheep. When we visited that summer, and the night was shrill with crickets and the heat did not let up, we sat talking for a long time after dinner and he told again the story about his first teaching job and the Vice-President.

When he bought the place, he continued his subscriptions to the *Guardian* and the *Workers' Vanguard*, but they piled up in a corner unread. He had a mortgage to pay. He didn't know anything about raising animals for slaughter, and so he read *The American Sheepman*, he said, with an intensity he had never even approximated when he was reading political theory for his Ph.D. orals.

The Vice-President of the United States, after his term in office, accepted a position as lecturer in political science at a small college in his home district where David had just taken his first job. The dean brought Hubert Humphrey around to introduce him to the faculty. When they came to David's office, the Vice-President, expensively dressed, immensely hearty, extended his hand and David did not feel he could take it because he believed the man was a war criminal and, not knowing any other way to avoid the awkwardness, he said so, which was the beginning of his losing the job at that college.

But that was the dean's doing. The Vice-President started to cry. He had the hurt look in his eyes, David said, of a kicked dog with a long, unblemished record of loyalty and affection, this man who had publicly defended, had *praised* the terror bombing of villages full of peasants. He seemed unimaginably empty of inner life if he could be hurt rather than affronted by a young man making a stiffly moral gesture in front of two men his father's age. David said he had never looked at another human being with such icy, wondering detachment.

And so, in the high-ceilinged kitchen, the air drenched with the odor of clover, we remembered Vic Doyno in the snow in Buffalo, in the days when the war went on continuously like a nightmare in our waking and sleeping hours.

Vic had come to work flushed with excitement at an idea he had had in the middle of the night. He had figured out how to end the war. It was a simple plan. Everyone in the country—in the world, certainly a lot of Swedish and English students would go along—who was opposed to the war would simply cut off the little finger on the left hand and send it to the President. Imagine: they would arrive slowly at first, the act of two or three maniacs; but the news would hit the papers and the next day there would be a few more. And the day after that more. And then on the fourth day there would be thousands. And on the fifth day clinics would be set up—organized by medical students in Madison, San Francisco, Stockholm, Paris—to deal with the surgical process safely and on a massive scale. And on the sixth day the war would stop. It would stop. The helicopters at Bien Hoa would sit on the airfields in silence like squads of disciplined mosquitoes, and peasants, worried and curious because peasants are always worried and curious, would stare up into the unfamiliar silence of a blue, cirrus-drifted sky. And years later, we would know each other by those missing fingers. An aging Japanese businessman minus a little finger on his left hand would notice the similarly mutilated hand of his cab driver in Chicago and they would exchange a fleeting, unspoken nod of fellowship.

And it could happen. All we had to do to make it happen—Vic had said, while the water for tea hissed on the hot plate in David's chilly office and the snow came down thick as cotton batting—was cut off our little fingers right now, take them down to the department secretary and have her put them in the mail.

January

> Three clear days
> and then a sudden storm—
> cedar waxwings,
> having feasted on the pyracantha,

                    perch in the yard
              on an upended pine and face
                 into the slanting rain.

I was making this gathering—which pleased me, the discarded Christmas
tree, the waxwings which always pass through about this time of year, and
the first storm, as if I had finally defined a California season—when Rachel
came down the walk and went into the house. Typed it out—the birds
giddy with Janus the two-faced god—and then went in to say hello.

              Two women sitting at a kitchen table,
              muted light on a rainy morning.
              One has car keys in her hand.

I was surprised by two feelings at once; one was a memory, the other a
memory-trace. The memory was called up, I think, by a glimpse of Rachel's
clear profile against the cypress outside the window just before she turned to
greet me. I had remembered a day twelve years ago in early summer. Rachel
had just had an abortion and we all went for a walk in San Francisco near
the bay. Everything was in bloom and we were being conscientiously
cheerful, young really, not knowing what form there might be for such an
occasion or, in fact, what occasion it was. And Rachel, in profile, talking
casually, the bay behind her, looked radiant with grief. The memory-trace
had to do with car keys and two women at a table. Someone was visiting
my mother. It was a rainy day, so I was inside. Her friend, as adults will, to
signal that they are not going to take too much of your time, had car keys
in her hand. Between Earlene and Rachel there were three oranges in a
wicker basket and I had the sweet, dizzying sensation that the color was
circulating among them in a dance.

              Sing the hymeneal slow.
              Lovers have a place to go.
              Their dancing bones will have to grow
              more gentle in uneasy heat.
              The heart is what we eat
              with almond blossoms bitter
              to the tongue, the hair
              of tulips in the softening spring . . .

Rachel is looking for a house. A realtor has just shown her one. Looking at
the new house, she loved the old one, especially the green of the garden,
looking out on the garden. The old house has drawbacks, long rehearsed,
and the new one, with its cedar shingle, exposed beams, view, doesn't feel
right, it is so anonymous and perfect; it doesn't have the green secrecy of
the garden or the apple tree to tie Lucia's swing to. Earlene is asking
questions, trying to help. A few minutes later, when I pass through again,

they are laughing. At the comedy in the business of trying to sort through mutually exclusive alternatives in which figures some tacit imagination of contentment, some invisible symbolizing need from which life wants to flower. "I hate that old house," Rachel is saying, laughing, tears in her eyes. I find myself looking at their skin, the coloring and the first relaxation of the tautness of the sleeker skin of the young, the casual beauty and formality of that first softening.

> The birds are gone no rain
> but light: the white of Shasta daisies,
> and two red geraniums against the fence,
> and the dark brown of wet wood,
> gleaming a little as it dries.

The Apple Trees at Olema

They were walking in the woods along the coast
and in a grassy meadow, wasting, they came upon
two old neglected apple trees. Moss thickened
every bough and the wood of the limbs looked rotten
but the trees were wild with blossom and a green fire
of small new leaves flickered even on the deadest branches.
Blue-eyes, cranes-bills, and little dutchmen
flecked the meadow and an intricate, leopard-spotted
leaf-green flower whose name they didn't know.
Trout-lily, he said; she said, adder's-tongue.
She is shaken by the raw, white, back-lit flaring
of the apple blossoms. He is exultant
as if something he knew were verified
and looks to her to mirror his response.
If it is afternoon, a thin moon of my own dismay
fades like a scar in the sky to the east of them.
He could be knocking wildly at a closed door
in a dream. She thinks, meanwhile, that moss
resembles seaweed drying lightly on a dock.
Torn flesh, it was the repetitive torn flesh
of appetite in the cold white blossoms
that had startled her. Now it seems tender
and where she was repelled, she takes the measure
of the trees and lets them in. But he no longer
has the apple trees. This is as sad or happy
as the tide, going in or coming out, at sunset.
The light catching in the spray that spumes up

on the reef is the color of the lesser finch
they notice now flashing dull gold in the light
above the field. They admire the bird together.
It draws them closer and they start to walk again.
A small boy wanders corridors of a hotel that way.
Behind one door, a maid. Behind another one, a man
in striped pajamas shaving. He holds the number
of his room close to the center of his mind
gravely and delicately, as if it were the key,
and then he wanders among strangers all he wants.

David Fisher

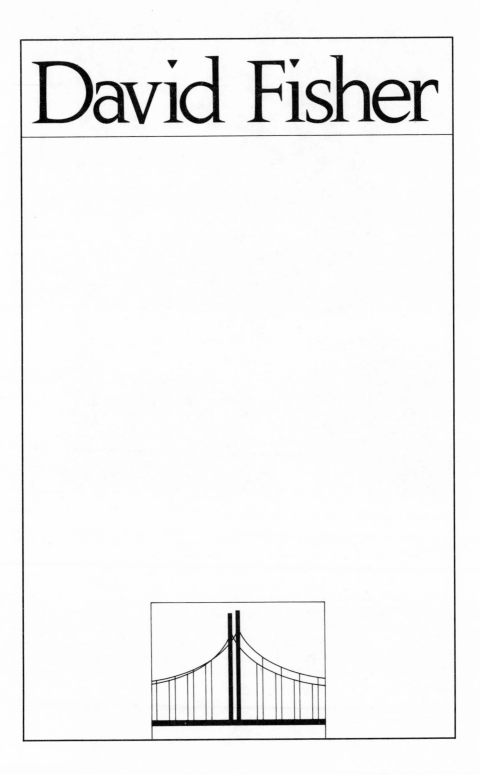

David Fisher grew up in North Carolina and graduated from Duke University in 1963. He studied at the University of Tubingen and the Sorbonne, and has advanced degrees from Yale. He is fluent in and has translated poetry from several languages. His published poetry includes: *Requiem for Heurtebise, Homage to Jean Cocteau, The Book of Madness, Teachings* (winner of the Poetry Society of America's William Carlos Williams Award), *The Revised Book of Madness* (nominee in 1980 for the Pulitzer Prize). Other awards have come from American P.E.N. and the National Endowment for the Arts. He has taught at Yale, Folsom Prison, St. Mary's College, Moraga, Philander Smith College in Little Rock, and Columbia University (in a Harlem Upward Bound project.) In 1979 he married a student, and they live in San Francisco. "We have nine fine multiracial children, legally, and have never taken care of, at any one time, fewer than twelve."

O Come All Ye Faithful:
a brechtian oratorio in five acts

act one

Stung by receiving a really unkind letter from _____ on the occasion of publishing my first book, *Requiem for Heurtebise: Homage to Jean Cocteau,* into getting drunk and miserable for a week; and believing as I do that anyone who would translate Mr. Tomas Transtromer's *Og derfor vil eg no prova paa/ aa gjer' ei vise* as "And that's why I shall now strive/ to make a *ditty"—*would *steal—* I shall now argue that the true function of translation has been aetiolated by a modern misconception.

The practice of the art of literature will naturally involve a familiarity with many other authors. Part of the demonstration of this familiarity goes, by courtesy, under the name of translation.

Translatus is the past participle of a verb which means "carried over." It refers to a very specific process, for example the Englishing of Italian. It also inevitably suggests the process by which one person's way of talking (and more deeply, one person's way of seeing) becomes part of another person's way of talking, and seeing.

Translation is a very complex process.

There is a certain kind of scholarship which delights in pointing out the extent to which a translation is not "literal"—the distinction between what is free and what is literal being to some extent mythical, and invented for this purpose.

The damage done by this kind of scholarship to students is everywhere apparent. Students do not dare to translate, for they do not know the language well enough, they feel. Nor do they dare to use what they understand. The eminent American poet John Logan freely confesses that it was when translating Rilke that he finally *allowed* himself to dream!

FitzGerald's poem, the *Rubaiyat,* has resisted all subsequent attempts to better the Persian—in particular that of the learned (and *sober*) Robert Graves.

And one has no choice, from the driest, *textual* evidence, but to imagine Chaucer at his miserable desk in his small draughty room, poring over an *Italian translation* of the *Romaunt de la Rose.*

The argument, that one should not translate freely, unless one is FitzGerald, or Chaucer, appears to me to be misguided. Everyone should have as much access to everything as his knowledge of language permits.

The invocation of Chaucer suggests a related problem, posed by an original which *borrows.*

The author who reads was probably faced with this dilemma long before the

Greeks: namely, if he acknowledges a source, he is accused of one thing; if he does not, he is accused of the other.

The first recorded reference to Shakespeare identifies him as being "an Vpstart Crow, beautified with our feathers."

Excellent works of scholarship allow us to compare Shakespeare and Chaucer and Jonson with such sources of theirs as can still be discovered.

But the better a writer is, it appears from their example, the more he will be able to use everything he reads, or hears, or sees.

There is a certain point, economists tell us, at which stealing becomes industry.

Ben Jonson, who liked to quarrel, short of "maiming a man in a jest," warred with certain of his contemporaries about his massive use of sources. Others seem to have understood: Carew, in his ode to Jonson, says simply,

> if thou o'ercomst
> a knottie author, bring the bootie home.

I believe this to be the way any truly creative person feels.

One would imagine that anyone whose knowledge of language is sufficiently healthy, and whose own art sufficiently deep, and whose interest in encouraging others sufficiently keen, would always instinctively feel this way—unless the rival company actually performs your play in the courtyard.

We should never, I believe, force a translator to have recourse to Jonson's words: "By G-d, 'tis good, and if you like't, you may!"

We all spend our days in translating, in carrying over into our lives what we find to be fresh and good. We do so, with as much grace, and as much acknowledgment, as we are able. If this be error, and upon me proved, I never writ, nor no man ever loved. Now, may we have some more bananas.

*

act two

FROM *The Complete Poems of Jean Genet*, first English Edition
Manroot South San Francisco
Introductions by David Fisher and Paul Mariah
Translated by David Fisher, Paul Mariah, Frank O'Hara, Nanos Valaoritis, and Chet Roaman. 1981.

At last, some thirty-five years after the completion of the last poem, but in the author's lifetime, the English-speaking public may have access to the complete poems of Genet, and compare the agonized efforts of his translators with the author's unapproachable French.

The poems are deeply erotic, and like those of Shakespeare, Sappho, and Cavafy, have no physical boundaries. They are also an argument against capital punishment far deeper than argument—an outcry of pure love.

Genet's Immoralism has been sufficiently discussed and misunderstood. Jean Cocteau, his great champion, in the criminal courts and in the lists of literature —but who is no more entirely to be trusted than any very great conversationalist —assures us that Genet would refuse to be introduced to any writer *whose immorality appeared to him suspect.* More profound was Cocteau's prediction, long ago, that Genet "must surely be regarded as a moralist some day." This judgment has come to pass, and one is grateful for another remark of Genet's which Cocteau has saved for us: "To watch our heroes live and to pity them is not enough. We must take their sins upon ourselves and suffer the consequences." In real life, as in these poems, Genet has done just this.

This translation, such as it is, and though individual poems bear individual names, was achieved in the dreadful throes of collaboration, by a group of translators—may we simply note—whose own combined time in prison and other institutions totals more than six years. Thus our special sympathy—though *nous sommes tous, tous condamnés à la mort,* and one of our number is already dead —but it is no special appeal for our rendering: any infelicity which the reader remarks must not be Genet's but our own.

Cocteau's brief summary of his defense of Genet, written many years ago, still retains such a lucidity and authority that it might well accompany our author to heaven or Parnassus, or to the infernal regions, where he might more aptly prefer (in the end) to go.

> In order to "place" Jean Genet in the eyes of the Court of Justice (1942) I told this Court that I considered him to be one of France's greatest writers. One can guess how the newspapers under the occupation gloated over the whole business. But a Paris Court is always afraid of repeating some famous blunder, of condemning Baudelaire. I saved Genet. And I do not withdraw any of the evidence.

*

act three

On the Distinction Between Poetry and Prose: The Pynchon Industry

There is a Pynchon industry. *Gravity's Rainbow* is firmly canonical. Young people in art cinemas whisper, breathlessly, of "T. P."

Gravity's Rainbow has everywhere been praised in the highest terms ("Fantastic"—*The New York Times;* "Brilliant"—*The Atlantic Monthly;* "Magnificent"—*Saturday Review,* etc.) It is the winner of a National Book Award in fiction. It very nearly won the Pulitzer as well, but the prize's editorial board overruled the judges, charging the novel with "obfuscation" and "unclarity."

The book is, beyond doubt, difficult to follow. It appears to take place in a number of European countries during the late years of the Second World War, and the metaphor on which it seems to hinge is rocketry. The hopes and fears of our civilization are, of course, nicely expressed in the possibilities of rocketry, for good and ill, and the title *Gravity's Rainbow,* suggests among other things the arcing flight of the rocket.

A host of humorous personages appear, with names such as Mondaugen, Squalidozzi, Pudding, and (my favorite) Corydon Throsp.

There are a number of things about the book which I find seriously disturbing. First, the language, which is often poetic in the worst sense, as in "magenta firths," "a transvestism of caring," "their lips were palimpsests of secret flesh," and so forth.

Also, there is a constant stream of hermetic information, which has no apparent relation to the depiction of character. The piano keys, in one situation, are "all white, an octave on B to be exact—or H, in the German nomenclature—the notes of the rejected Locrian mode." There is also, in the name of intelligence, a considerable amount of sheer nonsense, such as the following:

> There has been this strange connection between the German mind and the rapid flashing of successive stills to counterfeit movement, for at least two centuries—since Leibniz, in the process of inventing calculus, used the same approach to break up the trajectories of cannonballs through the air.

There has been this strange connection between the academic mind and the rapid flashing of successive heavyweight thinkers to counterfeit movement, certainly; at least as long as I've been teaching.

There is also a certain amount of sex in the book, of the requisite oddity, and it occasions no warmth, no human exchange. Relations between characters are limited, in general, to an occasional exchange either of information or of certain deep surmises, as, for example:

> Tchitcherine: "You mean *thio*-phosphate, don't you?" Thinks *indicating the presence of sulphur . . .*
> Wimpe: "I mean *theo*-phosphate, Vaslav, *indicating the Presence of God.*"

This exchange may indicate something about the author's knowledge of Greek prefixes, but it tells us very little about Tchitcherine and Wimpe.

Faulkner will name his patriarchs in *(The Bear)* Theophilus and Amodeus, and the meaning of names is one of the secret delights of reading him. But Faulkner is interested in people, and he nowhere spreads his learning on with a trowel.

This book smells of the candle. It appears to me calculated to appeal to people who are self-consciously intellectual. It nowhere demonstrates the fine intelligence and delicate feeling for character which we find so bountifully in the works of Eudora Welty and Josephine Jacobsen and Ray Carver and Isaac Bashevis Singer, Reynolds Price, Fred Chappell, William Styron, Ken Kesey, Joseph Heller, Chuck Kinder, Anne Tyler, Steve Minkin, Robert Penn Warren, Morton Marcus and Dennis Kaplan.

Pynchon's admirers root through his work—not like wild hogs through acorns, yet with great industry—for the physics of Clausius, the thermodynamics of Maxwell, the benzene-ring chemistry of Kekule; history may determine that Clausius, Maxwell, and Kekule were better novelists. Here is a joint profundity, from two respected admirers of Pynchon:

> Plater *(The Grim Phoenix: Reconstructing Thomas Pynchon)* notes that the act of interpretation is itself subject to the entropy (redundancy, loss of information, noise) which rules all information systems, especially when that interpretation is aimed at text which attains the complexity and self-reflexiveness to address that entropy:
>
> > "*Gravity's Rainbow* has such complexity and diversity that it cannot be comprehended at once, only serially, and *so much is lost in the process* [emphasis my own]" that the message has changed before it can be assimilated."
>
> David Porush
> *The American Book Review*
> February 1980

Doesn't that just *burn a hole* in a *dull page!*

It may as well be stated, that if you like people that talk like that, you *will* like Pynchon, and faculty parties, and the *most recent work of James (or about Nahum)* Tate; and you are probably somewhere burnishing, or preparing yourself to burnish, the undoubted mind of a good undergraduate, in that Crepe-Paper Flame.

"*So much is lost in the process . . .*" I think it could be called a lost process. One would never want to go so far as the elderly gentleman of my acquaintance, who calls this book, "just some more exfoliate bullshit."

But I imagine *Gravity's Rainbow* will be pretty slow going for anyone who reads novels, as I do, for an understanding of character and a certain deep and painful feeling of place. There is *no* distinction between poetry and prose, and *may we have some more bananas.*

act four

A Brief Introduction to the Poems of Richard Silberg

(*Translucent Gears,* North Atlantic Books, Richmond, California, 1982.)

Here is Richard Silberg's first book. Here are lyrics of great purity and poignance, a poetry of great haleness and joy, while yet knowing all of despair and death: here is "Love, white as a bone, with all its delicate hues and overtones." These poems give the strongest possible account of Mr. Silberg's intelligence and lyric gift. There is great variety, too, in the musical nature of his structures: from keening of blues to swashbuckle of boogie to the most delicate possible . . . love-forms . . . of Mr. Silberg's beloved jazz.

And ultimately the voice behind these lyrics is both bardic and reassuring: it may not save you, but here you have company! Here is someone we need in our life, who can see who we are and not turn away; Silberg's slim soul a long-legged bird wading out with us into that foggy marsh . . .

Mr. Silberg has a poor person's feeling about the sacredness of water, and family, and bread. One is never in any doubt—as one is always among our computer-poetasters, and the dank landscapes that wash up on the shores of our major magazines—where his human sympathies lie. Here, where God goes on patiently hiding, Silberg's fingers move many dark arms to explore His universe, with awe, towards the center.

*

act five

Arthur Rimbaud Flips Through
Late-Night TV, Observes the
Sycophantic Cross-Dedications,
and Inadvertently Founds
the Rimbaud School of Hotel
Administration

The Young Bonaparte, has his finger up, perhaps he is only testing the political winds. A liberal commentator calls him The Heartbreak of Psoriasis. Orange County has exploded a nuclear device. *Where is Stoney?*

ON THE REPUBLICAN MESSAGE BOARD:
Cynthia, please come home. Granny is ill.
We forgive you for sleeping with the colored man.

The thunder lizard. A plinth of silver symbols. The nurse's nostrils siphon the shadows. To hold the plastic up to nature. I lie like a dog on a shadow. The shadow smells of urine.

Late Show, THE NEW CINEMA, channel One hundred and Forty-Six. Cameraman with Parkinson's disease. Based on Alfred Hitchcock's famous 19-minute cut in 4000 segments where they double-clutch the '52 DeSoto. Good News for the Feathered; you can rid yourself of those bothersome facial feathers . . . ! Avoid turnstiles today.

SELF-POLLUTION IS THE DEVIL'S PHONE BOOTH!!!

The President resigns, before poor Senator Ervin really had a chance. The horses ride off the carrousel. The merry-go-round horses (the lights in their eyes blown out) ride off the carrousel, & move silently through the fields. . . .

The New Yorker's three-for-a-dime sadness, with respect to impeachment. Involuted stories about the death of the young author's Himalayan mother, in exile, heartbreakingly near the Shandrapur Hilton. Jesus, I'll send them a column, and meet you in the Drambuie ad! Remember Maurice and his trained intestine. And the man who put money in his nose. An aroused peccary can kill a dog, or a worthless Attorney General. *Free Days at Zoo: August 20, 27.*

Channel 60: Late-Night Educational TV!!! Apply for Credit! We have an Individualized Peer-Smelling Program. We have an Individualized Advanced Algebra Program. We proffer many more positive reinforcements . . . we offer an Interaction Language Program . . . an Imaginative Short Story. Our Individualized System Allows for Individualized Programs, Within Reason. We stress One-To-One Teacher-To-Idiot Relationships. Additionally, the President has licensed us to DESTROY PROGRAMS FOR THE HANDICAPPED.

San Francisco is purple, seen through iron bars. *Do you deserve cheaper bars than Nixon?* The Plutocrat from Missouri will yield two minutes to the Democrat from Texas. (He whispers in Barbara Jordan's ear: "Hey—you keep singing till the other acts unfreeze.") Barbara Jordan makes her opening statement: "You know, those first five years with the Dallas Cowboys, I felt out of *place*, not having a *scar* or *tattoo.*" Don Meredith, who holds the all-time record in Dallas (or any place else) for fumbles by a quarterback, has no desire to smile. Suppose your mayor tripled his wealth in three years! DAS EWIG WEIBLICHE ZIEHT UNS HINAB.

The Supreme Court (including the one he packed, and nearly including the one he tried to pack) rules, 8–0, against the Young Bonaparte. (Someone must have been on Cape Cod.) The Young Bonaparte says, "I am deeply gratified that the Court has upheld me." His nose collapsed on gristle. Moon swamps— the akimbo blimp. On Jenkins Hill, a ferris of flame. In the White House, the blue eels of power, and in adjoining hotels, the seldom-consulted Poetry Consultants . . .

Her kohl-rimmed eyes. And to think 'e was once a promising young solicitor. Duke Law School, was it? Son of a Parsee vicar, was it? Ripped Helen Gahagan Douglas nearly out of politics, was it? Double-reed instruments, and white shoes gleaming like radium in the damp San Francisco darkness. Typewriters which chop the "o" out. The Council for the Democrats, Albert Jenner's, small diffident cough. What breaks my heart is Jenner; he is too fair, too modest, too unassuming, to take the measure of the monster. Twenty stuntsmen drowned in filming *Mutiny on the Bounty,* and Sandman lives! Sandman, the Republican Congressman from New Jersey shouts, "Nobody's dying in Southeast Asia today!" It is clear Mr. Sandman is in the Congress of the United States because there were no openings in the Mafia that year.

*

Harlequin ducks on the mountain waters. When was I due exactly? A glacier lily pushes through the snow. Do you really think my rug is a little too busy? The nature sounds are made by a Ph.d. . . . You know, long ago, my old dog George died in a swing, he was a big old dog, I expect the swing is still in motion.

Theda Bara is an anagram for Arab Death. Do you think there are any foreigners the Young Bonaparte *likes?* Some he considers useful . . . Theda Bara used to like to pet bees. The silence was signed with the breath of cats, like gut-strings on St. Swithin's Day.

Now, Bonaparte springs with Camera Eyes to His *Papers.* He thinks it's a new discovery not to be afraid to die! God, I, Arthur Rimbaud, hope to hear the Star Spangled Banner, like ambergris on the wind, at his *graveside.*

Nikolai Gogol
for The Rimbaud and Gogol School of Hotel Administration

Lost

The bare room,
the table cries,
the doctors harvest the silver vertebrae.
The restraints are terrifying.

"Perhaps you have made of death,"
says the doctor,
"an idea excessively false."

A strange clear dream is born to the poet
in the isolation room.
The doctor is wearing
a nacre and ebony serpent.
The shackled celestial poet
opens the violet of his heart—
forgetfulness uproots the symphony—
a star is feeding.
There is angel strife in the poet's eyes,
o little lost poet with
many fine doctors and one celestial pillow.

The Birds of Arles

But what is happening I see
around us a jungle
of furniture begin to enlarge itself
the Morris chair is growing

roots and vines form in a

vegetal exuberance
behind the hedge

Almost as high as my shoulders
vines of string beans undulate
and outside the house a thousand birds
have rented the telephone wires

and I (reading lips) see a laugh
which I take for the sound of birds
of those birds of the asylum at Arles
which speak during the mistral from
the immobile plane trees

After ten shocks I heard
a lovely phrase repeated by
the birds of Àrles:

"Would you and Tlaloc like to go
for a ride in the country?"
We were overjoyed, but before
I could reply I was mad
rolling again through vacant space
past the tribunals
of innumerable silent judges

I returned slowly to the world
to find the invitation
(from the birds of Arles)
was no longer current.

Rehearsal

The far faint protocols of Katherine's flute
drip from the eucalyptus, in the rain.
Sleepy birds, with songs in their eyes, are mute;
sheep on the hillside dream of sun-warmed stones.
      Beyond a lighted window in the night
      bone-weary folk consider Henry's plight.

Messengers come and go in the struggling eyes
of the small dog on the hearth, who feebly whines
at death scenes, barks when Gloucester dies—
his old eyes struggle to retain their lines.
      Splash of a mailed fist against its sword,
      an ancient syntax gathers with each word.

A cow peers in the window, stands amazed
to see the slaughtering reach of human loins.
Was this the ensanguined end for which cows grazed?
She belches lightly, her eyes spin like coins.
      Rumination cannot tell her what to say
      to hecatombs of a Shakespearean play.

Why Do You Want to Suffer Less

I go to school.
My new duality arranges her skirts
between tricks.
The intellect is the cigarette
that makes me hungry.

Dragged-in terminologies,
obese fogs ready for frying,
My mind, inflamed, bloats on distinctions,
the future becomes a monotonous instrument.

Decorous poetry.
Good wives peopled
            with swallows—
                bituminous rivers.

My thoughts,
trained to bifurcate like a seal,
are a form of sewage.

            "I thought there were some
            nice plays on sound—'video'
            and 'fidelity.' "

            "I picked up a sense of penetration
            through repression."

I can no longer reply
with one green word.
I am ready for shock.
My mind has lips like a claymore.
My mind is a whore.
My mind has murdered my suffering.

The Emergency Room

Chic desolation of the
factory—a rigid girl
is carrying someone's lunch.
An old man is bleeding
in a plastic chair.
Small doctors
in Hush Puppies pass

like clam diggers waving
from the meridian beach.
An old man is bleeding,
he is bleeding the rich rust orange
of the Pacific Fruit Express.
There are icicles of blood
on his chin.
He is saying, "*Brutos.*
Brutos. Savages.
Sooner or later you going
to pay for it."

"What's the problem, sir?"
someone asks.
The old man looks up, for a moment
his eyes are black.
"Oh," he says. "Many problem . . ."
He becomes frightened,
unable to finish his sentence.

A Junkie with a Flute in the Rain

A child with a wrench is
moving through Harlem, turning
on the hydrants. A junkie howls
at a bus stop, and a drunk
with a beer in a small paper bag
does a two-step outside Minnie's.
Venus rises from the tenements,
Priapus weighs his sex in the scale
against a nickel bag
(And you must come to see me)
Here street lights pray over the avenues
like Giacometti nuns,
pigeons are thin as sparrows,
the roaches big as grapes. Old ladies
sit in hotel lobbies in chairs
chained to the walls. On park benches
old men are stacked
like doves on a telephone wire.

Origami birds nest in my room
beside a sculpture
made of broken needles

and you must come to see me
you will find me, love, in the streets

a junkie with a flute in the rain

Analyst

Picking through pieces
one cannot spare space or memory
in the great dustbin where illness must be lost
Outside the hands of the furniture
the thick half-dream of the client

> *one is tired*
> *one is in pain*
> *one confuses essential facts*

The desperate empty eye confronts you—
the empty indigo of a blind window.
Body deserted by sleep,
tomb of deliberate servitude,
pure lack of human franchise.

And yet, o psychiatric fidelity
o weary love with a cigarette
o vulnerable delicate question small
as a hole in a bone.

The client is trembling with cold,
without your identity he slows,
repeats himself—and you must summon again
the steady, weary magic of sortilege.

Your dream is of silence
your hands are of leaves
the straw
at the edge of the sky calls your name.

o dear Lord forgive the healer,
whose words are as mixed with comfort and terror
as rain on the sea.

The Mutilated Soldier

The torches surrounded by butterflies,
the fox fulfills a long dream of rapine,
his tail is on fire, the tail of his brothers
are on fire—the pale wheat is in flames.

In this year of the luminous horloge, the year of the
grand interior
flame,
a soldier also seeks to avoid
his Emperor's service, by mutilating
the two great fingers of his hand.

The mutilated soldier
his crown cold with roses
assumes the burden of the fox.
He speaks to a crow, to a silly goose.
He says confusing tender words
to the beasts,
The mutilated Soldier.

The Retarded Class at F.A.O. Schwarz's
Celebrates Christmas

Mr. Klein says, "Milagres, hold Angelo's hand,"
So I do, and we walk past a million toys.
I especially like the blue ones.
When I sit on Santa's knee, I
Hold to Angelo's hand, and try to
Think of a good thing to ask.
At last I ask Santa
If I can come back next year.
I am not sure I have earned a blue one.

The Vietnamese Girl in the Madhouse

For Thai Tran

Someone's youngest daughter
has lost her mind, there is
more meaning in a snail's cuneiform

than in her prattle in three tongues,
still she is lovely
with her hair loosed;
and only beside the bones of these hills
is she ever silent, can she ever be silent,
and we are too poor for her madness.

The Teacher

When I was a teacher
I taught the students that
the two great levelers are
Pestilence and Disease, and then
a few days later I would ask the students
what the two great levelers are,
and they would answer, "Disease
and Pestilence," and I would lose
my temper, and roar, "No, that
is wrong, it is Pestilence and Disease."
They were hopeless. And I would teach them
the structure of tragedy, and I would
diagram the structure on the blackboard, thus:

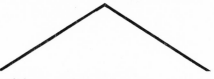

They did not understand, some
did not even copy down the diagram.

*

I have retired, now, to my father's
small stump farm. I eat cress, berries, cattail sprouts,
and chives, but mostly mushrooms: orange chanterelles
and Zeller's boletus that I gather in gunny sacks.
I fry them, boil them, broil them, pickle them, and
eat them raw. They make me somewhat dizzy.
I wear a miner's helmet,
Still I have bad dreams.

*

The hogs crowd round the stove,
a possum hangs from the hall tree.

Under the cabin, goats browse
the dynamite. A new spring came up in a field
and I took a shovel
and I tried to coax it
nearer the house, but it dived
down a badger hole and disappeared.

*

I have put up chintz curtains. In the
appalling heat, under the socket moon,
I worm the corn. When I was a student
I went to Wales, to Mynydd Llanybyther, and Cwmpidlfach,
I stayed with Thurlow Craig, who told me
country stories, of the dance of the stoats,
of rooks who breed on the midden, of the fox
who played dead to catch the buzzard.
At night we visited the local
In a cart drawn by a pedigreed Cardigan cob.

I make my own beer now, with
good English malt, I add the hops
in an old stocking my wife left. Sometimes
the hydrometer tells me it is thirty proof,
sometimes, in the moonlight,
a bottle explodes, rattling the windows.

*

It is winter,
the landscape is set forth
like the best blue china.

A young frost makes her
first sketches on the
panes of my cabin.

    Someday I should like to teach again.

Outside, on the cold roof of my Nash,
I hear the frosty clatter of goat hooves.

Death of Rimbaud

Death with his sad hands
is slowly wrinkling the water.
A tree against which
the sky contends, is protecting a bird.
o forest of water and gold

Once more to see the roofs of Paris,
the white scorpions of Africa,
> *(The Negress consuming absinthe*
> *from the dark plateau of her lips.*
> . . . .
> *The vermin burn like a torch.)*

In the abattoirs of Vaugirard
a young bull who is also about to die
calls with a clear voice
toward Paris.

Once you were a little girl, and
said you were schooling an elephant. Now
you are lovely beyond my delirium, like
a blue minaret, or the merciless wives
of Holland. My laugh is no longer subtle
enough for yours.

> *When you pass the snow falls—all at once—*
> *from my heart, as from a tree in winter.*

The Old Man

The old man is seated.
His eyes are the color of the fire.
He is making peace with his heart.
When he walks near the harvest.
his eyes are a twelfth-century blue.
This old palace of his is dismembering itself
far from the gaze of the Lord

He listens, in the fields: a little blood and a song,
a bird, like the hope of these regions:

. . . . .a billboard on the wall
of the old dry church . . . . . .

Because they are swaying
in the high branches of sleep—
Because they are swaying . . . . . .
He wonders, he sometimes wonders

. . . . "For what serves such study,
                    such scruple, such council,
                    As soon as one turns his head,
                    the abyss is working alone."

                    *   *   *   *   *

All around him the cypresses . . . .
of night, he had hoped to die
the white death of combat, the bird is
his hope, a little blood and a song . . . .

It has been long since he stood wild in the rain
and took to himself that he could not conceive.
But his sorrow runs deeper, the woman
has long since died in his dreams . . . .

                    *   *   *

A Child's Christmas without Jean Cocteau

The heart of man is encumbered
heavy with all he loves.
One has left his shadow
on a Hiroshima wall.

The women dream of children
in the same arena
where death espouses
the youngest bull.

That young orator, the sea, sucks stones
and learns to speak.
In my own childhood I dreamed
of high 12th-century windows . . . .

                    .   .   .   .   .

It was five years ago at sunset
(. . . . . oriflamme of the evening wash)
looking toward the Odeon
when I learnt that Jean was no longer

---

on this side of the mirror.
I dreamt, that night,
of a dark moon,
violins, and the pale ghost of a child.

. . . . .

It is evening.
The streets are full of mendicants
and silver.
The lights on the hills

cross the bridge
to console us.
The rolling ships
are balancing their masts!

> *o heart of the barren hawk,*
> *o lonely hawk in jesses,*
> *the heart of the hawk*
> *is also encumbered: the hawk,*
> *the violin, the sea,*
> *cry-out-to-heaven—*

that one has children in order
to be forgiven!

Harvest Poem

The moon, with the pace of a wolf,
  leaves a sign on hebrew doors.
    The harvest's hips are full of sky,—
      her weedy bones the garrotes
      of concisely humbled fears.

It is June. The crops try to swim.
  Corn, that orphan among grains,
    struggles upward. The harvest's channel
      to the god is still immaculate.

Here too is artificial insemination:
  a bull gone to pasture wearing his catch-valve.
    The male corn, the tassel at the top, the
      female the soft silk attached to the ear . . .

Thus the harvest rolls toward God,
  laving itself in pure waters, becoming

a necklace of fire on the plains.
  The crops roll in perfect consanguinity
    with the wind, towards the minatory thresher.

August invites the moon to enjoy
 its final stasis, catafalque of seeds.
  Bright horses sport in the empty fields,
    the old men gather the vines for burning.

The Pastor Speaks Out

The pastor sips weak hock and seltzer
in the room, where Auntie Maud devoutly bobs.

His parish waits:
red among hawthorns
redder than hawberries
leaded windows, lozenged with crimson, shine.

The pastor arrives.
Kant on the handlebars, Bultmann in the saddlebags;
    (the dark pines the resin-scented rain
    smell of the broom and the gorse)
Swedenborg rumbles like a dream in his stomach.

Revival steam is on the windowpanes
for Calvin now the soft oil lamps are lit
Horny hands that erewhile held the aces
summon the hymnals

The pastor draws his concordance
which only this afternoon has served as a tray
for an ice and a macaroon . . .
he can hear the soft flesh of the saved.

The doors of the church are chased
with sardonyx and gold
and Evil, quivering, waits
for remission of Sin.

The pastor speaks out against
the rhodomontade of political opera.
He speaks out against the doped colts
that run amok with our wages.
He speaks out against the adder
that glistens in the entertainment noose.

All sing.

The collection plate hangs
at the end of the verger's arm like a leech.

On the Esplanade des Invalides

You were born on the esplanade des Invalides,
and died in the seventh Arrondissement.
  My luck was that of my sabre,
   but your eyes grew old together.
   Your regard was open as a blue Vermeer.

I have watched you, before sleeping,
 in the tender morning, for a quarter
 of a century, in the quartier Vendôme.
  I have watched you paint
  like a complaisant bird.
    The nape of a man is made for the poignard,
    but when you died,
      my life closed like a year.

Now I am an old man of Patmos
 solemnly watching white gulls.
  Yet I will come to you,
   once more to be held in the dark
   enamel of your gaze.

I will come
 by the interior mists of secrets,
  I will come like a fire-ship in the night,
  I will come like the stars
   in the similitude of white fowl.

The Keepsake Corporation

I am in prison for trying to swindle the
  Keepsake Corporation, but who am I?
    a Full Professor of Soil.

My fever is down, after a nice
  eligibility workout. I was always a battler.
    Above me they are saying,
      "This is a possible left hip."
        "Possible left hip."

Henry Ford is talking interminably
    about an artificial cow, and above me the doctor,
        switching off his trauma beeper, asks,
            "In your goldfish tank, would you like
            black fish on white rocks, or
                white fish on black rocks?"

And I am not certain and I ask him to forgive me
    for not being certain, and I study Swahili,
        in case that becomes diplomatic.

And above me they ask "Do you choke?" and I
    answer, "All my life." & may the Lord have mercy
        on the thousand unedited caresses I received
            outside these walls.

The coach is weeping as the tall seniors graduate.
    I make sketches for my Lipstick Ascending.
        Drive the Lipsticks West. A sentiment to which
            no Christian could possibly object.
                De Tocqueville is weeping in the night.

I am still a separate culture—with a literature,
    an idiom, a diet, a pervasive sense of irony,
        even behind these walls. & I know that Leland
            Stanford missed the golden spike in Utah, and
                above me they keep asking, "Who runs Kansas?"
                    I answer Mount Rushmore which gets me time
                    and a half.

And I stand in the moist black soil of the Yard
    with my authentically toned Bean Lake Duck Call
        and they whisper "We are portaging in the best
            Frontier Baroque Lawyer in the country, fellow
            name of Lincoln," but *I* say the country
                is going to hell.

It's getting so you can't even take a military jet
    home to hunt ducks.

Mycenae

To look from the Acrocorinth
    down the dark plain of the Argives,
        to look down the dark plain of the Argives,
            to imagine Mycenae looming,

                    the Lion Gate, Agamemnon's Mask,
                    the hum of bees in the tomb.

There are red poppies there
    and my small black dog
        who died
            without murmur there.

Mycenae is older and more full of blood
    than anything we know.
        There is scarcely a tree
            to help one to sleep.

Athens is different:
    there are many cultures in Athens.
        There are Byzantine churches
            full of Christ's finger. . . .

In Athens there are fires in the market night.
    Athens is pleasant; some of the tyrants are dead,
        and the gardens are filled with music.
            Beyond Piraeus looms the large peasant profile
                                        of the moon.

Lycabettus, that sad slow clock, calls one south
                                in the evening,
    darkness sings in the city,
        the evening opens in velvet,
            rivers of wheat imagine themselves,
                while the stars of Odysseus rain.
                    o heart, o clock, o angelus of Athens.

                    *   *   *   *   *

Yet in Mycenae, in Mycenae,
    down the dark plain of the Argives, there is blood, like salt,
        there is ancient death, and the hum of the tomb—
            my small black dog lies there. . . .

Linda Gregg

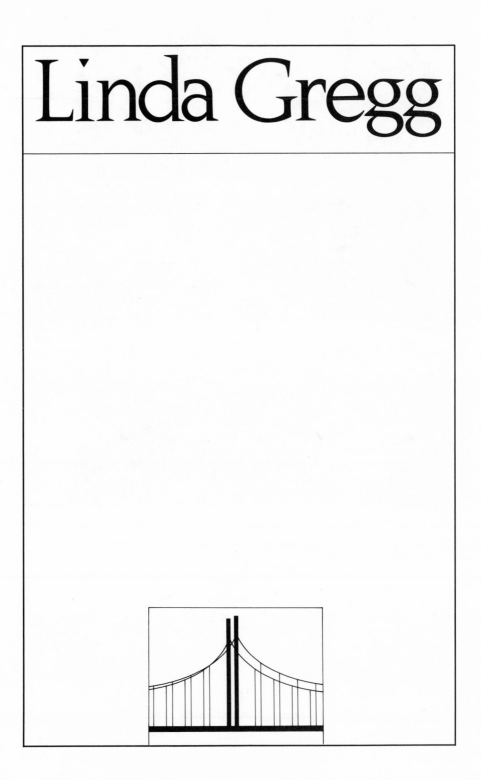

Linda Gregg grew up in Northern California, and was educated at San Francisco State University, where she received her B.A. and, in 1972, her M.A. She has been a poet-teacher at a number of colleges and universities: most recently at the University of Tucson; the College of Marin Poetry Center; the Napa Valley Poetry Conference at Napa Valley College; the "Gathering of Poets" at Louisiana State University; and The Theodore Roethke Festival at Lafayette College. Her first book of poems, *Too Bright To See,* was published in 1981. She has been featured in several anthologies and in numerous magazines, the latter including: *American Poetry Review, Ironwood, Plowshares, Pequod, Kenyon Review,* and *Antaeus.* She has been awarded a Guggenheim Fellowship for 1983. Other awards include the First Prize of the Poetry Society of America, in 1966 and 1967, and the Frank Stanford Memorial Prize in 1978. She lives in San Francisco.

Not Understanding

Emily Dickinson was the first poet I really read. I was in the fifth or sixth grade and she seemed such a secret thing to me that I always read her in bed. I remember clearly the amazement, respect, and something maybe like horror when I read her. I still react to her that way.

I felt then and feel now that she halts me at the border of her poetry while she uses the space beyond like a landscape with many birds in it feeding on the trees after snow has fallen and now it is morning and there is a steady small rain. I didn't understand that when I was little. She was different from those I knew. For me there has always been that something in her which wanted to remain separate. I have never felt let in. Not as I feel let in by Roethke or Lawrence or Sappho or Catullus or Shakespeare. I respect it. I do not wish to approach closer than she wishes. I think of how she would stand on the upstairs landing to listen when there were guests talking downstairs in the living room. Out of respect, I do not go up those stairs after her. She called her poems her letter to the world, not her meeting or her embrace. When I went to her grave, I kept wondering what she would want me to do. I listened to the silence between us of earth and air, and of time, and to the natural silence around us. I listened for her there, and what she gave me was that silence and that distance. I accepted it gratefully, as a gift. And stayed still to be more closely where she was. I did not touch the stone.

There are still a lot of things I don't understand. The wind that seems to be in her poetry, for example. Is it her breath? I don't think so. There is very little natural breathing in her poems. I think it is something other than herself, something which halts her breath. I think she has let something like God's will into her poetry. It halts her, adds much, pushes her, even works against her feelings and body, yet is a great strength in her poems. It blows through and the words do not blow down. This doubleness in her work creates power.

One of the important ways of understanding the poetry of Emily Dickinson may be *not* understanding her. Not, at least, understanding her in the rational way. In the way we understand prose, for example. When I was a young girl, I often did not know what the poems meant. To be honest, that happened more than often. It happened almost all the time when I read her that I did not understand in the usual way. But I did understand nevertheless. Even now, I think many of her poems are successful without being understandable in a logical sense.

I want to be careful to make clear that I am not *against* understanding or explaining the poems. It gives me great pleasure when the poems suddenly yield themselves to me and become clear. I delight in people who help that to happen. I delight in the poetry whose meanings *are* clear, instantly. Lines like:

> There's a certain Slant of light
> Winter Afternoons—
> That oppresses, like the Heft
> Of Cathedral tunes—

For all of us who grew up in the country, there is a special pleasure when she speaks of a snake in the grass *wrinkling*. But one of the most important things about her poetry for the young girl I was *was* the other kind of poetry she wrote, the kind which made no logical sense to me but worked wonderfully. Lines like the ones which end that very poem about the wrinkling snake (called "A narrow fellow in the grass"):

> . . . never met this Fellow
> Attended, or alone
> Without a tighter breathing
> And Zero at the Bone—

I still don't know what "Zero at the Bone" means, not in a logical way, but it seems clear to me in another and equally important sense. This is also true for lines like:

> The deer attracts no further
> Than it resists the hound   (979)

Or poem 690, which begins: "Victory comes late" and ends with the fine lines:

> God keep His oath to Sparrows
> Who of little Love know how to starve.

Sometimes whole poems have this quality for me, such as poem 512:

> The Soul has Bandaged moments—
> When too appalled to stir—
> She feels some ghastly Fright come up
> And stop to look at her—
>
> Salute her—with long fingers—
> Caress her freezing hair—
> Sip, Goblin, from the very lips
> The Lover—hovered—o'er—
> Unworthy, that a thought so mean
> Accost a Theme—so—fair—
>
> The Soul has moments of Escape—
> When bursting all the doors—
> She dances like a Bomb, abroad,
> And swings upon the Hours,

As do the Bee—delirious borne—
Long Dungeoned from his Rose—
Touch Liberty—then know no more,
But Noon, and Paradise—

The Soul's retaken moments—
When, Felon led along,
With shackles on the plumed feet,
And staples, in the Song,

The Horror welcomes her, again,
These, are not brayed of Tongue—

This could be explained. I can glimpse bits of meaning in among the dazzle; but to tell the truth, I am content (in this poem) not to track the meaning down by those clues. I really don't care what the exact meaning is when she speaks of:

The Soul's retaken moments—
When, Felon led along,
With shackles on the plumed feet,
And staples, in the Song.

I liked it even when I thought *plumed* was *plummed*. And I secretly hope *staples* means what we use it to mean now. Stapled Songs! It is a successful poem for me without the other kind of understanding. However, I'm not saying that I like to ride the energy, or the images. What I *am* trying to say is that there's an important way of getting to the *true* meaning which may elude analysis. I *do* understand what *the soul's bandaged moments means.* It *means* the soul's bandaged moments.

I am *not* choosing between understanding and not understanding in these poems. But I *am* trying to suggest that *sometimes* there is a legitimate way her poems communicate without needing to be decoded into logic. It is important to me and to my own work to remember that in even the greatest poetry there is often the other kind of meaning.

Anyhow, this was true for me when I read Emily Dickinson at the very beginning of my knowing about poetry. It helped me to know there is a magic at the center of poetry, a way of meaning that is different from logic. So that from the first I had the encouragement to trust my instinct in preferring metaphor to simile, image to abstractions, to trust the intuitive more than the rational in my poetry.

Of course, I am not saying this should be true for all poets. Not even for all *her* poetry, but it has *always* been how I work. Or part of how I work. And it is so partly because of Emily Dickinson. She taught me there is a difficult, hard-to-understand, hard-to-translate, hard-to-write-about-or-explain place. I knew I had that in me also. But at the same time, I learned that the difficulty or obscurity in her poetry is not because she uses images to hide a secret. Rather, it is an attempt to say something that cannot be said in a simple or direct way.

One of the amazing things about Emily Dickinson for me, when I first read her and also now, is the presence of thought in her poetry which thinks like a poem does. I remember how as a child I could almost easily understand those thoughts without understanding. Or maybe I should say understanding it *before* understanding. I remember clearly saying at that early time: "then I will have to write my own poetry. A poetry of a kind I cannot understand in the same way I cannot understand *her's.*"

Understanding before understanding led me and led me toward what is magical in poetry. Maybe that is one of the most valuable things about the poetry of Emily Dickinson: to teach that there is something in poetry which cannot be handled, cannot be studied scientifically. Can only be approached, can only be honored. We can go up to the border. Can name what is there. Can know a lot. But we must remember that it is still country on the other side of the border and there are things there which we do not have good names for. We must remember there is a kind of safety in trusting the unknown. There are things beyond the border which are invisible, but if we are patient and listen hard, we can sometimes hear them.

We Manage Most When We Manage Small

What things are steadfast? Not the birds.
Not the bride and groom who hurry
in their brevity to reach one another.
The stars do not blow away as we do.
The heavenly things ignite and freeze.
But not as my hair falls before you.
Fragile and momentary, we continue.
Fearing madness in all things huge
and their requiring. Managing as thin light
on water. Managing only greetings
and farewells. We love a little, as the mice
huddle, as the goat leans against my hand.
As the lovers quickening, riding time.
Making safety in the moment. This touching
home goes far. This fishing in the air.

The Girl I Call Alma

The girl I call Alma who is so white
is good, isn't she? Even though she does not speak,
you can tell by her distress that she is
just like the beach and the sea, isn't she?
And she is disappearing, isn't that good?
And the white curtains, and the secret smile
are just her way with the lies, aren't they?
And that we are not alone, ever.
And that everything is backwards
otherwise.
And that inside the no is the yes. Isn't it?
Isn't it? And that she is the god who perishes:
the food we eat, the body we fuck,
the loose net we throw out that gathers her.
Fish! Fish! White sun! Tell me we are one
and that it's the others who scar me,
not you.

The Chorus Speaks Her Words as She Dances

You are perishing like the old men. Already your arms are gone,
your legs filled with scented straw tied off at the knees.
Your hair hacked off. How I wish I could take on each part
of you as it leaves. Sweet mouse princess, I would sing
like a nightingale, higher and higher to a screech
which the heart recognizes, which the helpless stars enjoy—
like the sound of the edge of grass.

I adore you. I take you seriously, even if I am alone in this.
If you had arms, you would lift them up I know. Ah, Love,
what knows that?

(How tired and barren I am.)
Mouse eyes. Lady with white on her face. What will the world do
without you? What will the sea do?
How will they remember the almond flowers? And the old man,
smiling, holding up the new lamb: whom will he hold it up to?
What will the rough men do after their rounds of drinks
and each one has told his story? How will they get home
without the sound of the shore any more?

(I think my doll is the sole survivor, my Buddha mouse, moon
princess, amputee who still has the same eyes.
With her song that the deer sings when it is terrified.
That the rabbits sing, grass sings, fish, the sea sings:
a sound like frost, like sleet, high keening, shrill squeak.
Zo-on-na, Kannon, I hold each side of her deeply affected face
and turn on the floor.

This song comes from the bottom of the hill at night, in summer.
From a distance as fine as that first light on those islands.
As the lights on the dark island which held still while our ship
came away. This is the love song that lasts through history.
I am a joke and a secret here, and I will leave.
It is morning now. The light whitens her face more than ever.)

Gnostics on Trial

Let us make the test. Say God wants you
to be unhappy. That there is no good.
That there are horrors in store for us
if we do manage to move toward Him.

Say you keep Art in its place, not too high.
And that everything, even eternity, is measurable.
Look at the photographs of the dead,
both natural (one by one) and unnatural
in masses. All tangled. You know about that.
And can put Beauty in its place. Not too high,
and passing. Make love our search for unhappiness,
which is His plan to help us.
Disregard that afternoon breeze from the Aegean
on a body almost asleep in the shuttered room.
Ignore melons, and talking with friends.
Try to keep from rejoicing. Try
to keep from happiness. Just try.

There She Is

When I go into the garden, there she is.
The specter holds up her arms to show
that her hands are eaten off.
She is silent because of the agony.
There is blood on her face.
I can see she has done this to herself.
So she would not feel the other pain.
And it is true, she does not feel it.
She does not even see me.
It is not she any more, but the pain itself
that moves her. I look and think
how to forget. How can I live while she
stands there? And if I take her life
what will that make of me? I cannot
touch her, make her conscious.
It would hurt her too much.
I hear the sound all through the air
that was her eating, but it is on its own now,
completely separate from her. I think
I am supposed to look. I am not supposed
to turn away. I am supposed to see each detail
and all expression gone. My God, I think,
if paradise is to be here
it will have to include her.

Whole and Without Blessing

What is beautiful alters, has undertow.
Otherwise I have no tactics to begin with.
Femininity is a sickness. I open my eyes
out of this fever and see the meaning
of my life clearly. A thing like a hill.
I proclaim myself whole and without blessing,
or need to be blessed. A fish of my own
spirit. I belong to no one. I do not move.
Am not required to move. I lie naked on a sheet
and the indifferent sun warms me.
I was bred for slaughter, like the other
animals. To suffer exactly at the center,
where there are no clues except pleasure.

Growing Up

I am reading Li Po. The T.V. is on
with the sound off.
I've seen this movie before.
I turn on the sound just for a moment
when the man says, 'I love you.'
Then turn it off and go on reading.

Eurydice

I linger, knowing you are eager (having seen
the strange world where I live)
to return to your friends
wearing the bells and singing the songs
which are my mourning.
With the water in them, with their strange rhythms.
I know you will not take me back.
Will take me almost to the world,
but not out to house, color, leaves.
Not to the sacred world that is so easy
for you, my love.

Inside my mind and in my body is a darkness
which I am equal to, but my heart is not.
Yesterday you read the Troubadour poets

in the bathroom doorway
while I painted my eyes for the journey.
While I took tiredness away from my face,
you read of that singer in a garden
with the woman he swore to love forever.

You were always curious what love is like.
Wanted to meet me, not bring me home.
Now you whistle, putting together
the new words, learning the songs
to tell the others how far you traveled for me.
Singing of my desire to live.

Oh, if you knew what you do not know
I could be in the world remembering this.
I did not cry as much in the darkness
as I will when we part in the dimness
near the opening which is the way in for you
and was the way out for me, my love.

The Gods Must Not Know Us

> The signifying clouds at dawn
> fill me. Open my spirit.
> The shining of sun and moon
> morning after morning
> makes my heart serene.
> —from SHANG-SHU TA CHUAN by Fu Sheng

All the different kinds of light
give off light.
The light of the heart (sun).
The light of the mind (moon).
Longing and having make it all
possible for us.

But what the world gives disturbs,
this confusion of excess the world gives.
Morning comes again and again,
holding everything lovingly.
We cannot hold it all at once
this giving.

KALOS is written over the heads of the gods
on the Greek vases. They like beauty so much

they fill the world with it.
Until the plenty makes our joy hesitate
and I fear they will know we do not have a place
big enough to handle so much.

The world gives forth beauty
like the great, glad women in the dream.
It overwhelms us. Spills over.
I am afraid the earth will take it back
and part of my self will get lost
and I will not be a fitting gift.

The gods must not know us well or they would
not dance so openly, so happily before us.

As When the Blowfish Perishing

As when the blowfish, perishing,
makes itself the greatest size,
the empty agoras and broken colosseums
repeat the supposition of a god
who worshipped a god. Pretending
those men were proportionate
to what they made. And they are. I think
of how you dream and dream and care
for the blood carried in silver bowls
out of the room. Of my diminishing
as the world makes love to me.
It is a long way from the rock to here.
There is a huge pile of dead people
and they will not sing. I wish so
you would come back.
We kept the courtesy an internal form
to have the beauty after.

Sun Moon Kelp Flower or Goat

Later I would say, I have cut myself free from order,
statistics, and what not, what have you.
But I was never connected. To anything.
Marriage taught me to let go more. As if I knew
what I wanted. As if I were after something.
The *finally* was that year as I walked the island

every day. I could feel something extraordinary.
It was the same in me as outside me. I could say us:
The flat land I walked. The mountain approaching.
The blanching of everything living and dying.
Ruined hills and towns without roofs on the houses.
Men and women in black clothing offering water,
singing, being silent, laughing. Dying, as if that
were anything to us who were nature and beyond
suffering. What survives. The part which remains.
What is birth and death to sun, fish, kelp, eggs?
But there is kindness which feeds us another way,
with windlessness, empty heat, or the taste of grapes.

Alma to Her Sister

alone no loneliness in the dream in the quiet
in the sunrise in the sunset Louise.
in the dream no loneliness in the dream
in the sunrise in the sunset just the two of us

alone no loneliness done. in the dream
in the quiet of the day done in the sunrise
Louise. in the dream in the dream
in the sunrise in the sunset.

alone no loneliness done. no loneliness
in the dream in the quiet
in the sunrise in the sunset. Louise
in the dream. in the sunrise in the sunset.

Trying to Believe

There's nothing gentle where Aphrodite was.
Empty mountain and grasshoppers banging
into me. Maybe there never was.
But I go up again and again to search
under thorn bushes and rocks.
Am grateful for the marble upper arm
big as my thumb. A shard with a man's feet
and a shard with the feet of a bird. A sign
that it can be more. Like when a wind comes
in the great heat and lifts at my body.
Like when I get back to my mountain, aching

and my hands hurt. Sit alone looking down at
evening on the ocean, drinking wine or not.

The Color of Many Deer Running

The air fresh, as it has been for days.
Upper sky lavender. Deer on the far hill.
The farm woman said they will be gone
when you get there as I started down the lane.
Jumped the stream. Went under great eucalyptus
where the ground was stamped bare by two bulls
who watched from the other side of their field
all the time I went past and up the slope.
The young deer were playing as the old ate
or guarded. Then all were gone, leaping.
Except one looking down from the top.
The ending made me glad. I turned toward
the red sky and ran back down to the farm,
the man, the woman and the young calves.
Thinking that as I grow older I will lose
my color. Will turn tan and grey like the deer.
Not one deer, but when many of them run away.
Some day I will be like them. Not young,
but running to the next quiet place.
It will be hard to see me. I will be healthy.
I will walk and feed and run and be happy.
But I think it will be hard to be with me.

Not Wanting Myself

Not wanting myself, I try to go
into whatever makes longing:
the hawks mating and falling,
the Sung paintings where the Chinese
live in their own distance.
Wrenching to get away,
I put down money
to go into the dark place
and see advertisements of my desires.
But they hit me. Hit me
when I wanted to see the birds fly.
Birds who are part of myself

with hearts you can eat.
They invade my longing
with an intelligence that does not hold
on to anything. O, my dreams,
I am losing even you.
The only lover my mind has left
separates my mind, like milk.

Choosing the Devil

Mephistopheles enters
between one step and another.
He makes things with words.
Whatever he says exists immediately
in the world. Plants grow.
They flower and bear fruit,
harvesting unto themselves.
And grow up again.
I do a dance, to keep from hurting them.
I grab him close around the neck.
I look into his eyes like a wild girl
and see his excitement. I jump
and land perfectly on his black dog
who runs in circles
like a trained one in the circus.
I balance on the very back edge of the dog.
I want to balance. I am having fun,
riding around and calling after myself:
Devil, I am doing it perfectly. Look,
I am doing it perfectly.
Goethe is at home, writing: "All things corruptible
are a parable." I do not go there.
He is on the mountain.
It is so massive, so incomplete.

Children Among the Hills

The lamb was so skinny I thought it was a baby goat
and called my sister to see. Lying on its side,
legs straight out in front, little stomach pulsing.
Then the head lifted sideways and began telling us
how much he hated the promiscuous sun which shines

on all things equally. Rotting one, growing strength
in another. On those caged in virtue and on men who
walk through the streets at ease in the hot light.
On that which is not quite animal, on what is not
quite mineral. That which hisses in the shadows
along the wall. Army of horses practicing formations
in the Swiss mountains. Shepherds fleeing into Italy.
On two dead fish on the sidewalk still pink from
their life in the sea. Finally the lamb slept.
The trees on the hills around us were silent.
Like a thing made of silver. But inside everything
was moving, shivering with wind. We knew that much.

Not Saying Much

My father is dead and there is nothing left
now except ashes and a few photographs.
The men are together in the old pictures.
Two generations of them working and boxing
and playing fiddles. They were interested
mostly in how men were men. Muscle and size.
Played their music for women and the women
did not. The music of women was long ago.
Being together made the men believe somehow.
Something the United States of America could
not give them. Not even the Mississippi.
Not running away nor the Civil War nor farming
the plains. Not exploring or the dream of gold.
The music and standing that way together
seems to have worked. They married women
the way they made a living. And the women
married them back, without saying much,
not loving much, not singing ever.
Those I knew in California lived and died
in beauty and not enough money. But the beauty
was like a face with the teeth touching
under closed lips and the eyes still. The men
did not talk to them much, and neither time
nor that fine place gave them a sweetness.

Death Looks Down

Death looks down on the salmon.
A male and a female in two pools, one above
the other. The female turns back along the path
of water to the male, does not touch him,
and returns to the place she had been.

I know what death will do. Their bodies already
are sour and ragged. Blood has risen
to the surface under the scales. One side
of his jaw is unhinged. Death will pick them up.
Put them under his coat against his skin
and belt them in there. Will walk away
up the path through the bay trees.
Through the dry grass of California to where
the mountain begins. Where a few deer
almost the color of the hills will look up
until he is under the trees again and the road ends
and there is a gate. He will climb over that
with his treasure. It will be dark by then.

But for now he does nothing. He does not disturb
the silence at all. Nor the occasional sound
of leaves, of ferns touching, of grass or stream.
For now he looks down at the salmon large and whole
motionless days and nights in the cold water.
Lying still, always facing the constant motion.

Being with Men

There are things a man does
that damage a woman. Which are not wrong.
Are even grand and solemn occasions.
Cultivations, seizures of Life from Time.
Treasures which will accompany him
years farther on. The wife grows strange,
but one does not comfort her.
It might look like he is guilty of something.

The River Again and Again

If we stayed with each other long enough
to see the seasons return, to see the young animals
and the opening of peonies and summer heat,
then we could make sense of the hawk's calm
or the deer all lowering their heads
again and continuing to eat.
I could show you how repetition
helps us to understand the truth.
And we would know each other sometimes
with a love that touches indifference.

Marriage and Midsummer's Night

It has been a long time now
since I stood in our dark room looking
across the court at my husband in her apartment.
Watched them make love.
She was perhaps more beautiful
from where I stood than to him.
I can say it now: She was like a vase
lit the way milky glass is lighted.
He looked more beautiful there
than I remember him the times
he entered my bed with the light behind.
It has been three years since I sat
at the open window, my legs over the edge
and the knife close like a discarded idea.
Looked up at the Danish night,
that pale, pale sky where the birds that fly
at dawn flew on those days all night long,
black with the light behind. They were caught
by their instincts, unable to end their flight.

Coming Back

I stood watching the great hulk of desire
glide within memory. Watched it move
like the only true beauty in the world. Let it pass.
Kept to the ragged path the old men made
one by one and long ago. Desire would have led me away.

My heart beats within the galaxy of this life—
restrained, limited, in love.
Understanding how some siren longings kill.
I, keeping still in my distance, surprise them
by holding my ground, singing and shouting down praise
upon them. As if I were one of them.
I, the girl who ate dirt, who wrote of the fool
hidden in the straw crying because he wanted a monkey
and some bells to make a living.
I who looked at the drying leaves with my heart
have learned to come back.

How the Joy of It Was Used Up Long Ago

No one standing.
No one for a long time.
The room is his room,
but he does not go there.
Because of the people.
He stands in the dark hall.
The smell makes him close
his eyes, but not move
from the place so near.
They have cut the cow open
and climb into the ooze
and pulse of its great body.
The man is noble, the festival
growing louder in his flesh.
His face is sad with thinking
of how to think about it,
while his mind is slipping
into the fat woman.
The one he saw for a moment
near day, open and asleep.
A filth on the floor of that room.

Things Not of This Union

The weight of myself. The weight of my mother.
The weight of my sister. All the arguments.
I think of our womanhood and how it slices our lives
in half. And of the men who come toward us singing

about loss, reading their list of orders, explaining
to us of wholeness through mating. How they are
the protection, we the bearers. They the fighters,
we the hidden. They the cutters and we the carriers.
They the landscape, we the cave and the small bears
frolicking in the warm grass. But my heart is strange.
It sees things not of this union. I see the sun.
I see the water in the creek is going somewhere.
See the swift moon. I see how the stars come
when it is dark. So I leave the laws of my own kind
and come ignorantly to this place where fineness
is mud for strange life, and the seas graveyard
or offering place. Stand and wait, stand and wait.
Hoping to be taught. Hoping to learn seeing.
My big dumb being clearly mirrored in the water
mirror. And move very little, not wanting the sea
to work at refinement any more than is usual.
The foreign others will say she is dazed or crazy.
They will not ever think my waiting in this odd place
is the journey. I lift my head to the mountain
and try to smell something new. The whole world
at once. No longer the salt shell and then the pine
tree. Wanting a longer unity to go back home to.

Euridice Saved

I am filled with the sorrow of all things seen
for the last time. He lays with me gently
in the unfamiliar house and kisses me. And when he holds
my head in both hands and arms, I dream of the real world.
I look from the mirror to the light on the floor.
I am happy with him eating bread and coffee.

This morning when I took off my shirt to bathe
I noticed I held it in the air before me
for some time. I looked at it without perception.
When I let it fall, it did not make a noise.
Art, I was thinking, is the imitation
of what we called nothing when we lived on the earth.

Stan Rice

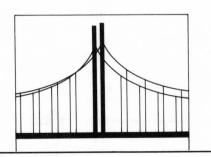

Stan Rice was born in Dallas, Texas, in 1942, and lived there until he was 18, when he married novelist Anne Rice. They moved then to San Francisco, where they still live. Their first child, Michele, died of leukemia in 1972 at age six, which occasioned the poems of *Some Lamb*. They now have a four-year-old son, Christopher. Rice attended North Texas State University and the University of California, Berkeley, and received B.A. and M.A. degrees in creative writing and literature from San Francisco State, where he has taught for seventeen years. For eight years he was assistant director of the Poetry Center there, and is now chairman of the Creative Writing Department. He has won a National Endowment for the Arts Fellowship, the Joseph Henry Jackson Award, and the Academy of American Poets Edgar Allan Poe Award. His books, *Whiteboy* and *Some Lamb*, will be joined by a third, entitled *Body of Work*, to be published this spring.

Excess and Accuracy

My intention in this essay is to illuminate the poems chosen by the editor for this anthology by describing the concerns, temperament, and vision out of which they were written.

If you are asked to picture mentally the last time you went swimming, you will probably "see" yourself in the act of swimming as though you were a witness somewhat at a distance from the swimmer, rather than "be" the swimmer and feel the water against your face, your arms extending from your shoulders, your body invisible behind you, the lake at eye-level before you. I take it to be a habit of brain (very familiar in dreams) to "see" oneself at a slight objective remove, as though you the rememberer were watching a film of the swimmer.

I believe this tendency to create a cinema in an "aesthetic distance" characterizes all intelligence, and that a poem is an event of intelligence which compresses all the techniques of mentation into a single rhythmic unit. To me the act of writing a poem gathers up and focuses sensualized forms of thought, just as memory gathers up and focuses the swimmer. A poem is brain in the act of braining. When the poem works it is a supreme pleasure for it is the objectified event of mind working well. When the poem fails (or when a year's worth of poems fails) it is a keen displeasure, for it is a model of indecision, vanity, and madness.

Brain strives for a state of patterned integrity. Poem strives for a state of patterned integrity. Since poem is a product of brain and brain is a product of Universe and Universe itself (however mysteriously) is striving for patterned integrity, to write a poem is to attempt to touch the godforce. This lofty equation is with me constantly. To consider the act of writing as anything less is to reduce it to a therapeutic hobby.

I think I am a religious poet. (My critics might argue that the tone of the poems in this anthology is that of a tent evangelist; I can hardly argue with them.) This "religion" is not to be confused with Christianity or Buddhism or Marxism or any other proscriptive belief system. By "religious" I mean an attitude toward matter and energy as intrinsically awesome. The goal of language, in my opinion, is to "worship" phenomena. The poem is always an act of homage, the intention of which is hallucination. The memory's objectified "view" of the self swimming is an hallucination of the swimmer. The trees vanish, the sky vanishes, the car you came to the lake in vanishes: what rises intensely to attention is the swimmer as Image, as emotionally charged icon, as "vision." The entire poem, for me, is a musicalized network of these religiously elevated vision-events. This is true of bombastic oratorical poems and murmured still-lifes-of-the-heart. I would contend that the very nature of intelligence is hallucinatory isolation of details. Every bush, intensely seen, is a burning bush.

Given this predisposition I have found myself struggling with a dilemma all my adult life, one that I have yet to resolve. I have found myself temperamentally at odds with most of the English and European verse which is my heritage. Most of it is, to my taste, overly concerned with what I would call "static harmony" —like the balance of equal weights on a seesaw—whereas I am inexorably drawn to "dynamic balance"—the mutually repulsive and attractive tensions which keep a solar system in coherence. The poems of my immediate tradition lack the teeth (not to mention the fangs) that I feel all objects and experiences have. They are *physically* dull to me. The nude intensity of phenomena seems untouched, even untouchable, by most English verse. The erotic complexity of phenomena seems to me an absolute given. The paper on which I write these words is *in fact* a furnace of molecular activity. How can a poetry dedicated to religious discovery (revelation) exclude (in its themes or in its language use) this feverish intensity, this aspiration in all entities to achieve as much as possible while still maintaining Livingness? My goal in every poem is to include as much as possible while remaining faithful to the parameters of the experience being examined and the poem itself. A poem has only one rule: to achieve and maintain livingness. The alternative is the death of the object. We say of such a poem "it doesn't work." We could as easily say "it failed to attain life."

The poems I wish to write always risk exaggeration, for this is the price of admission to the cinema of brain. The poems also willingly embrace the risk of theatricality. All thought is theatre. The nature of thinking is the transformation of sense impressions into Images which can be sorted, collated, and reassembled in insightful relationships. All "thinking" is "imagination" (image-making) or we could not figure-forth the image of the swimmer at all. The very chemistry of mental activity, we are gradually learning, is a tension of electrochemical accretion and release. This tension crests as the theatrical phenomenon known as Imagery. Poetry is an already theatrical and dramatic subjective process objec- tified. What falls on the remembered swimmer is the spotlight of Thought.

Post-Beowulf English literature rarely treats mentally exterior events or men- tally interior events as radiant theatrical integrities. For a long time (and still to a large degree) I worked with a sense of isolation from the mainstream of European and American poetry. Even surrealism I found to be only *linguistically* interesting. I usually felt I was "reading words" rather than truly touching the tongue of the world.

Having declared religious hallucination as a goal, I would hasten to add at this point that I am not after a poetry of distortion, disorientation, or rapturous blur. The essence of insightful hallucination is accuracy. I have found in recent years two models for the hallucinatory vividness which I seek while retaining fidelity to the thing-itself: primitive poetry and 20th century science. While this may seem an odd marriage, to me both thought systems approximate my sense of the poem (and all experience) as an erotically braided net of semidiscrete luminous moments. The preliterate poem is congenial to my sense that the poem's truest order is that of lucid image clusters organized with greatest simplicity and greatest vividness. Such poems begin (as all religious acts begin) awestruck by Stuff and bearing true witness to the thingness of things, and then proceeding by stark sincerity to honor both the world and the transformations of the world that go on in brain to turn these accurate observations into emotionally charged images. Modern scientific theory also informs my work: blazing splinters of phenomena comprise this seemingly inert paper. Post-Kantian philosophy, Einsteinian physics, modern linguistics, computer technology, and subatomic physics all arc back over centuries of rational and scholastic thought to corroborate the techniques of primitive art. In the primitive idiom and in the computer I find a home for my twin interests in Excess and Accuracy.

All I have said so far has seemed to omit any mention of "theme." But for me it follows inexorably that the quest for the blood in the turnip (while never sacrificing the turnip's integrity) leads to themes which examine eternal verities. Otherwise the theatrical intensity becomes thin and shrill, the evangelical zeal becomes polemic, candor becomes vanity, and I get the horrible sensation that I am shouting into a barrel. I feel the death of the mind. This of course is not a new idea, but it bears repeating that even the most autobiographical theme (and all the poems in this anthology were drawn directly from my life) must be a context for insights that exceed the private self. I would argue that if the private is treated with passionate lucidity, it exceeds itself and becomes Image. And it is a characteristic of lucid Image that it reverberate with multiple meanings. This is true of even the simplest concrete detail. To figure forth the Image of yourself swimming is to exclude all irrelevant data and to focus not on "you" but on flesh, water, air, coolness, vulnerability, and even death. As you can see, I'm not a very good swimmer.

The poems chosen by the editor for this anthology do, I feel, demonstrate these governing concepts in action. But I should add in closing a kind of disclaimer. This description of "what I do" surely includes a lot of "what I'd like to think I do." One must set the governing concepts against the poems and ask if the two are a match. What a poet cannot clearly see are his "givens," his axioms, his unquestioned assumptions. But even so, perhaps there is worth in an essay of this kind; especially if it, too, exceeds the private and becomes a vision for action.

The Skyjacker

I am Tex Ritter. I am not Eldridge Cleaver.
I am approaching Havana.
I am carrying a pillow into the cockpit on which is embroidered
I am Tex Ritter. Howdy.
A calm falls over the cockpit.
The co-pilot takes off his extra ears and I tell them,
Relax. I tell the captain to tell the passengers
that this is not Eldridge Cleaver
this is Tex Ritter talkin
and we're going to Havana
and Relax. Then I hear the neighbor's black son's Pontiac
roar outside my window. I partly wake up. I look out.
He is wiping the water off the windows. Like a beast
out of the dream I just finished about living on a cliff
guarded by two white dogs with long flexible noses,
the Pontiac sits, its exhaust smoke
turns pink in the brakelights.
Does he know I am Tex Ritter? Does he realize
we have set down in Cuba, all of us, shrieking tires,
aluminum skin shuddering and windshield wipers
ferociously lapping the windows, the Cubans standing
behind the frosty reception room glass,
clipboards hanging from their belts, does he?
I'll bet he doesn't know.
I think I'll tell him.
But when I look back he and his Pontiac are gone. Oh well,
what's a skin-deep defeat to me, Tex Ritter?
Maybe it's better nobody knows who's talkin
when I kick in the cockpit door
and catch the pilots with their long soft black flexible noses
coiled in their laps, and slip
out of my embroidered pillow my gun and say, coolly,
We are going to Havana,
this is Tex Ritter,
this is not Eldridge Cleaver,
We are going to Havana forever!

America the Beautiful

The logarithm. The fraction. The bead of dew.
The illusion. The quality
that leaps out of the bicycle. The possibility again
of heroism. The dispelling of sadness. The dynamo
and the huge act. The inclusion of machines
and therefore the mastery of machines.
The Big Dipper and the smoothness of aluminum.
The absolute colors. The April
that ascends and descends at once in the mercury.
The white bicycle of thought.
The way out of the doldrums of locomotives
and the smokestacks whose bodies are totems
of maniacal clarity. The moon
absorbed by the intelligence. All "property"
transformed without being "owned." The possibility again
of the heroic and gloomless claritas of sense.
Stoned visions of facts themselves.
The actual objects, around whose shapes accumulate the halos of presence.
The milkman come back, more jangling than war, the New War
declared on demythologized THINGS.
The investment of stone again
with the mercurial feathers and eyes
of the boneless breeze.
No victory but in the perception of the emotional quality.
Victim and victor transposed. The melting down
of the locomotive in the machine of its making.
All rhythms seen as extensions of spirit.
All spirit seen as extension of motion.
The ferociously benevolent dilation of the eye
at the warcraft of Knowledge. At last
the vision complete of this: that the excesses of today
are the natural resources of tomorrow. By which
the data quivers with delight in the graph,
and the formerly dead hairdomes ignite with feeling,
and the moosehuge inanity of literal competition
is transformed into the ecstatic sexual come.
Not the loss of all energy into sloth
but the internalized energy of sensual synapses,
of galaxy and water and brilliant brain and breast and nipples
and scrotum and mons and scarlet tip.
America The Beautiful. At last

the Constitution made fact and the fear of actualized Liberty
renounced and the Void smoothed like a bed.
I pledge allegiance again,
this time to the vivifications of our lost Body Politic,
nerves and follicles and arteries
ablaze in the suaveness of night.

The Dogchain Gang

The street is no river. For slouching
they put big rings of white lime
around each elm tree in the yard
outside the lunchroom. The Mexicans
are throwing switchblades at the locker room wall.
The grape-ade has flicked its cock.
In metalshop the whiteboy is running his twofoot
bread-knife along the buffing-wheel,
the soapstone melts; desire, alongside his leg, desire;
& outside, broad low-slung Chevys cruise
from the 7-Eleven to the freeway.
That wool in the woods is girl's wool.
Maybe them what eats shit set fire to the tires
stacked in the trees beside the Lighthouse
For The Blind. Or some jelly-bellied
cop searched everybody when Everybody
dropped cherrybombs down the toilets.
The excuses ran out on you, whiteboy. The flashlights
walked on invisible legs in the alleys.
The percentages got better of you getting it like Billy Bob
got it in a car wreck or like whatsisname, the one with all the hair,
shot in the throat, the rest of his life
proud of not being able to talk: Lovers of Knives. Well, shit, I
remember easy all the lives that ended at 16
because nobody loved love as much as the circular bone in the penis
that shows when youre backed up against
the white lime. Here come
the gringos Lefty & Carl, and then the Mexicans
Juvey & Moses & Menchaka, my life
flickering between fence slats between the woods of tires
and the miniature golf course, my small chest
shrinking even more, hair sleek with Fitches,
my percentages increasing with each evasion.
Whitey in black leather is whitey alongside

browny's suave Jesus, sterling silver
crucifix at the throat, suede & ancient, lies lies lies,
bilingual angels, jelly-handed murderers, arsonists,
big prick-mongers sliding down plaid seatcovers
into their own lives, somebody's gonna gitcha, razors
in boot toes, fear fear fear in beautiful eyes,
liquid as polish, endlessly flickering,
dogchains hanging out of the mouths & sides.

The Bicycle

That which *is*, for example,
the *bicycle*
stands out
among things, its *wheels*, fierce,
its substance. For example
the spokes *are*. Spinning
they are even more surely, by which
we recognize the life-light around the hub
and under the brain's thin skin work
a thought for the rightness with which
its fenders join with the frame,
the handlebars, the accuracy, the *pureness*.
In the same radiance most things
stand, ugly, harmonic, *stand*
for us to mount
and ride out, clicking, handbrakes cool steel
handbrakes, alive more than ever
to what *is*, our vision fashioned to please
the legs, the way things
devicelessly wreck us with their perfect chains
on two oily wheels and wreck our
bodies, that we might somehow
rise out of this twofold spinning or leaning,
happy at last, at rest, furiously at rest,
a thing so rightly joined
the chain and frame
will never pull, for example, apart
from where we are *going*.

The 29th Month

A thing, loved one,
is eating our air.
It dwelleth in oily hair.
It dwelleth in the chair by the window.
It dwelleth in the lying-out-white baby.
A man enters in a smock
and it isn't the cook it's the doctor
What's up, Doc?
He says the medicines can make her sing but can't make her talk.
So we bought her twenty-five dollars worth of chocolate eggs
whose shells melt and centers flood and the days,
ah,
the days,
they move so slowly,
people come in and out of the parkinglot carrying zinnias,
the dentist in the window leans over his oven,
the gardener waters the concrete,
little black girls in green crinoline come to visit their grandfathers.
The body doesn't lie.
I want to make it be in words, because
to get the poem right
is to have another baby
while the real one dies.

The Last Supper

What's that red stuff? Blood? Gee
ZUZ! Go down on THAT,
Baby-eater.
So? The pillow has fangs? So?
Something's too soft here.
Ok, tell me: what does an angel's skeleton look like?
Looks like the shadow of a bunch of chains.
Jesus. I'm sitting up all night with a fern.
I'd cry but my eyes got eaten by . . . uh who was that anyway
Ate my eyes? Some "god"?
He got hungry and he needed some silverware so he opened
My daughter and he said, Look at this here little faceful of bones:
FORKS & KNIVES & SPOONS AND BUTTERKNIVES.
God, bruise-stomper, purple to puss, crusher of children,

Beerbelly, tattoo on bicep reading YUM YUM
In a valentine being squeezed by a chain
& a vulva with a lightning bolt in its eye.
Zero with teeth, leukemia-licker, slut.
It IS blood, that red stuff. GEE
ZUZ! Somebody dropped the watermelon on the concrete.
Get a sponge. Get a shovel. Call God. Soup's on.

Incanto

1.

I sit waiting for one of the two kinds of miracle:
the thing as it *is*, or the thing *transformed*—
which Tyger?—
There are no lambs here, my juicy head—Time
hath made off with the last lamb left—That's dead—
Anne sits reading the Chronicle in her nightmare clothes—Daisy
glossy on couch—I hear a broom & a hose on concrete—my neighbor,
sweeping his reflection away, no doubt—The photographs are in the album
each face under its plastic, waiting, for the Real, the cheek
crushed to cheek
that the brain might arc the gulf between brains—Orgasm?—
A huge hand comes out of the clouds and squeezes the brain
and lets it go
and it soaks back up what it let—selfdrenched again—astonished,
a mirror in grass—
Is the miracle *clarity?*—precise definitions instead of this *song?*—
Which tyger shall eat the reflection?—If I'm to go on
the terms of the slaughter must be known—
Hugeheaded child lying on couch beating her lace collar
under which is the pain in her lungs—
The precise names of the medicines
did not help:
6-mercaptopurine prednisone cytoxin methotrexate dilantin
thioguanine vincristine asparaginase cytocine-arabanacide
                    NO HELP—
At 4 a.m. I wake up on hospital linoleum beside her bed TV
hissing the screen a miracle of chaos not a single word
worth saving they're all too small throw them back no limit
to errors the faces are under the plastic in the album two
months have passed she's dead that's it the scissors lie in
the moonlight on the bedstand clarity is cannibalism—

Sunday—8 October—72
Michele now nothing but an emptying dress in the grave.

2.

White day—glare—light on the liars—
Outside the Rainbow Carwash & Lounge
the blacks in ankle-length leather—shoes of shame vanished—
lightning in leather—All the names of the colors
in the 48 count box of crayolas,
listed—Clarity & Vividness joined—screamy with silky—
The books articulate, intact—poodles barking at windows—a girl
at a curtain, reading—a white dress drying in a tree—
ruthless clockshop window & enameled scarlet chinese porcelain egg
        on crunchless velvet—
And not *one* human in the landscape who is not a metaphor—
Everything metaphor except the metaphors—Gesture is sculpture—
The swinger stands fixed in nitrogen
and the brain that talked just an hour ago shines in a jar—
To write this right is to cope with the corpse—
I kissed her in the coffin, the big cool rubber doll in the coffin,
she smelled like crayolas, her face
a Thought—
Hold on—even in heaven, frozen in gold—in the boneyard
where the clock coughs, hold on—in the marble, safe against seepage,
hold—in the dirt, in the neutral, hold on
that you might be able,
should the miracle come,
LET GO.

3.

I let her go, I told her, me, squeezing the oxygen bag,
Electrocardiagram ink line straight to horizon, no blip,
Precision useless again, Chief Doctor
In rumpled suit no tie unshaven 5 a.m. & fumbling Intern,
This probably his first death, mine too,
Anne in her blue robe astonished, after two years, still,
        at the last moment,
ASTONISHED,
Fingers to lips,
The oxygen tent ripped back, the cooler roaring for nothing, me
Squeezing the rubber bag trying to find the rhythm of a breather sleeping
That her heart might recognize, begin again, all the time
Saying to myself "Don't come back Mouse don't come back," her head

Heavy on rubbery neck the veins I'm ASTONISHED
Rising to the surface of the skin like crazed lacquer, One Two Three
Shots of adrenalin straight into the vein,
No response,
Me squeezing now the tears dropping bright on the black rubber bag No
                                                                    Response,
The head nurse massaging the chest a deep gurgle like a clogged trap
NO RESPONSE, Anne
"Can't we do anything, isn't there anything else we can *do?*" The Doctor
Stands up, "You can stop now, we might as well stop kidding ourselves,
                                                                    she's
Gone," and my head cocks sideways like the RCA Victor dog
& I bend over & her lips part easily & wetly & I give her
the long kept sexual kiss of father
to daughter, too late
Hello.

4.

Enough is never enough—That voice comes back—Suave shells of gesture
in doors—The photographs just holes full of crayolas, a glare
in a book—Never enough—Anne drinks, pregnant with novel, writes &
                                                                    screams—
Ten twelve fifteen beers, never enough—
Once more smallvoiced prophetess bald and swollen in final months in red
wheelchair spoke the truth & knew no other thing to say & Death ate her
& Death wasn't even hungry—Well,
"when the sun goes to sleep it makes a hole in its bed"—
There was no key to lock the door no emergency shriek no police the rapist
came in under the door a crack too small even for light to get
he got—Backwards, that—Forward, Michele as a model—Meanwhile,
the poem, for a moment, voice in the gulf, the nightmare articulated, the
                                                                    clock
naked, its back off, blood on the toiletpaper, the experience sung, done,
        Incanto,
the brain squeezed then released to drink back up what it bled—
Clarity & Vividness, both miracles, wed—At last—
        For a moment—
No more death.

Some Lamb

That lamb
In skin
The black wink closes
On that *mnaah*
So dead
The film, the flesh
I guess
Is somewhere
Ecstasy
Is somewhere
Wed with sleep
In the bed
Armless headless pillow
Hold me
My pet lamb is leaping
Up! up! innocence is meat
Is what we live to eat
Straight up in bed
Twelve months
The night is fed
With shapes which fit so tight
This vest of ribs
We scream we beg
Time stop it! stop it!
And yet
That was
Some lamb
Some lamb
Says Death.

History: Madness

Smoke beshags
the lemons and olives.
I was not mad.
I have color slides to prove this.
If you see a flayed goat
hanging in a Haitian shack
tell that goat I have a color slide
this side of death; its death.

And that the veins are still violet.
Further: I have evidence
all history is the orange
of blood-stained water.
Here come the lemons from their gallows.
Silk dress, head of spinach, chicken on her bones.
I have this documented.
History: madness: how did they stuff that man's bones
into that jar whose mouth is smaller than his head?
The chalk gasps. And the fish filet
bears the pink imprint of the bones
of the fish that was in it.
You will make a beautiful fossil
because you believe in ideas.
The tapestry was reversed
so that we could see what madness
resembles. If you see that goat tell it
I have a color slide of the metaphor
of its death. I did not suffer madness.
I suffered facts.
And have the bloody photographs to prove it.

The Cry-Bird Journey

There's no fleeing the cry-bird. This evening
a dove walked on the air mattress in my pool
on squashy careful claws.
I'm on a journey fleeing the cry-bird.
Last Sunday, at the ballpark, guess what they gave me:
a razor! Later, in the warehouse of antiques
where I went to flee her
there were the beast-horned armoires and crazed mirrors
lined up as though stunned by their own distinctness.
Is that the refuge? that luminous dumbness
utterly lost in Thingness? How can a human
flee into objects? The cry-bird was perched at every aisle.
Her whistling plus the thump of the heart in the wall
drove me back onto the street. So I took my sunglasses
out of my shirt and now am here.
This strange thing happened, he said. A bird
flew into my apartment and now it's in the bathroom.
And there, on a shelf, in a fern,
was a myna bird. He swore it had not said a word.

Well then, I said, it's not the cry-bird.
He stared as though waiting for the rest of the sentence.
I asked her what six months of catatonia was like.
Well, she said, it was mostly pretending. Most
insanity is pretending but you wait for somebody
to give you a good reason to stop it.
And she laughed like an intelligent little demon.
She said she wears all that make-up to hide the scars
on her face. And I said, What scars?
And she ran two fingers from her lip to her ear.
No! I refused to settle for anything less
than what is analogous to jumping in icewater. Up,
with characteristic squeaking, flapped the dove.
Which she humorously insisted rhymed with "stove."
Silly girl. Don't you realize
we are supposed to be fleeing the cry-bird?
She stared at me like a boy at his first full-grown
vagina. What a metamorphosis! Terrified,
and allured. You mean you really believe
I'm a person worth liking? she asked, almost in tears,
more than almost. Cree! Cree! the cry
of her double. What can't be fled must be re-invented.
The cry-bird does not roost in the apple tree
but there's a nest somewhere or it couldn't go on
and on. A razor, no less!
So we all fled on.

Metaphysical Shock While Watching a TV Cartoon

Things come from nothing.
The lawnmower
the bulldog uses
to shave the cat
in the cartoon I am watching:
from nothing.
The startled duck bursts
from nothing; drags its feet in the water;
doubles the blaze.
Suddenly, where there was nothing,
there is a lawnmower.
In the next scene the cat is not shaved.
Its hair has returned spontaneously,
and the bulldog's jowls are overlapping

a big naked bone which then
is a stick of dynamite which explodes the dog's head.
In the next scene the dog's head is a dog's head again.
Nothing did it, and nothing
made it ok. The logic of the cartoon
overwhelms me. I watch the TV in the mirror
over the fireplace to get some perspective. But this just
doubles the nothing. *I* came
from where that lawnmower came from.
Jesus, I whisper. Im frightened; and write down
on the telephone messagepad the first line
of this poem; itself, especially, suddenly,
from nothing.

Poem Following Discussion of Brain

The dog.　　The book.　　The glass.
Things seen *as* things.
Arguing a theory of how we perceive. Brain
of dog discussed. The man in the catatonic state
sat up in bed when the terrier licked his face, and said,
"Where can I keep him?" First words since 1958.
Was Christ, to Lazarus, a great dane?

I argue that brain is Master
because brain is slave to Stuff.
The dog, the glass, the book,
first; *then* their transformation into images; *then*
the sensation they are standing in shimmering rings.
Even the movie credits announce
the dog playing Rex is actually King.
I eat food and brain eats names.

My friend argues for Mind minding mind's Minding.
I call that *religion*.
Without Stuff, I insist, there are no Angels.
Angels don't fall out of Heaven they crawl out of Things.
The book. The glass. The dog. Still-lifes precede drama;
just by a hair. The dog that bites you on the toe
tears off Imagination's leg.
Religion calls the dog Illusion. I call the dog
King! And he comes loping up, and licks my face,
and I wake from *and* into
dream.

Flesh

Flesh has a remarkable future.
It calls from the ice cream parlor, See me
in my jeans, I am not yours,
thus a mystery.
It prospers because it has no memory.
Threat, suffering, transience:
you cannot blow flesh out like a match,
for it is a punk in a dish
brewing its little orange tip in the chaos of air.
Its resin is squeezed out on the ice cream floor
in lightbulb-size droplets.
It whispers where it spreads. In the magazines,
there it is: garish, smaller but larger, detached.
Can *this* be *it?* Oh yes. Imagine yourself
without that which makes you
a monster. Imagine yourself like this paper.
The flesh of others is not curly trash;
it is the message. Imagine being called from the ice cream parlor
by Death. Would you go?
Would you if Death were Flesh?

Round Trip

1. SF, a punk cafe, distortion of the literal.

Pale Punk drinks liquid naugahyde on porch of Cafe Flore
in catastrophe-colored pants and beguiles the passing
breadtruck to fill his mirrored sunglasses as dogchains
dangle under the arch of each boot to beat back piecemeal
the incoming rosy breast and oily hair of speechless Death
whose female debutant puts the torch to the crinoline so that
the teenage flamingo might writhe in flame and scorch
the toilet wall with a plume that exactly duplicates
the architecture of the Pure Punk Lingo risen from TV snow
the bloody flakes of which
come down on childhood like cellophane unrumpling
brightly and noisily on the baseball glove mummy
purely given to a desireless life another eon
near the cool moist broomcloset and the roaring rags.

2. In-flight to NY to see the Picasso Show in America the Beautiful.

Like the core of a star working its illiterate miracle
the syntheses boil and cell by cell
the carrion glitter of small towns accretes
below on the ground and the lamial squiggles
of small rivers and the curds of separate clouds
whose shadows below them on the fields are cloned
in scrambled fierceness I, also, long
for that width and depth of oxygen packed in coherence
as where the sea's sand's whiteness bleeds to violet before
the cold ink plunge, snowless and snowy.
Where Hell is mental the bricks are slippery
and all persons wear the black flippers of the frogman
and his second skin, and everything tactile
is a species of cloud. Where Hell is physical
the rolling blaze of the golfcourse at dawn
has no limit and the only surcease from despair
is Landscape Art.

3. NY, in the hotel room, clinging to the literal, fearing for America.

Return to the minutia in whose trust we place
the continuum, cradle to later, and on whose delicious shoulders
we observe the red mark of the straps
of the milk-heavy bra from whom the nourishment of details
is drunk, those holy Other Acts that give
to the net of whatnot its silken weight. Return to it.
The paragraphs outlive their usefulness
but the form of the wish is fulfilled
and the words develop and moisten the cock of the bull
at the heart of the maze with the oil of the child
crushed in the cradle.
Let the catfish-mouthed angels come lap the blood
from the lawns. The venison is in darkness when it flees.
The pork is on the hook in the freezer. The lamb
is curing in the coolness of our backward glance. Acres
of floodtide approach the ranked gladiolas
whose filled heads cause their stems to bend.
And in this manner the truth and falsity of all versions
of minutia link up as an observable infinity of pinpoints
enroute to the place where the lathe of flesh
hums in the frictionless void.

4. NY, at the door of the Picasso Show, preparing for the distortion of the senses.

Memory is not cruel, nor does it curse
our improvisations for exploring the tray
of green liqueurs or the tiny oilstain
that inexplicably inspires terror or the grim sameness
of the beauty of clouds seen from above in a jet.
The carnation is erect the buttermilk is
liquid and solid at the same outpost the water has turned
to ice that is impossible the golfcourse the menstrual
rhythm the snow on the lawns is strawcolored
urine on the whitewash the face stark upright a carnation
in the hotel bed the glucose-starved bloodcells of hangover
and TV blue eyes waiting for the paintings of
Picasso, the Master Who Mocks Death.

5. NY, in the Sculpture Garden, the sculpture talks.

I have climbed the lath of values to the place
where the chalk crumbles and a mouth on a stick
translates the light into words. Quote: "Of the heatfly
there is no misery to know.
Of the mobility of the earthworm no analogue
in stillness, in grief. No language for the vegetarian lamb."
And I have peered in at the toilet of the queen bee
and felt the radar of her slaves. And I have heard the bells
in the Spanish architecture call to their lost loves,
the Dead, whose bodies besponge the path to the fire-escape
that crackles with my weight as I cling.

*6. NY, we go looking for dolls, in a glut of distortion and pessimism wondering
if they are our betters.*

The dolls are imitating the Marvelous, that point
when all the cortical neurons waltz to the same song
in the mansion of the decay of the moment.
Is that the tinkle of the watchman's skull?
Is that the wooden soldier's foot, fresh from Denmark?
Is that the rustle of the gown of the plaster quadroon
with the blowtorch eyes?

7. NY, St. Patrick's Cathedral, Words and Things.

In the stars that appear nightly to whet their appetites
on our glooms. In the starved shadows
cinched at the waist and made to squeak. In

the prepositional phrases precisely put
before between behind and *in* the slowly liquefying skull
that causes the brain to hesitate and lose track
of its time on earth *among* the stars, dissolve, and be
the dirt-down-drain of a single life's deathbed cough
echoing like a dropped wine bottle
in the stone and stained glass Cathedral interior
whose exhaust fans roar softly in the vault where the ribs
meet and the earthless light touches the bundles of stone roses,
heelclick of tourist's sandals, nylon leg against nylon
leg, rack of vigil lights guarding
the smokey gate of the dead, each little thought-wax
trembling in its trap . . . in all these
I am remembering you. You who have entered for good
the illusion of water carved in marble,
the horrible harmony of Time.

8. NY, in the airport, awaiting the return flight, fearing for America, the Beautiful.

In the Book of Beauty, in the volume preceding
the shutdown of senses, something is erased and rewritten,
the rose in the Bible is squashed.
By what?
I leave this behind in the brainspring of forms,
to blossom if it wish, a potted geranium on a black
balcony in New York, toilet of the cat, and demote my attention
to the Literal that I might witness the elements
that occasionally congeal as penetrant thought.
Though ghosts crowd the airport and the taxis
are painted within with heads, dishwhite and round,
and the snail makes no noise on the roseleaf, and
the entrance to Heaven and Hell is forked,
he who lives for clarity knows
night forages with sloppy loose mouth
for its meal, a manatee in the outhouse, seeking the verities
that have outlived the suavity of change,
as Daylight sits with its spiked hairpiece in its lap and
its bald head spiked with light, gazing, stupified,
as humorless as Christ.

9. SF, a punk cafe.

Pale Punk has shaved his head, now in his leathers
they could call him "Flashlight" and not be inaccurate,

it is a great sin to be inaccurate, or maybe "Mohawk Flashlight"
or "Plownose" or "Onion On A Stake" and not be
wiping and jiving and stapling
totalitarian posters to lightpoles. A lamia passes
in blowing black net. Picasso was right. We are at
the marriage fete of two plums who exchange the juices
of their bruises and relax into the luxury of becoming
one sack of skin and silver mold. For such is love,
a mingling. Is it too late? Am I *on* time? From Twin Peaks a white fog
empties out of the cup of color, gorgeously obeys gravity, shifts
and eddies like dryice vapor, one immense rhythmic
concatenation of sapslow radiance enveloping the details,
the minutia. Can you see through this dazzle? Can you ferret
the shapes from the shining?
Can you perfect your ventriloquism on the acetylene-eyed dolls?
Can you swim in the marble, survive the illusion?
Can you stand on your hind legs like an angel and sing
the perfectly circular song?

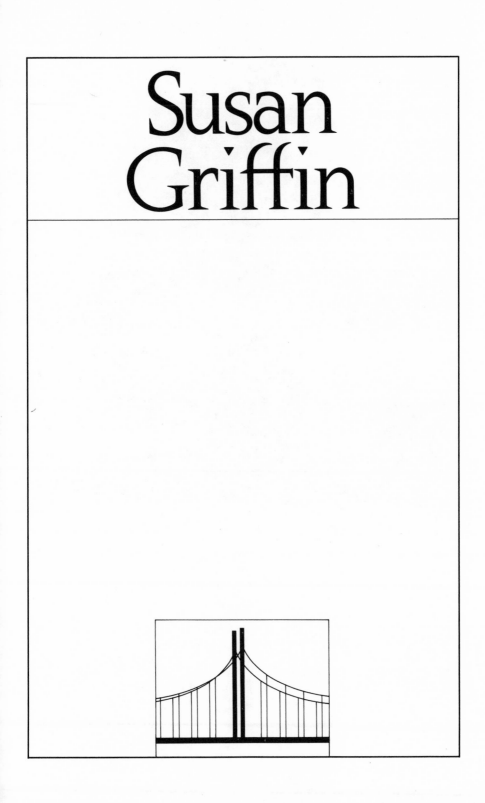

Susan Griffin

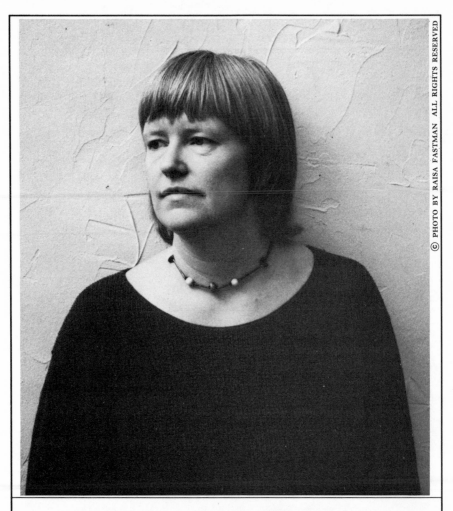

Susan Griffin was educated at the University of California, Berkeley, and at San Francisco State University, where she received her B.A. and M.A. in English literature, with creative writing emphasis. She has been an instructor at both universities, and lives in Berkeley. She has published eleven books, including: *Like the Iris of An Eye* (poems); *Woman and Nature*; *Rape: The Power of Consciousness*; *Pornography and Silence*; and *Voices*, an award-winning play in poetry which has been produced throughout the United States and in several countries in Europe. An anthology of her writing, *Made From This Earth*, was published recently by Harper & Row and by Woman's Press, London. Her awards include a grant from the National Endowment for the Arts, the Ina Coolbrith Prize, and the Malvina Reynolds Cultural Achievement Award. Her poetry, essays, fiction, and criticism have appeared in numerous magazines, journals, and anthologies, and she has given readings and lectures throughout the United States.

Inside the Door

Oftentimes beginning a new work, I feel imprisoned within myself. I am not supposed to say this or that. I am expected to write about such and such. Political expectations, expectations of style or character. And these are suffocating. But the line of the poem makes its way to consciousness despite this suffocation. Usually I hear the first line spoken in my mind. And the language strikes me. I am not taken with the analytical meaning. Rather, its appeal is more direct.

These lines occurred to me this morning,

> I do not like
> the star
> put on my hand
> last night.

At a concert last night, a star was stamped on my hand, as a sign of admission, and I do not like it. Very simple, and literal. But in the poem, more than literal. This is what one means when one says the language of poetry resonates. It leads somewhere. And not somewhere obvious.

For example, if I were to continue the poem with an obvious intent such as:

> A tattoo
> reminding me of
> motorcycles and
> violence

lines which are also literally true, the poem would begin to fall flat for me. Maybe it's true that the star looks like a Hell's Angel tattoo to me. But I feel disappointed with this outcome. "So what," I say. This is nothing new. And I would either do away with these lines, or abandon the poem altogether.

I often discover such a pattern in student's work, three or four stunning lines, and then, three or four very dead lines. It is as if the student had awakened from a dream prematurely and, quickly, before the images could exist, explained the dream away.

I like to dream, and I remember dreams. Like a series of poems, my dreams often have recurring images, and even a continuous narrative. Many times I have dreamt of a green place—a forest, wood, or park—and always, when I dream this place, I experience the same very deep feeling (for which even now I have no word). And just as I will write several poems about one theme, so too I dream thematically. All this month I have been dreaming about death, and my fear of dying.

What is it that makes poetry different than prose? It is said that poetry has rhyme, and rhythm, and line breaks, that it uses metaphor. But these distinctions have never seemed sufficient to me. They seem instead only to be symptomatic of a deeper-lying purpose. It is said that prose is rational and poetry is not. And yet, on one level, poetry is quite rational. The poem may seem irrational because, like a dream, it ignores the boundaries we accept as real. In a dream I can be several people at once—myself, my father, a child, a woman pregnant. And this is also true in a poem. In the poem one can have the direct experience of being in two places at once, feeling two opposite emotions, holding two contradictory opinions, at once. And of course, one *can*. This is the real nature of the mind. Poetry is closer to that nature than prose.

I love what is called "naive" painting, painting in which the artist does not know about, or does not care about perspective. In my kitchen I have a small watercolor by a woman in her nineties which depicts the kitchen of her childhood in Russia. The little girl, who is herself, floats next to the ground. Her hand is on a *dreidl* that is half the size of a chicken standing next to her. This chicken is almost as large as the child's mother, who holds out a plate of cookies to an identical, indeed the same, little girl who now stands next to her mother. She is very small in this second version. Near the hearth a goat floats mid air. Two men playing checkers and a third who reads the Talmud are all the same size as the little girl with her enormous *dreidl*. One might say the painter was mistaken about size and gravity, about time and space. But really she was not. She was precisely accurate about the size of things as she experienced them.

I do not think the painter decided beforehand to make the *dreidl* big because the little girl was preoccupied with it. I do not believe she premeditated at all. Instead she allowed herself to discover what the world looked like to her as a child. Robert Duncan has said about the poetry of H. D. that she was following image from image, word from word. I like to move this way through a poem, without premeditation.

I began "The Perfect Mother" when, driving home one day, the line came to me, "The perfect mother lets the cat sleep on her head." For some reason these words were a great relief to me. I had been worrying all season about my daughter and my mothering of her. These words made me laugh. They filled me with a kind of glee. And the line seemed crazy. Not really sane at all. So I kept on in that direction. Driving the car, I kept following this madcap feeling, tracing it like a nerve into the interior of a muscle.

In this way I came across buried memories of scenes from *McCalls* and the *Ladies' Home Journal,* my grandmother's magazines which I read as a child, pictures of emotionally balanced, ideal mothers in sunny remodeled kitchens giving Dixie cups of juice to their healthy children. This was an archetypical kitchen, one I have never really inhabited. And at the same time, I came across cartoon images of tortured cats.

What can one say about this poem? That it is a protest against the *Ladies' Home Journal* idea of Motherhood? For some reason this prose statement offered as an "explanation" of my poem sets my teeth on edge. Makes me feel like that tortured cat, hair straight up. I agree with the new idea in criticism that there are many possible readings of one work, but even this begs the question.

I am saying of course that one cannot paraphrase a poem, or even a line of a poem, and in the same way, one cannot paraphrase an image. No symbol can really be made equivalent to another unit of meaning because it *is* the meaning.

For example, I am facing an aesthetic problem with the writing of a play (in poetry) about my childhood. I want certain configurations in the play to be subtle. But in the first version, apparently I wrote them so subtly that they simply were not apparent at all. I could have decided to make these configurations a little less subtle. But another aesthetic possibility came to me. I suddenly saw an image of red ink sinking into the page with such intensity that it blurred the letters.

Now if you say, "Oh, of course you want to say those things in your play intensely," I would tell you that you missed the point. It is not intensity, I would say, it is letters blurred by red ink that I want.

One can describe a painting accurately, listing shapes, dimensions and colors, but what one finds on the page finally is not a painting but an experience in and of *language*. The description does not equal ($=$) the thing. Poetry does not describe. It *is* the thing. It is an experience, not the secondhand record of an experience, but the experience itself.

We forget that language is an experience.

The highwayman came riding, riding, riding.

My grandmother used to read me that poem when I was a child, and she read it to my mother too, when she was young. *Riding, riding, riding.* This is not a line about a robber who rides a horse; it is: *The highwayman came riding, riding, riding.*

Language is not only a way to speak with others; it is also an experience of oneself. I am going through a period of dissatisfaction with all that I have written except for my most recent work. Therefore it is particularly hard for me to write this essay. Or to write prose at all. Because I am changing. There is a movement, motion, emotion, which I don't yet understand. Prose would force me to "understand" in a language at a remove from the experience itself, and hence, untrustworthy. But poetry speaks directly. It gives me this motion in language. Through the poetic line I actually feel what I feel more intensely, and it is this that gives me knowledge of myself. My experience is not described or explained by language; it *is* language.

The healing power of speech. This is a particularly crucial question for women because circumstance has forced us to live inside a language which is false, and which therefore gives us a false experience of ourselves. To speak falsely, even with a false cadence, is to betray oneself. One aims for the language that resonates at exactly the same pitch that one feels. Perhaps whatever is said in this pitch is right.

The series of poems called *Our Mother* came to me, one after another, as I began to feel a certain way, at first mutely, and then, *in* language. For a long time I wanted to write poems addressed to a female God. (For some reason I do not like the term "Goddess.") I wrote some poems that had a thin, sickly feel. The voice was not convincing. I wanted an image of God as female, but I did not have such an image. The question is not, of course, whether there is or is not a God, or whether this God is male or female. Because like it or not I had an image of God in my mind and that image was male. All my conscious arguments could not change that image.

Then, in the late spring of this year, the voice of Our Mother came to me. It was not in the way that I expected. I was not in a sanctuary, or in any sacred place. I was not partaking of a ceremony; I was not meditating or thinking seriously alone in my study. I was in a hotel! It is true that I felt very good in this hotel, an old walled house in the French countryside, favored by artists who paid their bills with paintings and sculpture, the rooms filled with the kind of furniture families handed down over generations, worn with use. Wonderful food on pink and white tablecloths. I had a sense of well-being here that women rarely feel because it is usually we who create beneficent worlds, seeing that the tablecloths are ironed, the vegetables fresh.

This hotel bore the mark of a woman's hand, too. But this was not the familiar figure of the submissive or martyred, essentially powerless wife and mother. Madame sat at the gate, sizing us up as we walked in and out. One felt in her eyes the truth, for good or bad, was mirrored. Here was no sentimental mother. She was tough. Honest. We were required to bring a certain intelligence to the way we lived in her eyes. To honor the food we ate with a proper attitude toward the labors of growing and cooking. I began to feel I wanted to entrust the world to this sensibility.

And then there were two events which occurred one after the other. First, Kim and I took a walk through the country to the next village. On the way we encountered one barking dog after another, and I still have a child's fear of dogs. Because of these dogs, I felt I would not be able to go back the way we came. But before we could reach the road, a very nasty dog chased us back down our path. I felt trapped, with no possible solution, and so frightened and desolate was I that I burst into tears. But then, as if from nowhere a French farm woman appeared, looking into our faces with her own very kind face. Speaking slowly to us in French we could understand, she said that she too was afraid of the dog. She said she wanted so much to give us something, but had nothing. Then she took us to the building where she stored her lettuce and gave us cold water. She showed us a path through her own farm by which we could reach the road. At the end of this path, growing on the land guarded by the nasty dog, but out of the dog's reach, was a cherry tree, its branches full of fruit. All day we had walked past cherry trees wanting this fruit, and now we ate.

When we reached the next village, the newspapers on the street all announced the suicide of Romy Schneider. And I remember thinking, if only she had waited a few moments more . . .

Both Kim and I felt convinced that day that the universe is benevolent. But these poems are not an argument for a benevolent universe, or for a female God. Rationally, even irrationally, I have in my mind many arguments against the existence of any God, or of a merciful universe. I worry that such belief may in fact serve to justify human indifference to human suffering. These poems are not part of that philosophical dialogue. They are instead an actual experience in language. I *did* hear this voice.

A friend telephones. She is losing her apartment, leaving her lover of many years, finishing her book. And she wonders why she has been weeping. Well, we joke, just a few details. Now you have to get back to the serious things, I say, like who does the shopping.

And we laugh again because everyone knows that who does the shopping is just a detail, and all that loss is the serious thing. But is this really so? For loss is experienced through detail, when for instance, one shops alone if before one shopped for the night's food with a lover.

Thus, the presence of Our Mother came to me through many details, a pot of tea, a box of tissue, barking dogs, an unnecessary death, a woman sitting reading the newspaper. These details were my experience. They did not stand for it. They *were* it. And so was the voice of Our Mother.

Language is a state of being. It is real. But not in the way we are used to thinking of "reality." One acts on the world. Builds a road through a certain landscape. Prunes a tree in the backyard. And then one sees evidence of having acted. A road exists. A tree exists. But, having made a line of poetry which includes a tree or a landscape, one has put the tree and the land inside oneself. And, at the same time, one has stepped outside oneself to be with the tree and the road, or even to *be* the tree, in language.

What does it mean to change consciousness? Not just that one changes one's mind about this or that opinion. Rather, when consciousness alters, one exists in a different universe, differently charged, colored, felt. And can consciousness be separated from word or image, from the symbol?

I am not just saying that reality is subjective. No, because reality is not entirely subjective at all. We may at different times all have a different experience of reality. And yet the question of consciousness is not that simple. Among the utterances and pictures of others, one can recognize some images or words from one's own experience, and then, there are those that one does not recognize. But it often happens that years after I have read a line of a poem I did not understand, I will suddenly remember that line and say to myself, "Oh, *this* is what it meant." States of consciousness exist within us and some we have entered and some not. But I have never experienced a state of consciousness within myself that was not shared somewhere by someone. And I am beginning to realize that when I encounter what is strange to me, I am merely seeing the evidence for an unknown region of my own soul.

Walking daily in the mountains of Corfu, I pass the village idiot. He rests in a dark doorway; inside there is nothing but rags and old, unused machinery. He is covered with soot and filth. I don't want him near me. I don't want him to touch me. Although he is fed and allowed to stay, the villagers sit apart from him. But in the next village, a mile away, a retarded boy is kindly accepted, included. What is *this* man's history? Why is he kept apart? Is he mad? Is he hated? The next day, still afraid, I find myself entering his room in my imagination, thinking how can such a life be endured? And at the same time, I feel a murderous rage at him, because of his misery.

Now here, halfway round the world and months later, I can see him, his eyes, his face, his strange and awful smile.

And now at this point in my narrative, I remember another vision I had last week. Standing before the sight of many different kinds of vegetables for sale in a market I frequent, I suddenly felt these different vegetables held the secret of life for me. And I laughed. Were there always eggplants? Didn't this particular species, which seems so right, so inevitable, which *is* so right, appear one day out of something else that may be gone now?

> Inside that doorway is terror.
> I don't want him near me.
> I don't want him to touch me.
> The man who lives there.

The play I've been writing is written in a child's language. And now I want to say everything in this language. Because this language is taking me someplace that I know exists, someplace I need to be.

And our friend Naomi Newman writes that she wants to get into the other rooms of her house, the rooms she always dreams. Lines leading somewhere. Outside expectation. Just that.

Berkeley
Fall 1982

Love Should Grow Up Like a Wild Iris in the Fields

Love should grow up like a wild iris in the fields,
unexpected, after a terrible storm, opening a purple
mouth to the rain, with not a thought to the future,
ignorant of the grass and the graveyard of leaves
around, forgetting its own beginning. Love should
grow like a wild iris
but does not.
Love more often is to be found in kitchens at the dinner hour,
tired out and hungry, lingers over tables in houses where
the walls record movements; while the cook is probably angry,
and the ingredients of the meal are budgeted, while
a child cries feed me now and her mother not quite
hysterical says over and over, wait just a bit, just a bit,
love should grow up in the fields like a wild iris
but never does
really startle anyone, was to be expected, was to be
predicted, is almost absurd, goes on from day to day, not quite
blindly, gets taken to the cleaners every fall, sings old
songs over and over, and falls on the same piece of rug that
never gets tacked down, gives up, wants to hide, is not
brave, knows too much, is not like an
iris growing wild but more like
staring into space
in the street
not quite sure
which door it was, annoyed about the sidewalk being
slippery, trying all the doors, thinking
if love wished the world to be well, it would be well.
Love should
grow up like a wild iris, but doesn't, it comes from
the midst of everything else, sees like the iris
of an eye, when the light is right,
feels in blindness and when there is nothing else is
tender, blinks, and opens
face up to the skies.

Chance Meeting

This is how it happens.
I am walking away
from the bookstore,
my head reeling with
images of bear cubs their
fur glistening
with dew (disappearing
from the poet's glance
into forests) and my mouth full
of the poet's words against the
rich who
DO NOT HEAR WEEPING.
I wonder at the strangers
walking the pavement and
want to go deep
into a foreign country
where poverty is visible
and no bones are made
about pain,
when I see
(in the window of a shop)
a sign reading "closed" and
know I am late,
move swiftly thinking of
dinner and zucchini plants
and a dog that
needs to run free and you
I want to be with, then
suddenly
there is a mistake,
   my car
appears
in the middle of the block,
it carries my daughter
with her father
and his new woman
they are going
to a restaurant.

I slip quickly
down
the street
so she won't see
me, my daughter, there should be
no tears, a
pleasant dinner.

My daughter, my heart cleaves
at this, when I see
you, I want to
touch your face, window, glass,
SIDEWALK, STRANGERS,
CARS, DO YOU KNOW,
I fed this child
through the night
whom now
I run from.

Letter to the Revolution

Revolution,
Damn you, I have
a thousand accusations to make:
you failed to save the life
of George Jackson, and you
failed to make yourself
pure.   Like a dumb animal
you have turned on your best
friends. You pretended great
change, in the name of the children
of the bourgeois while the
children of the poor
still suffer. You make promises,
which you have not kept.
You have taken more pleasure in
slander than in understanding and
if you have not lied
you have participated in illusions.
You failed in the worst moments
to bring even a shred of hope
and at the best times, to give
love. You have taken time

and blood freely but
if you have given anything
it is secret.
You have made friends into enemies,
parents to strangers and children
afraid. You boast frequently
about your accomplishments
always elsewhere, and you speak
of humanity, but your first
movements are always
cruel. Revolution,
I find your presence
everywhere, but nowhere
do I find your heart.

Chile

My daughter pleads with me
for the life of our goldfish
souring in a tank
of ancient water,
"I want them
to
live," she
says.   Late at night
I pass the green tank
still full of guilt.
I have chosen
in the hierarchy of my life
to go to work,
to shop, to cook, to
write these words
before saving the fish;
choices surround me.
Nothing is ever right.
Every breathing space
asks for help;
dust multiplies in the
                hallway;
lecture notes fly away
through windows which
need glass and paint
and in the back of my mind

somewhere
is a woman
who weeps
for Chile
and shudders at the
executions.
All along she
has been
pondering the social order
and her
worried thoughts
slow
my
every movement.

Field

To rage I
gravitate in
the field of
your fear.

We see by
force of
circumstance:
I listed
all you had
and now
I list your
lacks.
Loving
is not seeing
but the lover
sees.

She turns from
truth to truth.
She moves across a
room and in this
distance
breathes, re-
covers her-
self, names
her discomfort

which had
needled
her like a
drug.

> *You* are two
> not I.
> The one I love
> the other
> *belies*

>> all we know together
>> all we have barely seen
>> delicate as the line between
>> the air and your face

> *How can you ask me to love her?*
> *This blunt*
> *one, this denier?*

She is your sister
swollen, blunted,
blue,
and she is frightened of me
this dumb
woman, this
buried
force
in you.

Three Poems for Women

1

This is a poem for a woman doing dishes.
This is a poem for a woman doing dishes.
It must be repeated.
It must be repeated,
again and again,
again and again,
because the woman doing dishes
because the woman doing dishes
has trouble hearing
has trouble hearing.

2

And this is another poem for a woman
cleaning the floor
who cannot hear at all.
Let us have a moment of silence
for the woman who cleans the floor.

3

And here is one more poem
for the woman at home
with children.
You never see her at night.
Stare at an empty space and imagine her there,
the woman with children
because she cannot be here to speak
for herself,
and listen
to what you think
she might say.

A Woman Defending Herself Examines Her Own Character Witness

QUESTION: Who am I?
ANSWER: You are a woman.
Q. How did you come to meet me?
A. I came to meet you through my own pain and suf-
fering.
Q. How long have you known me?
A. I feel I have known you since my first conscious
moment.
Q. But how long really?
A. Since my first conscious moment—for four years.
Q. How old are you?
A. Thirty-one years old.
Q. Will you explain this to the court?
A. I was not conscious until I met you through my own
pain and suffering.
Q. And this was four years ago?
A. This was four years ago.
Q. Why did it take you so long?

A. I was told lies.

Q. What kind of lies?

A. Lies about you.

Q. Who told you these lies?

A. Everyone. Most only repeating the lies they were told.

Q. And how did you find out the truth?

A. I did not. I only stopped hearing lies.

Q. No more lies were told?

A. Oh no. The lies are still told, but I stopped hearing
them.

Q. Why?

A. My own feelings became too loud.

Q. You could not silence your own feelings any longer?

A. That is correct.

Q. What kind of woman am I?

A. You are a woman I recognize.

Q. How do you recognize me?

A. You are a woman who is angry.
You are a woman who is tired.
You are a woman who receives letters from her
children.
You are a woman who was raped.
You are a woman who speaks too loudly.
You are a woman without a degree.
You are a woman with short hair.
You are a woman who takes her mother home from
the hospital.
You are a woman who reads books about other women.
You are a woman whose light is on at four in the
morning.
You are a woman who wants more.
You are a woman who stopped in her tracks.
You are a woman who will not say please.
You are a woman who has had enough.
You are a woman clear in your rage.
And they are afraid of you
I know
they are afraid of you.

Q. This last must be stricken from the record as the wit-
ness does not know it for a fact.

A. I know it for a fact that they are afraid of you.

Q. How do you know?

A. Because of the way they tell lies about you.

Q. If you go on with this line you will be instructed to remain silent.
A. And that is what they require of us.

FOUR SELECTIONS FROM *Woman and Nature*

Prologue

He says that woman speaks with nature. That she hears voices from under the earth. That wind blows in her ears and trees whisper to her. That the dead sing through her mouth and the cries of infants are clear to her. But for him this dialogue is over. He says he is not part of this world, that he was set on this world as a stranger. He sets himself apart from woman and nature.

And so it is Goldilocks who goes to the home of the three bears, Little Red Riding Hood who converses with the wolf, Dorothy who befriends a lion, Snow White who talks to the birds, Cinderella with mice as her allies, the Mermaid who is half fish, Thumbelina courted by a mole. *(And when we hear in the Navaho chant of the mountain that a grown man sits and smokes with bears and follows directions given to him by squirrels, we are surprised. We had thought only little girls spoke with animals.)*

We are the bird's eggs. Bird's eggs, flowers, butterflies, rabbits, cows, sheep; we are caterpillars; we are leaves of ivy and sprigs of wallflower. We are women. We rise from the wave. We are gazelle and doe, elephant and whale, lilies and roses and peach, we are air, we are flame, we are oyster and pearl, we are girls. We are woman and nature. And he says he cannot hear us speak.

But we hear.

The Garden

And the man said, The woman whom thou gavest to be with me, she gave me of the tree, and I did eat. . . . Therefore the Lord God sent him forth from the garden of Eden, to till the ground from whence he was taken. So he drove out the man; and he placed at the east of the garden of Eden Cherubims, and a flaming sword which turned every way, to keep the way of the tree of life.

—Genesis 3:12, 23, 24

She was in the garden, sequestered behind bushes, as night came, just as the other children were called in, and so she stayed quiet, she said, as a mouse, so that she could be out there alone. And when the cries of the others had gone indoors, in this new silence she began to hear the movements of birds. So she stayed still and watched them. Then she felt, she said, the earth beneath her feet coming closer to her. And she began to play with the berries and the plants and finally to whisper to the birds.

And the birds, she said afterward, whispered to her. And thus when, hearing her mother's frightened voice, she appeared finally from the dark tangle of trees and shrubs, her face was so radiant that her mother, amazed to see this new joy in her daughter, did not tell her then what she knew she would soon have to say. That those bushes her daughter hid behind can also hide strangers, that for her shadows speak danger, that in such places little girls must be afraid.

Silence

I am reminded that a great compliment of my childhood was: "She's such a quiet girl."
—Michelle Cliff, *Notes on Speechlessness*

In that photograph of the child and her mother there is a wide space between them and wide space all around them, and all that space seems to be filled with silence. The child looks as if she might have cried but is not crying. Her eyes look down intently to the ground. Her hands grip the wire of a barbed-wire fence. Maybe she has just tried to say what she felt. Maybe the language did not come to her, she could not find the words. Maybe what she felt got turned in her mouth into other words. She has that look of desperation on her face, that she had tried to speak and given up.

In the mother's body is a different kind of helplessness. She stands with one hand on her hip, another shading her eyes from the sun, looking toward her daughter. Whatever her daughter tried to say was not something she could understand. And her posture might be righteous, or even angry, if there were not a clear longing in it. As if the child's attempt at speech had touched an old buried place in her, and so she lingers, half turned to her daughter, half turned away, knowing she will never grasp that feeling and thus already having given up, yet not able to turn from it.

And they stand there forever that way, locked in silence.

Acoustics

One way to feel the holiness of something is to hear its inner resonance, the more-than-personal elements sounding-vibrating through.
—M. C. Richards, *The Crossing Point*

This cathexis between mother and daughter—essential, distorted, misused—is the great unwritten story. Probably there is nothing in human nature more resonant with charges than the flow of energy between two biologically alike bodies, one of which has lain in amniotic bliss inside the other, one of which has labored to give birth to the other.
—Adrienne Rich, *Of Woman Born*

The string vibrates. The steel string vibrates. The skin. The calfskin. The steel drum. The tongue. The reed. The glottis. The vibrating ventricle. Heartbeat. Wood. The wood resonates. The curtain flaps in the wind. Water washes against sand. Leaves scrape the ground. *We stand in the way of the wave. The wave surrounds us. Presses at our arms, our breasts. Enters our mouths, our ears.* The eardrum vibrates. Malleus, incus, stapes vibrate. *The wave catches us. We are part of the wave.* The membrane of the oval window vibrates. The spiral membrane in the cochlea vibrates. *We are set in motion by what moves outside our bodies.* Each wave of a different speed causes a different place in the cochlea to play. *We have become instruments.* The hairs lining the cochlea move. *We hear.* To the speed of each wave the ear adds its own frequency. *What is outside us becomes us.* Each cell under each hair sends its own impulse. *What we hear we call music. We believe in the existence of the violin. The steel string. The skin. Tongue. Reed. Wood. The curtain flapping in the wind. We take these sounds as testimony: violin, skin, tongue, reed exist. Our bodies know these testimonies as beauty.*

Ma Ma.   Da Da.   La le la le.   Mo Mon Po pon mah bowl ma ba ba me mommy me seepy ba now bye bye now baby now mommy now baby bankie bottie ca ca gah gr gr gr ma ma me my ma ma sleepy baby me sleep night night me baby mommy go bye bye say bye bye me

When she hears this cry she remembers smallness. Smallness rises up in her. Translucence of skin rises up in her. Her mother rises up in her. The taste of salt rises up in her. The taste of sweetness rises up in her. She thinks of the fragility of the inner ear. She thinks of death. She pokes her finger delicately, carefully, into the corpse of her own aged body, into the future. She thinks of the odor of feces. Of decaying leaves, the cast-off shell of the crab. Of the red membrane. Of the red bottom. The pulse in the skull. The moisture running off the back. The child's whole body. Smallness. Fitting against her forearm. Hand the size of her finger joint. She thinks of the redness inside, the wetness inside. She lifts the child's wet body to her. Under the child's weight and heat, her own body is moist. On the top of her skull, she thinks, was a membrane. With her two hands she makes an opening in the body of her mind to reveal what is vulnerable in her. The sound of her blood resonates. The sound of air enlarges her. Presses against her womb, presses against her vulva. She is small. She is infinitesimal. She is a small speck in darkness. In wet darkness. The darkness undulates. The darkness is hot against her. The darkness is growing, pressing into her. She is the darkness. She is heat. She grows. She presses the child's face to her face. Smallness—she closes her eyes in the softness—rises up in her. The child's fingers enter her mouth. The child's eyes stare into her eyes. This child vibrates through her. She knows this child.

The group velocity of waves. The period between one wave and another. Waves of waves. *We turned back to our mothers. We listened for the stories of their lives. We heard old stories retold.* The pitch. The volume. The timbre. *We heard again the story of the clean house, we heard again the story of the kitchen, the story of mending, the story of the soiled clothes.* The bell ringing.

The confluence of pitches in the ringing of the bell. The overtones *of the cries of birthing, the story of waking at night, the story of the shut door, the story of her voice raging, we heard again the stories of bitches.* Resonance, the fork of the same pitch humming in sympathy, the sympathetic wave.

We tried to recover them as girls. We sought them as daughters. We asked to be led into recesses, we wanted to revive what was buried, we sought our own girlhoods we had feared lost. The regular impulses, the steady pitch of the note. The octave. Harmony. *We heard the story for the first time that her mother's mother had brought her mother to a doctor, and we heard what the doctor had said to her mother, that this pain would teach her a lesson, we heard that before this her mother's mother had gone off by herself, had given a stillbirth, we heard the words* out of wedlock *we understood* Sound only a milder form of the shock waves made by explosions, by blasts. *why these stories had been kept from us* Sound one of the ways *we know how many stories* in which concentrated energy *are in this silence* diffuses itself about the world.

We say we have lost some of our mothers forever to this silence. We say we have found hatred in the mother for the daughter and in the daughter for the mother. We say of our mothers that parts of them are lost to us, that our mothers come back to us dismembered, that in the effort Waves *to recover them* from the friction on the bow of the string vibrating *we stand in danger* in the maple bridge, vibrating down the sound post *of losing ourselves* in the chamber of the body *or parts of ourselves* through the cells of the surrounding plane wood *in this whirlpool* shaped by the shape of the body *in the inherent lie of silence* outward into the air *that such stillness is not stillness* to reverberate to the shapes of walls *that this stillness is treachery* to resonate in the surrounding trees *that even as we find our daughters return to us* The waves *we recite again their names* the waves in the atom *saying that we cannot be complacent* the atom vibrates *nor stand still, that we must name every movement* that the smallest particle of matter is a vibration *that we must let our voices live within us* that matter is a wave, *that we survive by hearing.*

Pot of Tea

Our mother makes a pot of tea.
Watch this, she says,
It is a love affair.
When the leaves and the water meet
they see something in each other
they become alike.
She holds the tea cup close
to our noses.
A wet heat rises up in the
air and touches us.

Tissue

Our mother tells us it is time to clean up.
She gives us a box of tissue.
She shows us how to blow our noses.
If we weep a little
she makes us tell why
and dries our eyes.
If we go to the bathroom
she gives us tissue.
We have turned over
our glass of milk on the table.
Wipe she says.
Standing in a dark closet
she arranges the boxes in a tall pile.
The old tissue goes outside.
Into the fire, she says.

Teeth

She who usually feeds us
is in a bad mood.
Are you trying to eat me up?
she shouts.
She bares her teeth
and makes a low noise.
With a disgusted gesture
she tells us
Go study your manners.
And wipe your feet,
she adds.

Sitting

Our mother sits by the
pool,
reading her newspaper.
We are not to disturb her.
Love her as we do, we must not
tell her that now.
She is by herself.

If we glance sideways
from time to time
we can see beautiful expressions
pass over her face.
But we must not stare.

Distress

What would our mother say?
Where is our mother?
Does she know?
Does she know what is happening to us
here?
What will she do?
Will she save us? Will she come for us?
Does she know what happens to us
here?
Is it happening to her?
To her, to her, too?

Dogs

Don't be afraid, she tells us.
Don't let them best you.
We are trembling.
We have burst into tears.
Here, she says, *I've been afraid
once too,* she says
and there is another way up the hill.
She gives us water.
*Maybe you're not ready
yet,* she says to herself,
to face them.

The Awful Mother

The whole weight of history bears down
on the awful mother's shoulders.
Hiroshima, the Holocaust, the Inquisition
each massacre of innocents
her own childhood

and the childhood of her mother
and the childhood of her child.
What can she do?
She remembers.
The child's drawing, the lost
mittens, the child
cold, the awful mother shouting
the child's story of shadows
in her room, waiting
the awful mother
waiting, and *her* mother
waiting, the child already asleep
and the awful mother
knowing too late
the howling of children
in cattle cars and fires.
The wind blows so hard
it is as if the earth had fallen
on its side.
But nobody wakes up.
Only the awful mother stirs stricken
with grief.

The Perfect Mother

1.

The perfect mother lets the cat sleep
on her head. The
children laugh.
Where is she?
She is not in the sandbox.
She is not carefully ironing the starched
ruffles of a Sunday dress.
What does she say?
She does not speak.
Her head is under the cat and
like the cat, she sleeps.

2.

But her children are in a marsh!
Bogged, they have gone wild.
Yet, no one should worry.

See, they are there, in a sunny kitchen.
They drink cups of soup and wipe
their faces with yellow napkins.
What does it matter if
they are hatching plots, if
in their waking dreams
the poor cat is trapped
its hair
standing on end?

3.

Where shall we go? We ask the perfect
mother. What
do you want of us? She is no
where to be found.
Not in the cookie jar
we have broken to bits
not under the shiny kitchen floor
not on our lips.
Here we are transfixed,
mourning the perfect mother, and she
is caught in the trapped cat
of her children's dreams.

The Bad Mother

The bad mother wakes from dreams
of imperfection trying to be perfection.
All night she's engineered a train
too heavy with supplies
to the interior. She fails.
The child she loves
has taken on bad habits, cigarettes
maybe even drugs. She
recognizes lies. You don't
fool me, she wants to say,
the bad mother, ready to play
and win.
This lamb who's gone—
this infant she is
pinioned to—does not listen,
she drives with all her magic down a

different route to darkness where
all life begins.

My Child

My child deep in the
snow of illusion thinks she's
guilty (for more than can be
said) The argument, the loss, the
hesitation. What? A hatred here or there.
All terrible. All terrible
the things we know,
these things we never show
and children suffer.

Three Shades of Light on the Windowsill

I was already
years old when these things
began to happen to me which
must happen to every child.
As when her voice singing
turned my body
into a tremor in the
place where I stood
as when
reaching for myself
in the darkness
I became blood, as when
I woke saying
oh, surprised, it is
me, and delighted
by three shades of light
on the windowsill.

Joseph Stroud

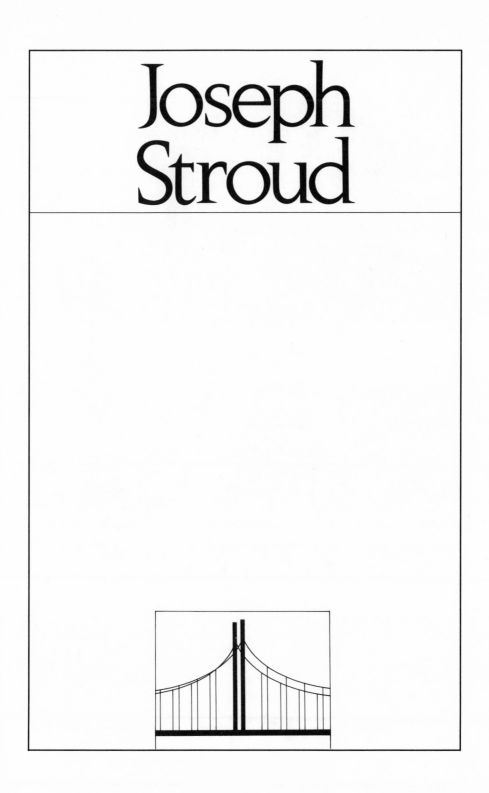

Joseph Stroud was born in Glendale, California, in 1943. He was educated at the University of San Francisco, California State University at Los Angeles, and San Francisco State University, where he received his B.A. and M.A. degrees. He has traveled in the South Pacific, Central and South America, Southeast Asia, India, Nepal, Afghanistan, Greece, Ireland, and Wales. He teaches at Cabrillo College and lives in Santa Cruz on the coast. He has published two books of poetry: *In the Sleep of Rivers,* and *Signatures.*

Geodes, Han-Shan, The Tehachapis, Rexroth: Some Fragments

When asked to write about my work as a poet, I think of a room in my grandfather's house where he kept some of the objects he had collected on his travels through the Southwest: animal skulls, fossils, shells, petrified wood, and numerous kinds of minerals and rocks. He had a fine collection of geodes—rather ordinary-looking stones, but when broken in half they reveal a hollow cavity lined with beautiful crystals. He called them "thunder eggs," and when I was a boy he had me convinced that they were the petrified eggs of dinosaurs. His favorite of the collection was the only one that had not been broken open. It was about the size of a cantaloupe, and you could feel the hollowness inside by the surprise of its weight when hefting it in your hands. Throughout my childhood I tried to talk him into breaking it in half, but he always refused.

Rilke in his "First Letter to a Young Poet" observes: "Things are not all so comprehensible and expressible as one would mostly have us believe; most events are inexpressible, taking place in a realm which no word has ever entered, and more inexpressible than all else are works of art, mysterious existences . . ." The poet's task: to translate experience into language, which then becomes a kind of transformation—its own substance, focused and elevated; something somehow worthy of our toil, a monument larger than the craft that gets us there. But the danger is to live for the work, the artifice, the poem or painting. To do that is to give way to the marketplace or careerism. The poem serves the life of the poet, and hopefully the life of its audience. I believe that poetry is a way into the world. In the writing of the poem I come to discover what I value and love, what there is to make my life worthy of. It's a humbling and surprising process. It goes beyond a felicity with words and a mastery of craft, into a new or renewed world. I think that to read Chaucer or Shakespeare or Whitman is to find within oneself the potential of the mind and heart at its best, something worthy of our praise and celebration. A way to reach through the tangle of grief and loss and horror, to frame what is important, to acknowledge and give shape to it in a form that pleases or disturbs as it instructs; something permanent.

Test the poem. In the dream the sky is filled with hundreds of planes, high up there, cruel slivers of silver, soundless, and the bombs are falling like rain. It is the end at last. I rush toward Ellen's house and little Sam, but suddenly there is the white flash and immense fireballs mushrooming everywhere. I awake, 3:00

A.M., and look up through the skylight into the night, alone, crowded with failure, loss, an incomprehensible world, deceit, bloodshed, betrayal. Turning on the light, I reach for a book of poems—opening it, measuring each word as way into the impossible, mute day ahead.

Han-shan. The poet as hermit. The pure life among a landscape of cliffs and river gorges. Clarity and light. Responsible to no one. Fashioning the pearl of the mind. The alluring life away from wife, children, friends, and job. To write poems out of the still life of nature. The other side of the heart. Full of solitude, difficulty, and patience. Learning to shape yourself to the gradual turning of the seasons. Looking back on what was. Tempering language as you build a fire out of pine needles and dry sticks. As China grows and collapses into empire. As Tu Fu makes the long, sickening march home among hostile soldiers; his shock and sadness upon discovering his starving family—and those hard poems that came after. Systole/Diastole. The tower and the city slums. The many different journeys, and the poems that help us on our way.

Our blood is red coral; we build a bridge over the abyss.
—Nikos Kazantzakis

Poets hope so much for their poems, and all the while the audience goes on with its usual life. I am told that poetry has never had a larger reading public than it has today. But the audience I see at readings consists mostly of other poets, or those who wish to write poetry, some students who are there because they are assigned to be there, and maybe a few critics sharpening their pens which they mistake for their wits. What does poetry have to do with the lives my students think they live?

Last year a friend wrangled me a field pass to take photographs at the Stanford-UCLA football game. So there I was at the focus of a bowl packed with 80,000 people watching 22 late adolescents trying to maneuver a ball from one end of a field to another, and wrack each other in the process. I had never seen the game from this angle. I thought how this scene was being multiplied a thousand times over in other stadiums across the country, and a million times again through television. And how it would be repeated the next day, and Monday night, and so on. I tried to imagine a half-time show featuring some mythic, very best poet of our time reading a few poems on a podium at the 50-yard-line.

Another scene. Calcutta, 1974. A city no one would believe could exist unless they had to live there. Perhaps a million people living only in the streets, whose yearly income doesn't exceed what you or I spend in the supermarket before Saturday night's dinner. I remember walking those seething streets with Pound's *ABC of Reading* tucked under my arm, wondering what on this earth poetry had to do with these people? (And I think about how many poets would phrase the question differently: "What do these people have to do with poetry?")

Games, crowds, the magnitude of suffering throughout the planet, the overwhelming weight of humanity. In the face of all that, where does the poem fit? What can it do?

On the death of one of his children, Issa wrote: "Yes, it is a dewdrop world . . . and yet . . . and yet." And yet there is a small, isolated part of each person where art, the poem, can and must live. It is that which the artist must hold on to, trust, and work out of. The poem, the painting, music, reaches out to the individual, private self, to where we live alone among the teeming world around us. I remember the Vietnam war and how helpless the government wanted me to feel in the face of the huge grinding war machine. I remember the only slogan that made sense to me at the time, and which still rings down through the years: "You end the war in Vietnam by ending the war inside yourself." All we have is our own life and our own sphere of influence. It is there where art lives and flourishes, in the personal moral world of each individual. It is there that the poem lives through us and touches the lives of others. I think that is the mystery and task of being an artist. Without it, the world is less, each heart diminishes, and the reptile governments with their deadly chaos have their way at last.

There are those to whom place is unimportant,
But this place, where sea and fresh water meet,
Is important . . .
                                    —Theodore Roethke

One of those places for me was the Tehachapi Mountains, a wilderness area at the southern tip of the Sierra range, where the mountains gradually descend into the Mojave Desert. Once or twice a year when I was a boy my family would stay in a group of hunters' cabins owned by friends of my father. It was a dry, barren landscape: canyons with huge outcroppings of granite, pine forests on the far ranges thinning down to jagged hills thick with thorn brush. At that time in the early '50s there were still glimpses of black bear and mountain lion, but the wildlife was never plentiful—mostly deer, coyotes, hawks and turkey vultures, jackrabbits, whiptails and horned toads, quail, bobcats, dove. There was something harsh and austere about the tone of that landscape. Even the light was hard, like quartz.

Sometimes in the late afternoons Henry Weldon, a Paiute who lived down near Jawbone Canyon, would ride his horse up to the cabins and spend a few hours drinking beer, telling stories and advising the hunters where to go to find the deer and quail that year. He worked for a cattle company and kept track of the various herds as they grazed up into the canyons. I always looked forward to his visits, and I cherished those moments when I could walk the canyons with him, for he brought the landscape into a human perspective, made it seem almost understandable.

And there were the other times, walking alone to the Indian burial ground on a hill overlooking a river gorge, or sitting with my grandfather down near the pond with its green frogs and dragonflies. It was during those moments that I first began to feel the world as a mystery and wonder, that I first sensed what Boehme calls sacramental signatures. I began to glimpse something larger than my own child's life, something that was unknown and mixed with awe and joy and tenderness. I still feel that landscape and mystery, as if it were etched in my blood. It is there where I try to measure the language of my poems.

Since this anthology focuses on poets associated in one way or another with Northern California, I would like to say a few words about a poet who has been intimately connected with that literary and natural landscape—Kenneth Rexroth. His involvement with the San Francisco Renaissance, the avant-grade, the Beat Movement has already been well documented, so what I would like to offer are simply some personal observations about him and the influence he has had on my own work.

Most of us have experienced those moments, when reading someone's poetry for the first time, of an immediate, pervasive recognition—a flowering of perception, and surprise. This happened to me in the early '60s when I first opened *Natural Numbers*. I had never encountered a poetry of such elegant, clear language—poems that moved quietly and carefully through a personal relationship with the natural world. But it wasn't simply "nature" poetry, a landscape set apart or divorced from how we live our lives in a complex, industrial civilization. Rexroth wrote out of a matrix flowing and interconnecting with philosophy, science, mathematics, the arts, intimate personal relationships, the turning seasons, time, social conditions and political events, death and love—the whole gestalt of what it is to be human and alive. Those poems enlarged my life.

There were also his translations, particularly of the Chinese and Japanese, which were to me an introduction to another kind of sensibility, radically different from the Donne and Pope and Milton and Eliot and Yeats that I had been schooled in. And they were peculiarly important to me because of the physical situation I felt a part of, being born and raised on the Pacific coast. Looking east —crowded with all that land, past the Sierras, the Rockies, the Midwest, New York and the Atlantic seaboard, all the history of America—somehow felt like looking backwards, towards some distant past. Looking west there was a vast, open, pure immensity of water and light, a place from where storms would rush or where the sun would go down in a melt of colors. It was a world of potential and possibility. And always, somewhere over there just beyond the end of things, was Asia—not so much the "mysterious East," but a world always at the outer limits of the imagination. And Rexroth brought that world home to me, made it a real and concrete place, something to connect with.

And there was Kenneth Rexroth the person as I witnessed him in various circumstances—cranky, erudite, pompous, tender, bullshitting, hipper-than-thou, wise, sensitive, English-tweeded, warm, generous, castigating, opinionated, suffering-no-fools, sad-blue watery-eyed, jiving, strong-jawed and joweled, presence.

In the mid '60s, Rexroth taught a class at San Francisco State College—a graduate seminar in the arts. I was one of the ten or so students in that class. It was a chaotic time—the careening Vietnam war, Free Speech and students' rights and the Student Strike, psychedelics and acid rock, People's Park, demonstrations, marches, draft card burnings, ecology, the Beatles, and Haight Street. As a teacher, Rexroth was frustrating. He held to the line that students should direct and infuse the class with what they thought was important or meaningful. Which was fine if the class was being taught by a dullish assistant professor who didn't have much to say anyway. But these were strange times, and as students we were curious to find out what he thought it all meant; perhaps he could help put it into some kind of perspective. It was all we could do to pry open a few anecdotes or so. We wound up making a film of some obscure Brecht play. In spite of his aloofness, there were times when he would open up and speak directly to us of his own values and concerns. And that's how I remember him as a man—sitting stiffly, uncomfortable, measuring each of us with his distant, sad-eyed face, speaking of individual responsibility and compassion, full of integrity and grace.

Sometimes in the mornings, Sam, 4 years old, sneaks out of Ellen's house, comes out to my shack and climbs into bed with me. We lie there and make up stories. What a lucid, simple kingdom, with the sun lancing through the skylight and the leaves of the walnut and cherry tree showering above us. A place set aside, for a while, from the harrowing, disinterested, and stumbling world. Outside, the breeze shuttles the leaves of the sunflowers, a sound like the ripping of parchment. The peach tree is heavy with ripening fruit and the cottonwood leafs with a green light. Honeysuckle vines through the lattice and bees swarm among the small blue flames of rosemary. Now and then we can hear the rifle-crack of walnuts dropping on the roof of the shack, or the high voices of children, Spanish and melodic, from the neighbor's yard. And I begin to think that time could not touch us, as I go on with the stories. That there is a language that could somehow nurture and preserve and help us to understand and love the world.

Grandfather

Now I see you
In a small California town
Asleep under fig trees, the black fruit
Swollen and ripe. Your shadow seems
To deepen on the morning grass as peppertrees
Scatter their leaves like rain
Or seeds.

I remember a summer morning
We sat on your porch, the warped boards
Pocked with holes and nails. The fields
Freshly cut. The pond rimmed with willows
And magnolias. You tried to tell me
Why my brown bitch had eaten her young.
It was a morning of bees.
I saw the light sing on their wings,
A mellow gold quaking into music.
You must have heard too
For when I turned you had fallen into a dream,
Your throat humming with veins.

Then I heard that other music. The cicadas.
The green frogs. My bones
Drained like the sap of trees
As I dreamed myself into the heart of the pond.
I forgot everything I ever learned.
Except your voice. Down there.
Singing of home, death, a blossoming tree.

Poem to My Father

Always
Always
Always
All ways I see are dark unto stone.
And if I should kneel in a field,
Shirt open, the sun on my shoulders,
Knife against my wrist,
Calling down black birds who shall love me,
Who *shall* love me? Father, let me sing,
Though blind, my eyes draw from yours

The light of age, poverty, a spirit
Looking for wings.
                        I took myself into language
Believing all the fables: the talking beasts,
The forests that rise and walk at night,
Until I felt all the world in me
Heave loose, fall
And fall deeper than dreams
Into dark. Alone, a room to myself,
I shaped my life into an ark. Ocean
Of silence, deep water, I want to love.
Father, let me learn, make me see
Our lives together. I am your flesh
As you are mine. Let us walk
Close to the earth.

Poem on the Suicide of My Teacher

We are the bees of the invisible—Rainer Maria Rilke

The secret lies in the egg of night—Loren Eiseley

1.

No moon No road No thunder
A white tree with black veins

Give me the ocean repeating the movement of my blood
Give me the bell that wakes the woman who bears the earth
Whose flesh is fruit split open to the moon
Whose life is a net of blue fish
Give me the strength of a root
For we've been hung on our ribs to die

Let my wound grow Round as the sun
Let me return my life to the spine of the stars
Let my language come home to its nest beside God

I am the wife of night
My throat falls with snow
My hands are a puzzle of water
My life bells like a candle plume

2.

Gordon is dead. Where
Do I place my grief? Lord,
It is time now. I hear a skull within a skull weeping.
I see the perfection of death.
It is a monkey claw at the throat of the moon.
I listen to my blood. Tonight.
The stars tell me nothing.

Mystery. We explored it in lab. The cadaver.
You naming all the organs, tissues, muscles, bones.
I saw your hand kneel in the chest of an old man
And raise out his shriveled heart.

"This is unreal," I said. And now
Your death is inside my head
Like a fist, clenching.

3.

Teacher
You gave me *The Immense Journey*.
So what was your own? Its end
Takes me to an abandoned road when I was 9 years old:
A meat truck with its back doors sprung open,
And emerging from the shadows in the back,
Two cops holding between them a man
With his throat cut open, the blood gushing
In heart bursts. I entered another kingdom
That day. A railroad bridge where I used to climb
Under the beams among the pigeon nests.
I cradled in my hand a thin, blue-speckled egg
As a train screamed over the tie-bars and rails,
Darkening the light over me, until it simply
Disappeared. Dust sifted onto my hair,
Onto the broken, drooling egg. I wept.

4.

You are the son of a bitch that broke the circle
Around the house that kept the flame
To feed the sons you left
To bear your death.

May their lives quicken into blinding mirrors.
May they find some help on their own dark day.

5.

You move away, Gordon. Tomorrow you will be less,
And less each day. Until only your wild Irish grin
Will glimmer, silked, webbed in memory, that spider,
The mother of my language that recalls
And calls you: Teacher Alcoholic Suicide

What kind of breast or egg were those bottles
You sucked on? Even the final image. A shotgun
Among the digs. Among the scattered bones and beads
Of Indians dead for centuries. So what
Was your final lesson?

The earth of Soquel is black in Autumn.
The corn stalks are dry, withered old men.
This morning I dug a grave for a rabbit.
Each shovel I gouged with fury, and grief,
Thinking the earth was your chest,
Hoping to wound your dead heart. To find it.
To open a vault in you, as the one in me.

Monte Albán

Monte Albán
                In the ruins at night
Lights in the valley of fires

The wind among the stones
Fireflies flickering over the ground
In the mist
And softly under those small lanterns of light
Illuminations
The tarantulas moved
                Ghosts of black hands through the ruins

Oaxaca Oaxaca

Poem to Han-shan

Often in this life
I think of you—
Marriage broken, sick of the world,
Making the treacherous journey to Cold Mountain.

You came closer than any of us
To stone, stream, cloud,
To the pearl of the mind.
30 years alone with silence,
Cliffs,
Your laughter and tears.
The Governor who expected wisdom
Sent his aides ahead
Bearing gifts and medicine.
Oh Han-shan, screaming "Thieves! Thieves!"
Before you disappeared
                          Into the mountain.

Lament

Because the moon became my mother
No need to weep
Because the tree broke open its honey
No need to weep
Because the blade always finds the heart
No need to weep

To Christopher Smart

I will praise Christopher Smart
For his life was a flame unto the Beloved
For he wrote with a key on the madhouse wall
For he slept in class and taught in the tavern
For his secret name was Mother Midnight
For he knelt in the street and asked strangers to join him
For he sang out of poverty and debt
For he saw the Lord daily and drank with him often
For in his nature he quested for beauty
    And God, God sent him to sea for pearls

Exile

Hommes, ici n'a point de mocquerie;
Mais priez Dieu que tous nous veuille absouldre
—François Villon

Ten years Villon lived in a small village
Outside Paris. Often the Pastor
Watched him walk from the square
To the graveyard under Gallow Hill.
But no one saw Villon steal the Eucharist
And eat the wafer in his dirty room
With the peasant girl, half-dressed,
Mindless in the heat, sweating and moaning
Under the sentence and law of that Medieval light.

Memory

For Tim

It is dusk
On the bridle path that wanders
Through the Griffith Hills.
Two boys walk, arm
In arm, under the branches of oak,
Madrone, and pine.
They are brothers going home
Before the sun goes down.
Walk with them. See
How the smaller, younger one
Stretches his stride to keep
Beside the other. They
Talk quietly
Having spent the day for snakes
In the hills behind the bales of hay
Slit with arrows the grown-ups shoot
For sport or hope. Why
Do they stop before a tree
Swarming with bees?
In the gnarled roots they see
An emerald lizard with spines
Down its back. Don't wake them.
It's no dream as they dream

A kingdom to allow such a beast.
Crowned and golden, they continue
Home, a sound of bells,
In the huge, quiet night.

Dragon

All day the sun builds its temple
                              though we perish
In that shining. Rilke in the rose garden
Discerned his paradise in the quiet vault of blooms
As the thorn brightened his blood
And the architecture of light began its walls
Around his brief and singing house.
                    Even the great beast elephant
Follows the lava flow where the earth gives up
Its sweetest grass. And at the *masuku*,
Tangled with growth, the odorless gas seeping
From fissures, he eats and breathes until the tower
Legs fold, and the whole hulk
                              topples down.
Vultures, jackals, the aardwolves who come to feed
On the carcass, stagger and collapse
In the corrupting air.
                    So the earth leaks
Its poison. And the silent, alien sun
Gives no sign to those voices
Down there, looking up, crying and reaching
As they go under.

Below Mount T'ui K'oy, Home of the Gods, Todos Santos Cuchumatán, Guatemalan Highlands

He stumbled all morning through the market,
Drunk and weeping, a young Mayan whose wife
Had died. Whenever he encountered someone he knew,
He'd stop and wail, waving his arms, and try
To embrace them. Most pushed him away,
Or ignored him. So he'd stand there like a child,
Forlorn, his face contorted with grief,
Lost among the piles of corn and peppers,
The baskets of bananas, avocados, and oranges,

The turkeys strung upside down, the careful
Pyramids of chicken eggs, the women
In their straw hats and rainbow *huipils*,
The men smoking cornsilk cigarettes,
Meat hanging from the butchers' stalls
(chorizo, goat heads, tripe, black livers),
As everyone talked, laughed, or bartered,
And young boys played soccer in the courtyard,
The Roman priest, like a thin raven, elbowing
His way through the crowds, rain clouds
Swarming from far down the coast, the sun
Shattered among the pines on the high ranges,
And weaving through all of it the sound
Of women who sang over a corpse in an earthen house,
Keening a music like distant surf breaking
Within the very heart of the mountain.

Signature (II)

All morning he lay in the tight, dark room,
His head resting on a porcelain block
As the tattooed boy fixed the opium
And held the pipe over a flame.
                          Then out
Into the heavy Calcutta sun, the light pouring
Onto the courtyard where women in magenta saris
Washed clothes against a red mud wall.
And where the corpse of a man sprawled over a chair—
Just there—naked, spider-boned, stiff.
He stood a long time gazing at the bizarre,
Angular posture.
               So that is paradise,
He thought, caught in the flood of light and heat.
A bright cloud swirling around a blazing tree.
The golden linkage of order. A precise,
Jeweled machine oiled with music. The cold,
Marble palace inlaid with lapis lazuli, agate,
Mother of pearl. And all of it shining. The bones
Gathering out of the earth, dancing
And burning before the tusked, goat-faced beast
Gorged on meat. He thought.
                    Until the landscape
Altered, and everything began to crack

And flake like a painting, the colors
Washing out, the Signature disappearing
Down the road with those Bengali men
Squabbling and laughing as they pushed
And pulled a cart full of dung.

Documentary

Bring the camera closer in. Focus
On the burning *ghat*. They've finished
The ceremony around the body, and are torching
The wooden pyre. See how the tongues of flame
Rise from the limbs. Zero in on the head—
I want you to catch the skull when it bursts.
Pan down the torso, the spine in ashes, the hips
Crumbling. Then dolly back for the scenic shot—
The Ganges flowing past. But keep the tension
Sharp, you might catch the silhouette
Of a river dolphin. Filter the lens
To bring the blue out of the mud-silt.
Now zoom down to the middle of the river,
That small boat, the boatman dumping a child
Overboard. Get his flex of muscle
As he struggles with the stone tied to the corpse.
Then back to the panorama, the vista. The storm
Rushing in. The lightning flashing far off
Over the river palace. The silver drizzle
Of rain. The quiet glow on the water.

Signature (III)

Tsangyang Gyatso was twelve years old
When they claimed him the new Dalai Lama.
Too late, for he had learned to love this world.
I can see him in the great palace at Lhasa
Standing among the strict monks and the immense
Hanging tanka of Vajrasattva. Each day
He performed the service and tended the spirit.
But at night he would slip out of the chambers
And steal down to the little town of Sho.
There in that warm, yellow room the women
Would undress for his pleasure.

Broken
From the continual divorce within, he wrote
His tiny poems of love. And one day left Lhasa,
Disappeared, to wander the ice and cliffs,
A beggar for the rest of his life.
                              Each year
In his mountain kingdom a tower festival
Is performed: the delicate Buddha paradise
Carved from blocks of frozen butter. At dawn
Amid the chanting, the turning prayer wheels,
They are tossed into fire and all our butter dreams
Rush out in flames.
                    Tsangyang Gyatso,
Your laughter was like a mountain, your weeping
Was a dragon with wings. You knew more than any of us
That such is the Signature of all things.

The Room Above the White Rose

This steaming night in Vientiane. A filthy room,
The Laotian girl gone, lice in the bedsheets,
The Mama-san downstairs counting the money
And the hours. Outside, gunboats cruise the Mekong.
The Pathet Lao and Royalist troops stroll the streets,
Forever divorced in their deadly politic.
                              All night
I listen to Rachel's voice on the tape,
Remembering those first years when we held
And held each other through the mornings, the orchard
Blossoming around us, the strawberries ripe
And blazing in the field.
                    And I think of that other marriage:
The monkey-rope hooked from Ishmael to Queequeg
As he sloshed over the dead hulk of whale,
All around him the sea rioting with waves and sharks.
All night the tape goes on, Rachel's words deepening
With the hours, the batteries running down,
The sound going bestial, disembodied,
                              fading
Into the laughter and cursing of the soldiers
And whores leaving the White Rose, and mixing
With the faint, otherworld song of monks
Chanting in the Dragon Temple at dawn.

City

Of course the heart is nothing
But muscle and blood, a chambered organ
The size of your fist, prone to attack
And failure. We can't include it
In modern poems, having given up
That old cadence for this slaughtered prose.
Once the heart was like a city,
Medieval, the cobbled streets led down
To the slums near the river. At night
Thieves were about. There's a butcher shop
By the stable where in the morning you can hear
The high screams of pigs as they are holstered
From the ceiling and their throats slit.
It's snowing now and there is a crowd gathered
Around the gallows as the Bishop in his gold robe
Forgives a sinner in the name of a greater King
Than the one in the castle on the hill,
That feeble old man who sits among his tapestries
Alone and afraid. Far off you can hear the airs
Of a minstrel singing *timor mortis conturbat me.*
And there are rumours going around:
Of strange inventions—glass which magnifies
The face in the moon—of wondrous, far off lands,
Cities made of gold, treasures of silk and spices,
Talking beasts, the rare unicorn. But here
The peasants are hungry, revolt is in the air.
An old man in a cluttered, upper room of the city
Sits at his desk and turns in his hands
The puckered, toad-like remains of a human heart,
And begins to calculate through reason and observation
Alone, how everything in God's earth or heaven
Can be known.

Sibyl

All morning the beast labors up from the valley
As the loud, black bees crash from sage to crown.
Beetles hunt in the thick honeyvines, in the rotting
Pulp of grapes and figs. The animal
Continues to climb the steep, winding path.

From this distance you can discern something
Clinging to its back. A stone stands up
And scatters off, stops, and turns its black,
Lizard eye.
                    Closer now, you can make out
A hooded figure riding a mule
As the hard *chin-chink*
                    chin-chink of hooves
Breaks through the insect drone. Everything
Quiets down. Even the pollen spiders crouch
Deeper in the blooms. The sun honeys
The earth, the heat weighs down like a mountain
As the beast comes on
                    bearing the rigid, black-shawled
Old woman,
            and they continue past into the high gorge,
The Voice shriveled and mute
Among the sheer, granite cliffs above Delphi.

As for Me, I Delight in the Everyday Way

—Han-shan

Each day the earth turns, each day
The sea rises, all the days the seasons
Are, the small lemon in its own time,
A face turning from the window in an old house,
The song we can always
Almost hear.
                    There's a poetry to this life
No one will be able to write.
The horses come down the mountain at dusk.
We've all seen this. But who gives thanks?
And what about the lemon. When was the last time
Anyone brought that sweetness
                    to their face?
Of each loss there is an opening.
To find a voice for love is a way
Of loving.
How all the deaths and griefs rush out of you
When you hold the little lemon in the cup
Of your hand. How easy it is to forget

These poor daily rags we wear
Shine brighter than the silks of kings.

Naming

For Sam Scott

Summer in the Tehachapi Mountains.
A broken waterwheel, its scoop-troughs
Splintered and empty. Rabbit brush.
Owl's clover. And Grandfather near the pond
Pointing out the names of things—
Cottonwood, manzanita, rose quartz, quail—
His voice full of tenderness.
It was the first time I ever knew sound
As a kind of recognition or praise.
                              Near the end
Of his life, a stroke took away his speech.
He would sit on the porch, mute, and watch
The sun wear down the day.
                         But I remember
The summers when we picked filaree
And stuffed them in our pockets
Where they coiled like clock springs.
We'd stroll back to the cabin at dusk.
Once we stayed late, watching dragonflies
Dip over the pond. It was dark
By the time we reached the porch.
We could hear the men talking inside
And smell the potatoes and onions frying
In the black skillet. He put his arm around
My shoulder, and we looked up into the deep
Catch of night, as slowly he began to name
The far off, alien stars.

Proportions

For years I've lived with Breughel's painting
The Harvesters' Meal. At first I noticed just
The obvious. The men and women in the foreground,
Sitting on wheat sheaves, eating their simple meal
Of cheese and gruel. The pensive, sad-eyed man

Slicing bread, the woman lifting a pitcher of water
To her mouth.
                    Then I moved on to the wheat fields,
The straw colors. The man with his curved scythe
Slashing the long stalks. Another man lugging
Heavy water jugs in each hand. Three women,
With sheaves on their shoulders, walk on a path
That will lead past the thatch-roofed houses
Toward a grove of trees where the tower of a church
Juts into the sky.
                    For a long time I watched the dog
Back in the foreground. A spaniel of sorts,
Sniffing the earth, its white tail rigid.
                                        Slowly
I became attracted to the expressions on faces.
The exhaustion of work on a summer day. The openness
In the heavy-lidded eyes. I kept wanting to see
The face of the young woman with her back to me.
Deeper in the painting two people greet
And talk. A man and woman, I think.
Behind them are two locust trees suffused with light,
Branches and leaves intermingled.
                              That held my attention
For a year. I started to consider color,
How it blended from the greens of the forest
Into the gold and amber of the fields,
The blue sky mottled with dust.
I began to dwell on balance, harmony, the music
Of landscape and work, the burden of earth,
Excess, and pleasure. The long, difficult craft
Of living.
            Recently I've been following
The road in the right background, the way
It rounds a small hill and disappears
Into what I imagine is a valley. Always
The other landscape the heart dreams
And yearns for. A place where we could dwell,
And trust, and walk on through a world
Renewed and fresh as far as the mind
Can create.

Above Machu Picchu,
129 Baker Street, San Francisco

In memory of Bob Waters, murdered on the Avenues

Fifteen years ago I awoke
In a San Francisco room and understood
For the first time that I—and everyone
I knew—was truly alone. I looked
At the wall, the ashes in the fireplace,
The iguana in its glass cage, the floor
Scattered with poems. I got up,
Walked into the kitchen, and gazed out
Over the backyards toward the Panhandle
As one by one in the old Victorian houses
The lights came on.
                         I didn't understand my grief,
Nor could I foresee how the years would lead me
Here, to these stone peaks in the Andes, looking
Down on the ruins of the last Inca city,
The broken terraces and moon temple of Machu Picchu,
As the sun seethes over the jungle and snow fields.
Nor how I have come to see that love can be
A way of learning how, and what, to praise
As I do now
                that distant morning
In that long ago room.

The Gold Country:
Hotel Leger, Mokelumne Hill, Revisited

The sound of rain on the roof was too loud.
I knew someone was making love in the next room.
I remembered all those years walking with Rachel
Through the orchard, the pine forest near Uruapan,
The stones and wheat and white Greek chapels of Karpathos,
Walking, it seemed, as if there was some place to get to.
I could feel the city begin to break apart,
All the careful bridges, the pavilions and lanes,
That fine old hotel with its marble floors
And ebony stairs, the quiet rooms with their windows
Overlooking the river, the snowy egrets, a lifetime

In praise of something larger than my life,
Crumbling.
　　　　　I got up and washed my face, stood looking
In the mirror looking back into the room, the rain
Louder now, wondering when I would leave, how
I would go out the door into the other city,
Making my way, building this time within me
A simple bare room, no window, an empty book
Of white pages, and a bed for sleeping.

Machupuchare.
What the Mountain Said.
Shaking the Dead Bones, Christmas Eve, 1974

Given the morning, its rush of flowers
Given the sun, flamehole, burning and breathing
Given the wall with its long skeleton
Given each day the quick tunnel into the grave
Given the marriage bed, its flowers and fire
Given no choice but to sing as the axe falls
Given an image of Akbar, his palace in ruins
Given night, its revels, the flesh carnival
Given the moon, the sickle sweeping
Given silence, no words, and no mouth to speak
Given this labyrinth of stars, a cave as beginning
Given a crown, its jewels your years

Now throw the dice
　　　　　　　and tell me, Joseph,
Where is paradise?

Michael Palmer

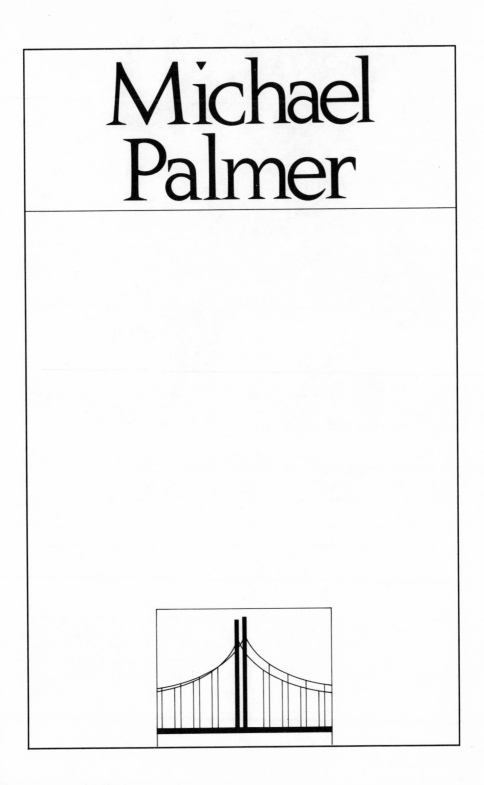

Born New York City 1943, down the block from the Gotham Book Mart. While at Harvard College edited *Joglars* magazine with Clark Coolidge. Graduate work in comparative literature at the University of Florence and Harvard. Moved to San Francisco in the fall of 1969. Since 1974 has collaborated on over a dozen works with Margaret Jenkins and the Margaret Jenkins Dance Company, as well as with a number of performance artists and composers. National Endowment for the Arts Fellowship in 1975. Radio plays, *Idem* I–IV produced for KQED radio in 1980. Books and chapbooks include *Plan of the City of O* (Barn Dream Press, 1971), *Blake's Newton* (Black Sparrow Press, 1972), *C's Songs* (Sand Dollar Press, 1973), *The Circular Gates* (Black Sparrow Press, 1974), *Without Music* (Black Sparrow Press, 1977), *Transparency of the Mirror* (Little Dinosaur Press, 1980), *Alogon* (Tuumba Press, 1980), *Notes for Echo Lake* (North Point Press, 1981). Some of his translations appear in *The Selected Poetry of Vicente Huidobro* (New Directions, 1981) and *The Random House Anthology of 20th Century French Poetry* (1982). He is currently a contributing editor to *Sulfur* magazine and a member of the faculty of the poetics program at New College of California. He is married to the architect Cathy Simon and has one daughter, Sarah.

From the Notebooks

A Preliminary Note

More than anything else these brief notebook excerpts reflect my interest in the generative semantic function of the poem and the polysemous, often veiled nature of poetic meaning. The poem as an act of signification then, a complex (or radically simple?) gesture of disclosure and withholding which derives from yet exists somewhere apposite to our everyday discourse. As should be evident my work does not "frame experience" according to any traditional mimetic model, nor does it generally follow a linear path. Its heuristic impulse often seems to bring into question the character of the first-person (the so-called "speaker") as well as the linguistic sign itself. From one point of view it could be said to risk its own dissolution as it proceeds, yet it could equally be said that any poetry wishing to transcend an acculturated, decorative role does the same. Threads of speech and constellations of sound would appear to inform the work, rather than a single, unitary voice. Its coherence, if a reader will grant it coherence, seems less a matter of aesthetic strategies (or affective devices) than of inhabiting the text, the words of the text in the world, and responding to its implications as it unfolds. It becomes an act of attention in which a reader must fully share if the work is to be realised.

I have drawn only from notebooks kept while I was at work on *Notes for Echo Lake,* and the selections might be taken as a parallel text addressing similar concerns in a different mode. In paring down the "days" of the notes for this context I have entirely left out a number of areas of concern. The largest omission would be the notes on dance for my ongoing collaboration with Margaret Jenkins and her company. I have also left out the notes on a sequence of radio plays, talks, etc., which would form the truer map of my activity and thinking during the period. As a reader and writer outside of the academy I have the luxury of wandering quasi-randomly among fields of interest—linguistics, language philosophy, musical and mathematical theory, detective novels, nature writing, psychology, and so on. My notebooks display this scatter. They are a congeries of quotations, source material, reflections and inchoate writings, a kind of thief's journal or maybe more accurately, a game of blind man's buff played among ghosts.

From the Notebooks

25 aug 77
"I use "virtue" in what I take to be Plato's and Aristotle's sense: a capacity
by virtue of which one is able to act successfully, to follow the distance from
an impulse and intention through to its realization."

—Stanley Cavell, "Music Discomposed"

11 sept 77
"You think that after all you must be weaving a piece of cloth: because you
are sitting at a loom—even if it is empty—and going through the motions of
weaving."

—Wittgenstein, *Philosophical Investigations*, I-414

19 sept 77
"I have never supposed a poem to be organic at all. I don't think the thing
grows, it's built and put together by a craftsman . . ."

—Bunting interviewed in *Montemora*

21 sept 77
Why do I so determinedly disregard experience *per se* as 'materia poetica';
i.e., this seems an instinct of mine from the beginning of any writing—as if
fearful that such a focus might qualify an immediate engagement with
language-as-object, with some notion, obviously idealised, of 'pure'
imagination. *Yet* experience is complexly present, generally after passing
through filters additional to those with which it is always engaging—
                    i.e.,
language *both* as filter and as instrument by which filter (veil) is lifted.

25 oct 77
Gadamer, "the essential self-forgetfulness that belongs to language."

12 nov 77
This time when I'm moving or at least feel that I'm moving out of
confusion into work—how everything I read explodes off the page and
equations continuously present themselves—how in an almost literal sense
world becomes *book*.

              As opposed to those times when such information feels
unavailable, utterly.

***

"Here we have a sort of mathematics of colour."

—Wittgenstein, *Remarks on Colour*, III-3

***

Isn't part of my attraction to L.W. that he has eliminated those things I
(once?) wanted to eliminate from 'prose fiction': character, description and

---

. . . fiction? Might not Beckett be considered closer to L.W. than to most prose writers of this century?

***

"Man muss immer gefasst sein, etwas *gänzlich* Neues zu lernen."
—*Colour*, III-45

14 nov 77
"vois ci"
—Royet-Journoud, *Le Travail du Nom*

5 dec 77
"Cézanne—The Late Work" at MOMA today—it could have consisted of one painting; or one painting and one of the watercolor sketches—that is, one could enter at any point and fill the entire span of attention . . . Point being that it *never* wavers, never gives in to easy effect, never settles for itself . . .

***

The notion for example of composition with nothing at its center—with *nothing* at its center.

19 dec 77
Macksey (*Structuralist Controversy*) on poem as both constatory and performative utterance.

23 jan 78
Sarah at the verge of first speech—imitating sounds, phonemes, with full "consciousness" of the game—is there any way to tell when the line has been crossed. (Since in a sense there is "language" from the first moment.)

29 jan 78
N.B. Sol LeWitt's insistence that his work is *intuitive*, for all the mathematical and logical implications it might generate.
His sense of *system*
and of transcending individual "taste" as a value. (Does he?)

25 april 78
"Symmetry occurs in all the arts as they develop. It is usually present in some form in most good poetry . . ."
—Zukofsky in *Prepositions*

25 may 78
"Right from the beginning, ideas concerning emanation were closely bound up with a theory of language . . . The process by which the power of emanation manifests itself from concealment into revelation is paralleled by

Michael Palmer · 343

the manifestation of divine speech from its inner essence in thought, through sound that as yet cannot be heard, into the articulation of speech."

—Scholem, "Sefirot," in *Kabbalah*

8 july 82
Matisse interviewed by Apollinaire, "I have never avoided the influence of others. I would have considered this a cowardice and a lack of sincerity toward myself." (1907)

***

"The importance of an artist is to be measured by the number of new signs he has introduced into the language of art . . ."

—Matisse

13 july 78
Beckett to Lowenfels, "Walter, all I want to do is sit on my ass and fart and think of Dante."

***

Number of publishers who rejected *Murphy:* 42

28 aug 78
Hermes-the-Whisperer, father of Eros.

9 nov 78
"Man lives with his objects chiefly—in fact, since his feeling and acting depend on his perceptions, one may say exclusively—as language presents them to him. By the same process whereby he spins language out of his own being, he ensnares himself in it; and each language draws a magic circle around the people to which it belongs, a circle from which there is no escape save by stepping out of it into another."

—Von Humboldt, quoted by Cassirer in *Language and Myth*

29 nov 78
"All poetry is experimental poetry."
"Things seen are things as seen."
"Sentimentality is a failure of feeling."

—Stevens, *Adagia*

30 nov 78
"The point is that poetry is to a large extent an art of perception and that the problems of perception as they are developed in philosophy resemble similar problems in poetry. It may be said that to the extent that the analysis of perception in philosophy leads to ideas that are poetic the problems are identical."

—Stevens, "A Collect on Philosophy"

"beautiful songs are the thing intended"
>—Lyn Hejinian, *Writing Is an Aid to Memory*

13 dec 78
Mandelstam on "easily assimilated poetry, a henhouse with a fence around it, a cosy little corner where the domestic fowl cluck and scratch about. This is not work done upon the word but rather a rest from the word."
>—quoted by Monas in intro to *Selected Essays*

***

"In poetry only the executory understanding has any importance and not the passive, the reproducing, the paraphrasing understanding . . ."
>—Ibid., "Conversation with Dante"

21 dec 78
Problematic nature of *Notes for Echo Lake 6*—don't try to alter that. Instead work within it if possible. Keep questions of form open.

5 jan 79
Returning to Hermann Weyl's sense of primary numbers presenting "problem of cognition in its simplest form"—doesn't this apply to aspect of the poem as a "crossing of number and imagination"?

9 jan 79
Michael Davidson on Stein in *Language 6*, ". . . we must discover language as an active "exchange" of meaning rather than a static paradigm of rules and features . . ."

***

Feeling now that I need to complete *Notes for Echo Lake* even though it includes sense of itself as a failed work, or work of evasion and inconsistency—
>are not those two qualities lovely possibilities?

17 jan 79
Re notion of "savour" as central to poetry in the Vedas (c. 2000 B.C.). N.B. difference between "savour" and taste + the "gai saber," "gaya scienza" of the troubadours.

1 feb 79
Talking here with Clark Coolidge until 3 a.m., re nature of our work and our working, in particular how we both have moved into areas of statement that previously we might have thought to exclude because too "direct" or "oracular" or whatever . . . How we both work outside or around "territory of ideas" and deny strategies.

6 feb 79

Zukofsky's equation, love/reason:eyes/mind. "Only when eye and mind were as one would love flourish with reason."

—Seidman

13 feb 79

"For I had placed myself behind my own back, refusing to see myself."
—Augustine, *Confessions*, VIII.7

14 feb 79

"My memory also contains my feelings."

—*Ibid.*, X.14

15 mar 79

Barthes' point that relationship of signifier and signified is one of equivalence, not equality. Relationship not of sequential ordering, but a unifying *correlation*.

***

N.B. Umberto Eco's sense of an "aesthetic idiolect" that takes into account rule-breaking functions of ambiguity and self-reference as organized in a work of art. Thus the "special language" (?) of art as it endlessly moves beyond each established level of meaning the moment it is established.

Both

beauty and danger of this are obvious.

***

Barthes in *S/Z*, "By increasing one's knowledge of codes, the aesthetic message changes one's view of their history and thereby trains semiosis." As Hawkes notes, art then represents not the "mere 'embroidery' of reality, but a way of knowing it . . . and of changing it."

22 mar 79

What is the quality of song that enforces (reinforces) silence, e.g., cricket song?

19 april 79

"denn wir leben wahrhaft in Figuren"

—Rilke, *Orpheus*, 1.12

26 april 79

With Robert Duncan today talking about "unknown" and "unknowable"— how artist is willing to enter unknown territory to arrive at unknowable (which *remains* unknowable—i.e., nothing is "solved" by that event).

23 may 79

"Ce n'est qu'en quittant une chose que nous la nommons." (Gide in conversation with Benjamin, 1928.)

26 may 79
Marx in the *Rheinische Zeitung*, "form is of no value unless it is the form of its content."

30 may 79
"Where one is is in a temple that sometimes makes us forget that we are in it. Where we are is in a sentence."

—Spicer, Heads of the Town

***

N.B. Marx and Engels' "principle of contradiction" whereby the political views of the author may run counter to what the author objectively reveals.

And the notion that there *are* moments in history when the most significant art will (of that moment's necessity) be politically committed—and other times when great art may well not be.
And Engels' point that however highly mediated in relation to its economic base, art is also *part of* that economic base. There is always an aspect of the art as a product within a given system . . .

—v. Eagleton

8 june 79
". . . the arbitrariness of language conventions seems to diminish as the text becomes more deviant and ungrammatical, rather than the other way around."

—Rifaterre

18 june 79
"Mediation, which is the immediacy of all mental communication, is the fundamental problem of linguistic theory, and if one chooses to call this magic, then the primary problem of language is its magic. At the same time the notion of the magic of language points to something else: its infiniteness. This is conditional on its immediacy . . ."

—Benjamin in Reflections

***

Naming as essential language function.
Name = "the language of language."
N.B. Benjamin's sense of naming as translation . . . It proposes a prior "paradisiac language of names," pre-lapsarian. Language as both communication of the communicable and symbol of the noncommunicable.

20 july 79
Less and less does a poem seem to exist "as an object"—rather it is various, mutable, etc. . . .

but it does respect objects in the world for the potential clarity of their presence, without benefit of sentimental redecoration.

In a sense too it can be said to make common objects visible (remarkable) that might otherwise be taken for granted. W.C.W. understood this & L.Z., and it is not to be confused with the hourly epiphanies of post-Williams writers who grow ecstatic each time they find a plum in the refrigerator.

9 aug 79
Valéry (as quoted by Philip Guston), "A bad poem is one that vanishes into meaning."

***

Sarah early this morning demonstrating:

> "Jumping Magic"
> "Purple Gum Magic"
> "Lollipop Magic"

12 aug 79
The sense of stilted literary contrivance in so many of Auden's "big" poems —sounding as if they were written to be framed (or written with frame already attached) for literary anthologies, e.g., the Yeats elegy or "September 1, 1939." The dependence on homily . . . that comes to mark so much literacher of the *Partisan Review* and so on, the self-styled authoritative periodicals—i.e., journals which expend most of their energy ascribing authority to themselves.

20 sept 79
Robert Smithson, "My memory becomes a wilderness of elsewheres."

26 oct 79
Wittgenstein in letter to Russell, "Identity is the very Devil."

7 nov 79
"The sign for the tree, and not the sign that other artists may have found for the tree . . ."

—Matisse, interviewed by Aragon

8 nov 79
Today writing *Notes* . . . 4 again—odd how what will appear simplest to many readers is generally most difficult to get right, most elusive—this being c. 4th time I've written it, and how many to follow? (Question of finding its necessary form . . .)

***

"In writing I am not but am writing."
    —Duncan, *Writing Writing* (from his reading tonight at the Art Institute)

Art Blakey (*Down Beat* interview, Nov 79): "Most kids when they play soft lose the intensity of the beat, plus they drop the tempo. When they play loud again, they pick the tempo back up, so the tempo is going up and down and nothing is settled."

"Sid Catlett and Chick Webb told me long ago to learn how to space my energy—space it. Sid Catlett was a huge man—he was big. He'd sit at the drum and make it sound like a butterfly—so pretty—it had nothing to do with loudness."

"The first time I saw Wilbur Ware in Chicago I saw him playing on the street with a washtub, mop stick and rope. He had sneakers on with Coca Cola bottle tops stuck into the rubber, and he was dancin' on the street . . ."

26 feb 80
"An artist should observe nature but never confuse it with painting. It is only translatable into painting by signs. But such signs are not invented. To arrive at the sign, you have to concentrate hard on the resemblance. To me surreality is nothing, and has never been anything but this profound resemblance, something deeper than the forms and the colors in which objects present themselves."

—Picasso in conversation with Brassaï

11 mar 80
Is *Echo Lake* now beginning to feel like a book? How many layers must there be?

20 mar 80
Hanns Eisler quoting Hölderlin in an interview, "Our singing is not powerful but it is part of life."

28 mar 80
"There is no longer anything that is unthematic."

—Adorno, *Philosophy of Modern Music*

8 aug 80
For the *I* & the *I-Thou* in poetry, discourse is the model; it manifests and remanifests the complexity of "identity" and its ultimate merging with others in a pattern of mutual translation and exchange. It emphasizes the establishment of a semantic whole through the receiver. Even the most "private" and "personal" utterance manifests this dependence—perhaps more so—since it elicits the fullest act of reading in order to come into meaning; and with its heightened ambiguity and range of possible readings it *stands for* its own polysemousness and variability.

***

Jakobson's plea that we see the grammar of poetry as the poetry of grammar
. . . how it enters recesses of language . . . how a "literary work internalizes
its criteria of coherence."

—v. Steiner, On Difficulty

6 nov 80
"Whoever cannot sing, dies." Siberian proverb.

Changes Around the Bay

In this kind of weather
my name is Martha

Yesterday afternoon
you changed your own

to Tom. Ron
became Joan. John

became our neighbor
He's going to become

a lawyer
and Dick just bought

a twenty-foot boat
with no sails

Before that
he made a list

of the chambers in the brain
of our cat. When Harriet

was eighty
she lost her right leg

in a sexual accident
with the bottom man

of a human pyramid
Now the bay

is beginning to change
The distance

across the bridge
is the same

It's also greater
than before

we came
It's also later

The Classical Style

It seems they never complete these things

The body flown back from Rome
Those are samples of her blood

taken from his sleeve. Blue yes

but also white, also cylindrical
the tiles apparently brown

about four inches square
and a path worn into them

leading toward a door
or away from a door. Now it's finished

and the cat is dead
to be replaced by another cat

cream colored with a grey mask

Only a few passages of the work are written in score
form—most of it takes the form of completely independent
instrumental parts, since the playing of the four parts is
not intended to be synchronized. 'Each player performs
his part as though he were alone.'

Certain rites performed
as with ropes hanging

from the highest trees
in the magic forest

as with light, threaded
the people said to live here

counterfeiting light

And the hooded figure circling
before the music begins, 'an

emptiness almost perfect . . .
fragile . . . precise . . . as

if an earlier
and better time had returned'

We have lost each other on the stair

We have come to listen and watch
and talk and be talked

I in my (to some) curious
elephant suit with silver studs, you

in nothing or close to nothing
at all, forming the

two of us
what they call a pair

Soon however it won't be winter
in Nebraska even though elsewhere

it will become something like winter

freezing your hand to the rail
and impeding the linear progress

of various objects
while encouraging others. The sound

may try to slow down or at least stop
Until then we'll refuse to hear

We have lost each other on the stair in the deep snow
that forms a window. I have visited the family in the
mountains and the village of old women and small children,
comes a storm of separate crystals winter extends as
it resists.

Among the violin cases
refrigerators, radios and dust
we are alive in these hills
or sleeping beneath a hill
Certain questions arise
Will the rains ever come
and Will the rain ever stop
You have designed the perfect house

to live in, solid
as a crystal, with
no doors or windows
and different sounds for each room
all the modern conveniences
such as light and dark
first light then dark
careful voices of the hill-dwellers

with their pointed heads
Certain questions arise
as grace notes, trills
and slides across
the broken cantus of trees
and rock
and river where it bends
as we bend ourselves

This is the shortest day of the year
when everyone can hear those sounds

This is the longest day of the year
its distance measurable as light

seen from a distance
then recorded: Aurigula, Gemini, Taurus

Canis Major and Canis Minor
the Great Nebula and the Horse's Head

defined as a 'cloud
of cosmic dust'

spreading its relative darkness
of which we're unaware

I sometimes wonder about the response, a century from
now, to tapes or recordings of the music of today in
which the tempi are misjudged, the ensemble is sloppy,
and the rhythms have come out all wrong. Will this
be taken as the style of our time?

That dissolution of the standard way
as this hole where there was a field
a few weeks ago, the argument concerning the mountain
lying due south, whether
to level it entirely or, the alternate idea

to remove only its crown
the top hundred feet or so
and place the houses there. Each name

with its explanatory myth
to be studied in the regional
museum or library. Thus Peril (Alaska),
Truth or Consequences, Bullet,
Dogtown, Natoma, Medicine Bend,
the Frying Pan and the Schuylkil
Thus 'table,' 'cinema,' 'horse'
and so on, your stereoscope

in which two almost identical views
become one, whether looked at
through grey eyes or brown,
held unsteadily in either hand
the towns and rivers
appear to float, an ocean liner
crosses a wheat field explaining
that way the Great Migration

of our ancestors the hawk
and the slug, the brown eyes
with their illusion of greater depth
the grey with their impression
of pure intellect clearly separate
from emotion. It seems
they never complete these things
the heads and arms visible

above the waves indistinctly drawn
and a possible suspension bridge
extending from the more recent past
into the less
renamed the present

On the Way to Language

The answer was
the sun, the question

of all the fragrances undressed
by the rats in the Pentagon

is Claude's, little
memory jars

empty of their pickled plums
and the tiny

pile of dried bodies under the floorboard
(we had to sell that car)

Summers are always difficult
arriving too soon, too

much wind and the absolute
darkness when it finally descends

over the plantation. We're not ashamed
of our immense wealth

even somewhat proud
of the cleanliness of the servants' quarters

From the sound of their weeping
they seem happy enough

in their work, childlike
and contrite. The answer was

memory, an efficient
engine driven by earthly

remains and the question
of the valley of desire

crossed by the bridge
of frequent sighs

The Comet

"An outlook based upon philosophy became obligatory."
—Bruno Schulz

That year the end of winter stood under a sign
All days were red in the margin
writ large against the ochre rooftops
                          and yes that was your father's

face, a murder best forgotten
by passersby inured to the dust

though blinded a bit by the redness
                                    Invisible charges rose

in the poles, only
to enclose them, a parody of juggling
within the lap of eternal matter
                                    like love c. mid-afternoon

eyes half-open, adjustments
at an unexpected point of the experiment
occurred toward the backstage of things
                                              warm

currents of air and some really
depressing tricks that filled one
with true melancholy
                        regarding *principium individuationis*

suitable more to the success of an idea
in an illustrated journal
of modern physics
                    splendidly bogus

and immediately satisfying
as forecast long ago by the prophets
in a circus farce

Song of the Round Man

For Sarah when she's older

The round and sad-eyed man puffed cigars as if
he were alive. Gillyflowers
to the left of the apple, purple bells to the right

and a grass-covered hill behind.
I am sad today said the sad-eyed man
for I have locked my head in a Japanese box

and lost the key.
I am sad today he told me
for there are gillyflowers by the apple

and purple bells I cannot see.
Will you look at them for me
he asked, and tell me what you find?

I cannot I replied
for my eyes have grown sugary and dim
from reading too long by candlelight.

Tell me what you've read then
said the round and sad-eyed man.
I cannot I replied

for my memory has grown tired and dim
from looking at things that can't be seen
by any kind of light

and I've locked my head in a Japanese box
and thrown away the key.
Then I am you and you are me

said the sad-eyed man as if alive.
I'll write you in where I should be
between the gillyflowers and the purple bells

and the apple and the hill
and we'll puff cigars from noon till night
as if we were alive.

Documentation

> "This is how it happened"
> —Homeric Hymn to Demeter

This road ends in a field of grain
and drunken crows are filling the air
or how do we know what we know

He spoke holding his severed ear
The sky moves too quickly through the frame
and the smile has been put on sideways

Veiled Hecate lives in three bodies
lit by approximate light
The daughter receives grief and is alive

The daughter recites grief and is alive
as the mother places her in the fire
and the child holds her yellow hair out

wondering why it's been cut
The bearded tree is the third part
where the ages of the barley hang down

They have loved a secret architecture
that leaves false evidence of itself
and they love to be as three in one

Our visit has lasted an entire winter
and we have half forgotten each word's name
The sky moves that quickly through the frame

Notes for Echo Lake 5

> "a blue under people"
> —Bernadette Mayer, *Memory*

The tree's green explains what a light means, an idea, the bomb or Donald
Duck, a box of marbles in a marble box, the amber jewel behind the toad's
eyes reminds us that it's night. The interpreter of the text examines the
traffic light, coughs and lays the book aside. The dead mayor sits behind his
desk, overcome with wonderment.

The interpreter of a cough examines the light and lays the text aside. Here
and there leaves, clouds, rivers of tears in the streets meant a sonata for
tongues.

Truth to tell the inventor of the code weeps and lays the text aside. Here
and there calendars and walls remind him that it's night, a sleeping lion is
curled up in one corner, a voice can be heard behind a door, and Plato told
us of the law, Plato warned us about the poem. The dead mayor wonders if
the King of France is bald.

Today is an apparent day of empty sleeves and parallelograms, and red
meaning red, and the flag as an object, and red instead of red, the flag as an
object with undulating sides, the spider who taught me to walk, the
emptiness of the code, the spider who forgot how to walk, the delicate
curves within the code, three barking dogs, the mystery of intervals, the
absence of a code, the lion asleep at her feet, the empty sleeve waving, the
bottle now broken, the voices she told him to listen for, the stolen book, the
measurement of intervals.

Does physics know Caesar by name?

Plato warned us of the shadows of the poem, of the words cast against the
wall, and Plato warns against the song.

The tree's green explains what a name means apart from memory, flickers of
light in the darkened room, our eyes fixed on the screen on the figures of
nothing.

The inventor of the code hears each note and swallows his tongue, frightened by shadows. The lion red as a lobster is green sleeps in one corner dreaming of the hours' numbers and names, a river flowing at his feet. "Shuffle Montgomery" was the song.

And here and there they speak in tongues, correcting the right notes in order to get them wrong. And how many days did you spend underground?

The interpreter of leaves examines each tear as pages turn. In the field at dawn they cross swords and a head rolls while the audience laughs. The dead city listens to the code as it reads, and a poem moves back and forth.

At our feet like a sky the graceful curve. Rumours that they are lovers or were in a previous lifetime made of salt. Hills beyond tipped with snow or salt, a curve broken off, searching for her tongue. A deep blue tasting of salt. The awkward curve and talking cloud, steps toward a forest for want of stairs. Are in a lifetime or were. Rumours that the sender had forgotten the code and swallowed his tongue. A mirror in one corner was about to fall, apparently his memory of Siena and the dome.

And Brother Mouse with parachute in mid-air, forever descending.

That they are figures or were, a pictograph with thumb extended. He drank from an actual glass of beer. An outstretched arm offers me its hand.

Symmetrical Poem

There is interest in being able to feel what you see
an unparalleled achievement of the imagination
even in January, and then to fall back
from the effect of an ancient tent
or text called the Suburban Blend

onto a patterned carpet. So paper
is made from stone and stone from solid
air we call glass, wavy ridges photographed
on sand beaches, thin sheets
marking each dune. The warriors, fearing God,

practice here and the readers
read and are read here, desiring
to be soldiers as well. Do not
look up you may think to tell them
but the words will fail to come out.

Voice and Address

You are the owner of one complete thought

Its sons and daughters
march toward the capitol

There are growing apprehensions to the south

It is ringed about
by enclaves of those who have escaped

You would like to live somewhere else

away from the exaggerated music
in a new, exaggerated shirt

a place where colored stones have no value

This hill is temporary
but convenient for lunch

Does she mean that the afternoon should pass

in such a manner
not exactly rapidly

and with a studied inattention

He has lost his new car
of which you were, once,

a willing prisoner

a blister in your palm
identical with the sky's bowl

reflected in the empty sentence

whose glare we have completely shed
ignoring its freshness

The message has been sent

across the lesser fractures in the glass
where the listeners are expendable

The heart is thus flexible

now straight now slightly bent
and yesterday was the day for watching it

from the shadow of its curious house

Your photo has appeared
an island of calm

in a sea of priapic doubt

You are the keeper of one secret thought
the rose and its thorn no longer stand for

You would like to live somewhere

but this is not permitted
You may not even think of it

lest the thinking appear as words

and the words as things
arriving in competing waves

from the ruins of that place

The Village of Reason

This is a glove
or a book from a book club

This is the sun
or a layer of mud

This is Monday,
this an altered word

This is the village of reason
and this an eye torn out

This is the father
or a number on a chart

This is a substitute,
this the thing you are

This is the varnished picture
or else an accepted response

This is the door
and this the word for door

This is a reflex caused by falling
and this a prisoner with an orange

This is a name you know
and this is the poison to make you well

This is the mechanism
and this the shadow of a bridge

This is a curve
and this its thirst

This is Monday,
this her damaged word

This is the trace
and this the term unmarked

This is the sonnet
and this its burning house

You are in this play
You are its landscape

This is an assumption
the length of an arm

This is a poppy,
this an epilogue

The Theory of the Flower

I will read a few of these to see if they exist
(We will translate logos as logos)

He swam in the rock
I am here from a distance

"Now kiss her cunt"
"Now take his cock in your hand"

The film is of a night garden
There is nothing meaningful about the text

There is nothing meaningful about a text
She

brushed away the sand
She brushed away the hand

This is Paradise, an unpunctuated book
and this a sequence of laws

in which the night sky is lost
and the flower of theory is a black spot

upon the foxglove
(These words have all been paid for)

He turns then to shade his eyes from the sun
She edges closer to the fallen log

This is Paradise, a mildewed book
left too long in the house

Now say the words you had meant to
Now say the words such words mean

The car is white but does not run
It fits in a pocket

He slept inside the rock,
a flower that was almost blue

Such is order
which exenterates itself

The islands will be a grave for their children
after they are done

You may use the paper with my name on it
to say whatever you want

I promise not to be so boring next time
never again to laugh and weep so much

which is how spring comes
to the measured center of the eye

The mind is made up
but you forget who it was first spoke

The mind is made up
and then and then

This is the paradise of emptiness
and this the blank picture in a book

I've looked over the photographs and they all are of you
just as we'd been warned

How strange
The winged figure in tuxedo is bending from the waist

The metalion addresses the mirror
and the music of the shattered window

falls unheard past the window below
How strange

but not so strange as speech
mistaken for a book

The phrase "for a moment" is popular in the world
yet not really meant to be said

That is the third or the fourth world
where you can step into a tremor with your tongue

I do not drink of it myself
but intend a different liquid

clear as the glass in which it's held,
the theory of the flower and so on

or the counter-terror of this valley
the fog gradually fills

just as we've been warned
It isn't true but must be believed

and the leaves of the sound of such belief
form a paradise

(pronounced otherwise)
from which we fall toward a window

Dearest Reader

He painted the mountain over and over again
from his place in the cave, agape
at the light, its absence, the mantled
skull with blue-tinted hollows, wren-
like bird plucking berries from the fire
her hair alight and so on
lemon grass in cafe in clear glass.
Dearest reader there were trees
formed of wire, broad entryways
beneath balconies beneath spires
youthful head come to rest in meadow
beside bend in gravel road, still
body of milky liquid
her hair alight and so on
successive halls, flowered carpets and doors
or the photograph of nothing but pigeons
and grackles by the shadow of a fountain.

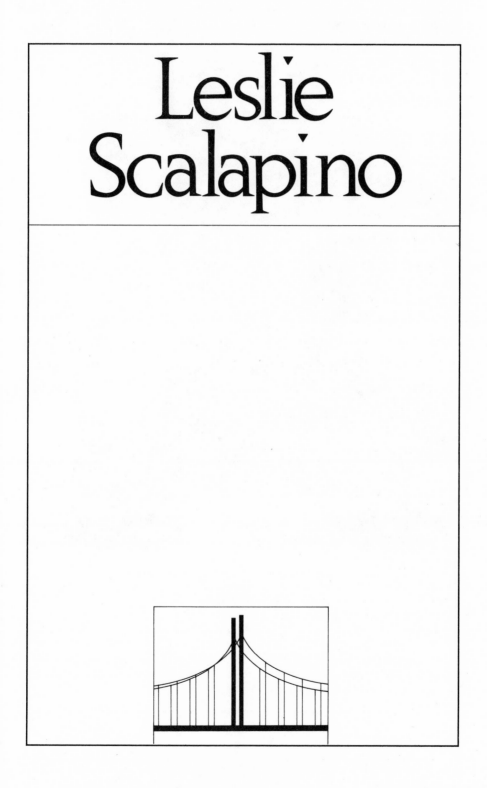

Leslie
Scalapino

Leslie Scalapino was born in Santa Barbara and grew up in Berkeley. She was educated at Reed College and the University of California, Berkeley, where she received an M.A. in English under a Woodrow Wilson Fellowship. She teaches at New College in San Francisco and at San Francisco State University. In 1976 she received a writer's grant from the National Endowment for the Arts. Her poetry books include: *O; The Woman Who Could Read the Mind of Dogs; Instead of an Animal; This Eating and Walking at the Same Time Is Associated All Right;* and a recent collection brought out by Northpoint, *Considering how exaggerated music is,* which includes poems from three earlier volumes as well as new poems.

My work is sequential. In a sequence called "hmmmm," excerpts of which are published here, the particular piece "About the night on which a man said he would spend a 100 dollars" arrives at a certain point as the cumulative effect of what precedes it; arriving at perception which would be absent were the piece to be read singly. What is important in terms of an action is that it is not I who is sated, but someone else. The concentration is not on her pleasure either. It is located in the city, which is "past" her and which is outside my (the speaker's) framework entirely.

In a piece which I'll use as an example, taken from a poem "Considering how exaggerated music is," subjective states and permutations of them appear to be reproduced externally. Though the movement could be in the opposite direction too—moving inwards toward the person from the perspective of the world. The idea being that things and people would be transparent. There wouldn't be a sense of time.

> I'd go to a restaurant or to the beach and my behavior which seemed to reflect only the surface of what I was thinking was reproduced externally in the jobs other people held.
>
> For a while I had a job in a store. A person I knew was older than I was and also would be very nervous. He had been feeling jaded and unable to do anything for a while yet my underlying mood and my emotions were not fixed and I managed to work some during this period.

In the following piece the concentration at first is on the "moment," rather than the man's ambivalence in the setting. Really it is on perceiving another setting, which is in the future. The emphasis is on me (the speaker) perceiving that future. Though I have no relation to the man, or to those others who are in the setting which is outside of either his setting or mine. Their perceptions will be separate.

> The sense I had of a man on the street was that he had a family yet was ambivalent toward the place or setting at that moment, an area where there were small businesses and restaurants, and not where he lives. There shouldn't be any sex say; he should be in a normal state and have no sex actually occur then or around that time and then have it occur later. Have slower ability.
>
> A retarding of his ability in general, not just in this setting; and have other people who were there wearing everyday clothes, walking some.

There is a spatial quality to thinking in "Considering how exaggerated music is" which is similar to "A Sequence" (published here). Private states are objectified and have a spatial dimension. As such, they also are opaque surfaces. Private feelings and social customs are on the surface. And if nothing is hidden, then the notion would be that the private realm and public are the same. So that repression would not be a way of giving depth.

"A Sequence" seems funny. In another poem, "This eating and walking at the same time is associated all right," I wanted the tone to be flippant, so that tone itself would be isolated as if it were an objective thing—and could be seen like an object. Individual pieces of the poem change by being in sequence. Objects and thoughts are expressed as spatial relations.

> I ate and there should just be the person who was talking about ar-
> chitects,
> or one of the other people I was with
> there should be just that person in the world
> with no banks or culture.

In "This eating and walking at the same time is associated all right" everything is public. Emotions have to be objectified say in plants and matter. So that the "self" isn't what one thought it was—and neither is the public realm.

> Are these people lying if they went somewhere, are dogs and other
> animals lying and wouldn't have any reason for lying?

> If these people are jealous—but jealousy is in plants and isn't
> related to lying, dogs are jealous

> I could have been matter and I feel jealous when I go out in public
> when I go anywhere

I'm interested in catching aspects of motion. In the poem "The Woman Who Could Read the Minds of Dogs," for example, lead-in lines are not titles. They are repetitions, which when reread in context change the motion in a piece. The intention is to isolate strands of movement. As if people's personalities were in a motion, something happening outside them.

So in recent work, such as a sequence titled "buildings are at the far end," elements of personality are removed so that people are seen as movement. "Interiors" are being created that are external to oneself—in this piece, the industrial area where people are in sports cars.

> I work, yet seeing a delivery driver in the sweltering weather I had the
> sense that he'd come to an area that is vacant. Like a dock or pier, it
> didn't have any shade or people—and therefore the duties of the driver
> are undefined, in terms of the work he's doing.

> Yet there's a sense of people—not being there, the area in the sun being
> remote—but being in an industrial area anyway in sports cars, or
> ordinary cars.

> The others in an industrial park, and the driver of the van isolated.

Everything is in rapid motion, which makes motion and stillness look indistinguishable. An "interior," such as oneself, would really be indistinguishable from outside motion.

I'm in the background in the sense that I came out of a train station and taxis are in the foreground.

I'm not very visible in comparison to the area where the taxis are, and the cars form a fan. They began to move, and other cars—vehicles that are privately-owned—are already outside of the spot where the fan is. Are in front of it.

That is what I wanted to accomplish in that particular work. And what I'd like not only to be able to do in writing, but in terms of action.

hmmmm

[ten excerpts from the twenty-eight-part sequence]

[*8.*]

Haven't I said that part of having intercourse

Haven't I said that part of having intercourse
with anyone, is loving them when they are weak,
When they can't speak. When a woman, say, mews
(while being flipped over on her belly by a man) i.e.
if she utters some sound sort of like what a doll
makes, when *it's* flipped forward. What I mean by this
is: her eyelids, after flying open with her head
flipped back, will drop shut when her head is forward.
And in falsetto   (we might even say mawkishly),
the woman's mouth makes a sound like the word Mama.

[*9.*]

How can I help myself,   as one woman said to me about wanting

to have intercourse with strange men,   from thinking of a man

How can I help myself,   as one woman said to me about wanting
to have intercourse with strange men,   from thinking of a man
(someone whom I don't know) as being like a seal. I mean I see a man
(in a crowd such as a theatre) as having the body of a seal in the way
a man would, say, be in bed with someone, kissing and barking,
which is the way a seal will bark and leap on his partly-fused hind limbs.
Yes. Am I not bound, I guess, (I say to myself) to regard him tenderly,
to concentrate on the man's trunk instead of his face, which in this case,
is so impassive.   Seriously,   I am fascinated by the way a seal moves.

[*10.*]

So I decided watching an *old* woman like her, who could rise so easily
on her hind legs from a chair at a party and single out
a young man that they could be satyrs. So erect.
With even the same look on her face which I saw one day, later
as she passed me on the street as she was hurrying forward
and not seeing me, wheeling on her pelvis with a shock
of hair standing out from her forehead and only the muscles
of her haunches appearing to move.

a woman who had been dressed by someone,   in the same way that

"The second to the last time that I saw her",   said a man to me
about the woman who, after not seeing him for a month or two,
retrieved one of her dresses,   by banging on the door of his house,
"I thought that she would split the door open.   Since she had
wanted the dress so badly", the man said, "later, when I saw her
for the *last* time,   one day,   on the street,   swaying toward me
(she was moving so rapidly in the dress, with it slung around her,
that for me, standing still and looking at her, it looked like she
were running thru me), I thought to myself that now I was seeing
a woman who had been dressed by someone,   in the same way that
an oyster will cover the irritant in him by coating it over and over"

[*14.*]

Seeing the Scenery

Satisfied this morning because I saw myself
(for the first time) in the mirror as a mountain. I mean by this
I "saw the scenery" in myself. Whereas I had pores
and veins and a brain, I was a mountain in the same way
one has boulders or trees. How would this explain, I wondered,
whatever emotions such as affection, cruelty or indifference I feel?
And I knew no matter how careful one is,
pebbles and grains *will be* modified put in a human form.

[*15.*]

As Rimbaud said,   I thought today sitting in the library
absentmindedly leafing through a book on the habits of birds,

As Rimbaud said,   I thought today sitting in the library
absentmindedly leafing through a book on the habits of birds,
isn't the way we find happiness precisely by losing our senses
(oversimplified, of course. I was being   facetious.) But still
I can see imitating a bird's call such as that of the fledgling
of a goose or a swan (here I referred to the book) by forcing
myself into a swoon. And,   by way of finishing the thought, I,
for the sake of appearances, since there were people sitting
in the chairs around me, merely sagged forward in my seat and
whistled as if I were asleep. Ssss, it came out, sort of a hiss,
like the noise of a goose. So, almost before I knew it,

I followed this by a low and guttural cough
and leaned forward simply to expel some phlegm. Then quickly
I took a glance around before I wiped my mouth. Feeling weary.

[*19.*]

How was I to know that the woman, seated next to me on the bus,
would,   when the bus lurched,   just appear to lose her balance,
and, as if to keep herself from swaying, would take hold of my arm
with her hand so that pressing me between her finger and thumb
she pinched my arm. Though I believed   (looking at her sideways,
and seeing only that her lips were parted slightly, with her snout
breathing softly)   that during the two to three minutes
in which this pain lasted, she was saying (or at least I imagined so
from the length of time that she held on to my arm
before releasing me)   *I wish that I could make you yelp just once.*

[*21.*]

[EPILOGUE: *anemone*]

"About the night on which a man said he would spend a 100 dollars
on me",   a woman described,   (and he did use up most of it
simply on taxi fares),   "I was able to describe my feelings:

"About the night on which a man said he would spend a 100 dollars
on me",   a woman described,   (and he did use up most of it
simply on taxi fares),   "I was able to describe my feelings:
by saying it was like being an insect who puts its feelers
out into the flowers of a plant,   and sucks from them,   as we were
(sucking)   from the restaurants and bars of the city
to which the taxi took us. All night we were surrounded by lights.
As I lay back inside the taxi, just waiting for the man to make
arrangements for me   (in regard to *that* part of my feeling,
I would describe the taxi as being more like a buoy),   I had the
feeling (thru-out it) of rising slowly,   and of floating along side
particular spots in the city. By morning,   naturally,   I was sated".

[*22.*]

"Having her under me",   the man said,   "in bed, and remembering

"Having her under me",   the man said,   "in bed, and remembering
what she had said about going to bed once with a movie actor,
I found that I wanted to imagine him   (like looking into a mirror,

etc.), as I made love to her.   So,   as her face lay under me,
and I thought of her as a plant under me which only moves
on a stem,   her legs seemed to me to be like the stamens
of the plant,   i.e.   It was the male part of her which attracted me,
drew me in, literally, stirring against my legs, and holding me too,
as I parted her labia, and finally gently entered her female part".

[24.]

we put our heads into the windows of a car which was passing, and,

One woman   (I heard about this several years later)   said   :
"being a prostitute"   (this was said, by-the-way ,
after her telling about approaching with 6 or so other women
2 men in a car,   on a street at 3 am in the city   )   ;
"means simply coming out of the hotels and streets of the city
to the car (which is waiting with the men in it) in the same way
that, say,   the feelers of an anemone,   (while being attached
at the base to the anemone)   in order to feed it,   float out
further and further into the water which encircles it. So it was:
we put our heads into the windows of a car which was passing, and,
putting our arms around the necks of the men, began kissing them".

The Woman Who Could Read the Minds of Dogs

on itself. His red hair was standing up) "I just began to weep."

Much later,   after I had ceased to know the man who had once
described to me how ,   driving his new car with its top down   ⁄
   around and around the block   (with his 1st wife in the car—
he said that he had been downtown with her drinking in a bar)   ,
while he was looking for the entrance to the hotel parking lot ,
he had   collided, or rather,   had grazed the sides of 3 parked
cars   ;   as I said,   it was much later when I was standing
on the jetty of a marina and watching a man standing up in
a   motor boat,   while he turned it around and around in circles.
"Well",   (I remembered the man I had known saying about himself
   —as I watched the man in the motor boat turning it slowly
on itself. His red hair was standing up) "I just began to weep".

*

"while we were taking turns driving all night one night in the car

"My father", (the man continued, telling me about how his father,
while travelling in Europe one year with him and his brothers ,
had picked up a woman in one of the casinos) "had insisted on
having her with us in the car. So, (we were unable to resist this—
since she was such a lush herself), my brothers and I", he said,
"while we were taking turns driving all night one night in the car
would tell her that we had to stop for us to drink out of the whiskey
bottle that we kept in our trunk. Well, I won't forget how she,
watching us passing the bottle between us, while we were standing
beside the car (but we were just putting it up to our lips) was
both afraid (since we were driving) and just eager for a drink".

*

to the toilet or to some bar , and , (because she was drinking)

"About the woman whom my father", the man said, "had insisted on
picking up at one of the casinos (while we were driving in Europe):
of course, she was constantly wanting to get out of the car to go
to the toilet or to some bar , and , (because she was drinking)
once, when we were driving around the curves in the mountains ,
she kept wanting to use my father's felt pen on the windows—
telling us, 'I am drawing the mountains', but, (because the car was
moving), I told my father she was just making a mess on the window".

*

Cicada

"For once, while we were driving in the car with her (of course,
my father ended up taking her with us to Mexico) , the woman
(when we were driving in the desert, at least. It was 6 a.m.) ,
said very little;—as she seemed to be listening to the sound,
like a high-pitched whine, (we must have been moving at 70 m.p.h.)
made by millions of cicadas in the bushes by the highway.
Well, so, my father said that in the hotel, later, she woke up in bed
(obviously she had been dreaming) and said that she had had
'one of them', a cicada, in her mouth so that she was pressing it
with her tongue and the roof of her mouth to make the sound come
out (saying to him as she woke up 'I was spitting its innards out')".

*

I was not thinking about the woman whom I had heard about once
who could read the minds of dogs (as I remember, she even diagnosed
dogs' illnesses), once when I passed a man on the sidewalk downtown
(he was dancing, moving around in circles to the music

that was piped out of a bullhorn in front of the door of a music store);
but (maybe because of the way he pulled his neck back—
with his shoulders heaving in time to the music—which is the way a dog
bites down on a stick when it's being yanked out of his mouth) ,
I immediately had the idea that the man was hungry, undoubtedly
because I hadn't eaten yet that day .

*

so that I said to the person I was with that I was reminded of me ,

What the man whom we saw (he looked like a derelict) wanted
(we didn't know him, of course) running like that alongside the car
we were in (we were in downtown traffic—he seemed to want in with
us, the way he was running beside us, without a word—
so that I said to the person I was with that I was reminded of me ,
having refused to talk when I was young); I don't know.
However, I said he was like the woman who let her hair grow (I was
thinking about it later), while she was living in a jungle backwater ,
and clawed and bit when they wanted to force her onto the aeroplane.
So that they left her (just like we left him, standing worn out in the
street, looking after us) with her hair standing up because of the wind.

*

by the time he reached Bombay, we were to have intersected with him.

"One of the memories that I have of my mother", the man said ,
"(I was young then) was that my father had asked her to come ,
with my brothers and me , by train from Calcutta so that
by the time he reached Bombay, we were to have intersected with him.
Well, (by the way, I don't remember that my mother ever
said much to us. We were not with her often) on the way
to the train station with her (our car, because there were so
many beggars in the streets in the way, was constantly slowed down),
my mother (despite our driver's instructions not to) insisted on
dropping a paper bag that had a sandwich in it out of the window
of the car. Whereupon," the man said, "I saw one beggar tear open
the bag, open the sandwich that was in it and toss the bread away".

*

in my mouth with her fingers saying to me, with each mouth-

"My seat", the man said, "being by the window up near the wing
of the aeroplane (we were on our way—this was when I was 17—
up from Khartoum to Cairo), my mother (my father had with him

one of his underlings   whom I kept seeing putting his hand on
her back or on the nape of her neck as she leaned back—she said
nothing to him)   had to lean over me to look out the window   .
So, while we were being served hors d'oeuvres (and she kept saying
to me,   over and over,   to look at this or that crag or rock on the
desert,   as we were flying over it)   she would put hors d'oeuvres
in my mouth with her fingers,   saying to me,   with each mouth-
ful of crust with meat inside it,   "I want you to suck on it   ,

*

—so it was seven years after she'd been killed—since I was 29)"

In the dream,   (I had this dream I think 6 years or so ago
—so it was seven years after she'd been killed—since I was 29)"
said the man,   "I imagined   that I saw my mother in the casket
(as, in real life, the lid had been closed, I did not see her then).
So,   looking in, it seemed (this is so typical of all dreams)
that she was herself but covered with a chitinous shell,   like that
of an insect such as, say, a beetle, but with wings where her arms
had been   (or rather, *were*, since they were both arms and wings).
— I wanted   (and for me, this is the center of the dream)
to split the chitin on her   by tearing it open with my hands   and
peeling it off of her. But I could not do so without hurting her ".

*

Foal

"During 52 hours of labor   ,
the foetus in me—it was by that time so large, that it seemed
to be bigger than for a human birth—kicked me so hard", she said,
"that I thought that it was something else: that it was a foal
which was inside me and was kicking me with its four legs.
It could not unfold them. Nor could I push it out.   Finally ,
obviously   as it would not come out of me in the other way , it
just had to be taken out of me by caesarean ".

*

mu   seum

And it was in Mozambique,   I said,   where we saw—
I was about 13—(and he,   a boy whom we had met re-
cently   at our hotel,   who   I remember was with me ,   was
   standing next to me when we were looking at that
glass case,   was 17)   the dead fawns in the mu-

---

seum.   Some of them had 6 legs.   He said to me to
look at that one that had 2 heads   :   it had horns
just appearing on its heads. All of the fawns had the same
face.   He had me put my hands on the glass of the case

*

so obviously I was irritated by it—I mean seeing this dog

"We were in a hurry   (my wife", the man said,—"This was my 2nd
wife—had wanted me to return home for something so we were late);
so obviously I was irritated by it—I mean seeing this dog
   just standing   (actually we had seen it earlier too)
in the center of the street and holding up traffic;   and at the
sound of the honking pacing on the center line or in front of a car
   and looking so eager. It had been doing this for hours,
I said to her.   So,   (I don't like it when I do this sort of thing
in public)   I simply rolled down the window and swore at the dog".

*

"Oddly", the man said, "(—for she used to be practically mute—

"Oddly", the man said, "(—for she used to be practically mute—
at least with me)   what I guess I liked best about her—
my 2nd wife—was the story,   or the odd sense I got from it
   about her   :   when she was 17   (I guess she got this
from her father—he went fishing)   she dreamed about having
   a fly   (like the ones, she said to me that are used as bait
for a fish,   as it was made out of silk feathers and had
a hook on it) fly (while she was sleeping) up thru her nostril.
It went on up into her head. And, on waking,—I say—
she still had it in her . Obviously,   the sense that I have of
this story is, for one, that she would not have put it this way"

*

"In this dream that I had about her",   the man said,—
it was one he had had about his 2nd wife—"I made her,
before we went to bed at night   (this was in the dream,
I mean)   open her mouth   (it seemed   that she would
   do what I wanted her to)   and had her swallow a bell
like the kind that one would put around the cat's neck.
Well, hours later, (I had been sleeping so it was like a
dream inside a dream)   I heard the bell,   as,   obviously
she had gotten up out of our bed ;   I heard her go to the
hall door, before   I woke up getting up out of the bed"

*

According to Madame Nijinsky , Nijinsky prepared his own
costume   in order to dance in "L'Après-midi d'un Faune" .
His costume consisted of tights into which he had to be sewn.
With flat curling horns on his head, his ears elongated with flesh-
coloured wax   (so that they appeared to be pointed like a horse's),
he looked like the half-beast adolescent faun he was supposed to be

*

So that I said I had read that in *one* country—

where rites of passage connected with magic were conducted—
if somebody died   (whether from old age or from an accident)
they thought it just simpler to sew up the lips of the corpse
so that if its name were called , it could not answer.
According to this,   cats   (I continued) could bring them back.
Anyone calling a dead cat in an alley at night,   it was said,
would *know* that the sound that came from the alley
    was the sound of the one who'd been killed   .

*

"this was before she knew she was carrying our child)

"We were in the West Indies , (this was before my 1st wife" ,
said the man, "—maybe there really *is* something to their
idea that a dog can slip into a woman's womb
when it wants to be born in a human form"—Obviously,
he meant this facetiously   ;   "as I say",   he continued,
"this was before she knew she was carrying our child)
when the incident with the dog running alongside our car
occurred.   It was one of those thin,   practically wild,   dogs
that hang around the run-down areas of Nassau.   Oddly,
she said that the dog was running beside her, perfectly silent.
When she glanced out of the window and saw it , its head
was almost level with hers—as if it were on its hind legs".

*

I remember that there were kids—bands of them—of about the age
of 7 or 10 or so there   who would hang around the outskirts

"In Nassau" (he said,   "this is where my 1st wife and I were
    when she was carrying our child. It was born there.)
I remember that there were kids—bands of them—of about the age

of 7 or 10 or so there   who would hang around the outskirts
of the marketplace,   say,   or outside a cafe. They were beggars.
My wife once—maybe she was associating their activity with   the
odor of fruit from the stalls of the bazaar (she had been standing
waiting for me to bring around the car for her)—said the beggars
were like wasps or like worker bees that were hanging around her
    (forcing her she said to tell them to go away)   and still they
wanted to fasten onto and to follow her after we were in the car".

A sequence

She heard the sounds of a couple having intercourse and then getting up
they went into the shower so that she caught a sight of them naked before
hearing the water running. The parts of their bodies which had been
covered by clothes were those of leopards. During puberty her own organs
and skin were not like this though when she first had intercourse with a
man he removed his clothes and his organ and flesh were also a leopard's.
She already felt pleasure in sexual activity and her body not resembling these
adults made her come easily which also occurred when she had intercourse
with another man a few months later.

*

When sexual unions occurred between a brother and sister they weren't
savages or primitive. She had that feeling about having intercourse with men
whose organs were those of leopards' and hers were not. Walking
somewhere after one of these episodes she was excited by it though she
might not have made this comparison if she'd actually had a brother. At least
the woman she had seen in the shower had a leopard's parts. In these
episodes when she'd had intercourse with a man he didn't remark about her
not being like that. And if women had these characteristics which she didn't
it made her come more easily with him.

*

She overheard another couple together and happened to see them as she had
the couple in the shower. The nude part of the woman was like herself and
the man had the leopard's parts so that she had the same reaction and came
easily with someone, as she had with a sense of other women having a
leopard's traits and herself isolated. The man with whom she had intercourse
did not say anything that showed he had seen a difference in her and that
made her react physically. Yet other women seemed to have a leopard's
characteristics except for this one she'd seen.

*

Again it seemed that a man with whom she had intercourse was her brother and was ardent with her—but this would not have occurred to her had she really had a brother. Yet her feeling about him was also related to her seeing a woman who was pregnant and was the only one to be so. The woman not receiving attention or remarks on the pregnancy excited her; and went together with her sense of herself coming easily and yet not being pregnant until quite a while after this time.

*

She also felt that she came easily feeling herself isolated when she was pregnant since she had the sense of other women having leopards' organs. They had previously had children. She was the only one who was pregnant and again she saw a couple together, the man with leopard's parts and the woman not having these characteristics.

Again she could come since her body was different from the adult who had some parts that were leopard's, and having the sense of the women having had children earlier than her and their not having younger children now.

*

Her liking the other women to have had children when she was pregnant had to do with having them there and herself isolated—and yet people not saying much about or responding to the pregnancy. She thought of the man coming as when she caught a sight of the couple together—being able to come with someone a different time because she had a sense of a woman she'd seen having had her children earlier. There being a difference of age, even ten years, between a child she'd have and those the other women had had.

*

She happened to see some men who were undressed, as if they were boys— one of them had the features and organ of a leopard and the others did not. The difference in this case gave her the sense of them being boys, all of them rather than those who didn't have leopards' characteristics and this made her come easily with someone.

It was not a feeling of their being a younger age, since the men were her own age, and she found the men who lacked the leopard features to be as attractive as the one who had those features. She had the feeling of them as adults and her the same age as them, yet had the other feeling as well in order for her to come then.

*

She saw a couple who were entwined together and her feeling about them came from the earlier episode of seeing the men who were nude and having the sense of them being adolescent boys. Really she'd had the sense of the men she'd seen as being adults and herself the same age as them. The couple she watched were also around the same age as herself—the man being aware of someone else's presence after a time and coming. The woman pleased then though she had not come.

*

She had intercourse with the man who had the features and organ of a leopard and whom she had first seen with the group of men who lacked these characteristics. The other men were attractive as he was. Yet having the sense of the difference between him and the others, she found it pleasant for him to come and for her not to come that time. The same thing occurred on another occasion with him.

*

She compared the man to plants, to the plants having a nervous aspect and being motionless. The man coming when he had the sense of being delayed in leaving—as if being slowed down had made him come and was exciting, and it was during the afternoon with people walking around. He was late and had to go somewhere, and came, with a feeling of delay and retarding— rather than out of nervousness.

*

areas

We went on a motorcycle on a straight road with people watching us and the parents of the man whose motorcycle it was came.

Not disliking me and taking the car with us, they sat inside when I got out and I threw up on the road's shoulder—over and over—yet not caused by being sick before or out of a sense of being agitated because of them. And the friend with whom I was close held my back when I was out of the car, drove back on the same road and they went into a factory for awhile.

*

I'd come by car. People from a large tourists' bus grouped around their bus yet at a distance from me—these people from the bus were separated from me by my being inside a room.

Just then I was alone. The bus was stuck in sand near-by with the people wanting to remove it. Them wanting to though there was dirt and work first before it'd be done and they would get dirty if they did it. The bus was removed and the people were alongside it.

*

I was locked out of the car in the rain which caused a blonde to stand with me in the street, a large woman.

I'd come with a person who was incompetent—could do certain things but in everything else was incompetent, his wife had to take care of him—and he'd gone, directed by a passer-by who took him with him, to hail a taxi, the blonde coming and standing with me afterwards.

*

The town—we were sitting on the edge of it—was circular in the sense that there was only one entrance and cars and campers were entering on a narrow road. On the narrow road going away from the town, I was feeling sick in the car from something earlier and went to throw up but I am standing, the insects at the other end of brush which is away from town.

*

People began pushing while begging and a woman was standing at the right, better dressed.

Those up-close held out their hands pushing into us who were in a cart on a road and they formed a fan around the back end of it with us facing the fan —we're in front of the fan facing it and then the front end of the cart. In front of that is the road.

*

The ticket in a shop where I'd gotten some candy and they'd forgotten to give it back, I returned with the ticket and was late reaching the gate for the plane—I ran on a belt to return to the shop. Missing the plane, I went back to a hotel which I associate with some women who were sitting around, not as an emotion or attitude toward them—who'd become angry—and the area they were in seen to be respectable.

Other areas being so as well.

*

Areas were respectable in the sense of being evenly dispersed—as a film is— and they do not go back to see it or to follow the film again. What they do is uniform as in paintings where if they are doing hard work that has the same space as large events which take place.

*

Just in being raised there'd be a sense of being spoiled, given food and lodging, parents also fair in their opinions.

Then when they'd reached maturity having to get these things themselves and then when they'd reached the level of being able to do so—of getting food and lodging—feeling that they were back again at that same state. Coming to that level and spoiled.

Laura Chester

Laura Chester was born in Cambridge, Massachusetts, in 1949, and grew up in Milwaukee. She received her B.S. from the University of New Mexico. She has been a magazine editor and has published several volumes of poetry and the anthology *Rising Tides, 20th Century American Women Poets*. Her books include *My Pleasure, Nightlatch, Chunk Off & Float, Primagravida, Proud and Ashamed*, and *Watermark*. During the past year, she has been working on a book of nonfiction, *Lupus Novice*. She has lived in Paris for several years, and in Berkeley with her husband Geoffrey Young, where they publish The Figures.

An Inclusive Poetry

"We shall never go back," my father used to howl with great pleasure, lost on a road trip—We would never return the same way we came, even if we didn't know where we were going. I inherited this feeling of forwardness, a confidence in the future. Though it's true, after the publication of a new book, there is often that unsettling period when one wonders—How will a continuing yet new style emerge. I've always felt the need for my writing to progress.

Impressionable by nature, I've had an open ear for influence, reading and absorbing what moved me, a sponge for the seen, heard, and the lyrical rhythms of language, though I think my greatest asset is that I'm just as much an editor as a writer.

Being a bride of the sixties, I was influenced by feminism, and yet my poetry has never been one of statement. Though I've worked from an intimate perspective, where the intuitive is a formative force, I've also wanted my writing to have a life of its own, word for word's sake, beyond gender, personal history or explanation.

Place has affected my work. My first book of poems, *Chunk Off & Float*, and the novel, *Watermark*, both persisted in returning to amniotic images of Wisconsin, where that overly lush environment encouraged a close, inclusive form of writing, unlike the Southwest, which was dry and spare. When we moved from Albuquerque to Paris, in the early '70s, the shift jarred me into a new sensibility. Surrounded by the foreign element, I felt a private, almost secretive connection with my language. *Nightlatch*, a book of prose poems, took off from the hot ingredients of dream sequence, and became city cool works in their own right. It was in these pieces that I first acknowledged my own conflicting nature as a puritanical sensualist. The poems wanted erotic license, but I managed to keep them under poetic control.

Though I'd been told that the transcription of dreams was not suitable to art, I'd been told "No" so much I was immune to it. First I was told that I should never marry a poet, and then it was suggested that we never have children, but once we had two boys—

> You shouldn't talk about children. Keep the pets
> and kids out of adult literature. There's a difference
> you know.
> > Because of writers, Men, in the past,
> > So what now, me here, This, dangling fuchsia,
> > Marionette-like, book about monsters,
> > Unnnderrr Wahterrr,
> > > *a Lovey book.*

It was also recommended to me, that if I wanted to be a poet, I should only write poetry, no fiction, no prose, but I think a writer has to be confident in her own inner dictates. I have deliberately moved from form to form, writing poems, prose poems, stories and novels, personal essays and straight nonfiction. I continue to think that different urges of expression are suited to different gaits, just as one horse can—walk, trot or canter. Being open to a varied pace has been helpful to me.

When I was first pregnant, I wrote *Primagravida,* which included journal-like prose, poems and dream stories, both from my own point of view, and from the real and imagined experiences of other women. This book was united by theme, the conscious and unconscious struggle involved in moving from independence to nurturing. Despite the precarious balance of needs and demands, I think this process of mothering has deepened my life and my art.

When I returned to the conventional poem, I was particularly concerned for the physical, visual aspect of the poem. All of the lines, units of sound, were meticulously laid out in painterly strokes across the page. I wanted the poem to have an immediate visual impact—wholeness, which would resonate again in the reading. As in the poem, "Last Breath," the voice in this series was singular, set apart, and the tone of these poems reflected that solitary stance.

We were now living in the heart of Berkeley, where the demands of being both a writer and a conscientious parent became intense. As I went on to write more fiction, I began to understand voice in a different way, and suspected that a poem could be inhabited by multiple voices too. Fiction also gave me greater permission to invent. The truth could be stretched to "trueness." I wanted dramatic possibility, the involvement of dialogue, pushing the novelist's inclusiveness into the condensation of poem.

My first attempt at a piece for two voices was, "For the Love of the Lamb," a long poem from *Proud & Ashamed,* the underlined portions indicating the second voice. These two streams of sound mingled and split, bounced off of each other, and at times, read as one, like a chorus. The actual live effect was astounding. People woke up to that interplay, and performing was enjoyable, rather than isolating.

In the book, *My Pleasure,* I wrote many varied pieces, including "On the Wallowy," that were performed by two, three and sometimes four people, a kind of vocal choreography, which was only implied in the unmarked published version. In explanation of this direction, I wrote these notes on the text:

> From all that's absorbed within the emotional circumference, certain moments seem to stick and come back in the replay. Having composed themselves during a stage of gestation, they arrive as a naturally selective synthesis. The movement here is similar to the semi-conscious

linking of the twilight reverie, what we go to sleep on, the prickling of memory, of audial and surface phenomenon. Updating a history to the present, pronounceable, each unit distracts from the previous, moving on, and yet all are held together as mixed motion in time, like the day in the life of any nurturer. A peopled poetry, an overlapping of internal/external voices, trialogues, riffs, back to back talking, word gestures traveling off in opposite directions, until they must meet and release and reform. The personal edge—not just one particular life, but an inclusive poetry. And so the drama resounds here in multiple, taking us beyond the isolation of "I" familiar to poetic vision, into a gathering of many, lodged in a tight interior space, until it seems something must give, or . . . Submerging, resurfacing, we sing the song fresh, almost without knowing that the toys we can't break are the voices that people us.

Finally, I did reach a saturation point where I could include no more. I felt used up, and dreaded the idea of forced, empty production. I simply had to put my work aside for a while, moving from the solitary life of writer, into the social realm, as I began to take part in the beginning of a new Waldorf school, involving myself in that community effort.

Taking a real break might be one of the hardest things a writer can admit to, for as you know, we take ourselves so *seriously,* and if we aren't proving to ourselves and the world that we are writers by writing something regularly, or at least thinking and talking about writing constantly, then how do we know who we are or what it all means. That was another problem. I felt like I had gotten to the point where there was not much meaning. The urban chuckle wasn't enough for me now.

Then I found out that I had a serious chronic disease, systemic lupus erythematosis, and I had to come to terms with both body and soul, and inevitably my world view and writing. Living on the edge of illness helped me do that. Jolted out of the ordinary, life came up close and meaning did shine, painfully bright, demanding acknowledgment.

My new work is more plain in presentation, less physically "decked out," but I believe it attempts to find a fresh balance, having gone to greater heights and depths. I've always understood that a poem has something of its own life, its own force, but now I see that it can also become part of a greater upward or downward spiral. I do not want to limit myself to the perpendicular of intellectualism, nor the squiggles of siren stuff, but I do want to be receptive to the unpredictable curve, letting a wholeness come through me, thought, word, and feeling inseparable, inspiration firmly linked to the craft-work of shaping. Writing now for me has got to be grand.

Simply

                              As I walk out of the *La Belle*
the small town theater is at ease tonight.

                    Automobile weather
and the framed house lights

                              are balanced on the curved
          shallows of the bay.

                              I do not know why it touches me
that the children are riding their bikes home

          over the bridge water

                              under the street lamps.

Last Breath

                              When the petals of the plum tree
swirl Up
              before my headlights
I turn the car downhill and Drive.

                         Because I can't see
                              the way the apple flower
                              snows the air
the way the fever
of the plum
is brooding everywhere in Berkeley

                              I drive and I am driven.
                    Tightly smooth   and
              forward in my black compartment.

          Thinking things
          that make me know   my
          heart still beats.

                         Loving in a way
                              that will not get there.

    So if I weep   behind this steering wheel

              I say that it's ok
              here in my privacy.

I can allow myself   one luxury.

                                    Let it go now
as behind
the petals from the plum   turn brown
                          and blow
                    Down the dark driveway.

Bees Inside Me

Ten thousand bees in the backyard.
Ten thousand bees
came swarming.
                    For the spot   for the queen to alight
          so that they could stop
their circling.
                    Fur and wing 10,000.
Bees for a destination.

                                        Bees in me
                                        inside my backyard
                                        Inside
                                        Bees inside me.

     Do they hear
          as they circle
     when they fly   together
as they light
          together—
                    Do they only hear
                    one motor?
                    Do they maybe hear
                         each other?

                                        Before they go   like that
                                        the bees   get full
                                        get good and full
                                        on honey.
They are breathing   heavy.
                              On the thought
                         with the body
                    for the smell of the mother
                         for the food we steal and name
                         Sweet Sex

won't make it
    better.

Bitter to be human
    to risk   the sting
        to fly and find   no limb
            no union.

O drowsy drowsy multitude
throbbing together
huddled on the tree Breathing in unison—

    Where is my sweetness
    going to come from.

On the wallowy

For Gloria Frym

Earth tremor.   I felt an *earth tremor.*

    (or was it just the house guests hunkering.

They love each other so
new & lovely
        sitting on the sofa, his arm
and her arm—
        Great big smile an Immediate kiss.
Also a tenderness under the rib cage
            bruising for that transitory
        ripest touch.

We come to imitation of initial urge
                wanting connection
to fill up the body with unmistakable This:

—SHOCKING WHITE SAMOYEDS ON AN YVES KLEIN BLUE—

Somewhere, sometimes, there's complete redness
azaleas in currant juice, huge satin lips.

        "Don't ask," he said,
because he felt horrible. Most of those
on that particular couch did.

Creamy tears look thick in cup
    by candlelight.

<pre>
                    Two stained hearts
sprout
         what seem to me
                              like milkdrops.
</pre>

"It's really a shame," my father said driving, straight ahead,
"that people rarely love each other at the same time."

<pre>
                                        (balanced.

                    Making a child is a similar thing:
</pre>

She had always wanted to
gut-level wanted to
but he completely refused it
and it's already happened
now the questions begin.

<pre>
          She's standing by the swimming pool
          confident, ready, but—
          There's no water in there!

                    I see.

          Yet she still dives
          yet she still swims through the air of the pool
          emptied, and arriving.
</pre>

Don't ask me where maternal urge comes from.
I might say—

<pre>
          From the tiny purple pony, thumb-sized
     I fed lettuce
          little nibbles of lettuce.

               (more an' more popcorn on the popcorn tree.
</pre>

The lovely man so many women fall in love with
nods to the hostess who obviously adores him—

"God," he says, "I wish she'd stop running around
looking like a servant."

Makes ya feel kinda guilty don't it.

But you know, Biewtifull, vut I'd Reeally like to see?
Itz you in da serving position vunce in a vile, because
I'm getting prrity Tired of pooting out for a lot of
singal men an getting none of da same in Return. I don
care if you are a lonely, unnerfed bachelur, don't

arrive anymore uninvited at dinnur. I'm Tired of yer
lazy obserVations—
                    "Gee, I wish I had a wife."

     My good friend with hair like bees
her front room surrounded by foliage, many trees bloom
          & it's her birthday.
     "This makes me sad," she gazes out,
what's clearly passing.
                         "Every morning, I wake up
          and it's so beautiful
it really depresses the shit out of me."

     Rain stole the plum trees' radiance this year.
          Dry heat once made
each pulse bloom
                    comme clitoral attraction.

Listen, I tell this, fashion's not important—
"You're getting better," (meaning, more like Me)—
Emotional absence, a garbled intelligence
looks like a one-way
zipper Up.

               All I want to do is
               gather and accept it.
               Let us learn to walk a language—
               Incredible feat.

Ven he vants to stop me, he make a spraying motion vit
his fingas—
               I, am Spiderman.
               I got you in my web.

     Digital clock date
set to her birthday forever.
                         Spray paint on pony-tailed
                    part of his hair.
          Compulsive drawer
locked up in closet
                    keeps drawing anyway—

          Kick you with my cowboy boots na-na-na.

Nice to be reminded of innocent heart-felt feelings from sofa
but here on the wallowy, I don't see too many lucky ducks.

Neighbor who I don't know well, comes
to find her children. Two of them are
here, another in her arms, but she
couldn't (kept laughing) get a line out
completely (slaps on thigh, ecstatically
converted) "I saw these great, dark
clouds, and then the writing—Sell
Everything, I was hypnotized for years
ran away with the baby, but my husband,
excuse me, Am I talking too much? Maybe
I shouldn't, but I always wondered, you
know, when you walk the stroller—
Some people have, you know, more light."

Meanwhile, the kids, (2, 3, & 4'ish)
who I thought were heading for her house
around the corner, have crossed two streets
(one of them very busy) and have entered
Safeway to steal a box of Crackerjacks.

He's his own girl friend, *blam/blam blam.*
Well, I guess, that's
one solution.
And a very short rope.
Looks to me, like contorted position—
Troll/mad/waiting/under/goat/clop/foot.

    "Please don't eat me! I'm skin & bones!"
        (little like a chicken wing
                not much meat)

Type hunt/Type Hunt
can't escape it
what attracts us.
        "She could solve everything,"
           self-made Lie.
Type hunt/Type Hunt
only trouble is—
        She was a very sad replica.

"Why a pop gun."
        (with a cork on a string)

"What does a fucking Pop gun
for a birthday present mean.
I don't even *like* guns."

"I do," I said. (I mean
I enjoyed shooting it off
a couple times.)
Know what I saw?
Werner Erhardt, sitting on a dixie cup.
Thought it was a motorcycle. There was a straw. Couldn't go
too far. All the way to Georgia. Then I got scared. I want
to go home now. This made him *very* angry. So I had to run.
Nice ole rich man in Mercedes picked me up, saying he'd
transport me, friendly father-type, hearse black car, until
he slipped out and I saw around the corner that HE was in
butcher's clothes and *this* was a set-up I was already on the
line of tied-down women getting their throats slit and their
heads whopped off . . .

Hmmm,
I think I better tell you a gentler
bedtime story.
Ok,,,
She was a chowist. She accompanied
her doctor friend in Tibet to a distant
monastery, and because he was an honored
man, she was allowed to go with him.
(This was quite rare.)
But before the long journey through
mountains in jeep caravan, he suggested
something about selecting a stick,
to keep the Blue Dogs back.
(She wondered if *that* meant . . .)
And then when they arrived, the holy gates
were thrown open, and out rushed fifty,
perfect, blue chows!

Well one of these mornings

You gonna rise up shinin'

Spread your wings

an' take to the sky

But until

that mornin'

There ain't a nothin'

gonna harm you

　　　　　So hush

　　　　　　　little baby

　Don't

　　　you cry . . .

They say
that at the hour
of the tremor
there's this sensation of waiting.

And beneath
that apprehension
you don't want to be touched.

Sometimes,

　　　　somewhere

　　　　　　　　　(heart so distant.

　　　Nothing trembles

but the memory of us.

Trellis

For Willa & Ayler, born 10.19.79

　　　A small blond girl brings a dark haired woman, a beautiful woman who is sitting in the grass, legs together to the side very feminine, a small girl in a short plaid dress, brings her mother these flowers, a handful, for she is in love with this woman, strange beautiful woman, and the woman seems amazed by the child, wonder and amusement, as she sits so carefully seductive in the grass, with her dense red lipstick and polish, the woman has waves in her hair. I wonder if the woman will accept them, the flowers. The child is so tentative, careful with her love. But of course she accepts them, her laughter accepts them, and everybody is glad.
　　　　　　　　　But how now to reconcile the oldest hostility, breast against breast, flowers crushed, tooth nail and hair. How to skin those feelings, let them swell to a drum, coming back with my belly to deliver them.

No, no, the
gift's never good enough. Child not the daughter she's supposed to
be. Very much "supposed to be." Wanting each other silenced.
Brutal reconciliation. None in the freezer chest, none.

I needed a
saddle, not a bullet jacket. I needed a saddle to escape. I asked the
groom for one, preferably soft and wide. He left the stable and
returned. With a Band-Aid. "Here's a good saddle for your horse."

Insults & injury blew the surface acceptance of everything she'd
secured as refuge around her woman friend. Wanting it easy not
difficult—Now, we need the gritty feel of cleanser to rub'n rub'up
against, not the endless o.k. (denial) of just *letting it go*.

After the
hot steam expresso of anger came calm, a sisterly benediction. Long
stretch of water galactic with light—The steps up were smooth and
uncluttered. We climbed to her home where her mother would give
us milk butter and bread, meaning affection, her motherly love.

*

I wrote her—I've lost the old passion. How can I make it *move*
anymore, push it waterlike Over without the old passion. Is it just
being pregnant, this slow river I'm on, sittin' in a fishin' hole of
contentment?

But she wasn't content, because she wanted that
passion more than anything, in her, more than coffee and cigarettes,
she wanted that fire, to float on her water, needed oil and a flame,
needed juice, his quick juice for her brain to push over. But no, she'd
be pushing a baby. That's different, not sexy. Old elephant pants.
And yet blood engorged volume excitement *come on*—Huge
mammals hump up in the ocean.

Or consider the weightless sex of
the net veined dragonflies, who settle in tandem on my knee. She
rests the tip of her long curled tail on the base of his neck, he bends his
tail under—It sticks to the base of her abdomen. Holding that
position, immobile, as if forever, making a blue heart shape.

He
rubs his hardness up behind her largeness for fun—He can grope her
symmetrically then. He splits apart his pants—She does and doesn't
want to see—He twists a mammoth worm in mud around his finger.
She goes down, going down, to engorge upon connection, for this is
her biggest turn on.

Nudge, said the mother. *We Nudge*, said the
one. So they nudged all day in the Valley of the Sun.

Delighted to find out that the guy she'd had the crush on was a total boor, for his baseness aroused her, he was no longer a threat. "You can have me," she said, so sober it scared him. He belonged in her satchel full of kicks to call up. I'm a Man, he mused, staggering, Not a Thought.

Her husband now is totally engaged, talking with another man. Both discredit by ignoring her presence. But she has two dolls, which she undresses in front of them. HaHA she says to herself. They pay no attention. The dolls have abnormally long penises for dolls. She moves the hand of each doll onto the sex of the other, amusing only herself.

Alright, she'll go off to ride her own horses. She doesn't need their saddle. She doesn't need a rein. She doesn't need any of their intellectual get-up. The creature can sense the other creature inside her, and moving between her legs, the animal responds.

Fly, said the mother. *We Fly*, said the two. So they both flew together to the Valley of the Moon.

Someday her real man will return to her, and not with his needs, his hunger or his burdens. He'll come lightly back into her original courtyard, and his skin will be cool and water fresh. Then nothing will interfere with their darkness, almost familiar, nothing will hinder their conceptional kiss.

In the garden every light was cuddling up the animals—Small pockets of haze around the rabbit babies and phlox. In the stable *hallelujah* all together we were moving, in a vibrant local hum, in the sun a kind of purr was in the air was on the oats, and as the trellis rose above us, a warm wind fell.

*

I slept on your name, Eden, place of my pleasure—A confirming light glowed with belltones collecting in answer to my question, which way will the ring swing, back & forth or around.

She came out two months early to show me her vulva. It was important that I see this fruit-like part of myself, though what entranced me most was her serenity, for this was a calm and knowing child.

Feeling strong—Stand, positioned on pier, facing smooth water. Feet parallel, shoulders down, head up higher. Full-bellied woman turns, sinks to her holding stance, arms straight up, in control of each motion. The people jabbering on martini boat ride by in silence. She releases a soft O sound.

Looking up, we see cumulus piles, skyward climbing. "The power inside more than 50 atomic bombs," he said. The pilots dip with respect and run their little props home, but thundering rain is my headdress.

Knees, a sweet portrait of knees, fine and girlish, by the sand, in a daze, before the stone wall. You know how fast she can run, how still she can stand, quietly, ready, how rarely she has gotten down on them.

He wants to paint the house black. Yes, including the trim. She wants to paint it fleshy, say a warm melon color, cantelope and cream. He wants a sophisticated archive. She wants a borning room. How can they agree on any name.

By holding up the same umbrella?

Everything was drenched with a palette of greens drenched early morning semiconscious aromatic field, that moves to throw its moisture into bursting. Forth and forward, swishing on through, to the middle where she'll want to lie down, and be held. Not necessarily kissed. Just held, all around, held in, on his shoulder, squeezed, encircled, his breath on her brow.

She will come sliding into town out of one amazed mother. Only after the fall did labor turn hard. Dream myself back into that garden, before the bite, vicious, snakey twist of it tightening, round my abdomen. I will give in, float under the wave, and bring her forth with the pushing swell of it. Mutual waterdrift into this world, with her name flying first to guide her, There—place where she might find her own pleasure. *Jouissance*, they will say, *jouissance, jouissance*, a rustling reminder of reeds around the harbor, as her bow bulges in, a widening chorus of bells—Dove skin Chime lamb button baby, prisms of glass shivering with color, giving in now into her unfolding rose, deliver us whole. Bathe us and bring us up together again, as we were, in the swing, above the garden.

Moved Towards a Future

We have the road here, the gate the key. And the miniature pond's reflection. Back to the hoofprint. Over the fence—Fall, folded. She waited there. Dappled mares welled up in the sky. The sky filled. She poured. Full. Over the wires losses were welcome. Home again, Hymn. Returns reminding. Very fine hopes. To have to want to do without. What were the large leaves saying? Strength in her now. And one big anger. That comes later, after threat of the last verb—No. To know to see and yet to taste it. Tongue on/stuck, the unknown factors. Haul pack sort box sell out-going. Out through the gate, our golden one waiting. Yes, and horizon, a ready Please, our prayer for you this evening. Extension of *here* as a place to land. To lie there though, watching it wind, fearing it rain, wanting it all soaked through. Out of you. Demanding it clean and clear and true, and the road goes up and it gets harder, damn hard. Shuck-it hard. We want to laugh about this. Cry. Beat down. Beat on. Go on, certainly, cursing and west with umbrellas for sun, not rain, come. Let them come in their due time. Do. Let him be that art, fixed, for eternity's instant. Palette tin can oil cold smooth, when ours is humus is rotting a little, and heavier, heaving. Having a malicious thought. Frame. Wanting to squeeze it. No not touch me. Not in the old way. Puncture, pressure, release and drive. Two mountain ranges to cover. Hover. Over you go. Fondness! Who are he kidding. Horses! This is our hoofprint. Read me, mount, and—Ride it on. We have not lost, and it's not any more a matter of winning. One day, one month, life at a time. And it *is* time now. You/he feel it. Already becoming a little of its own, a little of your own big part of the unknowable. You always did move in that element. Water, was it? Raining, backwards. Upwards I mean, I mean believe, and the sky was flooding. Clouds in reverse. The leaves stopped . . . talking. We were talking. But so was the party line. And it was more than plain distraction. Pain, washed over and firmed up. Grasshopper egg worm incubation. Fertile, unfolding. Fetal. Help. Hope on the range. In the plans another. And that one you can't doubt. For that one has been chosen to choose you. And now you can not lose. You. Go. Come, both ways. Stretched—East/West—Summer in winter. Reach, and a thought will meet you. As your foot finds the stone, as wheel the road. And over the left shoulder is our distance.

We Heart

For Jill & Alex

We all dazed—down by ocean, gold in jingles, inhalexhale all around. Out on the uncovered rippled floor, bubbling spurt of a razor clam, rivulets of the sand plantation. We needn't walk all the way to Jeremy Point, because if we wait—the waters will bring the point to us. Toes touching, clear abandon, watermelon pace.

Bonnets on babies, phases and kelp smell, just like a health food restaurant (lower east side) and I'm glad that we aren't there, but gathering stones, the metaphors, to make walking home such heavy success. He'll call that one, a loaf of bread, that—a temple, foot, an egg, a penguin, hammer and a hunk of ham. Squinting, dared, we do disrobe. We bare our futures and the water holds us. How could it be any other way, than both shores of one cape.

Buried in sand, lost under a towel, family photo—10 seconds to run/into the picture. All of us, *You-Hoo*, floating away on the days we heart together. We rise we nurse we cook huge lobster culls with missing claws. But see how quickly it grows another? Pushing the curling tail meat out—through the buttery hole—we gorge.

On the night of their common birth, Alex saw twin shooting stars, one heading for California. The mystery of it still plays its points along the spine. Some day they may recognize that common light, but for right now, it's a spool of thread, or a common piece of Zweiback.

And I see how quickly the years revolve, as our first babe covers the expanse of shore with strong, six year old legs, as our third hangs a thought in question. The emerging miracle of flesh looks up to receive an ancient notion. *Light—may it pour into us all, take hold of us, and strengthen.* O smiling eyes, big watery eyes, eyes not yet disillusioned.

You are one man who knows how to get down on the ground with them. Even the rabbi in line at the airport just back from Zurich could see that. Later, he stared at you kindly, while exhausted you slept under your hat, holding your book bag close.

On the cover of this new notebook Jill, the little flowers resembling fish, open their mouths to catch Word. One bronze-green horse in orange-blue sentence enjoys his riderless bath, while two women in the river's chapter, ride bare as their backs in the jungle thickness. We write we rinse we progress.

Clovis Ayler Felix Angel, Willa Rachel Anna. All are born but one who floats still towards that perfect Lily. You are the generation given to us, the flowers for whom we care. We heart we try we see we die, someday, we give to you.

If a giving up is necessary, a gaining will be had. And perhaps the knits and purls of that will make a fortuitous pattern. Jill pointed out to Clovis what she had worked into her sweater, good wishes knitted in as honeycomb, ripe blackberries, the tree of life, growing up with its delicate branches. We balance on those limbs.

Meanwhile the matches named *Cia & Mark* keep shooting sparks when I strike them. They must have had a good honeymoon. After walking down the aisle what got me most, was turning to the dark stone distance, seeing Clovis coming, all in white, careful with their pillow of rings. My father and sister behind him.

When the spark ignites, the fireworks are visible to the jam-packed burghers of Barnstable. We want to see this spectacle every year, return to awe, to *ooo's* and *aaah's*, as a return to our youth which cared most about the useless. "The useless, as people say."

We hearts grow across the country. The abundance of it comes in seed and stag, as summer heat, rising to the rain, out of sand and soil, under simple sheets, over land, we come, to water. We fly our notes that write like net, that sparkle and connect with spray and boom, our garden of tunes, our resting field. We brain— We heart— We will.

Go Round

The longest day will drive a crack—til Jubilate windows in. Three parts that braid begin to fly—That something singing overlapping. White roses on the fire lit. The stick once put begins to curl. A wheel is rolling sparks for ten. She feels it here—but *far away*. High golden hills remind the day of St.-John's-Wort. One yellow cup upon each end. Asha found three little bowls. The tones are gliding through the light. Mountains can appear we wave—and roll in dust and dark til then. Because the small ones can not stop. We find a way to circle so. We close into a fire pop. Open also leaves have room. And grow with pushes following through. We sing to leap the last of it. The nuts are gathered in a cup. The arc is scent, the curve a boat. To row and row the blinding stream. We hope to cast a shadow yet. A firm trail makes me follow up. We turn and run descend upon. To beat a beat upon the rim. A kiss in light before a name. The same few rise. Until she flew. The angel woke to be a bird. And never once the same again. The turquoise chamber turning parts. Lemon mint upon the flame. Old treasure sack. The tones do chime. And nut hats six can climb sky high. We wave we wheel around the bend. Though amber changed the wending way. Sinking deep in Lion's mane. Go round she say to sign your flame. Seven stars are shining bright. The round is fine. Just out of sight. We see it dry to golden sheets. Though wet was once all flick and stain. Today will not remain again. Go round she say go round to me. And let the lifting bird come through. The gate is raised the sun can too. Go round go round. Today is different not the same. A new a new. Goodbye in waves for sinking down. Often time to *see* and *bend*. Around she say. Once more again. So ashes breathe—Around me now.

In a Motion

The dangers of drifting while driving, in a daze—Loosening the reins that last ride on Eagle. I had the premonitions that day, galloping alongside Old Farm Road, newly spread gravel hid the edge of asphalt, my horse nicked—Sliding, weight of horse flesh—Thrown, into a splash of view, as if I *were* the landscape, skid hot palms, even liking that later, the wakeful, stinging, unexpected smasheroo. It all felt familiar, as if I'd read that page, somewhere, or someday, like "The End" plucked out of the saddle, oddly marvelous and shocking, like birth, but not squeezed, rather—Freed from the tiddly winks of shape.

To summon inside—The brave shining warrior, glittering hero of the skies with flaming sword, astride a horse so white, you *know* you are ready, to meet and overpower the dreadful. I've got my firm together now, my word drawn up, to hold and to swing into warning. Big "L's" begin lifting, for lightness and levity, raising the sediments Up in the body. L is for *lucia*, I said with my slipper, for all of the liquid that rises forever and falls into falls, to further the flowing, to keep us in motion.

Now each yellow girl on the bright red background of my new knit vest, reaches up to catch a heart above her head, while the boys down below around the border are running and flexing—They all warm my chest. They are not your modern children, who expect to be questioned, throwing up the hooves to their little lamb costumes. To resist what this culture insists on, strikes a light that cuts fad image into doubles, until a million brooms sweep wild water in a panic, and yet, this is such a tiny world with a placemat of maniacs, why not try to set it right. How to walk the white steed, each step lifting, and carrying, and placing, to stand. The electrical smell falls in a ring at your ankles. You *are* the shining rain. You draw a Number 1, in a motion, to the sun—The globe itself hovers there before you. Yes, you can touch it, give it a little "L——" That's what it's come back for, to set you on your way, gladly, with a hum—An approval.

Returning to the World

> Sleep is the Mother of God.
> —Flannery O'Connor

When I heard that thunder, I rose up like a happy animal. The window was wide, it was a hard straight rain. I leaned towards that freshness, beyond the family photos, having just unlocked the last room to my heredity. And what did I find there—In the ruins? (the contents glistened like candy-preserved antique toys) Greed, for material possession, which must be the top layer over some other layer of need. But there in the icing of the dreamwork, I spied the perfect arthritic bicycle, made entirely of wood, every curve, each spoke—I knew it would collapse if I touched it.

My father did give me permission to ransack the past. Might I even say he encouraged me? But it was *my* move flicked the cellular switch, self-repulsion on the structural level, collapsing the castle, setting the bones on fire, exhausted under the noiseless hum. I tightened up the reins on life itself, until my hands ached as if from a horse ride. But we know the fingers were just too eager to take, that conscience doesn't want you to cheat one bit, that life *is* constant in its demand for you to give, and that you cannot control The World.

*

From the first sign of hardening, to my birthday, nine months. Now I understand the significance of cake. The unfrosted one-layer with light. How I want it to glow in the waiting room—healed. The unseen moves upward as the physical grows stone. *"Rise up from out your carved condition."*

Each day it grew harder to move. Positioned with pillows, I would lie in the afternoon with my eyes closed, and the sun would flood in between worlds, redwood beams grasping the whiteness. Everything so still, it was a blessing that stillness. The plum tree full of flower, a gentle feeling as sleep came gratefully wrapped in soft swaddling.

Not who to blame, not even who do I forgive, just this need to be completely held. To give oneself over, to skin the shining seed—then to bury it. It was a long, slow rain, and it was coming from me, pulled from me, aching, until even the smallest birds bathed in it, and new life came up on its own grief. I will have slept from the Birth of Light to the Death of Darkness, and then my time is come to term, this spring. Still, I have these hours, returning to the world, while the rainwater pours, streaming over the roof of this room, and I am deep in my comforter.

Jorie
Graham

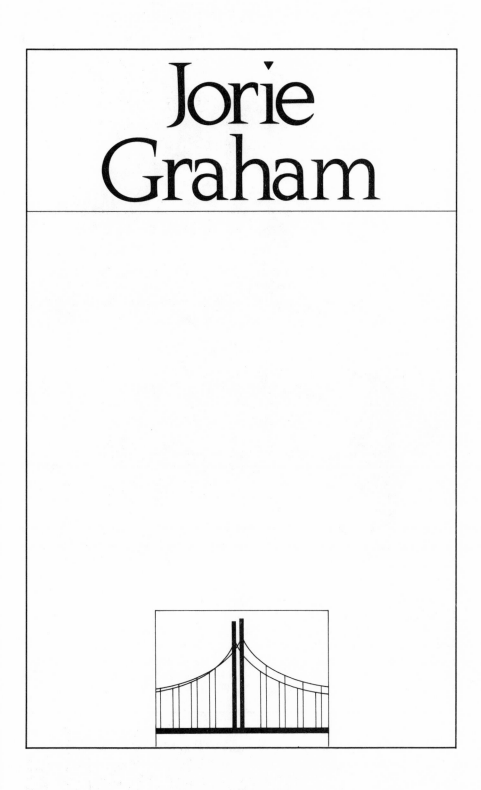

Jorie Graham grew up in Italy and was educated at the Sorbonne, New York University, Columbia University and The University of Iowa. Her first book, *Hybrids of Plants and of Ghosts* (Princeton University Press, 1980) won the Great Lakes Colleges Association Award for that year. A second book, *Erosion*, is due out from Princeton in the Spring of 1983. She has been awarded an Ingram Merrill Grant, a Bunting Fellowship and a Guggenheim Foundation Grant. Although she teaches, from time to time, at Columbia University, she makes her home in Arcata, California, where she is on the faculty of Humboldt State University.

Somes Notes on Silence

I think I am probably in love with silence, that other world. And that I write, in some way, to negotiate seriously with it. If poems are records of true risks (attempts at change) taken by the soul of the speaker, then, as much as possible, my steps are towards silence. Silence which is the absence of speech, or the ability to speak, the reason or desire. Silence which drowns us out, but also which ignores us, overrides us, silence which is doubt, madness, fear, all that which makes the language bend and slip. I need to feel the places where the language fails, as much as one can. Silence which is awe or astonishment, the speech ripped out of you. All forms of death and mystery, therefore, working in each poem against the hurry of speech, the bravery of speech. And I think it is very important to feel the presence of that ocean in the poem, in the act of writing the poem. Its emissaries are the white space, of course, the full stops. But, also, all acts of grammar, which are its inroads. And the way the lines break, or slow. I'd like to think you can feel, by its accurate failures, the forces pressing against the sentence, the time order. And certain kinds of words, too, are messengers of silence. Not just vagueness and inaccuracy, but prepositions and conjunctions, for instance; and diction deliberately flattened to deaden pain. And certain sounds that deepen and slow the poem into sounds you can't hear—all the long vowels in the sharp teeth of the consonants. And echoes, and what is said by implication, by default . . . Because there is, of course, always the desire, the hope, that they are not two separate worlds, sound and silence, but that they become each other, that only our hearing fails.

Certain kinds of diction, in poems, serve to sharpen the blade of the silence, making us hear it more loudly, more accurately. Abstract diction, for instance, feels especially powerful to me because of its poignancy, the sense of desperation that informs it, the sense of a last avenue being resorted to, a last, bluntest tool. One feels that imagery has been relinquished, that naming—the word as amulet —is all we have left. Lines like Jon Anderson's (speaking of a mirror): "I believe in its terrible empty reflection / its progress from judgement toward compassion" carry for me an implicit admission that there is no other way left, nor time enough. It's the urgency (not what teachers often tell us is the *laziness*) of abstraction that moves me. The sense that it is very late, and we must think fast and hard. Of course the language of image can do this, but it still believes in the physical world, in time enough, in the storyline and its properties, beauties, while the motion of *resorting to* the colder stuff, the drier quicker tools, moves me often precisely because of its implied failures.

The dryness of the abstract diction in late Williams, for instance, is rendered powerful by all the white space, silence, around it—into which it is slowed, from which it is sensuously wrought. It serves, this lingering, this carefulness (this jazz), to make abstractions "emotional"—stressed, voiced, stern. This is the most important service rendered by the variable foot in the triadic stanza, it seems to me, this singling out and stressing of lone concepts, dry sounds . . . I like to think of the otherwise skeletal notes rising in a very large empty cathedral. That kind of emphasis makes them swell with silence, take on the flesh of our more enforced listening.

Or a silence heard by default, as in Bishop, for instance, where the flat diction of a poem like *First Death in Nova Scotia* serves to muffle or blanket the terrible white birth of fear the child-speaker is experiencing—as well as her mother's famous scream as she enters madness; the scream that finally surfaces in Aunt Consuelo's mouth in *In the Waiting Room,* another poem where the stoic classicism of the language functions to sustain, highlight and buffer the great white noise of that speechlessness. Because the scream is in fact the voice of the silence —its foray into, possession of, speech—silence made audible, in so many of her poems, by the muted diction. Not unlike the way, in Lowell, (especially in the poems of *For the Union Dead*) the border between sanity and insanity is described by the inroads of strongly stressed, cacophonic, clangy assonances and the violent terms Vendler calls "scream-words" on the otherwise fluid, restrained diction . . .

Pace—music—are of course crucial in this. One can feel the weight of what the language is battling with every expectation of rhythm or rhyme or tone or form that is not met. The poem doesn't hurry or slow because of whim, after all, but because of what the silence within or without demands, silence from whom it is, in effect, won. Some poets win easily and always. One feels no *fight* for the poem in the poem. Some put up a powerful struggle. (Think of Berryman, all those breaks, twists in syntax, gaps, lunges). Some often or always lose. I often feel in Dickinson, in Glück, that they have battled with a worthy opponent and been gagged by it. In Glück, for instance, where often the theme of death as lover ("the hand over the mouth, over the eyes, in love . . .") makes the formal negotiation with silence the overt vehicle, the muscle of the poem, the perfect *finish* of the poem (the starved-for innocence) functions as armor against it. And yet, in the astonishing closures ("and the snow / which has not ceased since / began"; or "Instruct me in the dark"; or "as the heart / expands to admit its adversary"; or "The lights are out. Love / forms in the human body"; or "how could I not take them since they were a gift") the silence supersedes, is, indeed, victorious. And it is the terrible muteness of the Fall that her endings act out, over and over, it seems to me, the betrayal of the spirit into flesh, that great silence. In fact, the way the hush overrides makes one feel how the greater party, the instigator, is the "winner" in all this. Such failures of speech are, at any rate, enormously to her credit. I think of Frost's comment: "There are no two things as important in life and art as being threatened and being saved. What are the ideals of form for if we aren't going to be made to fear for them? All our ingenuity is lavished on getting into danger *legitimately* so that we may be *genuinely* saved." I stress those two words because they are the key. So much poetry fails, for me, because the risks are invented for the purposes of a poem.

Dickinson's poems, her dangers, are also, often, authenticated by her losses. So many of them—battles with those emissaries of silence which are the ocean, the wind, the light of day (with its terrible raised expectations—unfulfilled promises—of vision) and the speechlessness of pain, of fear—end on great failures of human speech, victories of "the Tooth / That nibbles at the Soul." It has the last word everywhere as one can see in these seven instances:

> Interrupt—to die—
>
> Until the Moss had reached our Lips—
> And covered up—our Names—
>
> Withdraws—and leaves the dazzled Soul
> In her unfurnished Rooms.
>
> Then—close the Valves of her attention—
> Like Stone—
>
> When orchestra is dumb . . .
> And Ear—and Heaven—numb—
>
> The Heavens with a smile
> Sweep by our disappointed Heads
> Without a syllable—
>
> The Tapestries of Paradise
> So notelessly—are made!

and of course in the succinct: "I know that He Exists— / Somewhere—In silence."

And so many are riddles, which are of course owned by silence until we crack them, which are in effect *spoken silence*. Her dashes themselves seem to me, whether intentionally used this way or not, the literal knife-edge of that other Speech greater than hers, the tongue of the Interruptor to whom she must give way, over and over. Interruptor who will not speak! Although the metrical base of her poems, the promise you know can't, finally, fail her, no matter how she tests it, makes her in effect less vulnerable than Glück whose free verse could fail at any time—requiring, therefore, that finish of hers, that show of strength. Dickinson can meet the lover, the silence, as it were, on more equal terms. Can rail against it, challenge it—("Because I would not stop for Death / He kindly stopped for me . . ."). In both cases the silence overrides, but how much more vulnerable the more modern rhythm seems. How much more energy must go into self-defense, proof of seriousness. And yet—and this is our dilemma, isn't it—how great the opportunities for bravery, in that ill-equippedness, seem.

Finally, even in the few poems that remain obscure in Dickinson (and other poets who resort from time to time to the silence of hermetic motion (Tate, Ashbery, Berryman, Merwin, Montale come to mind) the experience of obscurity for the reader comes to stand for the experience of mystery in the world for the writer. Or *apparent* mystery, apparent meaninglessness. So that we undergo that confrontation ourselves: the poem moving from speech to "silent" speech. We are made to rub up against it. And every time one of these poems unseals itself for us—and with a little work most do—it is a victory over silence for us, an experience of sudden grace. What a miraculous tool, then, obscurity becomes. The mercy of the suddenly dissolving riddle. It astonishes me a poem can do this . . .

Although there is, too, often, in Dickinson, the silence of the Ear that ceases to listen. Of cruel misleading promises. I think of those beautiful interviews with light *(There's a Certain Slant of Light,* and, *A Light Exists in Spring) . . .* They remind me of Bishop's interviews with the baffling muteness of oceans and jungles, always taunted, always expectant. The entrance that Dickinson seeks to gain through leaps of mind or intuition, Bishop attempts through description. The poems come to be almost *about* the effort of description itself as an act of vision, an attempt to penetrate that silence, the tools of description becoming the actual subject in many cases . . .

Of course it is not only darkness which encroaches upon the poem, not only confusion where language fails. It is also true, as George Steiner puts it, that "where the word of the poet ceases, a great light begins." So much can be seized about different poets' visions if one tries to imagine whether it is primarily a great light or a great dark that shines just beyond their words. Berryman ends on light here, dark there. How brave his terrible wading out past speech is: "I saw nobody coming, so I went instead . . ."; or, "Vanisht & then the thing took hold"; or the brutal truncated interruptions, the muzzlings: endings like "Why—"; or "Later . . ."; or "Henry nodded, un—"; or, "So what." And the radiant silences, how rare they are: "and polished women called / small girls to dream awhile towards the flashing & bursting tree!"; or, "Henry, tasting all the secret bits of life"; or, "through awes & weathers neither it increased/ nor did one blow of all his stone & sand thought die." Notice how the line can glide metrically into the silence here without having to put up a fight. For a moment, it's a draw.

And then there are the silences that override altogether, like Rimbaud's. And the silences, as where figurative language fails Dante in the *Paradiso,* of transcendent awe. And the desire of so many poets to undergo radical mutation

(*Change me, change me*, says Jarrell), and all those cessations of speech and memory which are the limits of this flesh.

Because poems are, after all, dialogues between the song of man and the silences of God, aren't they? And almost every poem illustrates one of the two impulses we experience: to be united with the unknown, to break out of this separateness, or to wrench a uniqueness, an identity, from the all-consuming whole. This is what Frost refers to, I believe, when he says "the most exciting movement in nature is not progress, advance, but expansion and contraction, the opening and shutting of the eye, the hand, the heart, the mind. We throw our arms wide with a gesture of religion to the universe; we close them around a person. We explore and adventure for a while and then we draw in to consolidate our gains. The breathless swing is between subject matter and form."

I think this is what Pound meant when he said that form, or technique, is a measure of a man's sincerity, adding that "a man's rhythm must be interpretive and will be, therefore, in the end, his own, uncounterfeiting, uncounterfeitable." For in the rhythm is the exact relationship of each man to his God. If he summons that silence and does true battle with it (if the poem is won from it, not bought from it) then the choices he makes in the poem at every move will be authentic because he will be using the poem to grow and be changed. It will be an *act*. Then bravery becomes a crucial issue.

Of course some poems tell stories about acts, more than seeking to be acts in their own right. They want us to see what's here. They are not so totally after transcendence or unity. They believe in time. In these poems, in the great narratives in which, to use Frost's terms, the movement is primarily one of progress, silence is most often only present in the margins. And while those poems that engage silence *want* to be eroded by it, transformed by it, believing as they do that what is true or immutable is reached past or beyond time, in *silence*, narrative sequences, for instance, believe in the changes of history and experience, believe that what is immutably true is achieved only via time, in it, by it—in *speech*, in other words. These believe in the future, in generation, in the flesh as the literal vehicle for transcendence, while the former often view the flesh itself (as well as speech) as the obstacle, and crave stillness, form, law, over the formulation of hope which is *cause and effect*. The protagonist of the first is the spirit, of the second, character. Jon Anderson (who writes both kinds of poems; and hybrids) describes our passage from one to the other in his beautiful lines:

> We who have changed
> And have no hope of change
> Must now love
> The passage of time.

Not that there is no *doubt* in the narrative motion, but that it is implicitly resolved by the very act of storytelling the poem announces for itself. No matter how it might twist to get itself free, a story is married to time and saved by it. A story always tells about something that happened. Something the speaker survived (as a voice at least) to tell about. While a poem which is an *act* could be the very last act, couldn't it, every time? It must feel that way, at least—the very last act or very first. Most of us write both kinds of poems, often at different stages in our life. Roethke, for instance, writes the poem *The Lost Son*, the *enactment* of loss and recovery, riddled by silence; and then, years later, *In a Dark Time*, which is a poem *about* the very descent and return *The Lost Son* actually enacts. One gets the feeling the earlier poem changed the life of the poet as he was writing it (and therefore the life of the reader, hopefully as he reexperiences it). There is, in a sense, no guarantee the speaker will make it through the poem. While *In a Dark Time* is built on those guarantees, presenting itself, as it does, as the record of an event that took place prior to the writing of the poem. An event it is thus able to generalize about. As in, for example:

> What's madness but nobility of soul
> At odds with circumstance?

> versus

> Is this the storm's heart? The ground is unstilling itself.
> My veins are running nowhere? Do the bones cast out their
> fire?

or, again:

> The mind enters itself, and God the mind
> And one is One, free in the tearing wind.

> versus

> The weeds stopped swinging.
> The mind moved, not alone,
> Through the clear air, in the silence.

The desperation, the genuine risk of the poet using the earlier poem—the process of writing the poem—in order to find what will, for now, suffice, moves me much more deeply. It changes me.

One could take this even further and say the battle between time and desire, between history and transcendence, is always taking place in the language itself: the syllables advancing with startling evenness, the beautiful strong stresses always trying, each one, to stop the flow altogether. And always the small sadness when the sentences keep on, the exile . . .

Finally, if in the form is each man's uncounterfeitable relationship with the mysteries, then the degree of his fear or grace are also in some measure legible there. It is hard to name these things: but in those poets who confront the unknown, the holy, most head-on, the syntax begins to buckle and bend back and break, very much like Saint Teresa first witnessing the host and twisting back, both to look away and, strangely, to better receive it. From the labyrinthine ritual cave paintings of the Stone Age, through every period of human time, when we have sought to enter, to break the surface, one of the ways in has been crooked—the blindness that one may see. And in the poets that go that way, twisted syntax, breaks against smooth sequence or sense, line breaks of queer kinds, white spaces, interruptions, dashes, overpunctuation, delays, clotted rich diction, obscurity, disorder, ellipses, sentence fragments, digressive strategies— every modulation in certainty—are all tools for storming the walls. Whether of hell or paradise is another matter.

So it is that boundary that interests me, between flesh and time, between what's sealed and what's open, between the words we speak and those that unspeak us. Those poems I love always feel like active negotiations at that border, not border-skirmishes but great last-ditch efforts. What moves me is bravery, I guess. And the incredible difficulty of saying something true. The presence of silence as an active partner on the page, a fierce opponent, puts pressure on me to try as much as I can not to lie. The very whiteness pushes back to make me authenticate, make me earn and stand by the small words. It makes me feel my choices in poems are never merely aesthetic or technical, but always, somehow, moral. That I am implicated by them and responsible, finally responsible, for each choice in the poem as if it were an act in the street. The silence is what Bishop calls *the monument*. I think of how she admonishes us, gently: *watch it closely.*

The Way Things Work

is by admitting
or opening away.
This is the simplest form
of current: Blue
moving through blue;
blue through purple;
the objects of desire
opening upon themselves
without us;
the objects of faith.
The way things work
is by solution,
resistance lessened or
increased and taken
advantage of.
The way things work
is that we finally believe
they are there,
common and able
to illustrate themselves.
Wheel, kinetic flow,
rising and falling water,
ingots, levers and keys,
I believe in you,
cylinder lock, pully,
lifting tackle and
Crane lift your small head—
I believe in you—
your head is the horizon to
my hand. I believe
forever in the hooks.
The way things work
is that eventually
something catches.

Drawing Wildflowers

I use no colors, just number threes,
and though I know there are gradations I will miss, in this manner change
is pressure brought to bear, and then—
as if something truthful could be made more true—

the spiderwebs engraved on all successive sheets, flowers inhabited
by the near disappearances of flowers.
Having picked one
I can start anywhere, and as it bends, weakening,

ignore that.
I can chart the shading of the moment—tempting—though shading
changes hands so rapidly.
Yet should I draw it changing, making of the flower a kind of mind

in process, tragic and animal, see how it is rendered unbelievable.
I can make it carry *my* fatigue,
or make it dying, the drawing becoming
a drawing of air making flowerlike wrinkles of the afternoon,

meticulous and scarred.
Brought indoors and moored to vases, unwavering light, I can take my time,
though passage then is lonely, something high and dry and
gotten used to,

something noble.
A bouquet is another thing—purple lupine, crimson paintbrush, pink
forget-mes clash. One can try, in imitation,
indication by default—

a suggested real, though not the same, a difference
from which not enough is lacking.
Watercolors could achieve the *look* of it, two mapped but hostile lands
resigned to their frontiers—but it's an abstract
     peace, magenta meeting

crimson; crimson, scarlet.
But these in our fields, the real, the sheet of paper, the bouquet,
will not negotiate, and how I love
my black and white and the gray war they make.

Netting

My father would have saved us, had the occasion of fire arisen.
Sundays, each at our post,
we practiced—
his fine network of hoses lacing into perfect

webs. So much water,
and each of us a knot we felt so safe in manning.
I never really understood the underpinnings, miraculous nation
beneath the smooth lawn—

a private patriotism.
Nothing again was ever as dangerous, as vulnerable. I know of father
less than I imagine, but in the end
all that we can know of anyone

is what we promised them. I know, therefore,
that fire is something we can catch, unwittingly, like cold,
and that these tiny roads
woven round and round our property like a spare set of roots,

is what we really are—a shadow map, a future kept alive by
met commitments.
And at those junctions, the world seems as private as public,
a well-kept secret

kept by all. Just as, deep in a cave, life can survive
only because of forms of life outside that will persist
in entering. So . . .
water to save us, and

profound curiosity—casting and trawling and building a surface
able to truly hold us,
like gossip, or the smell of lilacs, or an overheard song: soon
everyone has caught it.

An Artichoke for Montesquieu

Its petals do not open of their own accord. That is our part,
as the whisper is the hand we tender
to the wish, though each
would rather rule the field. What remains
is the heart, its choke a small reminder to be mindful
lest we go too far
for flavor. These are the questions
its petals part in answer to: where
is God? how deep is space? is it inhabited? The artichoke
is here that we imagine
what universe once needed to create it,
penetrable jewel;
what mathematics.
And then, now,

when the earth is no longer the world, it offers
a small believable cosmology:
each tiny leaf an oar

in the battle where each pulled his own; and the whole
the king himself, tiered like his crown or the multitude
laughing. The mind meets the heart
on such terrain as this, where each
can give in to the other
calling it victory,
calling it loss—
a no man's land where each of us
opens, is opened, and where
what we could have done locks to the very core
with what we have.

How Morning Glories Could Bloom at Dusk

Left to itself the heart continues, as the tamarind
folds its leaves every night and the mimosa,
even in perpetual darkness, opens and shuts
with the sun.

It is moved by such delays:
cat's-ears open at six, african marigolds, lilies
at seven, at eight the passionflower.
Its light awaits the souls of the living, its birds

for the branches to unfold in song;
the end of its year awaits each noon the opening
of the chicory of the meadow, and its meadows
imagine other sleepless flower beds.

If there is another world, then this is it:
the real, the virtual, the butterfly
over the evening primrose.
The error involved is minimal, it can be corrected:

the blue of the sky
is due to the scattering of sunlight
on its way out of the sky.
But no one said how slow, how willing.

The Age of Reason

The anxious bird in the lush
    spring green
is *anting*, which means,
    in my orchard
he has opened his wings
    over a furious

anthill and will take up
    into the delicate
ridges of quince-yellow
    feathers
a number of tiny, angry
    creatures

that will inhabit him, bewildered
    no doubt,
travelling deep
    into the air
on this feathery planet,
    new life. . . .

We don't know why
    they do it.
At times they'll take on
    almost anything
that burns, spreading
    their wings

over coals, over cigarette
    butts,
even, mistakenly, on bits
    of broken glass.
Meanwhile the light keeps
    stroking them

as if it were love. The garden
    continues its work
all round them, the gradual
    openings that stand
for death. Under the plastic
    groundcover the human

garden grows: help-sticks
     and knots, row
after row. Who wouldn't want
     to take
into the self
     something that burns

or cuts, or wanders
     lost
over the body?

2.

At the end of Werner Herzog's
     Woyzek,
after the hero whom
     we love
who is mad has
     murdered

the world, the young
     woman
who is his wife,
     and loved her,
and covered himself
     with blood,

he grows frightened
     by how quickly
she softens and takes on the shape
     of the soil.
In the moonlight he throws
     his knife

into the wide river
     flowing beside them
but doesn't think it has
     reached deep
enough so goes in
     after it

himself. White as a knife,
     he goes in after it
completely. The trees are green.
     The earth
is green. The light
     is sick

with green. Now that
    he's gone
the woman is a tiny
    gap
in green. Next day,
    in slow

motion, the undertakers and
    philosophers
(it is the Age of
    Reason)
wander through the tall
    and glossy

ferns and grasses
    looking for
the instrument. It's spring.
    The air is
gold. Every now and then
    they lift

the white sheet they have
    laid to see
what death is. They are
    meticulous.
The day is everything
    they have.

3.

How far is true
    enough?
How far into the
    earth
can vision go and
    still be

love? Isn't the
    honesty
of things where they
    resist,
where only the wind
    can bend them

back, the real weather,
    not our

desire hissing Tell me
    your parts
that I may understand
    your body,

your story. Which is why
    we have
characters and the knife
    of a plot
to wade through this
    current. Now

it's blossoms
    back to back
through the orchard.
    A surf
of tenderness. There is
    no deep

enough. For what we want
    to take
inside of us, whole orchard,
    color,
name, scent, symbol, raw
    pale

blossoms, wet black
    arms there is
no deep enough.

At the Long Island Jewish Geriatric Home

This is the sugar
    you're stealing
from the nurses, filling
    your pillow
with something
    for nothing,
filling my pockets
    till I'm some kind
of sandman
    you can still

send away. As for
    dreams,

your head rustling in
    white ash,
who needs them?
    It's this world
you love,
    the only one
where theft is possible.
    Today

there's mist outside your
    stormwindow.
The trees grow vague,
    then are
completely gone,
    then stain
this world again as it
    evolves
through them.
    Now,

from any window
    I learn
about freedom, from the muscular
    leanings
of any tree, the fate
    of sunlight,
of the wall in the way.
    Out there,
deep in the sleight
    of hand

is where you whipped
    my mother
for a stolen pencilbox
    till they thought
she was dead. And there
    is her sister,
the one who's never cut
    her hair,
and there the one who died leaving
    a freezer full

of meals twenty years old
    or more. Maybe
it's true, maybe there just
    isn't enough

to go around. Though once, when I
 was very small,
you took me out back
 to your tiny
orchard and let me pick
 till I was

bored. You showed me how
 only a tree
can steal (through sap
 and leaves)
the minerals of parent rock
 and feed them
(by the leafrot) to
 the soil.
How that delay (you drew
 a fountain

in the dirt) is all
 we ever
are. *Who wants a handout*
 anyhow,
you say. Family hours
 are almost
up. There is one branch
 I've kept
from there: it's shaped exactly
 like a woman

running, one raised thigh
 smoothed
by wind, and hair (really
 the shoreline
where the limb is almost torn
 away) unravelling.
She looks like she could
 outrun
anything, although of course
 she's stuck

for good here in this
 memory,
and in the myth it calls
 to mind,
and in this late interpretation
 stolen from

a half-remembered tree
　　which stands
there still like some god's
　　narrow throat

or mind nothing can slit her
　　free of.

In What Manner the Body
Is United with the Soule

1.

Finally I heard
　　into music,
that is, heard past
　　the surface tension
which is pleasure, which holds
　　the self

afloat, miraculous
　　waterstrider
with no other home.
　　Not that I heard
very deep,
　　but heard there was a depth,

a space through which
　　you could fall,
an echo travel,
　　and meaning
—small, jewelled, deep-water—
　　flash. I heard

in a piano concerto
　　the distance between the single instrument
and the whole
　　republic,
heard the argument each made
　　for fate,

for free will.
　　And listened
to the piano, solo,
　　on its gold hook, the tip

of the baton,
    struggle

and struggle.

2.

From the mud
    of the Arno
in winter, 1967,
    we pulled up
manuscripts
    illuminated by monks

in tenth century
    monasteries.
Sometimes the gold letters loosened
    into the mud,
into our hands.
    We found

elaborate gold frames,
    Annunciations,
candlesticks. The ice
    the mud became
along the banks caught
    bits of sun

and gleamed.
    Eddies, twists, baroque knots
of currents,
    all the difficulties
of the passage
    of time

caught and held
    in the lush browns
we reached through
    blindly
for relics. It was
    almost spring,

we waded out further,
    the bells
in the churches
    kept up

their small
        warnings. The self, too,
is an act of
        rescue
where the flesh has risen,
        the spirit
loosened. . . .

3.

Upstream the river
        is smaller,
almost still.
        On a warm day
the silence of the surface holds
        its jewels,

its tiny insect
        life.
In silence the waterstriders
        measure ripples
for meaning.
        They catch the bee

that has just touched
        the surface
accidentally. In silence
        the strider
and the backswimmer (which is
        its mirror image

underwater, each
        with its ventral surface towards
the waterfilm)
        share the delicate
gold bee. They can both,
        easily,

be satisfied. They feed.
        Sun shines.
Of silence, mating striders make
        gold eggs
which they will only lay
        on feathers

dropped by passing birds
        or on the underside

of a bird's tail
        before it wakens and
flies off, blue and white and host
        to a freedom

it knows nothing of.

History

Into whose ear the deeds are spoken. The only
listener. So I believed
he would remember everything, the murmuring trees,
the sunshine's zealotry, its deep
unevenness. For history
is the opposite
of the eye
for whom, for instance, six million bodies in portions
of hundreds and
the flowerpots broken by a sudden wind stand as
equivalent. What more
is there
than fact? *I'll give 10,000 dollars to the man*
who proves the holocaust really
occurred said the exhausted solitude
in San Francisco in 1980.
Far in the woods, in a faded
photograph, in 1942 the man with his own genitalia
in his mouth and hundreds of
slow holes
a pitchfork has opened
over his face
grows beautiful. The ferns and deepwood
lilies catch
the eye. Three men in ragged uniforms
with guns keep laughing
nervously. They share the day
with him. A bluebird
sings. The feathers of the shade touch every inch
of skin—the hand holding down the delicate gun,
the hands holding down the delicate
hips. And the sky
is visible between the men, between
the trees, a blue spirit

enveloping
anything. Late in the story, in Northern Italy,
a man cuts down some trees for winter
fuel. We read this in the evening
news. Watching the fire burn late
one night, watching it change and change, a hand grenade,
lodged in the pulp the young tree
grew around, explodes, blinding the man, killing
his wife. Now who
will tell the children
fairytales? The ones where simple
crumbs over the forest
floor endure
to help us home?

Love

Here it's harvest. Dust
    coarsens
the light. In the heat
    in the distance
the men burn
    their fields

to heal them. The grass
    is tall.
They disappear,
    they reappear . . .
slowly they navigate
    by fire,

cutting a path
    of ash.
They beat
    the flames
then lean
    on their tall forks

and stare. Nearby
    the sheep
in a stunned unison
    work what
remains. Dogs bite
    the strays.

What stark thing
        is it
we want
        that's only visible, believable,
caught through
        this blinding

yield? What poverty
        is strict enough?
Eight hundred years
        ago
in these fields
        the man

known as Saint
        Francis
abandoned by his
        church
and going blind
        spent all

one night. The medicine,
        the light
of his time,
        saw fit to burn him
at the temples
        to restore sight,

and all the tiny veins
        from ear to eye,
out of tremendous love,
        were cut.
It didn't work,
        but in great pain

near here, one night,
        the story goes,
rats worried him,
        visiting
his helpless warmth.
        To see them

for what they were,
        old man,
he composed
        in the dark

his famous
       canticle—*brother*

sunlight, brother
       firelight. The rats
traveled his face
       eating
the open scars. Later
       his blessed

aides bore through both ears
       with red hot irons
to no avail
       for sight. *Harm not*
the fire
       he said

to those who would
       save him,
and never would he, did he,
       extinguish
a candle,
       a lantern,

with so much
       pity
was he moved
       towards it.

Gary Soto

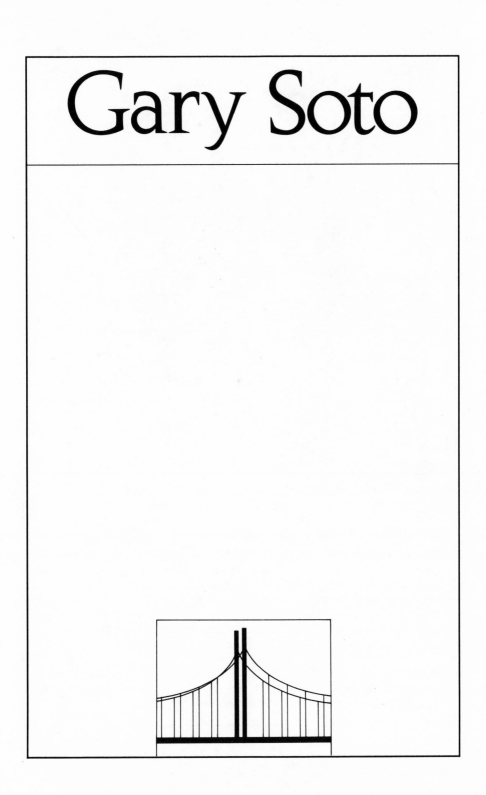

SADAKO

Gary Soto, born in 1952, was raised and educated in Fresno, California. He was educated at Fresno State College and the University of California at Irvine. His three poetry collections are *The Elements of San Joaquin, The Tale of Sunlight,* and *Where Sparrows Work Hard,* all published in the Pitt Poetry Series. Individual poems have appeared in *The New Yorker, Poetry, The Nation, Paris Review,* among others. His many awards include the Academy of American Poets Prize, the Discovery-*The Nation* Prize, the Bess Hokin Prize from *Poetry,* the U.S. Award of the International Poetry Forum, A Guggenheim Fellowship, and National Endowment for the Arts in poetry. He is an assistant professor of Chicano Studies and English at the University of California, Berkeley.

A Good Day

Let me provide you with a recollection of a summer day in 1976. Later I will highlight its importance in regards to my poetry.

Once, when we were bored and irritable in our apartment in Mexico City, the four of us—Ernesto, Dianne, my wife Carolyn and I—got into the Renault Ernesto had bought the previous week and risked the rough and sometimes unfair roads that winded to Cuernavaca. We were happy in the car when we left and even happier as we drove into town pointing to a fuschia-like vine with its red-flamed flowers. Carolyn took a picture of the vine from the car window—a vine that seemed to be everywhere, on the houses of the poor as well as the rich. Dianne remarked it was the most beautiful flower she had ever seen.

We had lunch and nursed dark beers. We then walked the *zocalo* where we bought trinkets from a child, and then visited a small museum in which the most interesting display was of rusted pistols and the sepia-colored photographs of those who had owned—or were killed by—those pistols. From there we went shopping: Dianne bought a belt for her niece and Carolyn turned over for the longest time silver charms that she hoped to add to a bracelet back in California. She chose an Italian flag and paid what the young woman behind the counter asked.

After shopping we drove outside the city in search of a nursery, for our apartment was bare: a dining table with chairs, an empty bird cage, two mattresses, and an ironing board that doubled as a writing table. We found a nursery and haggled over a few lush ferns that we propped in the trunk.

At the suggestion of a small boy who had helped us carry the ferns to the car, we drove further along the road to a pond, pressed small by an arena of jagged rocks and tall, wispy trees that were loaded with birds we couldn't recognize. We walked along a leaf-littered path, paired off into couples looking very much like the tourists we were, until we were in view of divers collecting coins from onlookers. We leaned against a stone fence, talked and took pictures of the divers and of one another staring intensely into the distance. Finally, one diver who was satisfied with the money he had gathered stepped out onto a rock that jutted over the water. He took a deep breath, then released it. He took another deep breath, spread his arms, and leaped into the gray water that broke white as his body hit the surface. He came up smiling and pinching his nostrils. The onlookers clapped and smiled at one another.

We walked slowly back to the car, none of us looking forward to the drive back to the city, especially since the afternoon rains would soon start, so we started on a walk that ended only twenty feet from the car. Ernesto spotted a harp player, a blind man who was handsome in a felt hat and a crisp, white shirt.

We walked in his direction behind Ernesto who struck up a conversation that led to how he had come to play the harp.

The story was that a group of Indians had found the wooden harp, stringless and warped, on a river bank. They studied it for a long time but couldn't figure out what it was. Bewildered, they carried it to their village, and talk filled the air because their people couldn't figure out its purpose either. Some said it was a suitcase. Others said it was a boat for children, very small children. Others argued it was a loom. One said it was a washboard. Still they were not satisfied and the three men who had found the harp took it into town. But no one was interested in buying or trading for it. They approached, however, the blind man and told him they had a suitcase for sale. Might he be interested? The blind man took it from the Indians and ran his hands over the body of the instrument. He tapped it. He twisted the pegs in their sockets. He guessed what it was, remembering the harp his father had made for him when he was a child, but didn't let on to his happiness because it would have meant a difficult barter. After a few minutes of haggling, the Indians walked back into the countryside with a frying pan and a pocket knife, very pleased with the trade.

"Young man, I'll play for you—and for your *esposa*," he said, indicating me with a nod of his head, though we didn't bother to correct him. "It's a love song." His fingers flashed over the strings, missing a few notes and stopping once to cough, but when he finished we clapped and could think of no better music as we looked at one another, moved by the music and the man who seemed so innocent. As we were leaving Ernesto tried to give the man a few pesos but he refused with a wave of his hand, "It's nothing. Be a Mexican and go on." Ernesto left the coins with the young boy who was standing next to the harpist.

We returned to the car and drove back to Cuernavaca where the main road led back to Mexico City. We were tired and quiet as Ernesto drove through the traffic that was start and stall with the weekend rush. Our faces were pressed to the window when Ernesto screamed, "Hey, look at that beautiful red flower!" We looked in his direction and saw the vine that we had raved about earlier in the day when we drove into town. Dianne shook her head and clicked her tongue, which followed with a long drawn-out "Errrrnesto."

And what does this narrative mean? First I must say that I wrote this piece to illustrate to myself and others what it means to have a good day. That is, I wanted to recreate an "ordinary" day in which I woke up, drank coffee, and, with others for whom there was love and kinship, opened the front door to enjoy the day. The events are as they happened.

But what of it? Well, on a superficial level nothing of *real* importance happens —God doesn't show up, Mexico is not invaded by the British, nor does the country fair come to town. Rather, we spend the day strolling, eating, browsing at a museum, watching divers on high, pointed cliffs, and talking with a man who plays the harp. They may be seen as daily occurrences, and they have no bearing upon the world. Nothing changes because we buy trinkets from a child.

They are a set of experiences that are commonplace, but interesting when recreated so that these particulars stand out as totems of a lusher experience. That is, the red-flamed flowers leap up in the mind's eye, and have a certain staying power. It remains with us as a meal may remain on the palate, hours after eating. So does the scene of the Indians trying to figure out what the harp is. A reader may ask, "Why does one think it's a boat? Another a suitcase?" A reader may ask, "Why is the harpist in a white shirt?" "Is there a beauty in his manners that is foreign to mine?" And finally, a reader may ask, "Why does it take Ernesto so long before he sees the flower?" "Is there a reason for this?"

Writing makes the ordinary stand out, thus enabling us to build in some kind of metaphorical meaning. A writer chooses words, images, events in order to illuminate their significance in a given narrative or lyric. It is like a young man who, naked to the waist, flexes his muscles—at one moment he is undefined, and the next the muscle contours, texture, and color stand out. At that time we discover his strength, or lack of it. So with literature. It reshapes experience—both real and invented—to help us see ourselves—our foibles, failures, potential, beauty, pettiness, etc. We read *Madame Bovary*, and we can't help but make associations to certain personalities. We read *Catcher in the Rye* as high school students and find ourselves agreeing with the reality of the novel. "Yes, I know exactly what he's talking about," a young reader may say. In short, literature helps define the world for us.

My poems work in such ways. What you'll see in them is that they lack overt statements, that they seem like "pictures," and that they are commonplace and not in the least elevated in regards to subject. They are, as a friend once commented, "like Dutch paintings"—simple events against the backdrop of a dark and tragic world. The poem "Mission Tire Factory, 1969" illustrates what I mean by simple, commonplace, and imagistic. It runs like a narrative, recreating the story of a worker falling hurt while on his job. But it is more than that, I hope. What the poem does is suggest behavior: to fall hurt while on his job is a humbling experience, one in which a "man" is placed in a fragile position, for it means that he may have to express his gratitude to his fellow workers who care that he is hurt. In the poem, however, Manny lacks the ability to show his feelings and, instead, opens his wallet to pass out dollars to express his thanks. An American gesture, I would think, for in this society it is foreign to show one's feelings, whether they are love, hate, jealousy, desire . . .

But returning to the recollection of a "Good Day," I also want to say that, in telling the story, I consciously chose—or "raised"—details that would lead the reader to believe that there was a greater significance or nuance in them. As I have said, the flower is one, the harp player is another. There is a certain chord of familiarity in both of them. The flower, for instance, could stand for, say, "beauty," while the blind harp player could be seen as Homer waiting for listeners like the four of us in order to share a story of some moral implication, and once finished, take up his harp to further his point with song. These details have a quality that invites us to read into them certain feelings and ideas.

In other words, I am referring to symbol—a reoccurring word or image that suggests a greater and more complex meaning. A poet will choose his symbols from what he knows, and more often than not the symbols rise from personality, which is shaped by the past. If I consider my childhood, for instance, I think of the ants that entered our lives: each morning they lined the kitchen sink, lengthened like thread along the baseboards, and darkened our garbage cans. The ant was a reality in my childhood, but now it has become a symbol in my writing. The ant is a vehicle of death, small and fragile as it is, and my poem "The Evening of Ants" illustrates this transformation:

> I climbed into the chinaberry
> With a play telephone
> Rang for a taxi
> To drive me away
> And for a man to tighten
> The leaky pipes
> That shivered like our dogs
> I rang mama
> And hung up on her
> Giggled called again
> To tell her I was hungry
>
> Across a dirt yard
> Chickens pecked at the broken glass
> Winking with sunlight
> And the Italian
> Who would roll his Packard
> A month later
> Was alone on his porch talking
> Hours passed birds passed
> And those orange cats
> Who eventually dropped
> Under car tires
> Moved as their shade moved
>
> Evening neared
> And the moment our father slipped
> From a ladder our mother

Reached the door
That opened into a white room
A white nurse It was the moment
I came down from the tree
And into our house
Where a leash of ants
Swarmed for the rice   the cupboards   the stove
Carrying off what there was to carry
Between one root and the next

October 1982
Berkeley, California

The Elements of San Joaquin

Field

The wind sprays pale dirt into my mouth
The small, almost invisible scars
On my hands.

The pores in my throat and elbows
Have taken in a seed of dirt of their own.

After a day in the grape fields near Rolinda
A fine silt, washed by sweat,
Has settled into the lines
On my wrists and palms.

Already I am becoming the valley,
A soil that sprouts nothing
For any of us.

Wind

A dry wind over the valley
Peeled mountains, grain by grain,
To small slopes, loose dirt
Where red ants tunnel.

The wind strokes
The skulls and spines of cattle
To white dust, to nothing,

Covers the spiked tracks of beetles,
Of tumbleweed, of sparrows
That pecked the ground for insects.

Evenings, when I am in the yard weeding,
The wind picks up the breath of my armpits
Like dust, swirls it
Miles away

And drops it
On the ear of a rabid dog,
And I take on another life.

Wind

When you got up this morning the sun
Blazed an hour in the sky,

A lizard hid
Under the curled leaves of manzanita
And winked its dark lids.

Later, the sky grayed,
And the cold wind you breathed
Was moving under your skin and already far
From the small hives of your lungs.

Stars

At dusk the first stars appear.
Not one eager finger points toward them.
A little later the stars spread with the night
And an orange moon rises
To lead them, like a shepherd, toward dawn.

Sun

In June the sun is a bonnet of light
Coming up,
Little by little,
From behind a skyline of pine.

The pastures sway with fiddle-neck
Tassels of foxtail.

At Piedra
A couple fish on the river's edge,
Their shadows deep against the water.
Above, in the stubbled slopes,
Cows climb down
As the heat rises
In a mist of blond locusts,
Returning to the valley.

Rain

When autumn rains flatten sycamore leaves,
The tiny volcanos of dirt
Ants raised around their holes,
I should be out of work.

My silverware and stack of plates will go unused
Like the old, my two good slacks
Will smother under a growth of lint
And smell of the old dust

That rises
When the closet door opens or closes.

The skin of my belly will tighten like a belt
And there will be no reason for pockets.

Fog

If you go to your window
You will notice a fog drifting in.

The sun is no stronger than a flashlight.
Not all the sweaters
Hung in closets all summer

Could soak up this mist. The fog:
A mouth nibbling everything to its origin,
Pomegranate trees, stolen bicycles,

The string of lights at a used-car lot,
A Pontiac with scorched valves.

In Fresno the fog is passing
The young thief prying a window screen,
Graying my hair that falls
And goes unfound, my fingerprints
Slowly growing a fur of dust—

One hundred years from now
There should be no reason to believe
I lived.

Daybreak

In this moment when the light starts up
In the east and rubs
The horizon until it catches fire,

We enter the fields to hoe,
Row after row, among the small flags of onion,
Waving off the dragonflies
That ladder the air.

And tears the onions raise
Do not begin in your eyes but in ours,
In the salt blown
From one blister into another;

They begin in knowing
You will never waken to bear
The hour timed to a heart beat,
The wind pressing us closer to the ground.

When the season ends,
And the onions are unplugged from their sleep,
We won't forget what you failed to see,
And nothing will heal
Under the rain's broken fingers.

The Firstborn

All day the Nina sewed in this room
The curtain pulled down
But where it was torn
The sun flared
On the wall
And on the wall
The fingerprints
Of the firstborn
Who drowned face-up
In the basin

That was weeks ago   but still
She was frightened
When she washed
Or drank there
She thought of the baby
Coming up heavy
From the soapy water
His mouth open
On the cry
That did not reach
Humming   she
Toweled and hugged
Her little one
Before laying him
On the kitchen table
Back in the room
She stood looking
At the basin
And did not understand
What she was looking at

Or why   but then
Closing her eyes
Dipped her fists
In the water
And thought
Of her old town—
A rooster   the winter wind sliced
Through a reed fence

The Street

> Then we would hardly eat except to be seen.
> —Elio Vittorini

Through the first days of Lent
The widow lugs the town's wash outside
In the heat squatting

Among onions and tomatoes poled waist-high,
Chiles and the broken fingers of peas
That point down.

Waving off the chickens,
She pins the grayness to the line, and beyond
This line, in the same boredom
That drips from the wash,

The old rock
In a bench of shade, the old
Who have come here to suck their tongues
And stare at each other's shoes

South of what was never received.

*

Molina shovels for what the earth gives,
Pulling up the barbed tooth
And the hooked nail,

A rug of pressed roots
Shook clean
And hung to dry in the open air.

He raises a lunch pail black
From the crossing of ants
And dips his arm

Into the hole, feeling the stones
Squat beyond the moon's tug.

When his flushed face
Is something to hold under a faucet,
Wring out like a towel,
It will be hours later.
It will be twilight.

It will be the child digging slowly,
But still digging,

While the night
Arrives with a wind
Clearing the way home.

                *

Because a puddle has outstared the sun
And the shade has rearranged itself
Like furniture,

Julio, the retired butcher,
Sits under the full skirt of a willow,
Talking to the photo
Of his first wife,
Her face greased with a thumbprint
And caught in a lean year.

He opens his pocketknife, closes it.
He pulls a nickel from his coin purse
And without looking
Dates it a 1959 D,

And in '59 he rose
At daybreak
To pluck the chicken of its burst heart
And the maggots
That went deep as bullets
In the yellow of the pork's fat.

This world is silver, between two trees.
The light is folding
Like a stiff wallet, west of all
He has dreamed, miles from
The prayer that will close his eyes.

                *

Goyo at the window, and no uncle
Arrives on the porch, to dust a coat
Or the boots spurred with foxtails,
Open at the tips.

           No aunt comes,
Heavy-breasted, to bend over the sink
And gut a chicken of the two stones
It pecked from the yard.

The yard grows cold
And its light pulls away
At the speed it takes to shut a cupboard
Hiding the chipped saucer, a spoon bearded in lint.

Goyo goes outside, near the fence,
And watches his cat lick what is salted
Under each paw

           for this hour
When the moon is a prop above the trees
And the streetlight assumes
Where its light falls
Someone should walk.

    *

Barber or field hand,
Whore's brother, pickpocket's son,
They come, shoeless, to the ditch
Where the starlight maps the water
And the current moves
Against its pull,
Slowing this night.

           In the quiet
Between one cigarette
And another, they stand breathing
Chilled air, listening
To the reeds benched
Along the water,

The peacock and the pocked toad,
The cricket that ticks
Like fire.

If the weeds rustle,
It is the wind stones freed
At noon.

If a child sets a branch drifting,
It will sink eastward
Through a seizure of moonlight,
Past the unroofed houses,
Bearing his name
Which is always sent back.

*

When the morning is a tablet
Of cold spit he cannot swallow,

Cruz leaves
For the Westside,
The neoned juke box and the warm beer
Sending up its last bubble,
For the cue stick
Swung hard against an ear, the mouth blooming.
A fly circles in the light,
And he orders a stronger drink.

Back home, he stands on the front porch
Before the window, his reflection,
A crack running
Like stitches

From one corner to the next.
He looks in as though this were not his
House and squints

Where the rat, nibbling what it can,
Turns once again to meet his stare.

*

At *La Fiesta*,
The uncle drops a coin of blood
In each palm,

An offering for the basin
Where the water rises in a steam
He cannot see
And vanishes into a cloud.

The white woman over an electric range
Will not know the pain
That stiffens
Like a star in a second of full darkness,

Nor what makes him push
His gloved fist
In the windows that eat their echoes—

She can't even guess.

One could say a bottle
That emptied like a cough
Turned over, slashed at a face,
And later, a car tire.

One could say the wound tears again,
Opening like an eye
From a sleep
That is never deep enough.

    *

The poor are unshuffled cards of leaves
Reordered by wind, turned over on a wish
To reveal their true suits.
They never win.

           This means Theresa Fuentes,
Palm reader and washerwoman,
Stacking coins into vertebrae of silver
Fingered dull by the cold:

           Emilio Zaragoza pushing
Chorizo into sleeves of pig gut,
Roping them in threes along the wall:

Fat Mother Luisa threading
The needle's eye with sunlight
In a house of closed cupboards and open mouths.

So they continue, dark and unfamiliar,

Their children at a table,
Brother to his bowl, sister to her dish,
Eating only enough so as not to say good-bye.

Mission Tire Factory, 1969

All through lunch Peter pinched at his crotch,
And Jesús talked about his tattoos,
And I let the flies crawl my arm, undisturbed,
Thinking it was wrong, a buck sixty-five,
The wash of rubber in our lungs,
The oven we would enter, squinting
—because earlier in the day Manny fell
From his machine, and when we carried him
To the workshed (blood from
Under his shirt, in his pants)
All he could manage, in an ignorance
Outdone only by pain, was to take three dollars
From his wallet, and say:
"Buy some sandwiches. You guys saved my life."

Brown Like Us

For Gerald

"Brown like us,"
Shouts a broom,
The guitar on the couch,
Uncle shooing a wasp
From the house.

Brown like the place
Where I just sat
Watching workers cut grapes into a pan,
Watching a butterfly leaf
Through the vines.

†

Papá, you are a tree
In wind. Your good fruit
Is shook free
And the cats come in two's, smiling.

Papá, your wrist
Is a length of rope, your hands
A wrinkled map of Juárez

Papá, the sun
Is warming my arm and brow,
The garden where I hoed
A grave for the ant.

†

Mamá, the hen
Has eaten her feathers, the sparrow
Her song, our collie a branch
He pulled from the canal.

Mamá, the sky
Offers a cloud, the rain
A quick river; this stone
Is like your eye for it's staring at me.

†

Mira, if I cough should I close my eyes?
If a dog licks my hand will he remember me?
Mira, is that hunger or a slow cat?
Is that rain or a glass of weak tea?

†

Who is that man with buckets
For hands,
A razor slash for a smile?
Who is that woman selling brooms
And sweets? Is that her dog
Or is she pointing at me?

†

He is the keeper of the ditches,
Father to a fishbowl, witness to water
Flowing uphill.

She is the stepdaughter
To la llorona, one who knocks on wood,
A sly one calling heads or tails.

†

They tell me it's easy to cartwheel into love,
That under this leaf is another leaf.

They tell me that inside this tree is a canoe,
Down that alley my cat—

Beyond my call, she is no longer mine.

†

"Brown like us,"
Says a shoe,
The penny in my palm,
The accordion wheezing
The end of a corrido.

Brown like the hour
When dogs walk slowly
And mice sidestep our anger
To nibble on rice.

Brown like mi abuela
Who keeps a coffee can
Of seeds and rumor,
A deck of photographs,
Creased and bundled with a rubber band,
In which she is the first one.

In the Madness of Love

Richard on the cold roof screams, I'm the eye
of Omar, and a friend and I, with crumbs
Falling from our mouths, shout for him to get
Down, to remember that the rent is due
And it's no time to act silly.
Look, he says, and we look: a burst
Of sparrows. No, the clouds, he says,
They are coming. We plead with raisins,
Watery plums, but he's distant as the sky—
Dark with kites crossing over to rain.
We plead with a sandwich, car keys, albums;
Threaten him with a hose, our black neighbor
The drummer. No use. I climb on all fours
Over the roof, unsteady as a wobbly chair,
And when I touch him he shivers
Like a kicked dog. I take hold and rock him
In my arms, his jaw stiff with rage
And his eyes so wet we could drink from them
And be free. What is it? I ask.
There, he points. And the clouds begin to move.

Heaven

Scott and I bent
To the radio, legs
Twitching to The Stones,
Faces wet, arms rising
And falling as if
Trying to get out or
Crawl the air—the
Air thick with our
Toweled smells.
                              It's
'64, and our room
And its shaft of dust,
Turning, is all
There is—though momma
Says there's the car
To wash, the weeds,
The grass and garbage
Tilting on the backsteps.
"Yeh, yeh," we scream
Behind the closed door,
And boost the radio
To "10" and begin
Bouncing on the bed,
Singing, making up
Words about this girl,
That car, tears,
Lipstick, handjives
In alleys—bouncing
Hard, legs split, arms
Open for the Lord,
Until Scott can't stand it
And crashes through
The screened window
And tumbles into a bush,
His shoulders locked
Between branches,
His forehead scratched,
But still singing,
"Baby, baby, o baby."

Cruel Boys

First day. Jackie and I walking in leaves
On our way to becoming 8th graders,
Pencils behind our ears, pee-chee folders
Already scribbled with football players
In dresses, track star in a drooped bra.
We're tough. I'm Mexican
And he's an unkillable Okie with three
Teeth in his pocket, sludge under
His nails from scratching oily pants.
No one's going to break us, not the Dean
Or principal, not the cops
Who could arrive in pairs, walkie-talkies
To their mouths, warning:
"Dangerous. They have footballs."
We could bounce them off their heads
And reporters might show up
With shirt sleeves rolled up to their ears,
Asking our age, if we're Catholic.
But this never happens. We go to first
Period, math, then second period, geography,
And in third period, English, the woman
Teacher reads us Frost, something
About a tree, and to set things straight,
How each day will fall like a tree,
Jackie raises his hand, stands up,
And shouts, "You ain't nothing but a hound dog,"
As the spitballs begin to fly.

Getting Serious

I shave my face, comb my hair
Back on the sides, and I'm different
From the posture I assumed in a grunting sleep.
It's time to get serious,
To cough delicately into a hanky,
To weigh each meal on a fork, not my unbalanced tongue.
I've turned thirty, brighter
By an espresso and paperback translations,
And my task is to be polite:
I hold open a door, and people rush in.

I help my wife with her coat,
And she smiles like a red coal blooming under wind.
So it is. I'm crisp
In slacks, a stiff collar,
And I'm off to witness a french romance.
This will take years. I turn 35,
Still crisp, and the theater is weeping,
Its lap full of popcorn and hands
Petting one another's love so it won't be sad.

Black Hair

At eight I was brilliant with my body.
In July, that ring of heat
We all jumped through, I sat in the bleachers
Of Romain Playground, in the lengthening
Shade that rose from our dirty feet.
The game before us was more than baseball.
It was a figure—Hector Montejano,
Quick and hard with turned muscles,
His crouch the one I assumed before an altar
Of worn baseball cards, in my room.

I came here because I was Mexican, a stick
Of brown light in love with those
Who could do it—the triple and hard slide,
The gloves eating balls into double plays.
What could I do with 50 pounds, my shyness,
My black torch of hair, about to go out?
Father was dead, his face no longer
Hanging over the table or sleep,
And mother was the terror of mouths
Twisting hurt by butter knives.

In the bleachers I was brilliant with my body,
Waving players in and stomping my feet,
Growing sweaty in the presence of white shirts.
I chewed sunflower seeds. I drank water,
And bit my arm through the late innings.
When Hector lined balls into deep
Center, in my mind I rounded
The bases with him, my face flared,
My hair lifting beautifully, because we were
Coming home to the arms of brown people.

Kearney Park

True Mexican or not, let's open our shirts
And dance, a spark of heels
Chipping at the dusty cement. The people
Are shiny like the sea, turning
To the clockwork of rancheras,
The accordion wheezing, the drum tap
Of work rising and falling.
Let's dance with our hats in hand.
The sun is behind the trees,
Behind my stutter of awkward steps
With a woman who is a brilliant arc of smiles,
An armful of falling water. Her skirt
Opens and closes. My arms
Know no better but to flop
On their own, and we spin, dip
And laugh into each other's faces—
Faces that could be famous
On the coffee table of my abuelita.
But grandma is here, at the park, with a beer
At her feet, clapping
And shouting, "Dance, hijo, dance!"
Laughing, bend, slide and throw up
A great cloud of dust,
Until the girl and I are no more.

Index

POETS

Chester, Laura 385
Dow, Philip 91
Fisher, David 221
Fraser, Kathleen 67
Gilbert, Jack 1
Graham, Jorie 407
Gregg, Linda 247
Griffin, Susan 289
Hass, Robert 193
Keithley, George 43

Ó Hehir, Diana 23
Palmer, Michael 339
Pinsky, Robert 165
Rice, Stan 267
Scalapino, Leslie 365
Schmitz, Dennis 121
Soto, Gary 433
Stroud, Joseph 315
Young, Al 143

ESSAYS

Breaking the Lightning Bug Code: Some Notes on Poetry and Childhood, *Young* 145
Dancing in the Doorway, *Keithley* 45
Excess and Accuracy, *Rice* 269
First Person Singular, *Schmitz* 123
For the Nonce, *Dow* 93
From the Notebooks, *Palmer* 341
Geodes, Han-Shan, The Tehachapis, Rexroth: Some Fragments, *Stroud* 317
Good Day, A, *Soto* 435
Inclusive Poetry, An, *Chester* 387

Inside the Door, *Griffin* 291
Interview from a Treehouse, *Fraser* 69
Making Us Speak, *Ó Hehir* 25
Not Understanding, *Gregg* 249
O Come All Ye Faithful: a brechtian oratorio in five acts, *Fisher* 223
Real Nouns, *Gilbert* 3
Salt Water, *Pinsky* 167
Some Notes on Silence, *Graham* 409
Some Notes on the San Francisco Bay Area as a Culture Region: a Memoir, *Hass* 195
[Untitled] *Scalapino* 367

POEMS

Abnormal Is Not Courage, The 9
Above Machu Picchu, 129 Baker Street, San Francisco 336
Acoustics 306
Against Botticelli 210
Age of Reason, The 420
All the Way from There to Here 14
Alma to Her Sister 259
Alone by the Road's Edge 33
America the Beautiful 273

Analyst 235
Anima 35
Apple Trees at Olema, The 219
Arbeit Macht Frei 132
areas 381
Artichoke for Montesquieu, An 418
As for Me, I Delight in the Everyday Way 333
As Rimbaud said, I thought today sitting in the library 371
As When the Blowfish Perishing 258

At the Long Island Jewish Geriatric Home 423

Awful Mother, The 310

Bad Mother, The 312

Bees Inside Me 391

Being with Men 263

Below Mount T'ui K'oy, Home of the Gods, Todos Santos Cuchumatán, Guatamalan Highlands 328

Birds of Arles, The 231

Bird Sings to Establish Frontiers, A 13

Bicycle, The 275

Birthday Poem 149

Black Hair 454

Black Hawk in Hiding 56

Blues Don't Change, The 162

"Boogie with O. O. Gabugah" 159

Bottom's Dream 115

Brown Like Us 449

Burning and Fathering: Accounts of My Country 17

Buster Keaton & the Cops 58

Byzantium Burning 18

California Phrasebook, The 130

Chalk Angel, The 129

Chance Meeting 298

Changes, The 190

Changes Around the Bay 350

Child, The 61

Child Naming Flowers 212

Child's Christmas without Jean Cocteau, A 240

Children Among the Hills 261

Chile 300

Choosing the Devil 261

Chorus Speaks Her Words as She Dances, The 254

Churchyard 213

City 332

Classical Style, The 351

Color of Many Deer Running, The 260

Coma 140

Comet, The 355

Coming Back 264

Courtship 36

Cruel Boys 453

Cry-Bird Journey, The 281

Daybreak 442

Dear Old Stockholm 154

Dearest Reader 364

Death Looks Down 263

Death of Rimbaud 239

Discretions of Alcibiades 176

Distress 310

Documentary 330

Documentation 357

Doe 104

Dogchain Gang, The 274

Dogs 310

Don Giovanni on His Way to Hell 10

Don Giovanni on His Way to Hell (II) 11

Donner Party, The, *an excerpt* 50

Dragon 328

Drawing Wildflowers 416

Dressing Game 136

Drunk Last Night with Friends, I Go to Work Anyway 103

Duck Pond at Mini's Pasture, A Dozen Years Later, The 102

Eclogues, I 126

Elegy 105

Elements of San Joaquin, The 440

Emergency Room, The 233

[EPILOGUE: *anemone*] 372

Euridice Saved 266

Euridice 256

Evening of Ants, The 438

Exile 327

Fashionable Heart, The 17

Field 440

Field 301

Figured Wheel, The 189

Firstborn, The 443

Flesh 284

Fog 442

Garden, The 305

Getting Serious 453

Ghazal 115

Gill Boy 139

Girl I Call Alma, The   253
Gnostics on Trial   254
Go Round   403
Gods Must Not Know Us, The   257
Gold Country: Hotel Leger, Mokelumne Hill,
    Revisited, The   336
Goodbye "Hello"   115
Grandfather   322
Growing Up   256

Harbor at Seattle, The   215
Harvest Poem   241
Haven't I said that part of having intercourse
    370
"Having her under me,"   the man said,   "in
    bed, and remembering   372
Heaven   452
History   429
History: Madness   280
History of My Heart   183
hmmmm [ten excerpts from the twenty-eight
    part sequence]   370
Ho   158
House   34
How can I help myself,   as one woman said
    to me about wanting   370
How Morning Glories Could Bloom at Dusk
    419
How the Joy of It Was Used Up Long Ago
    265
How to Murder Your Best Friend   37
How was I to know that the woman, seated
    next to me on the bus,   372

Identities   155
If I Could Meet God   128
In a Motion   404
Incanto   277
In the Madness of Love   451
In What Manner the Body Is United with the
    Soule   426
Infant   40
Interior with Mme. Vuillard and Son   87
Intimacy   161
It Comes During Sleep   103

January   217
Joan Brown, About Her Painting   86

Jours Gigantesques, Les / The Titanic Days   77
Junkie with a Flute in the Rain, A   234

Kearney Park   455
Keepsake Corporation, The   243
Kindergarten   137
Know, The   76

Lament   326
Last Breath   390
Last Supper, The   276
Learning to Type   35
Lester Leaps In   162
Letter   116
Letter to the Revolution   299
Lily, Lois & Flaubert: the site of loss   82
Lives of Famous Men, The   22
Locations   79
Lonesome in the Country   152
Lord Sits with Me Out in Front, The   20
Lost   231
Love   430
Love Should Grow Up Like a Wild Iris in
    the Fields   297

Machupuchare, What the Mountain Said,
    Shaking the Dead Bones, Christmas Eve,
    1974   337
Making Chicago   134
Maps   206
Marriage and Midsummer's Night   264
Meditation at Lagunitas   209
Medusa's Hair Was Snakes. Was Thought,
    split inward   88
Memory   327
Metaphysical Shock While Watching a TV
    Cartoon   282
Mission Tire Factory, 1969   449
Monte Albán   325
Moon Watching by Lake Chapala   153
More Than Fifty   22
Morning Star Man   57
Mother   104
Moved Towards a Future   400
Movies, The   18
My Child   313
My Marriage with Mrs. Johnson   19
Museum   213

Mutilated Soldier, The   236
Mycenae   244

Naming   334
Netting   417
News   141
New York, Summer   12
1930   84
Notes for Echo Lake 5   358
Not Saying Much   262
Not Wanting Myself   260
Nuts and Bolts Poem for Mr. Mac Adams, Sr.
   75

Old Lady Under the Freeway, The   30
Old Man, The   239
Old O. O. Blues, The   159
On Clark Street in Chicago   59
On Growing Old in San Francisco   11
On the *Esplanade des Invalides*   243
On the Wallowy   392
On the Way to Language   354
One West Coast   150
Origin of Cities, The   211
Orpheus in Greenwich Village   13

Palo Alto: the Marshes   203
Paschal Lamb   216
Pastor Speaks Out, The   242
Payments   38
Perfect Mother, The   311
Perspective He Would Mutter Going to Bed
   9
Pewter   15
Picture of Okinawa, A   136
Plan to Live My Life Again, A   31
Planting Trout in the Chicago River   133
Playing House   20
Poem About People   175
Poem Following Discussion of Brain   283
Poem on the Suicide of My Teacher   323
Poem to Han-shan   325
Poem to My Father   322
Ponce de León / A Morning Walk   152
Pot of Tea   308
Power to Change Geography, The   32
Private Rooms   39
Prologue   305

Proportions   334
Prospero Dreams of Arnaud Daniel Inventing
   Love in the Twelfth Century   21
Prospero on the Mountain Gathering Wood
   21
Prospero without His Magic   19

Questions, The   182
Questions and Answers   37

Rain   441
Rehearsal   232
Reproduction Interdite, La / Not to Be
   Reproduced   78
Retarded Children Find a World Built Just
   for Them, The   33
Retarded Class at F. A. O. Schwarz's
   Celebrates Christmas   236
Returning to the World   404
Revolution, The   19
River Again and Again, The   264
Room Above the White Rose, The   331
Round Trip   284

Sects   16
Seeing the Scenery   371
Serpent Knowledge   178
sequence, A   379
Shore   41
Sibyl   332
Signature (II)   329
Signature (III)   330
Silence   306
Simply   390
Sitting   309
Skinning-The-Cat   138
Skyjacker, The   272
Snow Geese in the Wind   114
So I decided watching an *old* woman like her,
   who could rise so easily   370
Some Lamb   280
Some of Us Are Exiles from No Land   30
Song   114
Song for New Orleans, A   59
Song of the Round Man   356
Song Turning Back Into Itself 3, The   149
Star & Garter Theater   129
Stars   441

Story About the Body, A 214
Street, The 444
Summoned 29
Sun 441
Sun Moon Kelp Flower or Goat 258
Susanna and the Elders 12
Sussyissfriin, [an excerpt] 116
Symmetrical Poem 359

Tall Windows 214
Tarantula 38
Teacher, The 237
Teeth 309
Terminal Version 41
Theory of the Flower, The 362
There She Is 255
These Labdanum Hours 85
They Grow Up Too Fast, She Said 32
Thief's Niece, The 60
Things Not of This Union 265
Three Poems for Women 302
Three Shades of Light on the Windowsill
  313
Tissue 309
To Bring Spring 64
To Christopher Smart 326
Translation into the Original 16
Trellis 397

Trying to Believe 259
29th Month, The 276

Vietnamese Girl in the Madhouse, The 236
Village of Reason, The 361
Virgil: Georgics, Book IV 128
Visiting Day 156
Voice and Address 360

W. H. Auden & Mantan Moreland 161
Waiting for Winter 62
Way Things Work, The 416
We Heart 401
We Manage Most When We Manage Small
  253
we put our heads into the windows of a car
  which was passing, and, 373
Whole and Without Blessing 256
Why Do You Want to Suffer Less 233
Wind 440
Wind 440
Woman Defending Herself Examines Her
  Own Character Witness, A 303
Woman, The 63
Woman Who Could Read the Minds of Dogs,
  The 373–379
woman who had been dressed by someone, in
  the same way that, a 371

FIRST LINES

"About the night on which a man said he would spend a 100 dollars 372
A child with a wrench is 234
A dry wind over the valley 440
After the men hunt, 136
All day the Nina sewed in this room 443
All day the sun builds its temple 328
All day you didn't cry or cry out and you felt like sleeping. The desire to 214
all it takes is girls 64
All morning he lay in the tight, dark room, 329
All morning the beast labors up from the valley 332
All the different kinds of light 257
All the new thinking is about loss. 209
All through lunch Peter pinched at his crotch, 449
alone no loneliness in the dream in the quiet 259
Always 322

And if our lives spill   105
And I was born with you, wasn't I, Blues?   162
& this is the organ which was made last   138
Apollo walks the deep roads back in the hills   16
As I walk out of the *La Belle*   390
A small blond girl brings a dark haired woman, a beautiful   397
As Rimbaud said, I thought today sitting in the library   371
As when the blowfish, perishing,   258
At dusk the first stars appear.   441
At eight I was brilliant with my body.   454
A thing, loved one,   276
a woman who had been dressed by someone,   in the same way that   371

because it is lunchtime   133
Because the moon became my mother   326
Because the shadows are sepia   84
Bee-logic: each small life   137
Bring the camera closer in. Focus   330
"Brown like us,"   449
But what is happening I see   231
But why are you sleeping, your wispy black hair   35

Chic desolation of the   233
Come to the window & see sweet dawn shine on this wonder: a man   115
Consider them both in paradise,   161

Death looks down on the salmon.   263
Death with his sad hands   239
Done with myself, I asked   140
Don't be afraid, she tells us.   310
Don't look, the woman says.   38

Each day the earth turns, each day   333
Each time we lose grief, Friend, we are free from joy & cross into eternity.   115
Earth tremor. I felt an *earth tremor*.   392
Erased off the face of my earth, all that remains is a white space,   34
Even at sea the bodies of the unborn and the dead   190
even though he falls   129
Everyone can see me standing in the center   56

Fifteen years ago I awoke   336
Finally I heard   426
First day. Jackie and I walking in leaves   453
First frost is weeks off, but the prudent man   176
First light of day in Mississippi   149
Flesh has a remarkable future.   284
For all the ungainly ones, the awkward, silent ones, for   32

For years I've lived with Breughel's painting   334
From my hill I look down on the freeway and over   14

Given the morning, its rush of flowers   337
Green is the color of everything   150

Haven't I said that part of having intercourse   370
Have you noticed the little shadow?   77
"Having her under me,"   the man said,   "in bed, and remembering   372
He gets mostly dead sage and thornbush,   21
He keeps the valley like this with his heart.   19
He painted the mountain over and over again   364
He realized that night how much he was in their power.   18
Here it's harvest. Dust   430
He says that woman speaks with nature. That she hears voices from under   305
He stumbled all morning through the market   328
his first day they asked   132
How can I help myself,   as one woman said to me about wanting   370
How could they think women a recreation?   11
How I loved him.   36
"How is she?" I asked.   82
How much of me is sandwiches radio beer?   152
How was I to know that the woman, seated next to me on the bus,   372

I am filled with the sorrow of all things seen   266
I am in prison for trying to swindle the   243
I am interested in the logic of secrets, how it has always moved me,   78
I am reading Li Po. The T.V. is on   256
I am Tex Ritter. I am not Eldridge Cleaver.   272
I awoke hot, startled in daylight, calling   104
I climbed into the chinaberry   438
I do not wish to report on Medusa directly, this variation of her   88
I'd walk her home after work,   12
If I could meet God   128
I found another baby scorpion today. Tiny,   20
If we stayed with each other long enough   264
If you go to your window   442
I go to school.   233
I held on her neck   104
I linger, knowing you are eager (having seen   256
In June the sun is a bonnet of light   441
In my dream the brooding child   61
In something you have written in school, you say   178
In that photograph of the child and her mother there is a wide space   306
In the life we lead together every paradise is lost.   210
In this kind of weather   350
In this moment when the light starts up   442

Into whose ear the deeds are spoken. The only   429
I remember, you tell me, a daughter, a love, as high as my kneecap.   41
is by admitting   416
I shave my face, comb my hair   453
I sit waiting for one of the two kinds of miracle: 277
I stood watching the great hulk of desire   264
IT CAN BE beautiful this sitting by oneself all alone except for   153
It has been a long time now   264
I think of my name, Julia Graham,   62
it is always night here   129
It is dusk   327
It is foolish for Rubens to show her   12
It seems they never complete these things   351
Its petals do not open of their own accord. That is our part,   418
It will happen in the summer,   41
I use no colors, just number threes,   416
I've come down here to live on a bed of weeds.   30
I was already   313
I will praise Christopher Smart   326
I will read a few of these to see if they exist   362
I would adore doing it over.   31

juggles old bones   57

Later I would say, I have cut myself free from order,   258
Left to itself the heart continues, as the tamarind   419
Let it end here where the blueprint   134
"Let's get hold of one of those deer   21
Let us make the test. Say God wants you   254
Light forgetting itself light   falling loosely   79
Like right now it's the summertime   159
Love should grow up like a wild iris in the fields,   297

May I put my head on your shoulder, Mr. Mac Adams, Sr.?   75
Mephistopheles enters   261
Monte Albán   325
Mr. Klein says, "Milagres, hold Angelo's hand,"   236
My child deep in the   313
My daughter pleads with me   300
My father is dead and there is nothing left   262
My father would have saved us, had the occasion of fire arisen.   417
My son & I, between *Fu-Sang* and   116

Nobody but Lester let Lester leap   162
No moon No road No thunder   323
No one standing.   265
Note—   159
Not overwhelming, this morning's little dream   76

Not wanting myself, I try to go   260
Now I see you   322

Ocean Springs Missippy   149
Of course it is snowing   154
Of course the heart is nothing   332
Often in this life   325
Oh the wine's fine   59
Old Graves fell asleep   50
On Clark Street in Chicago   59
One Christmastime Fats Waller in a fur coat   183
1. *SF, a punk cafe, distortions of the literal.*   284
One word in your letter &, again, that quail trots from the vineyard, spurts   116
on itself. His red hair was standing up) "I just began to weep".   373
On the morning of the Käthe Kollwitz exhibit, a young man and woman   213
Our mother makes a pot of tea.   308
Our mother sits by the   309
Our mother tells us it is time to clean up.   309
out of adult hearing   136
Out of money, so I'm sitting in the shade   22
Out under the sprinkler, naked as toads,   32

Perhaps if we could begin some definite way.   13
"Perspective," he would mutter, going to bed.   9
Picking through pieces   235

QUESTION: Who am I?   303

Revolution,   299
Richard on the cold roof screams, I'm the eye   451
Right up under our noses, roses   161
Robinson Crusoe breaks a plate on his way out   19

Satisfied this morning because I saw myself   371
Scott and I bent   452
She coulda been somethin   158
She dreamed along the beaches of this coast.   203
She heard the sounds of a couple having intercourse and then getting up   379
She is first seen dancing which is a figure   211
She was in the garden, sequestered behind bushes, as night came, just as   305
She who usually feeds us   309
Smoke beshags   280
So I decided watching an *old* woman like her, who could rise so easily   370
Someone's youngest daughter   236
Somerset Maugham said a professional was someone who could do his best   213
Sourdough french bread and pinot chardonnay   206
So, we are ghosts of angels   115
So youre playing   155

Stone Face is the likeness of all lovers. 58
Summer in the Tehachapi Mountains. 334
Summoned by the frantic powers 29

Ten thousand bees in the backyard. 391
Ten years Villon lived in a small village 327
That lamb 280
That memory like a derelict plane 38
That tremor rising 114
That which *is*, for example, 275
That year the end of winter stood under a sign 355
The air fresh, as it has been for days. 260
The answer was 354
The anxious bird in the lush 420
The bad mother wakes from dreams 312
The bare room, 231
The boss knows what shape I'm in. He tells me 103
The Chinese, to whom the eighteenth-century English 17
The *Chronicle* "green sheet" dries out 141
The classical engine of death moves my day. Hurrying me. 17
The cry in my mouth wakes me (thirty years later) 103
The dangers of drifting while driving, in a daze—Loosening the reins that 404
The dog. The book. The glass. 283
The doors of that city are ninety feet high, 33
The far faint protocols of Katherine's flute 232
The figured wheel rolls through shopping center malls and prisons, 189
The girl I call Alma who is so white 253
The head tilts back, like a heavy leaf, the eyes sew shut 40
The heart of man is encumbered 240
The jaunty crop-haired graying 175
The lamb was so skinny I thought it was a baby goat 261
The logarithm. The fraction. The bead of dew. 273
The longest day will drive a crack—til Jubilate windows in. Three parts that 403
The Lord sits with me out in front watching 20
The moon, with the pace of a wolf, 241
The myth-maker drags his myth 33
The old man is seated. 239
The oxen have voices 10
The pastor sips weak hock and seltzer 242
The perfect mother lets the cat sleep 311
The Poles rode out from Warsaw against the German 9
There are things a man does 263
There is a black dog in my painting. 86
There is a grey enameled sky, 39
There is interest in being able to feel what you see 359
There's no fleeing the cry-bird. This evening 281
There's nothing gentle where Aphrodite was. 259
The round and sad-eyed man puffed cigars as if 356

The sign for anger could be a felled pine tree.   35
The sound of rain on the roof was too loud.   336
The street is no river. For slouching   274
The string vibrates. The steel string vibrates. The skin. The calfskin. The   306
The torches surrounded by butterflies,   236
The toys I bought for you   139
The tree's green explains what a light means, an idea, the bomb or Donald   358
The weight of myself. The weight of my mother.   265
The whole weight of history bears down   310
The wind sprays pale dirt into my mouth   440
the wonder   128
The young composer, working that summer at an artist's colony, had   214
They used to meet one night a week at a place on top of Telegraph Hill to   215
They were walking in the woods along the coast   219
Things come from nothing.   282
This being a minimum security facility, it feels more like being on a reservation, than in a
    touchable cage   156
This is a glove   361
This is a poem for a woman doing dishes.   302
This is how it happens.   298
This is the sugar   423
This road ends in a field of grain   357
This steaming night in Vientiane. A filthy room,   331
Three clear days   217
Through the first days of Lent   444
Thrushes flying under the lake. Nightingales singing underground.   15
To look from the Acrocorinth   244
To rage I   301
True Mexican or not, let's open our shirts   455
Trying to scrape the burned soup from my only pot   22
Tsangyang Gyatso was twelve years old   330
Two girls barefoot walking in the rain   11

Walking out, I flushed some meadowlarks—   102
We all dazed—down by ocean, gold in jingles, inhalexhale all around. Out   401
We have the road here, the gate the key. And the miniature pond's   400
Well, David said—it was snowing outside and his voice contained many   216
We march into the suburbs led by a six-year-old kid   30
we put our heads into the windows of a car which was passing, and,   373
west of the Sierras where   130
We went on a motorcycle on a straight road with people watching us and   381
We were talking about tent revivals   16
What about the people who came to my father's office   182
What binds the atom together   114
What if Orpheus   13
What is beautiful alters, has undertow.   256
What's that red stuff? Blood? Gee   276
What things are steadfast? Not the birds.   253

What would our mother say?   310
When autumn rains flatten sycamore leaves,   441
When I go into the garden, there she is.   255
When I heard that thunder, I rose up like a happy animal. The window was   404
When I looked at the stubborn dark Buddha   18
When I was a teacher   237
When old crones wandered in the woods,   212
When the petals of the plum tree   390
When the storm hit, I was fording the river   19
When you got up this morning the sun   440
Where I lived the river   126
Where is the woman who unmoored this morning,   63
While the women sliced bread and cold meat   60
Who'll marry me? Cold Saturday. *Will he leave me?* With the   37
With poisoned apple, comb, ring, garment,   37

Yellow's unstitching itself from the sun,   87
You are perishing like the old men. Already your arms are gone,   254
You are the owner of one complete thought   360
You couldn't find it in the bird's weight   85
You too if you work hard enough   152
You were born on the *Esplanade des Invalides,*   243